So Far From Home

Also by Patricia Trainor O'Malley

Sacred Hearts Parish, Bradford, Massachusetts (1985)
A New England City - Haverhill, Massachusetts (1987)
Bradford: The End of an Era (1996)
Haverhill Massachusetts - From Town to City (1997)
The Irish in Haverhill, Massachusetts (1998)
Haverhill's Immigrants at the Turn of the Century (1999)
The Irish in Haverhill, Massachusetts, Volume II (1999)
Bradford College (2000)
Italians in Haverhill (2001)

So Far From Home
Letters from Ireland to Family in America

Transcribed, Edited and Annotated by
Patricia Trainor O'Malley

Foreword by Kerby A. Miller, author of the Pulitzer nominee
EMIGRANTS AND EXILES

Library of Congress Control Number: 2021911929

ISBN: 9798518136496

To my Irish Great-Grandmothers, Julia Donovan and Kate McCarthy, who said farewell to their children and watched them sail away to America, never to return home again. After all those years, we are connected again.

"You asked could I make to mass. I could, and to you if there was a road."

> — Julia Mahoney Donovan, Dreenlamane, Ballydehob, Co. Cork, Ireland to her son, Dan, in Haverhill, Mass.
> December 12, 1888

"If there was a road leading to that place, I'd walk all the way to see her, and all of ye."

> —Kate Keane McCarthy, Ballinlough, Leap, Co. Cork, Ireland to her daughter, Nora, in Haverhill, Mass.
> September 18, 1900

Table of Contents

Acknowledgments

To all the Donovan and McCarthy relatives in Ireland, England, and America. To the parish priests in West Cork who trusted me to handle their precious record books. To all the civil servants in the county and national archives, those professionals who shared their files and microfilms at University College Cork Library and Archives, and the Skibbereen Heritage Center, all of whom shared their personal experiences with local history. They never failed to answer my pleas for help. To Dr. Kerby Miller and Dr. Peggy Lynch-Brennan, who unstintingly offered their professional expertise and unfailing willingness to teach me how to turn what were close to indecipherable old letters into a coherent story of two Irish families.

You all have my enduring thanks.

And to Atty. Thomas Schiavoni, lover of all things Irish, who showed me that the letters could be Theater, as well as History; and to local historian, David Goudsward, who with Tom Schiavoni gave me the encouragement, leadership, and guidance to fight the challenges of age and vision loss to take "the letters" off the shelf, and, finally complete this book.

And you have my enduring gratitude and love.

FOREWORD
KIRBY A. MILLER

In the 1880s and 1890s, over 160,000 young men and women emigrated from County Cork. Many left West Cork, from the beautiful but impoverished countryside near the town of Skibbereen, where in those decades the population—earlier ravaged by the Great Famine of 1845-52—fell another 21 percent. Most of West Cork's emigrants found work in the United States—the men in industries, public works, railroads, and mines, the young women principally in middle-class homes as domestic servants. Memories of the vast majority have survived at best only as half-forgotten names or faded photographs. But thanks to Dr. Patricia O'Malley, the stories and words of her Donovan and McCarthy ancestors, who emigrated from farms close to Skibbereen, return to life and illuminate the entire Irish emigrant experience.

I first met Patricia O'Malley at a mutual friend's dinner party some thirty years ago. Since my academic career was devoted to studying Irish emigration, I was fascinated when she told me that her family had saved hundreds of old letters, most written to Dan Donovan or to his wife, Nora McCarthy, primarily by their parents and siblings in West Cork, or by Nora's former schoolmates, fellow emigrants, and domestic servants in the United States. Some years later, Patricia kindly let me read the letters and use them in my research. I was astonished by the richness of their descriptions of life in both rural Ireland and Irish-America, and so I am enormously grateful to Patricia for now making them available to a wide readership.

For Patricia O'Malley, *So Far from Home* has been both a labor of love and a triumph of perseverance. She has deciphered hundreds of faded pages of sometimes near-impossible handwriting, replete with what appears to us as idiosyncratic grammar, spelling, and punctuation, which often reflect the Irish (or Gaelic) language still spoken in the region. To provide genealogical and social context, Patricia has untangled dense and complex webs of kinfolk and neighbors on both sides of the ocean. *So Far from Home* thus represents many years of indefatigable research in Ireland and America, and many visits to libraries and to archives, and to relatives, tumbled-down cottages, and old graveyards in West Cork.

The letters themselves are replete with data of enormous historical and genealogical value. Most importantly, they reveal the joys and struggles experienced by wonderful but ordinary human beings in rural Ireland and urban-industrial America before the dawn of the last century. On the one hand, therefore, the letters of the Donovans and McCarthys provide windows of a sort into vanished societies. Yet, on the other hand, their triumphs and tragedies still resonate in our own world, in which increasing numbers of people still face the same powerful forces—rapacious landlords, bankers, creditors, employers, and the governments that enforce their edicts—that sent the young people of West Cork into lifelong exile.

Kerby A. Miller, Curators' Professor Emeritus of History, University of Missouri, is the author of many books and articles, including the prize-winning study, Emigrants and Exiles: Ireland and the Irish Exodus to North America (1985).

Preface

This is the story of two Irish families, the Donovans of Dreenlamane, Ballydehob, and the McCarthys of Ballinlough, Leap. Both homes were in south-western Co. Cork. They were ordinary farming families in nineteenth-century Ireland. The usual tools of genealogy provide us with the bare bones of the individuals in the story. We can learn about births, family names, marriages, and deaths. But, by a series of unexpected coincidences, we have been given flesh for those bones. The names and dates provided by genealogy have been given personalities, voices, and individuality. We know their words and ideas, joys and fears, inner concerns, and shared touches of humor because the Donovans and the McCarthys wrote letters to their family in America. And one Donovan and one McCarthy saved the letters. And that one Donovan, Dan, married that one McCarthy, Nora. And one day, their letters, along with boxes of old photographs of family and friends and boxes of ephemera, were found in the attic of a family home in Haverhill, Massachusetts by an inquisitive granddaughter who just happened to be an historian. The task of organizing and interpreting all these pieces of a family's past would be a research project both intellectually stimulating and personally satisfying. The genealogical material would provide history, but the letters would give the characters life by giving them voices. Their words, and the words of their correspondents, animated them and gave them a reality attainable in no other way for that time period before the advent of film. We get to know the parents, the brothers and sisters, the cousins, a few sweethearts, and many friends from school days in Ireland.

LETTERS

The letters in the Donovan and McCarthy collections were written, in the main, between the early 1880s and 1900. The great majority of them were sent to two young immigrants, Daniel Donovan and Honora (Nora) McCarthy, both of whom had followed older family members to the industrial city of Haverhill, Massachusetts. Dan and Nora had married in 1903, and their letters, each set packed into such available boxes as those that would have held writing paper or women's shoes. The boxes remained in the family home in the Bradford section of Haverhill, until 1977 when their caretaker, Julia Agnes Donovan, the eldest Donovan child, died. The letters, along with cartons of related materials, were transferred to the home of Dan and Nora's daughter, Lenora Marie (Donovan) Trainor, who lived just one street away from her family home.

Seventeen years later, while poking around in the attic of my childhood home, I noticed the stack of boxes, with the small boxes of letters perched atop. It was the best of good fortune that my mother, Marie Trainor, was still alive, still alert, and with a clear memory of who the people in the photographs were. Among them were the photos of all four of her Irish grandparents, all of the McCarthy siblings, and seven of the nine Donovan siblings. Marie still had fond memories of sitting with her mother and poring over a large plush velvet-covered photo album of her Irish relatives as her mother named off one after the other person in the photographs. Marie had never read any of the letters, much less looked at any of them. She would soon have a very thorough introduction to them. Her quiet daily life was soon disrupted with endless phone calls and visits that usually began with the words "Wait until you hear this!" or "Do you have any idea what this might mean," or "who this might be?" At the same time, I began to put the two family genealogies together, aided by the good fortune that a significant number of my mother's first and second cousins were still alive and in contact and thus able to cooperate as branch by branch the two family trees were erected. In another ten years, most of these close relatives would have passed on, including Marie, who died at ninety-six in 1999.

The Donovans were "comfortable" in comparison to many of their neighbors. Five of Dan's older siblings were already established with their own farms or trade and well along in filling their homes with the multitude of children that would give Marie Donovan Trainor over seventy first-cousins. Their letters to young brother Dan were replete with comments and complaints about the prices they could expect for their livestock and their crops at the local markets. The McCarthys had no livestock except for an old horse, one cow, and two goats. The family was not only poor; it was often on the edge of calamity. The letters to their children in America carried a persistent threnody of need: a pound for the rent, a pound for the bank, money for the man who owned the peat bog for permission to cut the turf that heated their little two-room cottage. None of the McCarthy emigrant children had anything equal to the leather money-belt filled with gold sovereigns given to Dan Donovan by his saddler brother, Tim, and his mother, Julia. And Marie had only ten or so cousins on her McCarthy side. The Donovans lived in Dreenlamane, Ballydehob on the Mizen Peninsula west of the market town of Skibbereen. The McCarthys were from Ballinlough, Leap, located above Glandore Harbor, and east of Skibbereen. The Donovans were farmers and craftsmen. Their widowed mother, Julia, had the satisfaction of having six of her nine children: Ellen, John, Mary, Julia, Tim, and Cornelius, Jr., settled in their own homes (insofar as an Irish Catholic could call their leased land their own). And all these children were within walking distance of the two-story stone house her late husband had built in the 1870s. This house was located next to the old Mahoney family homestead where Julia Mahoney Donovan had spent her childhood and where she and her husband had raised their own family.

Julia's husband, Cornelius Donovan, Sr. had been a successful farmer with a knack for breeding and raising livestock for sale in the local market. And when he died in 1882 from a strangulated hernia, he left his widow with an amount of money in the local bank. So when Julia, or one of her children, needed money to pay a tax or a loan, she only had to go to the bank and remove the required sum.

The McCarthy home was in a beautiful location, on a hillside overlooking Ballin Lake (Ballinlough). However, the house was not theirs, nor even a leasehold. It was a small cottage provided by the Skibbereen Guardians of the Poor (who oversaw the Poor Laws in the area). In other words, the McCarthys were a charity case. They had no farm, nor a share of a family farm, though they once had such. The father, Patrick, was an agricultural laborer dependent on neighbors, such as his older brother, Mike, for work.

The McCarthys had family within walking distance, just as Mrs. Donovan did, but they were not their own children but brothers, sisters, nieces, and nephews. When the first letters to be saved in the McCarthy Collection were sent to America, they went to two elder daughters, Mary and Ellen, who had emigrated in the early 1880s when the two were not yet twenty years of age. At that time, there were two daughters, Kate and Nora, and a son, Tim, at home. Within a few years, Tim and Nora would be in America, and Katie would be dead from tuberculosis. And Patrick and Kate McCarthy would be alone for the rest of their lives.

The McCarthys also had two older sons. Years before the first letters to be saved were written, the two sons, Jeremiah (Jerry) and Denis (Dinny), had gone to England. Jerry, the older of the pair, married a woman of Irish descent, fathered a daughter and two sons, and died before his thirtieth birthday of tuberculosis.

The first letter in the McCarthy Collection was from Annie McCarthy, the widow of Jerry, sent to his sisters, Mary and Ellen, encouraging them to come to England where work was plentiful. And the sisters should bring their parents with them so that, as Annie put it, they could all be together in one place.

The second son, Dinny, married an Irish native, Julia O'Brien in Wales, had two children there, emigrated to northeast Pennsylvania's coal fields, became a coal miner, and enlarged his family to three daughters and four sons.

The Donovan letters are filled with news about crops, sales prices for the animals they raised, the prices people were willing to pay for the butter the Donovans churned, and the eggs their hens laid. Monthly Fair Days in the market towns near their homes were not only a chance to meet and trade and socialize. The event also served as a local version of the "stock market," or what a large city would find in the business pages of the local newspaper. What were people willing to pay for heifers, for colts and foals, for pigs? Was it going to be worth it to cart animals to market if the offered prices were too low? All the letters written to Dan Donovan by his family seemed to focus on economic matters. Each of the Donovans who remained in Ireland was set up in his own farm or shop, or married a man with his own farm. Each house had its own growing family, which must have overflowed the small cottages that some of them had. Only three of the nine Donovan children – Hanna, Mike, and Dan – emigrated. None of them ever returned, not even for a visit.

Dan Donovan also had another set of letters saved for the future, quite different from those sent by his family. He received these nine letters from two female friends, Mary Ann McCarthy in Ireland, and Hanna Cronin, a former neighbor in Ireland and now a mill worker in Andover, Massachusetts. The young ladies were single-minded in their pursuit in writings to handsome Dan, and they were very bold in their hints: Dan was their last best hope in keeping them from becoming "old maids." Each of the girls, as well as Dan, were no more than twenty at the time of Dan's emigration.

Years later, his children would tease Dan about the collection so carefully packed away in an old stationery box labeled "Papa's Letters." That he would save his family letters was not the issue. Rather, their teasing and joking had to do with why he would so carefully keep the letters from old girlfriends, neither of whom he would marry.

The McCarthy letters had a quite different tone to them, especially those dated between 1894 and 1896. The writer was daughter Katie, who was in her early twenties at the time. Her letters are filled with news about their young friends, their dancing at the crossroads or in the loft of Tom Kingston's store in Leap, the gatherings at the McCarthy cottage, the impromptu parties with the donated kegs of liquor and ale. The McCarthy parents seem to have welcomed their children's friends and shared in the music and dancing in their tiny "charity" cabin.

There is no word of dancing or singing in the Donovan letters. Instead, there are reminders from Mother Julia to "keep away from bad company" and "stay away from the drink." The abstinence society, known as The League of the Cross, recruited many Donovans and their neighbors in the years the letters were being written. Only Dan's brother-in-law, Mick Hodnett, was willing to admit that "there will be no fun at the christening" (of brother Con Donovan's first child) because of all that had taken "the pledge."

The McCarthy letters are by far the more news-filled with listings of marriages, engagements, births, and deaths. There are regular reports: which friends would be soon sailing for Boston, who had returned for a visit (as sister Ellen had done), or those who returned to marry. They also reveal much better letter writing skills, so they can tell a better story. The McCarthy children were almost an entire generation younger than the older Donovan children. They had far better educational opportunities in the reformed school system supplied by the British government in the last quarter of the nineteenth century. Dan Donovan had nieces and nephews who were older than his wife-to-be, Nora McCarthy.

All of the letters in the Donovan Collection are from family members to relatives except for the nine letters from Dan's female admirers. The letters sent between 1885 and 1890 were sent only to young Dan. Three later letters to Dan came from a niece and his sister, Julia Minihane. All the other letters in the family collection were from Dan's nieces and nephew in Ireland to their siblings in America. And there was one long epistle from the widow of Tim the Saddler, Kate O'Donnell O'Donovan, to one of her three daughters in California. (The "O" begins to appear before the Donovan name in the 1880s, starting with Con, Jr.'s signature.)

The most distinctive difference between the two collections is the great number of letters from relatives and friends in the McCarthy group. This included those from three first cousins in Ireland, Julia and Mick McCarthy, children of Uncle Mike, and Denis Keane, whose mother was Nora McCarthy Keane. In addition, there are two letters from England: Annie, the widow of Jerry McCarthy, and one from her daughter, Katie, both in London, England. Another Katie, daughter of Denis, a niece in Pennsylvania, also wrote.

By far, the most significant number of non-family correspondents were the girlfriends of Nora who had become domestic servants in America, as Nora herself was. The majority of the young women had been her schoolmates at the Knockskagh National School immediately north of the townland of Ballinlough. Most notably were the fifty-plus letters sent between 1897 and 1900 to Nora from her friend Hannah Collins in Elmira, New York.

Hannah wrote so many letters to Nora that they were kept apart in their own stationery box. Hanna's grand-aunt had the "charity" cottage overlooking Ballin Lake next to the McCarthy's home. Hanna spent her teen years there, helping to care for her elderly relative, and any spare time she had was shared with Nora at the McCarthy home.

The letters from Nora's young friends are filled with life and pleasure. They share gossip of friends from home, those about to leave for America, or had already done so. They discuss plans to meet at weddings and dances in Boston. There are details aplenty about the life of young Irish domestic servants as they move about from post to post, ever seeking less arduous, more desirable employment. And in those years, there were many such positions. Not just with the wealthy Yankees, but with the growing middle class, many of them of Irish descent. And, as many of these young women had brothers in the vicinity, it is possible to obtain a sense of what the young male immigrant's experience was at the end of the nineteenth century.

Dan Donovan's Letters

Daniel Donovan (1864-1947) emigrated from Dreenlamane, Ballydehob, in County Cork, Ireland, to Haverhill, Massachusetts, in 1885. Within weeks of his arrival, he had begun to receive mail from home. The letters are from his widowed mother, five married siblings, along with those from his female friends. This box of "Papa's Letters" contained fifty missives written between 1885 and mid-1890. For the most part, the handwriting is difficult to read, and the spelling is often more erratic and creative than accurate, a tribute to phonetic spelling. Both penmanship and spelling would markedly improve as children in each branch of the family gradually assumed the responsibility for the correspondence with their uncle in America. Only brother Cornelius (Con), the closest in age to Dan, who had married a few months before Dan's departure, would have no children old enough to help within this time frame. His letters would not lose their distinctive, idiosyncratic style.

To this core of fifty Donovan family letters were added two letters to Dan and one to his daughter that had been saved in another box. As word spread among the branches of the family of this project, copies of five additional letters, written by family members to one another in the early decades of the twentieth century, were donated to the collection. Two of these letters are of particular interest as each gives an overview of all that was happening in the family's Irish branches. The first was written in 1911 by Lil Hodnett, youngest child of Mary (Donovan) and Mike Hodnett, to her seven sisters in Massachusetts with news of the particulars of the wedding of their only brother Richard, and the parts played by many of the groom's aunts, uncles, and cousins.

The second letter was written in 1919 by Kate O'Donnell O'Donovan, Dan's widowed sister-in-law. Kate was writing to her daughter Julia, one of three daughters living in California. Julia was about to be married, and her mother included an update of family news in her congratulatory letter. Within a few years, Kate and her two remaining daughters crossed the Atlantic and then the continent of America to take up residence in California.

NORA MCCARTHY'S LETTERS

Nora McCarthy Donovan, (1877-1953), from Ballinlough, Leap, County Cork, Ireland, came to Haverhill, Massachusetts, ten years after Dan Donovan did. During the third quarter of the Nineteenth Century, the Irish school system had been undergoing reform. The results show in the McCarthy Collection letters. The penmanship is clearer and more uniform. The spelling is much more accurate, as is the grammar. Like Nora, most of these writers, including those who wrote the letters for her illiterate parents, had attended the nearby Knockskagh National School and benefitted from the reforms. There is one exception to this rule. Mary Ann Donovan, a neighbor of Nora's in the nearby townland of Bawnfune, and an immigrant to Lowell, Massachusetts, had her own idiosyncratic style. She would begin every line of her correspondence with a capital letter, not just at the beginning of every sentence. I chose not to transcribe her style exactly, as it is simply a distraction.

There was no box labeled "Mama's Letters" nor any letters from old boyfriends. Nor did Nora undergo the teasing from her children that Dan apparently enjoyed receiving. Instead, Nora put her letters, tightly packed into two narrow boxes, originally used for women's dress shoes, or "slippers," and away from prying eyes.

Nora was one of four siblings in Haverhill and adjacent Bradford, Massachusetts, in the 1890s. Letters sent from family and friends in Ireland to any one of the four were circulated to all. The majority of them were saved by Nora in one shoebox. To these were added the many letters sent by her former mates at school, those sent by a young woman from the County Cork town of Clonakilty that Nora had met during the passage, and a miscellany of other friends. The letters of only four males, all of them first-cousins (Mike and Jerry McCarthy, Denis Keane, and Patrick Harding), offset the singularly female nature of the correspondence.

In all, there were one hundred and forty-six letters in the McCarthy Family Collection. They were written between 1884 and 1918. Sixty-seven were sent from relatives in Ireland, England, and Wales. Seventy-nine were from friends and relatives in the United States. These letters were tightly crammed into an old shoebox. Another box held the forty-three letters from Nora's friend Hannah

Collins. There is a second set of letters from Hannah to Nora written in the 1930s and early 1940s, but they are outside the scope of this project.

RESEARCHING THE LETTERS

Over the next dozen years after their discovery in 1994, the letters were transcribed and annotated. In some cases, the original spelling was so creative that the task became more of translation than transcription. In 1995, I made the first of seven extended visits to County Cork, Ireland. I still had second cousins on the Donovan side in the Ballydehob area, Cork City, and Dublin. And there were McCarthy cousins from a lateral line in the Leap area. Some cousins from this line had been more recent immigrants to the Haverhill area and were, perhaps, better known to me than the earlier direct relations.

My grandfather's childhood home, the Mahoney house, was still intact though no longer inhabited. That was also true of the later two-story house where he had lived for about ten years.

His brother Con and his wife, Brigid, had raised their family there until Con's death in 1929. His heir, Con III, a bachelor farmer, continued to live and work the homestead. He was later joined by his youngest brother, Mike, a retired Dublin police detective and another

bachelor. After their deaths in the 1970s, the property passed to their nephew, Cornelius Gerald, son of their sister Ellen/Nell O'Donovan of Ballinspittal, south of the town of Bandon. Gerald was a horse breeder and former jockey. His primary work was running his wife Kitty's tavern in Bandon. He chose to leave the houses in Dreenlamane uninhabited and use the fields for grazing his yearling colts and foals. The homes of Mary Donovan Hodnett and Julia Donovan Minihan were in ruin. The home of Tim the Saddler still stood in Ballydehob, where it was occupied by a bank. The family of Tim's only surviving son, Patrick Steven, had moved to the Dublin area in the 1940s.

The home of Dan Donovan's eldest brother, John, was still inhabited by his descendants through the line of John's sixth son, Patrick, and Patrick's sons, John and Tim Joe O'Donovan. The farmstead remains in Tim Joe's family. Tim Joe's two sisters also lived in the general area. Philomena, a retired rectory housekeeper, had a small cottage. Mary Twomey and her husband Jerry had a farm east of Ballydehob.

Tim Joe showed up at our B&B locale the first day my daughters and I arrived in Ballydehob. He drove us to all the family locations, both occupied and unoccupied houses and those in ruins. He guided us through the overgrowth to the pair of old homes where my grandfather had lived. We were able to enter the buildings and wander about. And Tim passed on the message that his sister Philomena expected to provide me with bed and board once my daughters had flown home. Mary and her family provided Sunday dinners for Phil and me.

And it was to Phil's house with its long monastic style table, where two generations of the family would periodically gather during each of my multi-week visits to talk about family, discuss the letters and the progress of my research, and pore over the album of family pictures I was collecting, as piece by piece, we re-created the Donovan family.

It was at Phil's house that we discovered a forgotten branch of the family. One afternoon, Mary Twomey paid a visit and mentioned that she had met Den Burke in town (Ballydehob), and he claimed that he was a cousin. We were all quite sure there were no Burkes on our tree. But Den had insisted. Mary and Phil remembered that Denis was the son of a Julia Schofield of Drishane. So, with that link, I paid a visit to the local county archivist and pore over the records. Den was right. His grandmother, Ellen Schofield of Drishane (where the Hodnetts also lived), was the firstborn of the nine Donovan children. She married in 1860, before Dan was born, and died in 1878, a day after delivering her only child, Julia. The latter would marry Denis Burke and mother, among others, our newfound cousin, Den Burke. And the Burke home became yet another Irish home where cousins welcomed me and provided yet more pages of information.

In a similarly serendipitous manner, I found links to the only other branch of the Donovan family that had no ties to Haverhill. This was the family of Tim the Saddler. Tim had died in 1902 before his fiftieth birthday. He left a widow and a house full of young children. One by one, his five daughters had gone to Oakland, California, to live with a maternal uncle. The last of his daughters and his widow, Kate, had joined them in the 1920s. There is no information that any of these relatives made a stop-over in Haverhill to visit their relatives. Over time, the memory faded.

One day, I contacted Joe Collins, a close cousin in Haverhill, to inquire if I could borrow any family photographs. He had no pictures but offered something better. Joe had recently been contacted by a lawyer in Ireland trying to settle the estate of the last of the Irish cousins from Joe's branch, the descendants of Mary (Donovan) and Michael Hodnett. He had contacted Joe because a letter from him was found in his deceased cousin's cottage in Drishane.

Could Joe provide the lawyer with the names and addresses of the surviving Hodnett cousins? The young lawyer from Dublin was Brendan O'Donovan, great-grandson of Tim the Saddler. I contacted our newly-found cousin and made arrangements to meet him and his wife and children during the summer when my children and I would be renting a house in Ireland. The visit was a grand success as we exchanged page after page of family information.

A few years later, in 2000, a Clan O'Donovan Reunion was held in Skibbereen attended by Donovans and O'Donovans from four continents. I was honored to be one of the featured speakers. I discovered among the audience members Colonel Bernard O'Donovan and his wife, Helena/Ena, from Cork City vicinity to my great delight. They were the parents of Brendan. And with that fortuitous meeting at the Clan Reunion, not only were all branches of the family tree connected, but I had made enduring friendships.

There were no immediate descendants of Nora McCarthy's family in Ireland. However, another branch of the family was still very visibly present. These were the descendants of Uncle Michael McCarthy and his wife, Mary Tobin. Uncle Mike had inherited the family farm at the southern end of Ballin Lake, a short walk away from Nora's family cottage. There are constant references throughout Nora's letters to her uncle and her cousins, especially Julia, Mick, and Patrick, known as The Shoemaker for his craft, the three closest in age to Nora, Katie, and Tim.

Julia and her brother Mick were among the correspondents to Nora. Julia took over the task of writing letters for her illiterate Aunt Kate and Uncle Pat when there were no more at the cottage to write for them.

Julia's granddaughter, Julia Anne Cullinane, provided an enormous amount of information about her McCarthy branch and acted as my connection with the surviving children of Patrick, known collectively as "Shoemakers," though none had carried on their father's craft. Julia Anne took me to Tullig and Drinagh to meet descendants of "Mary of Tullig," one of Uncle Mike's oldest girls. And, most importantly, she introduced me to John McCarthy, and his wife Noell and his mother Eileen, widow of Uncle Mike's grandson, John McCarthy, Sr. They were the current owners of the old McCarthy Family homestead, the site of many of the stories from home that were sent to America. Eileen and her children, all living in the area, provided enormous amounts of information about the McCarthys of Ballinlough, their relatives, and their neighbors. And to put all these threads of information together, it turned out that one of Eileen McCarthy's daughters had married a man whose brother had married Cousin Tim Joe Donovan's daughter. A third generation of Donovan-McCarthy connections!

When I made my first visit to the parish house in Leap and asked to access the baptismal and marriage records, there was some hesitation. Then the parish priest learned that I was one of the "Meenig" McCarthys, using the clan designation for our branch of the family. That gave me the same entrée I had received at the parish house in Schull once I let it be known that I was a cousin of the Donovans of Dreenlamane. To be allowed to sit for hours on end at a desk in the parish office, with total access to the precious records, was a rare privilege, and I made full use of my opportunity. The baptismal register in Schull was particularly rare as it began in 1808. In contrast, the earliest baptismal register in the parish office in Leap started in 1832.

Civil records began decades later in 1864, the year of Dan Donovan's birth. When I started my research work in Ireland, the Civil Records were available in the County Records Office in Skibbereen. Here it was my good fortune to have the services of the County Archivist, Seamus Ryan. He permitted me hours of his time, often giving me appointments in the evening after the office was closed when I could have his full attention. When I would offer him payment for his time, he would give me the name of one of his favorite charities and ask that I donate to it. Even after I had returned to the US, I would send the Archivist pages of questions about more names I had encountered, especially among marriages and deaths. I was never refused. With such incredible access to parish and civil records, I was able to pursue various studies, such as a family reconstitution of each of the families who lived in Dreenlamane during the period that the Donovans were in residence in the Nineteenth Century.

Piece by piece, I traced the families that Mr. Griffith had listed in his great Survey of 1851, from marriages and births before, during and in the immediate aftermath of the Great Famine through confirmation lists, marriages, and deaths from the Civil Register. All these records included so many additional names such as Witnesses, the person reporting the event, and so on. The end product was an essay published in the *Mizen Journal* from Schull. This was one of five articles of mine that the *Journal* published, based on both family and local topics drawn from my research.

When the County Archives were centralized in Cork City, appointments were required. A helpful genealogist from Kinsale, Nora Hickey, gave me her own appointment for my first visit, along with an introduction to the staff and information on setting up my own appointments. My intent in poring through so many records was to find out as much as possible about every name I encountered in the letters. I wasn't just filling out a family tree; I was filling all the nearby townlands with the friends and neighbors that the Donovans and the McCarthys encountered in their daily lives, and about whom the letter-writers in Ireland filled their epistles with "all the latest newses."

Visits to Cork City would include hours of research at the University College Cork archives, where my primary searches were in the 1901 and 1911 Census of Ireland. Overnight stays in Bishopstown, a suburb of Cork City, were courtesy of cousins Bernard and Ena O'Donovan, where we alternated tales of Bernard's career with the Army of the Irish Republic and my discoveries about our mutual ancestors. When it came time to go to Dublin to research property valuations at the national tax offices, I was welcomed to stay with Brendan O'Donovan and his wife, Dr. Noirin Noonan.

All these relatives in West Cork, Cork City, and Dublin provide me with bed and board, introduction to the local parish priests and access to parish records, and hours of good talk ("craic" they would call it).

During the years that I made my extended visits to research and visit my relatives, I was given lessons in how to understand such frequently encountered stumbling blocks as traditional Irish namingpractices. And I could expect explanations of the old "pishogues," or superstitions, encountered in the letters. They were able to figure out the creative spellings of Irish terms that our mutual ancestors understood but could not spell. Those relatives who were still engaged in farming provided great assistance in understanding the agricultural terms mentioned in the letters. In many cases, the described practices were no longer known or used by the next generation with their mechanized methods but recalled from their childhoods many wonderful nights were spent sitting around the monastery-style dining table in the cottage of cousin Philomena O'Donovan, and at Cousin Bernard's home outside of Cork City. There we indulged in great "lashings" of Irish tea and homemade brown soda bread.

One of the highlights of my years of research in Ireland was the day my host cousins and I visited a long-known neighbor but unknown cousin, Denis "Den" Burke, and his wife, Nellie Minihane, in Drishane. We renewed our family ties over, yes, cups of hot tea and brown soda bread.

Patricia Trainor O'Malley
Boynton Beach, Florida
June 2021

1990s photo of "lost" cousin Denis "Din" Burke of Drishane, with the author's host cousins, Philomena O'Donovan, front, and her sister Mary O'Donovan Twomey, originally of Dreenlamane, Ballydehob. Din's grandmother, Ellen Donovan Schofield, was the first-born child of Con and Julia Donovan. Because she died before Dan Donovan emigrated, she was forgotten by the later generations of cousins. Din, Phil, Mary, and the author are all second cousins.

Part One:

THE DONOVANS OF DREENLAMANE
And
THE DONOVAN COLLECTION

1. CORNELIUS AND JULIA DONOVAN AND THE DONOVAN FAMILY

Three peninsulas, the Mizen, Sheepshead (or Muintir Bhaire), and the Beara, shoot out into the Atlantic Ocean from the southwestern corner of Ireland. The Donovan family of Dreenlamane were from the Mizen Peninsula. At the southernmost tip of that peninsula is a great lighthouse. For decades, Ireland's emigrants had their last look at their motherland when their ships passed the beams of the light. The townland of Dreenlamane is located in the north-central section of the Mizen Peninsula.

Dreenlamane is sited between Mt. Corrin with its grazing lands, and its deposits of barytes, whose weight made it useful to sailing ships as ballast in the empty vessels they would sail to to North America to fill with grain and meat. Mt. Corrin is in the northern section of Dreenlamane, and all with land claims in the townland also had grazing rights on the mountainside. To the south was the towering mass of Mt. Gabriel known for centuries for its deposits of tin. Archaeologists have determined that miners in search of tin and other minerals came to Gabriel from as far away as the European mainland and as early as the Bronze Age. There are numerous relics of the Bronze Age in that part of Ireland. A not-so-well known one, except to the Donovans, was the ring fort in the south-east corner of the fields in front of the family home. Professionals would call it a "ring fort," but Dan Donovan would call it a "fairy fort," and had the evidence to support him for, so his story went, one night while riding his horse home, the horse refused to move past the fort, and young Dan had to turn about and approach his home in a roundabout way.

The patriarch of the Donovans of Dreenlamane was Cornelius, son of John Donovan and Julia Driscoll. He was baptized on July 4, 1812. He had at least two brothers: Jeremiah, baptized May 2, 1808, and Timothy, baptized January 7, 1810. We know all these details because the baptism took place in the Parish of Schull, on the east coast of the Mizen peninsula. The baptismal record dates from 1808, an unusually early extant volume. What is not known is the townland that the Donovans came from. That family name is more associated with the area near Skibbereen. That part of the Mizen peninsula is better known for Mahoneys and Driscolls, among others.

There were no more baptisms for John and Julia, or as she is called in the baptismal record, "Judy," a nickname that shows up over and again for the Julias in the family. So, Cornelius was the youngest and should he reach adulthood, he couldn't expect a share of the family leased lands.

Cornelius would marry on February 28, 1837. His bride was another Julia, Julia Mahoney, daughter of John Mahoney and Ellen Brennan of Dreenlamane. Julia was baptized on August 27, 1817. The only other Mahoney child in the Schull Parish record is her older brother Matthew, baptized February 24, 1815. [1] There were no other children born after Julia. If there were older children, they had to have been born before 1808. or outside of Schull Parish, and none of the neighboring parishes had Baptismal Registers as old as that in Schull.

Con and Julia's wedding was probably on the Tuesday before Ash Wednesday, the final day before the beginning of Lent during which time no marriages would be performed in the Catholic Church. That Tuesday must have been a busy day at the parish church because their marriage was the 28th of 38 performed that day alone. Scholars of the Great Famine often comment on the effect of a great population boom, spurred by early marriages and large families along with a spell of many years of good crops in the decades before the Famine. Thirty-eight marriages in one day in a small parish in rural Ireland would seem to underscore that theory.

We do not know much about the early years of Con and Julia's marriage except for the recorded facts of the baptisms of their first three children. They were not in the Schull Baptismal records but in those of the parish in Durrus in the north-west corner of the Mizen Peninsula with most of its authority extending over the nearby Sheepshead Peninsula. The first child, Ellen, named for her maternal grandmother, was baptized January 12, 1839, and was listed as living in Rosskerig. The second child, a son John (named for both his grandfathers) was baptized July 3, 1841, and his residence was listed as Clash. And the third child, Mary, was baptized May 11, 1844. Her birthplace was in Kilcrohane. All three townlands are along the eastern shore of Sheepshead Peninsula facing the Mizen Peninsula. When I expressed to a well-known Irish genealogist that I was puzzled by this display of a wandering life for Con and Julia, she suggested that it fit a pattern she had encountered frequently, that is it suggested that Con was a successful "cowman" whose services would be in enough demand that he and his family would be moving about from farm to farm. Con's later success in breeding cattle underscored the possible truth of this theory. In addition to Con's abilities, his wife, Julia, had the reputation of being a "much in demand" midwife. It is easy to infer that Con and Julia would find it fairly easy to be welcomed into farms in need of help.

The young but growing Donovan family shows up in Dreenlamane for the baptism of their third daughter, Honora, (known as Hanna) on January 15, 1847. It appears that the family moved into Julia's childhood home, a sizeable stone house, with a tin roof, not the proverbial thatched one. The left side of the house was one story with a pitched roof, and the right half was two stories high and in later year was used as a stable. There is no civil record of the death of Julia's mother, Ellen Brennan Mahoney so it is most likely that she died before the civil record began in 1864, and that may be the reason for the appearance of Con and Julia's family in Dreenlamane in her father's house.

One of the most inclusive recording acts in Irish history is Griffiths Survey, in which every field, every meadow, every house and its outbuilding in Ireland was surveyed, measured and recorded. This was as close as Great Britain came before the Twentieth Century to recording a census of the country it had stolen. When Richard Griffiths' surveyors reached the Mizen Peninsula in 1851, specifically the townland of Dreenlamane, they cited John Mahoney and Cornelius Donovan and Matthew Mahoney as sharing the taxes on the last unit in the townland. The great majority of the other farms beginning at the road south to Ballydehob were on a road heading west to Dunbeacon and Drishane. (A smaller number of farms were on the road heading east from the Ballydehob road. Con Donovan's eldest son John and his family lived in this part of Dreenlamane.) The farmhouses on the road to the west were on the left side of this road, primarily facing north to Mt. Corrin. The Mahoney-Donovan houses and fields were in the southern portion of the townland, facing towering Mount Gabriel and could only be reached by going south through neighbors' fields. During the Famine, a "make work" project had put a cart path from the road to Ballydehob, across some fields to the old farmhouse. (The pathway was still visible in 1967 when my mother and her sister made their first visit to their cousins at what was once their father's home. The path was grown over by the time my daughters and I made our first visit in 1996.)

A close reading in Griffith's Survey of all the listings of farms in Schull Parish in 1851revealed none that might have been that of Cornelius' father, John Donovan, or either of the two brothers, Jeremiah and Timothy, that we knew of from the baptismal records. However, a postal guide to businesses in Ballydehob in the 1870s lists a craftsman, Timothy Donovan, living in the village. That this might be Con's older brother, is suggested by the fact that Con's son, Tim, had moved to Ballydehob from Aughadown, Kilcoe, east of Ballydehob, following the death of his first wife in 1882. About the same time, the elder Timothy's name disappears from various guides to the village. There is a tendency in the Donovan family to pass on property to namesake children, so it is possible that a childless uncle Timothy passed on his craft and house to a namesake nephew. In turn, brother John would send his own son, Timothy, to be apprenticed to his brother Timothy and chose his next son, namesake John, as his presumptive heir even though the younger John had four older brothers.

The year of Hanna's birth, 1847, marked the beginning of The Great Famine. A second son, Michael, was baptized October 7, 1849 in the midst of its Great Famine. The Donovans lost no family members in the Famine, perhaps because of Julia's nursing skills. Michael, however, did carry the marks of a shortage of nutrition *in utero* for he was known as "the runt of the litter," a small man with a very bad stammer (however he fathered three handsome sons who all towered over him.)

A fourth, and final, daughter, Julia, was baptized in Schull Parish August 7, 1852. Irish naming tradition would have the first daughter named for her paternal grandmother, Julia Driscoll. As I learned, the exception to the rule is when both the paternal grandmother, and the child's mother, have the same name as they did. In the Donovan family. Assumedly, were a child to be given such a name while mother and grandmother were both alive, it would cause the death of one of them presumedly the older of the pair. From the genealogist's perspective, waiting fourteen years from the baptism of the first daughter, and passing over three daughters until bestowing the family name, suggests that the grandmother Julia had probably died sometime after the birth of Hanna (1847) and 1851. Needless to say, the repetitive choice in the next generation of the names of Cornelius and Julia makes it understandable why so many of them had nick-names (Con, Conny, Neil, Neilus, Courley, Curley, Sonny and Judy).

Three more sons completed the family: Timothy baptized February 25. 1855, Cornelius, Jr., baptized July 11, 1857, Daniel, born May 9, 1864. A church had been built in Ballydehob to service the members of Schull Parish who lived at that end of the Peninsula. Dan was the first of the family to have his birth entered in the Civil Records. He was seven years younger than the next in line, Con, Jr., and had three siblings (Ellen, John and Mary) who were twenty or more years older than he was. His mother was forty-seven, and had already survived the births of eight children, and a horrendous Famine. Family legend has it that the pastor of the parish, Fr. John Barry, publicly berated Cornelius before the parishioners for getting his wife pregnant. Whether the pastor's concern was Julia's age, or because of the size of her existing family, or because of her value to her neighbors for her nursing skills, the legend does not say.

The first break in the Donovan family occurred in the year after Dan's birth. The seventeen year old daughter Hanna had become pregnant and delivered a son, Cornelius, born September 3, four months after her mother had borne Dan. It took me three years of annual visits to Ireland, with regular stops at the County Archives in Skibbereen to find the birth. He was not listed under "Driscoll," the name by which my family would know him, nor was he listed under Donovan indicating his mother was not yet married. Conny was listed as the son of Hanna, and of Patrick Minihane, "who has gone to America." I had spent much time poring over birth records but I had never seen what amounted to a foot-note added to either a civil or church record. Neither had the helpful County Archivist. I only had to move my eyes an inch to the right in the Civil Record for an explanation. In the column where the name of the person providing the information was written, "Julia Donovan, midwife." The infant was baptized not in Hanna's parish church, but in the church in Goleen in the southernmost part of the Mizen peninsula. His grandfather, Con, whose name he shared, was the only godparent listed for the infant. Coincidentally, Hanna's oldest sister, Ellen Donovan Schofield lived in the townland of Drishane, in the Goleen parish, suggesting that Hanna had spent at least the latter months of her pregnancy at her sister's home. The next thing that is known of Hanna is a marriage record in St. Mary's Parish, Lawrence, Massachusetts of Hanna Donovan, daughter of Con and "Judy" Donovan to Patrick Driscoll, a resident of Andover, Mass., and a native of Ireland. So Hanna had been put on a sailing ship, perhaps with a purse of gold coins to support herself and her infant son in the hopes of finding the missing "Patrick Minihane." Instead she found an available Patrick Driscoll. Or, perhaps, they were one and the same person!

A second break in the family occurred in the early 1870s when Michael/Mick made the trip to Haverhill where his sister, her husband, Pat, and their growing family were settling and operating a boarding house, a billiards parlor, and a saloon. Whether Mick made a home with his sister or with one of his Mahoney cousins is not clear. But, clearly, his parents didn't think well of his opportunities in Ireland. Before he left home, Mick and his father had a formal photograph, a tintype, taken, the only picture available of Cornelius. Mick was hired by the Boston & Maine Railroad to clean railroad cars at the Roundhouse in Bradford, a position he held until h is death in 1914.

The 1870s were prosperous years for Con and his family and some of the profits went into the building of a fine stone, two-story house, in a Georgian style with enclosed fireplaces on each side of the house, and a fine tin roof. When I first visited, I questioned why the Donovan farm was referred to as "Spike." What did it mean? Did it apply to the farm as a whole, or just the house itself? Was it a Gaelic work that just happened to look like a familiar English word? No one knew, and the younger generation, well-schooled in Gaelic could not find a reference for the word. "Spike" it was, and "Spike" it has remain. By the time the house was livable, seven of the children were either married or had emigrated. Only the two youngest, Con, Jr. – the presumed heir, and young Dan who was in his early teens were still at home, along with their mother and father. Julia's father, John Mahoney, may have stayed in his old home, or moved to the new home as he was already a very elderly man. Mr. Mahoney lived a long, full life and died in 1881at the age of 103.

A long life was not in the cards for Con and Julia's oldest child, Ellen. Ellen had married Harry Schofield in 1860, before Dan was born. In 1878 she gave birth for the first time. She and Harry had a daughter, named Julia, born the 21st of July, 1878. Ellen died the next day of "puerperal convulsions," or childbirth fever. With all of Julia's midwifery skills, she could not save her own daughter. Ellen was only thirty-eight years old.

The next few years would see great changes in the Donovan family life. As mentioned, Julia's father John died in 1881. In October of the next year, Con, Sr., died of a strangulated hernia. He was seventy years old. His son, Con, already designated the heir, quickly arranged a marriage with Brigid Donohue of Goleen Balteen in February, 1885. His young brother Dan didn't need a fortune teller to let him know that as large as the new house was, there was no room for an unmarried younger brother, with no property of his own, and no trade as his brother Tim had. As for the other occupant of the house, Julia Donovan, who had handled the role of housewife and hostess for almost fifty years, what her new role in the new house was to be would be a much-discussed topic in the letters from Ireland to Dan in America.

2. *DAN DONOVAN LEAVES FOR AMERICA*

It was April of 1885, a good time of year to cross the Atlantic, and time for Dan Donovan to say farewell to his home, his family, and his friends. A few weeks shy of his twenty-first birthday, Dan was about to leave Ireland for a new life in Haverhill, Massachusetts. His father, Cornelius, who had died in October 1882, had done well enough both as a small farmer and a breeder of livestock that he was able to leave a modest inheritance for his family including his youngest child, Dan. Donovan's second youngest son, another Cornelius (Con) had inherited the family farm (or, more accurately in that time immediately before Land Reform, he had inherited the lease on the farm). Con, and his new wife, Brigid Donohue, had set up housekeeping in the family home. The signs were easily read by Dan – it was time to strike out on his own.

This left his mother, Julia. She had been the primary hostess in this family for many years. Her discomfort in adjusting to a new mistress of the house, was a problem that percolated through a number of the letters sent from home to Dan in America. Julia did have an alternative. She could always move back to her family home just west of the newlyweds for it had been vacant since the death of her father, John Mahone, in 1881.

Julia would miss her handsome, fair-haired, blue-eyed son. If such a term could be applied to the late nineteenth century, then it could be said that Dan was "doted on" by his parents, with his own horse and dog (Carlo), and some years of the schooling not available to his older brothers and sisters, but that was slowly returning to post-famine Ireland. Yes, she would miss her youngest, but she had three married sons, two married daughters, and hera widowed son-in-law all within walking distance (as measured by that age of much walking, and little transportation. Surely, there must have been horse-and-cart available for a woman in her late sixties, but there is no mention of such until one of the very last letters from Con to Dan.)

Dan had made the farewell rounds of his brothers' and sisters' homes all located within a few miles of the family farms. First, west to the townland of Drishane where his oldest surviving, and very pregnant, sister Mary, and her red-headed husband Mike Hodnett lived with their houseful of six daughters and one son. Mary, born in 1844, was old enough to be Dan's mother, and her eldest child, Katie, was only six years Dan's junior. Dan had made a second home at his sister's house, and always was welcomed for, surely, his help on the Hodnett farm was a great assistance. From the Hodnetts, it was a brief walk, or short trot on his horse, to Henry Schofield's farm. Henry was the widower of Dan's oldest sister, Ellen. She had died seven years earlier giving birth to the Schofields' only child, a daughter, Julia. Henry had since remarried and had a second family.

Dan's farewell to his sister Julia, was an easier journey for she and her husband, Johnny Minihane, lived in the townland of Cussivina, south across the fields from Dan's home. The small cottage was already crowded with six children, and Dan had often helped Johnny and Julia with the farm chores until their two oldest sons, Frank and Pat, were able to take on their share of the labor.

The visit to "Darraheen," his brother John's farm on the eastern slope of Mount Corrin in the north-eastern corner of Dreenlamane, was a difficult one, for Dan would not only be saying "good-by" to his beloved oldest brother, but he would be taking with him to America John's first-born, Ellen/Nell, who was only four years younger than her Uncle Dan. John and his first wife, Mary Murphy, had three children: Ellen, Cornelius and Julia. When Mary died, John found himself a strong new wife, Ellen Mahoney, and already the small cottage on the hill was bursting with John's "second family" of six children to bring a total of nine children and their parents (and the father of John's first wife and lease-holder on the farm.) Young Ellen Donovan must have found it easier to leave home, and all the crowding and noise and work, for she would be traveling not only with her handsome young uncle, Dan, but she would have the company of her good friend and neighbor, Mary O'Brien from nearby Dunbeacon. The two girls were sixteen, Dan almost twenty-one. The sad leave-taking was tempered by the anticipation and excitement of the week-long sea voyage on a steamship filled with other Irish emigrants, many of whom were their own age. And there was the new life ahead that each would begin in their ultimate destination, Haverhill, Massachusetts in America.

Dan's final farewells were saved for the day of departure. His brother, Cornelius (Con), and his new wife, Brigid Donohue, were now the master and mistress of the new family home. The old Mahoney homestead still stood but now its primary occupants were the cattle and horses the raising of which had provided the profits that built the new home.

There was a third house on the Donovan farm lot in addition to the old house, and the recently built house where young Con lived. It was the home of Dan's maternal uncle, Matthew Mahoney, his wife Jane, and their large family, half of which had already gone to the States. The Mahoneys and Donovans each had shares in the farmlands, pastures, and the rights to grazing on Mount Corrin. The two families were close physically and socially, and were in and out of each other's homes regularly. Dan's farewell to the Mahoneys was almost as difficult as that to his own siblings.

That left Mary Ann McCarthy. Mary Ann lived in Rookerrig, a distance away on the next peninsula, Sheepshead or Muintir Bhaire. It would not be quite proper to say that Dan and Mary Ann were courting, but they certainly were good friends, and Mary Ann definitely wished the relationship were closer. Dan decided not to make a farewell visit to Mary Ann, but he committed himself to writing to her after he was settled in America. She could be a very aggressive lass, and he didn't need that complication in his life right now.

Dan was a desirable "catch" and Mary Ann was not the only young woman who had hopes. He was a handsome, well-built, lad of moderate height. His bright blue eyes and his well-groomed brush of a mustache made him most attractive. Dan had attended the Dreenlamane National School and received much encouragement from the master, John Mahoney. He had no family farm to inherit in Ireland, but he would make his way with energy and charm in his new home across the sea.

So, on a pleasant day in late April, Dan, with his niece Ellen, and Mary O'Brien, gave their homes a final look, and headed for the nearby village of Ballydehob. It was almost as difficult for Dan to leave his dog, Carlo, and his fine horse. The immediate destination of the young people, and their accompanying family members was the home in the center of Ballydehob of Dan's brother Tim, known as The Saddler, for his trade of leather work. Tim was a successful craftsman, and owned a large home and workshop in the heart of the village.

Tim, like John, had lost his first wife, and one of his first children. His new wife, Kate McDonnell (also referred to as O'Donnell, or Donnell), was pregnant with the second child. Tim would drive the three young people in a wagon borrowed from a neighboring merchant to the market town of Skibbereen where they would board the train that would take them east to the port at Queenstown/Cobh.

There was one last farewell to make, and it was the most painful, for waiting at Tim's house was Dan's mother, Julia Mahoney Donovan. The family had survived the Great Famine, the death in 1878 of daughter Ellen, and the death in 1882 of their husband and father. Julia had already gone through the heartbreak of saying farewell to emigrant children twice previously. Daughter Honora (Hanna), born in 1847, had left in 1865 with her infant son, Cornelius who was only four months younger than his Uncle Dan. Hanna and her husband, Pat Driscoll, already had seven children by 1885, but would find beds for young Dan, and Ellen and Mary in their boarding house and home in Haverhill, a bustling industrial city in northeastern Massachusetts, where Pat Driscoll owned a few buildings including a saloon, and billiard parlor, in addition to the boarding house.

It was to the Driscolls that Julia Donovan's second emigrant child, Michael/Mick, had gone when he left Ireland in the early 1870s. A member of a later generation would describe Mike as undersized and "tongue-tied," i.e. with a speech impediment. In 1885, he had yet to marry.

The realization that the three travelers had a place to stay at the Driscolls' boarding house must have provided some comfort to the Donovan and O'Brien families. They were reassured that young Con Driscoll, and brother Mick and perhaps a Mahoney cousin or two, (brother Mick and the Mahoneys would be recognized by Dan), would meet their ship upon its arrival at the terminal in East Boston. The relatives would lead the travelers to the Boston & Maine train at North Station. About an hour later they would arrive at the railroad depot in Haverhill and Con Driscoll would direct them the two short blocks from the depot to their new home. One can't help but assume that sister Hanna and husband Pat and, perhaps, their older children would have been a loud and boisterous welcoming party for the travelers at the station. What a joyous procession they would have made from Railroad Square, east on Granite Street to the house at the corner of Essex and Locust streets.

Haverhill was a center for the manufacture of women's shoes, known as "slippers." Just three years earlier, in 1882, a terrible fire had destroyed the entire shoe manufacturing area, not far from the Driscoll's home. Now, the streets surrounding Driscoll's saloon and boarding house were lined with new four-story brick buildings all involved in the booming shoe industry or its related leather tanning, stitching, and cutting operations. The city was in the middle of an expansion not only economically, but in population and construction. Haverhill was attracting a sizeable number of Irish, French-Canadian and northern Italian immigrants to diversify the solidly "Yankee" core of its inhabitants.

Before Dan Donovan left home, he received a gift from his brother, Tim the Saddler. It was a leather money belt made by Tim, and, maybe with the help of Tim's apprentice, his namesake nephew and son of John, Timothy Donovan, The money belt was filled with the gold sovereigns (coins) that were Dan's share of his father's estate, and, one assumes, shares also for Mick, for soon after Dan's arrival, Mick married and immediately built a two-family home across the Merrimack River in the town of Bradford. It was near the Boston and Maine railroad depot and roundhouse in Bradford. Mick worked for the railroad as a laborer. Dan Donovan, with his secret horde of gold coins, could be a far more fortunate emigrant than most of the other young people who sailed with him. (Dan's youngest daughter remembered playing with the money belt as a child without ever knowing its origins or purpose, except that it was made by "the Saddler," whoever he was!)

And now, back in Ballydehob it was time to go. Mother gave her blessings and warned him, again, to "stay away from the drink," to write home as soon as he could, and to take good care of the young girls for whom he was now responsible. His brothers, Con and John, and brothers-in-law John Minihane and Mickey Hodnett, who had all joined in the walk to Ballydehob, gave their final hugs and kisses and words of advice. Into Tim's wagon Dan and the girls climbed. They were away. The great adventure had begun.

der, Miss Lucy Rodelle and others.

Arrived on the Bothnia.

The Cunard steamer Bothnia arrived yesterday from Liverpool with 24 intermediate, 781 steerage, and the following cabin passengers: Robert Brown, W. A. Randall, W. F. Fisher, Fred W. Brown, B. C. Creebman, Philip Lemorrtais, Sarah Darwin, Elizabeth Thayer, Elizabeth Young, Hosea Hewitt, Francis Howard, Jesefrin Swift, Harriet Freethy, John Freethy, Martha Freethy, Minnie Freethy and Constana Freethy.

The Boston Daily Globe notes the Bothnia's arrival on April 27, 1885. Unlisted are the, the passengers in steerage, including Dan Donovan.

Endnotes

1   *Dan Donovan's second daughter, Catherine Marion Hayes, had purchased a lovely print of a Rembrandt painting of a bearded man, titled "The Man in the Golden Helmet." From the first time he saw the print in Marion's home, Dan would always refer to it as "Uncle Mathew." The family knew nothing of said uncle and it became a family joke to refer to "Uncle Mathew." Imagine the surprise upon first going to Dreenlamane to find out there was indeed an Uncle Mathew Mahoney, who had lived immediately west of the old Mahoney home and most of whose children had gone to Massachusetts about the time that Dan had done so.*

THE DONOVAN LETTERS

Part I: D1 to D50
1885 to 1890

DOCUMENT D1

The first letter in the Donovan Collection, appropriately, was to Dan from his mother. Dan had sailed for America on 27 April 1885 on the S. S. Bothnia, and must have written to his home immediately for this response was sent only sixteen days after he sailed. It took about one week for a steamship to cross the Atlantic at this time. The phonetic spelling used by the scribe –either brother Tim or his wife Kate Donovan – can be somewhat challenging.

13 May 1885 – Mrs. [Julia] Donovan,[1] Ballydehob, Co. Cork, Ireland to Daniel Donovan, Haverhill, Mass.

Ballydehob
May 13, 1885

My Dear & loving children

Once more I inbrace [the] opprusunity of addressing ye with a few lines hoping in God the[y] will find ye are in the enjoyment of good health as the departure of this Leaves me & all the others at presant thank God for his goodness to us all.

My Dear & loving son Dan, I reseived your letter on 10 inst. which raised me once more from that Pat[h] I have so often gon true. Returning you thanks for your arrival and for his goodness to us all. Dear son I feel quit[e] strong now. I am down in Ballydehob[2] for the past week where the[y] do be often a good laugh nocked out of me. I am serting you did not forget Good Friday night last and all the funny storrys that Tim tells me rises my hart. 1 am thinking I will go across me self very soone. I am sorry I did not go with you as you had such a good pasage.[3] I felt as you did not say anything about Ellin as she did not wright her self. Her father feels trobled about it. I thought you wold give me a lot more information about Mick & Hanna & the family. When you are writing the next letter don't for get it. Lit me no if Hanna is very worn ore if Mike is any thing like the pitcure[4] that we have at home. Tell Hanna & Mick to excuse me for not sending anything to them. You no that I could not do any thing them days. Con and Bridget is pulling out Breare.[5] They have the coart[6] and all now to them selfs. All the boys & girls is the same as you left them. I was very glad how you stud so well to the girls going over. Tell Hanna that I would like to have her pitchure & Micks also & not for getting your own. I am sorry to say that it is probable that it will be the only sight I will ever get of ye.[7] A mothers advoice keep away from all bad company. Good by Dear childringfrom your most affectnet Mother Mrs. Donovan

ENDNOTES

1   *Julia Donovan was baptized in Schull Parish 27 August 1817, daughter of John Mahoney and Ellen Brennun of Dreenlamane, Ballydehob, Co. Cork, Ireland. She married Cornelius Donovan 27 February 1838, the 28th of 38 marriages recorded that day in the Schull Parish Register. (A Civil Register of Vital Records did not begin until 1864 in Ireland.) The Donovans had nine children, all of whom survived the Famine Era to adulthood. Con Donovan died 9 October 1882 of a strangulated hernia. He was 70.*

2   *She was at the home of her third son, Tim, a saddle maker.*

3   *Dan sailed from Queenstown/Cobh on the S. S. Bothnia and arrived in Boston on 27 April 1885. Traveling with him were his niece, Ellen, daughter of John Donovan, and a neighbor, Mary O'Brien, both 18 years old.*

4   *Welcoming Dan and the girls on their arrival in Haverhill was his older brother, Mike (1845-1914) who had immigrated in the early 1870s, and his sister Honora (known as Hanna, or Norrie), who came to Massachusetts with her infant son Cornelius in 1865. Neither Dan, nor his female companions, would have any memory of Hanna, and little of Michael. They were strangers, but they were family. Hanna (1847-1902) married Patrick Driscoll (1843-1891) in November 1865 in Lawrence, Mass. They moved to Haverhill and Pat operated a saloon and boarding house, and this place became the first home for family members like Mike, Dan and Ellen when they arrived from Ireland. Hanna had nine children with Driscoll in addition to her first child, Con, who was born the same year as his uncle Dan.*

5   *Con was the fourth of Julia's sons, baptized 11 July 1857. He inherited the lease to the family farm, known as "Spike," upon the death of his father in 1882. A little over two years later he married Brigid Donohue of Gunpoint and took up residence in the recently built two story stone main house, thus setting the stage for youngest brother Dan to leave. Con and wife Brigid were pulling out briar bushes at their farm.*

6   *Probably the Irish term "scoriachting," (pronounced "skwairting" that is, welcoming friends and neighbors for a visit whether spontaneous or planned.*

7   *Julia was prescient. Not one of her children ever returned to Ireland.*

Document D2

Dan's friend, Mary Anne McCarthy, from Roskerig on the neighboring Sheepshead or Muntuir Bhaire Peninsula, wrote the first of her five letters in June. Her tone is a bit coy as she wonders if he has been thinking of her. She appears to be well known to Dan's family and must have had some sort of acknowledged relationship with him.

4 June 1885 – Mary Anne McCarthy,[1] Roskerig, Kilcrohane to Daniel Donovan, Haverhill, Mass.

Roskerigh
June 4th 1885

My Dear and Beloved Dan,

It is with pleasure I set down to write you these few lines hoping you are well as this leaves me in at present, Thanks be to God.

My Dear Dan, I received your letter 2 days ago for which I return you many thanks also I can never express all welcomes I had for it although it took many a tear off of me when I thought of former days and it is little I thought when the saddler carried you out of Mahoney's at Ballydehob[2] that I wouldn't see you any more[3] but I hope in God we will see each other again too.

My Dear Dan, I am glad you had a nice passage going across but I suppose you were not thinking of me any time. y Dear Dan, I hope you are well as I would be more than delighted to hear of. My Dear Dan, you asked about cousin Ellen.[4] Indeed, I imagine she'll soon be a mother. She was very sick about a month ago. She said it was an egg that sickened her but Dan I said that it wasn't and that it was Mick that sickened her. I know you will laugh at it surely.

My Dear Dan, I mean to tell you that I was talking to Con a May fair day[5] and he told me that all were quite well. My dear Dan, I hope you will excuse me for not sending you my picture this time. I would but I would be afraid that you woudent get it until the next one whatever. Dan, I will send it for certain in the next letter and a few nice songs.

My Dear Dan, I hope you will write soon again and also I hope you will send me your own Picture. I would send you my own only I woudent like to send it in the first letter, afraid you woudent get it but I will be impatient now until I know will you get it. Dan if you like the songs you can tell me and I will send them to you.

My Dear Dan, leave me know was it in Boston you landed or did you see Maria from Whiddy. I suppose you remember the day of Mrs. Mahoney's funeral[6] that you were telling it to me.

My Dear Dan, I am quiet well thank you only the grief that I have after you but I suppose you haven't that for me. Dan I would give any amount to see you once more any way.

My Dear Dan, I will tell you all about Katty the next time. She didn't get married at all. Dan I will tell you a lot of newses the next time so Good by my darling far away. I send you my fond love and kisses and I hope we will soon meet. Dan we can write now as well as when you were at home.

Good By love far away.

Mary Anne McCarthy.

ENDNOTES

1   *Little is known of Mary Ann McCarthy of Rosskerig. She could be the daughter of Denis, a shoemaker in the village of Bantry, and Ellen Sullivan, and born 27 January 1865. This birthdate would make her a close contemporary of Dan Donovan. Her letters tell us she had a brother Denny who went to America in 1887, and sisters who lived in Auburn, Mass. Rosskerig is on the Kilcrohane (Muintir Bhaire, or Sheeps Head) Peninsula, immediately west of the Mizen Peninsula where the Donovans lived. Evidently she socialized with Dan quite frequently in the years before his departure for America.*

2   *Dan's brother, Tim the Saddler, drove Dan, Ellen and Mary to the train in Skibbereen. Mahoney's was a shop in the village of Ballydehob.*

3   *There is a suggestion here that Mary Ann was among those gathered in Ballydehob to say "farewell" to Dan and the girls.*

4   *Ellen McCarthy, daughter of Denis (deceased) of Roskerrig, married Michael Hosford on 10 February 1885. On the same date, Margaret McCarthy, a widow of Roskerrig, married Timothy Daly. Another related marriage took place on 10 March 1886 of Margaret McCarthy, daughter of Denis (deceased) of Roskerrig, to Eugene McCarthy, son of Michael of Roskerrig.*

5   *The 25th of the month was Fair Day in May in Ballydehob. There was a designated Fair Day each month in Ballydehob when local farmers would bring stock to the market, along with butter or other items whose sale would provide the money needed to pay the landlord.*

6   *Margaret Mahoney, wife of Joseph of Dreenlamane, died in 1882, aged 60. She died the same year as Dan's father.*

Document D3

Con Donovan was nearest in age to his brother Dan. There were more letters from Con in the Collection than from anyone else in the family. Most of them deal with farming details as well as family news. Mother Julia was with Con when he was writing this letter, added her own note to Dan.

14 June 1885 – Julia and Con Donovan, Dreenlamane, Ballydehob to Daniel Donovan, Haverhill, Mass.

June 14 1885
Dreenlomane

My Dear and beloved Sheldren,

I now take my pen in hand to writ ye these few lines hoping to find ye all in the injoyment of good helth as this note leaves us in at present, thanks be to God for his blesson to us all.

My Dear son, we reaved [received] your letter yesderday which gave us great pleasure to [k]now that you were well in health although it trebled us very much that you were not at worke thinking you may be unwell.

Dear brother, when I was reading your letter and seen you so trebled about home that I had to stop up and hand it to Bredgit to read it but if you feels lonesome or bad, you know where you left.

Dear brother I had the field carted[1] the day I got the letter .

[The following was written and then crossed out: "and that evening I felt so bad to think that of it."]

The brake[2] is the best of it. I have plenty staks in it and the rest of the field is meddling. Andrew[3] was with me carting it. I can not rite a bit with my fingers are cropt from markning the thrinches. They were so hard. I cut the turf yown bog and I had Mike Donnel[4] making hand turf[5] two days. I did not cut anything in Raheen.[6] [two rows of kisses]

I did not part with any of the stock yet.[7] If you cart a cow or hefer to the fair you would not be asked where you would you be going with them. It is the worse year to make money of any thing that ever come. Butter is for 6 or 7 pence a pound. I d not put any thing to the hill[8] this year. The mair is very well and will foal before the 20 of this mounth. Dear brother Dan, Johnny's wife[9] is very bad always and is not much yet. Some says it is the yellow ganders[10] she have and she had the opponion of two doctors and they sead it was not. The rent calling the 9 of June, we went in and Johny had to take it in the Bank, his name being in before its in your name.[11] We took it a ear rent. Tell Ellen to mind herself and tell her about her father. Tim have a young saddler.[12] His name is John. They are all well. John Minihane's horse[13] was hurt by a fall in the lackeene.[14] Himself was after him when he ran and fell with forse. We dont know is that it or not. His legs or lifess and can not rise without help. He is getting on these days. I have no more to say at present but remain brother,

Cornelius Donovan.

ENDNOTES

1

2   *The brake, or breac, is the rough ground where furze grows.*

3   *The only Andrew in the area was Andrew McCarthy, Dunbeacon. He was born in 1858, and married Mary Murphy of Dunbeacon in 1898.*

4   *Mike McDonnell, born January 1865, of nearby Coolagh Beg, was the brother-in-law of Tim the Saddler.*

5   *"Making hand turf:", i.e., shaping the peat into blocks for the fire place.*

6   *Raheenroe is the townland to the immediate west of Con's part of Dreenlamane. He probably had a field there.*

7   *There are numerous references to the accumulation of stock (cattle, horses) made by Con, Sr., and from which he derived a fairly comfortable living, all things considered.*

8   *The Donovan house and outbuildings are on the lower part of a slope on which are three fields, divided by hedges, or brush.*

9   *John Donovan (1841-1914) married, as his second wife, Ellen Mahoney (1855-1915) of Coomkeen in 1874. John was already the father of three. Ellen delivered her sixth child (John's ninth) when Patrick was born on St. Patrick's Day 1884.*

10   *Yellow jaundice.*

11   Either John Donovan had to take out a loan from the bank to pay his rent to the landlord, or take out some money from an account that had both his name and Dan's on it.

12   Tim and his wife Kate had a son, John, baptized 23 May 1885. Tim had fathered two sons by his first wife, Brigid Donovan, who died 20 April 1882. His younger son, Cornelius, died a year later. His older son, Michael, was taken in and raised by Brigid's family from Leighcloon. Tim married Kate in December 1881. They had a daughter Mary Ellen 31 December 1883. John was their second child.

13   John Minihane (1840-1923), of Cussovina, was Julia Donovan's husband. Julia was the sixth child and fourth daughter of Con and Julia Mahoney Donovan, baptized 7 August 1852.

14   "Lackeene:" a steep incline. Cussovina townland is flat ground so John and his horse had to have been some distance from home.

Document **D4**

Some of the most descriptive letters in the Donovan Collection
were from his sister Mary Hodnett and her husband Michael.
They appear to have been written by her husband Michael, or
Mick, who regales Dan with his troubles with his neighbors.
Dan's mother was visiting her very pregnant daughter Mary
at the time this letter was written and includes her own
message.

12 July 1885 – Mary and Michael Hodnett, Drishane,
Durrus and Julia Donovan to Daniel Donovan, Havcrhill,
Mass.

Drishane[1]
July 12, 1885

My dear brother,

We received your kind and welcome letter which afforded us
the greatest pleasure to hear from you and knowing that you were
in good health and also brother Micke and sister Hannah and
husband and family.

My dear brother, I hope that strange boss will take no effect of
you. I am glad you are not loosing weight. I hope you will continue
so. Dear brother, we got home to Ballydehob that day about one
o'clock.[2] Mother went home that day and went into her bed and
is there since. They said they would fix her bed on the loft. She
objected. Mary and I[3] told him to bring his bed and put it in the
barn so he did in a few days after and the young couple east since.

Mother is well. She came to our house last night. She was present
at the writing of this letter. She felt bad after you going. We went
east the Sunday after. We and the brothers and friends concoled
her. She is as well looking this day as I saw her these last 7 years, I
told her. So don't be troubled about her so much. She is all right.

Dear brother, we are not digging the spuds yet. The summer is
very dry and not hot. The gardens have not as much stalks as they
had this time last year. We were a few Sundays ago at the Saddler's

Christing. We had a very unpleasant day. The worst we ever had in that occasion. We had like to have it worst, and Mary coming out of the earth [hearth] at the Saddler's door her dress got fast, was thrown down on the guard stone and broke her ribes. She felt bad for three weeks after. She is well now. Ellen Mahoney[4] is getting on well. She will soon be all right. All the brothers and sisters of family are giving thanks to Providence.

Dear brother, you asked in some former letter did Jerry Neill interfere with me in the bog. No, he did not, but a worse serpent did. Mary Harnedy and her husband cut it unknown to me. I dried the turf and was draying it when she come with a stick and struck the place three times of it. I pulled if from her and broke it on my knee so I went to the turf and she and her brothers came and had no less mind than to tear me to pieces. So I summoned them, but they had old Sam and Jim Levis[5] to swear for them. Yellow Mary and Jim Levis swore that I choked her, threw her down and came down on her and she lost her senses. The Lord knows that I was as innocent of that charge as the Angels of Heaven. I had like to see the blackman but I worked them up and down. I made them perger themselves and well it was for me powder and ball was against me and wanted to fine me but I gave him tit for tat when I found I had to do it as he could do no good for them. He dismissed my case and the Harnedys and Murt[6] came that evening and cut the rest of my bog but if I had money I would take it to sessions where they would not play on me. They are trying to do all they can in me. They advised the agent not to take a half year's rent from me yesterday. The clerk he has is a cousin of the Harnedys, as you know is William Neil. They went to my dealer William Sullivan of Bantry told him that I was broke and he pushed me for next fare, the Devil will be ready for them in some future day.

From Mother

My dear and loving son dont be troubled about me. I am all right now. I am in good health and I am pleased in my mind when I hear from you and knowing that you are working and in good health and also it pleases me to know that Mike is so convenient to you. Let me know is with Hannah you are boarding. So I have no more to say at present but I send ye all my blessing across the Atlantic.

My dear brother, I hope ye will be looking out for some old house for me again the spring. I suppose I must make a run of it as all the Devils are so much against me. I am very much displeased over my situation at present. Mary will be expecting a letter from you. Before long, we may be able to convey some glad news to you. We may have an increase in the family. No more at present from your loving brother and sister,

Michael and Mary Hodnett[7]

xxxxxxxxx

ENDNOTES

1   *Drishane townland is a few miles northwest of Dreenlamane on the coast of Dunmanus Bay. Durrus is the nearest market village.*

2   *Refers to the day Dan left for America.*

3   *The Donovans had two houses at the home farm in Dreenlamane: the old farm where Dan and his siblings had been raised, and a newly built house where Con and Brigid lived. The old house was a sizeable two stories with a lower section on one side that was used as a barn, and an attached one story unit that may have once been a separate house. The mother chose to stay in the old house and leave the new mistress, Brigid, to her own home. Mother Julia would than make periodic visits to her four other children in the vicinity as they needed her help with new babies, and so on. Mary Hodnett was the oldest surviving daughter in the family, sixteen years older than young Con, and could "pull rank" on him as to the care of their mother. The new house was east of the original farm house. A third building on the property was the home of Uncle Matthew Mahoney and his wife Jane.*

4   *John Donovan's wife. The tendency to refer to married women by their birth name can be confusing.*

5   *The Neills, Harnedys and Levises were all Drishane neighbors of the Hodnetts.*

6   *Murt (Mortimer) Minihane of Drishane.*

7   *Mary Donovan Hodnett was the third child of Con and Julia Donovan. She was baptized 11 May 1844 and married Michael Hodnett (1844-1900) in February 1868. Mary died in 1908.*

Document D5
2 August 1885 – Con Donovan, Dreenlamane, Ballydehob to Daniel Donovan, Michael Donovan, Hannah Donovan Driscoll and family, Haverhill, Mass.

Derreenlamane
August 2, 1885

My Dear brothers and sister, husband and family,

I now take the greatest opershunity to write you all these few lines hoping they will find ye in the injoyment of good helth as this letter leves us all in at preasant, thanks be to God for his blesson to us all.

My Dear brother Dan, I receved your leer a few days ago witch gave us the greatest pleasure to now that ye were all well. Dear Dan, Ellen Mahony[1] is well now, thank god for it, and John Minihane horse is getting on a little.

Dear Dan, Mother is well and injoyment good helth, thanks be to God for it. (Don't read but what you like of this.) Sends her best love to you and Mike and Hannah and husband and famealy.

Dear brother Dan, I'd like you would not be working in such cloce place. I think I would rather worke oute in the country where I would have the open ear.

Dear Dan, the crops are looking very well now what ever they will do and I think that it will be a good year in spuds except had drie ground fore the yeare came dry.

Dear Dan, the mare have a mear foal, a very nice one.

Dear Dan, leave me now in the next letter is Mike going to get married or what [he] is up to or do you think have he much money. He must sum surely except he drink and now you ar working hard and now you now everything and don't card play or drink but as little as you can.

The tram is making to Skull and any man have but 10 shillings a week and few miners getting 12. Let me [k]now how ar the friends and neighbours getting on and how is Kate[2] making. I now would it be any use for me to send for the ten shillings she got going away. Let me know how is John Cronnan getting on. Mary Cronnan[3] is over before now.

[row of kisses] XXXXXXXXXXXXXX

Your mother and Sisters and brothers or all well and they all joynes in sending best love to you all.

Dear Dan, me and Bridget ar well and sends our love to you and Mike and hanna and family. How is Ellen getting on.

Dear Dan, let me now did Ellen see any of her sweeth [sweat] yet. I suppose the heat is taking some of it from her. She often told me that any work would not make her sweath. She sends a letter els where and she would send me one. I have no more at present but remain your ever truly, Cornelius Donovan.

(write with heast)

ENDNOTES

1   *Ellen Mahoney Donovan, John's wife.*

2   *Kate Mahoney, the daughter of Uncle Matthew Mahoney, born July 1865, had sailed on the S. S. Scythia to Boston in 1884. Her siblings, Jane and John, were already in Haverhill when Dan arrived in 1885.*

3   *John, born July 1862, and Mary, born c. 1863, were the children of Denis and Ann Cronin of Derryfunshion, west of Dreenlamane. John immigrated to Bradford in 1880, and Mary in 1885. Another sibling of John and Mary was Patrick who died of typhoid fever in Bradford on 14 April 1892. He was unmarried, 25 years of age, and a laborer.*

Document D6

Mary Anne McCarthy sent her picture to Dan. One could very well be she. Her parting words might raise an eyebrow on any one who assumes young Irish girls in the 1880s were modest and reserved.

20 August 1885 – Mary Anne McCarthy, Roskerigh, Kilcrohane, to Daniel Donovan, Haverhill, Mass.

Roskerigh
August 20th, 1885

My Dear and beloved Dan

It is with pleasure I set down to answer your kind and fond welcome letter hoping to God you are well as this leaves me in at present. My dear Dan, I received your letter a week ago for which I hope you will excuse me for not writing before now. I would only I was waiting to get my picture taken. My dear Dan, your letter was a month coming all to one day. My dear I hope you will like me know. Leave me know how will you like me. My dear Dan, it was in Ballydehob I on got it taken a Lady day.[1]

My dear Dan, I was speaking to Con and the Saddler and your mother. I was asking them about you and Johney Minihane said not to tell me any more about you for that I suppose I had a letter from you myself but I said I hadent. Your mother told me you were to come home again soon.

My der Dan, leave me know will you or not. They said they were all very well but I dident see Con's wife yet.

My dear and loving Dan, I hope you will excuse me for not writing before now. My dear Dan, leave me know how are you getting on or do you feel lonesome. I wish I was in one city with you this evening. We would have a pleasant evening but I hope we will yet. Please God.

My dear Dan I hope you will send me your own Picture now as I would be delighted to see one sight of you now. So I hope you wont refuse me now for it.

My dear Dan, I hope you wont delay this now if you can. We can write just as well now as if you were in Dirrelamane. My dear Dan, I thinks just as often about you as if I had you to see, Dan. My Picture was taken very Bad because it was a very Bad day. I woudent send it at all now only it would be too long to wait until I would go to Bantry.

My dear Dan I send you my Best love and respects out from my heart and my heart with them too. So no more at Present

Remember me when this you'll see though we be far apart,
while others have my company tis you that have my heart.

Also

That the dove of love mitent ever loose a feather
until you and I will be in one bed together. Amen.

Good By darling from your affectionate, Mary Anne McCarthy.

Kisses. XXX big ones. Send me the same.

ENDNOTES

1   *"Lady Day," is August 15, the Catholic Feast of the Assumption of the Blessed Virgin Mary. It is a tradition to try to go to the seaside on this day and bathe in the salt water for good health in the next twelve months.*

DOCUMENT D7

Dan's sister Mary had just delivered her eighth child, a daughter Annie, after a difficult three- day labor. Her mother was her experienced midwife and was still at the house to lend a hand. She took the opportunity of a letter writing session to add some sentences of warning to Dan regarding the evils of alcohol.

20 September 1885 – Mary and Michael Hodnett and Julia Donovan, Drishane, Durrus to Daniel Donovan, Haverhill, Mass.

Drishane
Sept. 20, 1885

My dear brother,

I received your kind and welcome letter which gave us the greatest pleasure to hear from you and to learn that you were well in health, thanks be to God for his kind mercies to us all. My dear brother, I cannot express my thanks to you for sending me the pound you send me. It was more than I expected from you so soon, though I consider if my folks in America knew my wants they would lend me a hand but thanks be to God, as they have not heard of my death. I thought last Tuesday it would be the tidings that would reach you all. I was unwell for three days not having no hope but hopes in God. You might imagine how I felt for [my] helpless family, but thanks be to God, I was alright. On Tuesday night about one o'clock my daughter was born.[1]

Dear brother, the reason I delayed not writing was to have a satisfactory account to convey to you, thanks be to God that sparing me to control my flock. Con and Kate Donnel[2] stood for her. Anne is her name. She is a very stu[r]d[y] infant. I don't feel very well yet. I got too much. I hope to be getting strong any more. Dear brother, I did not tell any one that you send me that pound but only Mother and Con. I knew that Julia[3] would be talking but the report of a registered letter goes far but we threw it on another seale.

My dear brother Dan I thought of the last baptism you were with me in Goleen.[4] I cannot tell you [know] how I was last week to be as I thought would be in care of a house full of orphans. But thank God it was quite the reverse. Your brothers and sisters are well and mother also. She is a brave soldier and as hardy as ever in what she went through last week. We all feel happy this morning for being able to give a good news to our friends in a foreign land.

Dear brother, I conclude by closing and sending you our best love and compliments. We remain your loving brother and sister,

Michael and Mary Hodnett

(Note from Mother Julia Donovan, sent with above letter)

My dear and loving son, I am glad that you are in study [steady] work. I hope you wont turn at the drink like your brothers at home and abroad. I hope you will keep away from bad company that would lead you ruin. If you were to see the times here at present, though since you went not long, you would be fonder of a shilling than of a pound before this. I feel proud to hear often from you. I send you my blessing to you all. Good bye. XXXX [Mother]

ENDNOTES

1   *Annie Hodnett, seventh daughter and eighth child of the family, was born 16 September 1885. Her mother, forty one, had been in labor for three days. It was her good fortune that her own mother was an experienced midwife. Annie's godparents were Kate McDonnell Donovan and Con Donovan. The Hodnett children were Kate (1870-1956), Mary Ann/Mamie (18873-1955), Ellen (1875-1967), Richard (1876-1952), Julia (1878-1967), Honora (1881-1925), Johanna/Hanna/Ann (1883-1970), Annie (1885-1979), and Elizabeth Mary/Lil (1889-1976).*

2   *Godparents for baby Annie were Dan's brother Con, and Tim's wife Kate Donnell, also spelled O'Donnell and McDonnell.*

3   *Mary's sister, Julia Donovan Minihane.*

4   *Drishane, where the Hodnetts lived, was a part of Goleen Parish that encompassed the western side of the Mizen Peninsula. The parish church was in the town of Goleen. The last child baptized before 1885 was Johanna, and Dan was her godfather.*

Document D8

Con reported on the failure of the Munster Bank and its effect on the various members of the family. He also included some details on the way in which packages from home were hand-delivered to family members in America, courtesy of the good will of emigrating neighbors.

11 October 1885 – Cornelius Donovan, Dreenlamane, Ballydehob to Daniel Donovan, Haverhill, Mass.

Derreenlamane
October 11, 1885

My dear brother Dan,

I receved your letter a few weeks ago and we were all glad to now that you and Mike and Hanna and her family were all well, as we enjoy the same at present, thanks be to god for it.

Dear brother Dan, I hope that you will escuse me for not answer your letter before now. The reasen was I got a soar finger but it never injure me of werkning, thanks be to god for it. It is well now. Dear brother, mother is enjoy good halth thank god.

Dear brother, I suppose you hear about the Munster bank. It did not troble mother a bit, for I told her not to mind about it, that she would never want for while the Lord would spare me helth but it will be soon all right with god help. I am going to send you a paper and you will see all about it and about the meeting in Ballydehob last Sunday, so much people were never seen together with baners and flags they march trough and froue. [to and fro] Dear brother, Nelly Schofel[1] is not going this year and the first opershunity we get you will have the ganse.[2] Bridget was not well this back two monts[3] which led me around a good deal. She is well now, thank god. Your brother and sisters and families ore all well, thank god.

Dear brother, what the matter with Ellen that she is not writing. God help her father to be weatning for her assistance. She promest to a help August. The closing of bank Munster [hurt] him very much for every one that owed money in the bank should clear it up.

It was no goke [joke] to make up 14 pounds with every thing etc. and the year been so bad. He sold the colt for 5 pounds and heifers for 2 pounds each. We all jynes in sendning you all our best love.

No more at present from

Your affectionate brother,

Cornelius O'Donovan[4] XXXXX XXXXX XXXXX

I cannot stop of dremen [dreaming] this week back. Write soon.

ENDNOTES

1   *Nelly Schofield was the sister of Henry of Drishane, the widower of Dan's eldest sister, Ellen, who had died in childbirth in 1878. In the 1860 Federal Census for Andover, Mass., there is a family of Schofield siblings, all born in Ireland. They included John, 18, Mary, 24, Bridget, 17, and Nancy, 13. John married and had a family. In later years, relatives from the Dunbeacon/Drishane areas will cite John's home as their destination in America.*

2   *A "ganse," or Guernsey, was a jersey (Irish) or a sweater (American).*

3   *Brigid Donovan was pregnant with their first child.*

4   *The "O" on Con's surname evolved from a small loop on the upper part of the "D" to a full scale capital "O." Few Irish names encountered while working on this letter collection had the "O" attached. By the early 20th century, most had them.*

Document D9
n.d. – Cornelius Donovan, Dreenlamane, Ballydehob to Daniel Donovan, Haverhill, Mass.

[The following appears to be an additional page to another letter. It was probably written in 1885 or 1886, before brother Mike was married.]

Dear brother,

We or all well in helth and mother is very well and sends her blessons to ye all. Let me know how John Cronan getin on or is he working. You spoke about Jen[1] the day you went away. She gave a great speech that day but in a short time after she got a sore foot and did [not] come out since. Let you and Cronan pray for her.

Jerry[2] send 3 pounds these days and said you would be soon home again. I sends my [best] to Mike and Hanna and family.

Good by for a while. Write soon.

Con Donovan

Dereenlamane

XXXXXXX XX XX

Endnotes

1

Jane Carey Mahoney (?-1904), wife of Dan's uncle Matt Mahoney of Dreenlamane.

2   *Jeremiah "Jerry" Mahoney, son of Matt and Jane, lived in Haverhill.*

Document **D10**

Dan sent Mary Anne his photograph in October 1885 and this kept her hopes alive that she might yet have a future with him. She starts to hint that she may soon be in America, and that she has no romantic ties with any one, not even the local constabulary sergeant She will repeat these hints in the next letters, but Dan does not appear to have encouraged her.

23 October 1885 – Mary Anne McCarthy, Roskerig, Durrus to Daniel Donovan, Haverhill, Mass.

Roskerigh
October 23rd, 1885

My dear and beloved Dan,

It is with the greatest Pleasure I set down to write you those few lines hoping you are well as this leaves me in at present. Thank god.

My dear Dan, I received your kind and welcome letter 2 days ago which gave me the greatest pleasure to see you once more. My dear Dan, I return you many thanks for your picture.[1] You looks beautiful, Dan. I hardly knew your face you got so nice. My dear Dan, you may say it was a welcome guest to me. My dear Dan, you were taken lovely. My dear Dan, I hope you are well and that you are thinking of me but they say out of sight is out of mind and that is not the way with me or I hope other with you. My dear Dan, I wish I was in that fine country of yours. You look so beautiful. My dear Dan, leave me know how are you getting on. I sends my best love to you but I hope it isn't in vain. My dear Dan, you may say that it is long until I will loose you now since I caught you once more. My dear Dan, please leave me know would you like to have I send you a nice tie. I would send it to you in this letter only I dident like to send it until you would tell me would you like it and what colour would it be.

My dear Dan, as many letters as ever we send to each other any one dident ever see one of mine and I have every one of yours yet. My dear Dan, I am to tell you that I am soon for leaving home but

I think I wont leave until after Christmas now. It is to myself to do what I please but Dan I will do whatever you will tell me do in the next letter.

My dear Dan, I think I would rather cross the Atlantic and to work in America than to stay at home in Ireland. My dear Dan, I could get the sergeant in the holy ground if I would like to take him and while grass is growing or while water is running I wont take a peeler.[2] My dear Dan, me mother is telling me take him but she might as well hold her tongue. Let them all go bedamed. My dear Dan, leave me know is America a good place for girls.

[no signature]

ENDNOTES

1   *Of the surviving pictures of young Dan Donovan, the one most likely that Mary Anne refers to is of a seated Dan, wearing a velvet-collared top coat over a suit and tie, and holding a bowler hat upright in his left hand. It strikes just the right note of a well-assimilated new immigrant who has shed all his "greenhorn" trappings. Dan sent a copy of this picture to each family member in Ireland, and Mary Anne.*

2   *A "peeler" was a policeman or constable, so named for Sir Robert Peel who founded the first police force in Great Britain. Apparently, Mary Anne had a sergeant in the police taking an interest in her. According to Guy's Postal Directory of Munster for 1886, the sergeant in charge of the Kilcrohane constabulary district was Bernard Dunne.*

Document D11

Dan's other female friend, Hanna Cronan, lived in nearby Andover, Massachusetts, about ten miles west of Haverhill. Hanna and her family had lived a short distance from Dan's townland in Ireland. Hanna worked in a textile mill in Andover, where Dan had gone to look for her. Hanna wrote in a more "proper" style, typical of what was expected of New England mill girls at that time who had to be conscious of "their place" and protect their reputations.

28 October 1885 – Hanna Frances Cronan[1], Andover, Mass, to Daniel Donovan, Haverhill, Mass.

Andover, Mass.
October 28:: 1885

Dear Dan,

I now take the pleasure of writing you these few lines in hopes to find you well. I am also well. Dear Dan, it made me feel bad to think I was not at my work a Monday when you went into my room. Did it scare you? I got many compliments for you that you were as good looking a fellow as they saw going into that room. I wished I was there at the time. I might never see you in there again. I wished I did. You were no shame. It let them to understand that you did not look like a green horn at all. Some of them said to me they would take you to be out here 3 years the less.

Dan I did not have much time to talk to you the last time you were here. I hope I will soon see you again and can talk. Dear Dan, this is one thing. I hope you will not go to the party to Mary Dailys at all. I will not go. It do not suit me be running to parties every where one is. Show this to no one please. Goodby with love to you, goodby. XXXX

I hope you will tell me did that girl from Mientervarew[2] write to you ever since you left home. This is the first letter I ever wrote to any fellow that ever breaded breath. Dear Dan, I hope you got along in Lawrence the day of the trial. I hope you will answer this and send me a correct address and tell me did you go to the party. I hope you will not for I know something. Dan, I hope you will answer my letter soon as you get time and do not let known to any person that I wrote. I shall say more the next time. Its late. Its 9 o'clock.

Dear Dan, I hear a news this after noon, a very bad news for me, a news that I shall tell you as soon as I will you see. O but if that news will come to pass, unhappy I will be. Good bye, Dan.

Write soon please and address to Miss Hanna Frances Cronan, Main Street, South Andover, Mass. No more at present from your affectionate friend Hanna F. Cronan. Good bye.

Write soon please.

Dan do not go to the party and have sence, please.

Good by Dan.

Remember me.

We will meet again, please God XXXXXX

ENDNOTES

1   *Hanna Frances Cronan was born in September 1864 to Jerry and Ellen (Regan) Cronan, Derryfunshion, a townland west of Dreenlamane, and near Drishane. She came to Andover, Mass. in the early 1880s and was working in one of the textile mills in that town, possibly the Stevens' Mill.. She may have worked in a weaving room, the noisiest place in such a factory, hence, her question to Dan as to whether he was scared when he was in the factory.*

2   *Muintervary Peninsula, or Sheepshead, where Mary Anne McCarthy lived.*

Document D12
16 November 1885- Hanna F. Cronan, Andover, Mass, to Daniel Donovan, Haverhill, Mass.

Andover
November 16: : 1885

Dear Dan,

I now take the pleasure of writing you these few lines in hopes to find you well. I'm also well, thank God for his Kind Mercies to us all. Dear Dan I received your kind and welcomed letter which gave me great pleasure to hear from you. Dear Dan, I cannot free all the questions you asked me till your face I'll see. I hope that wont be long, please God.

Dear Dan, if you did not go to the party I feels ever so much thankful to you but I hope you will not refuse the next invitation you will get. We are going to have a party up to Pat Driscoll's[1] the Saturday after thanksgiving. Annie Sullivan is going to give ye the invitation. She is inviting Johney Mahoney, Jerry Mahoney, Jerry Sullivan[2] and Dan Moynihan. And I told her to invite Jemmie Mahoney and Patrick's too sons,[3] Mickel and Dan Donovan, that's yourself. I hope they shall come. If you come make your self to home. Come pleas. If you comes, I hope we will have a good time. Doant you let on to any one no of it.

Dear Dan, I did not delay this letter as long as you did mine. Dear Dan, the next time you come into that room the girls will not have any quipines[4] on their heads. They are getting a mechine in there to get away the dust. I ante [ain't] going to work in there all my life, please God.

My dear and best love, I hope you will answer this letter with love. Dan do not go back on me if wind do not drive you woman would.

My Dear, I must draw my letter to a close for want of room. I will tell you lots of things when I will see you. I hope I will have a better time to talk to you the next time you come.

My Dear Dan, I only ask one word, forget me not. I feel ever so much thankful to you if you did not go to the party. Dan its bed time. I must bid you god night with love to you.

Good bye. No more at present from your friend Hanna F. Cronan

Goodbye for a while.   Forget me not. XXXXXX XXXXXX XXXXXX XXXXXX

Dan, no matter where you go on land ore on sea,
I'll share all your sorrows and care,
and when at night I kneel at my bedside to pray
I remember you love in my prayer.

Hanna to Dan

ENDNOTES

1   *Pat was Dan's brother-in-law.*

2   *The two Mahoney's were Dan's first cousins, and Sullivan was the son of another Mahoney cousin.*

3   *Jemmie was Dan's cousin and Pat Driscoll's two sons were Con and John, both nephews of Dan*

4   *"Quipines" – head scarves*

DOCUMENT D13

Dan sent copies of his photograph, and money, to his family members at Christmas. Con had the responsibility of distributing the gifts.

4 January 1886 – Cornelius O'Donovan, Dreenlamane, Ballydehob to Daniel Donovan, Haverhill, Mass.

Derreenlamane
January 4, 1886

Dear brother,

We received your kind and wellcom letter on Christmas eve which gave us all the greatest pleasure to hear from you all long with your pitcher.

Dear Brother, When I took out your letter and opened it and found your pitcher in it and did not expect any money so soon, you may be sure [I] did s[h]ed some soft tears that moment to see you stand. It looked as nice as when you left and nicer, and Mother was overjoyed to see you, and all your friends. You may say you got many a kis but we thought Mike would send his own and Hanna. Tell them that we would like to have them and we have all the rest.

Dear Brother, I delivered the money as you sed, to each of them. Bridget and mother returned you sevear thanks for your kindness to them and shall never forget for you. Dear Brother, all thought I had a good account from you. I felt very lonesome a Christmas night when I thought of the last night, but that can not be helped. The frinds and neighbour or all well in helth thanks be to god for it.

Old Jack Murphy and Misses Dempsey of Ballydehob[1] was berred on Christmas day, the Lord have Mersey on there soul. Dear Brother, the Saddler have the League of the Cross[2] these two months on. It is no harm for him. He is now dowing first reat.

Dear Brother, there was a ship racked to the west of bird's Island and every won from this west is ever rich from it with flour and meat. They took it with the boas [bows] and in a day or two it came into the shores in banks. Mikey have plenty meat and flour for this year and they all made lots of money of it.

It is sead hear that it is to Stantin's daughter that John Cronan is married.[3] I thought I would have a letter from him. Mother sends her blesson to you and Mike and Hannah and her family. It is a deal I lost with Ellen in fitting her out. That is every penny that was lost with her although you or her did not know it and she would send letters every where around and never send or lend to us.

No more at present.

Con O'D [two rows of Xs, kisses, across back page.]

Endnotes

1   *John Murphy was the father of John Donovan's deceased first wife. Anne Dempsey, 25, a shopkeeper's wife from Ballydehob, died 23 December 1865 of puerperal fever following childbirth. Her death was reported by her sister-in-law, Ellen Mahoney. The daughter to whom Anne gave birth was probably Ellen Dempsey, who is listed in the 1901 Census as a fifteen-year-old living with her aunt, Ellen Mahoney of Rathruane Beg, Ballydehob.*

2   *Tim Donovan had "taken the pledge" with the League of the Cross, an abstinence society.*

3   *John Cronan, 25, married Mary McCarthy, 24, daughter of Pat and Margaret, in Haverhill on 20 November 1885. Dan Donovan was Cronan's witness.*

DOCUMENT D14

When the Hodnetts sent their thanks to Dan for his Christmas gift, they included a lively description of the shipwreck which provided a supply of provisions to those willing to gamble that they would not be caught by the customs authorities.

24 January 1886 – Michael and Mary Donovan Hodnett, Drishane, Durrus to Daniel Donovan, Haverhill, Mass.

Drishane
January 24,1886

My dear loving brother,

I mean to communicate these few lines to you hoping the arrival will find you in as good a state of health as this leaves us in at present, thanks be to God for his goodness to us all.

My dear brother, I cant find words to return you thanks for your kindness to me. Though I wanted it, I did not blam[e] you. You had so many to distribute your hard earnings to and that you done honorably.

Dear brother, let me know are you in the same job always or how times are getting along with you. We are all well in health, thanks be to God.

My dear brother, we often think of you. When the Ibernian[1] struck in Bird island if you were at home you would be with us at that time. Bird Island is to the north of where Con one day was matching making with Miss Cotter. There was a deal of meat and flower [flour] in her for them that had help to bring it or save it on shore. She lies there still with the chief part of her cargo.

Dear brother, I am sure you will think of next fair day when we were drinking with James Hicky and Johnny Minihan rose a row. I am sure you often thinks of days gone by but I hope you are content. Let me know all particulars in your letter. Is sister Hanna kind to you or was it with her you Christmassed. We oftened talked of you that night though we did not hear of your letter until next day.

Dear brother, we will soon have a great day in Spike at the cristning.[2] Nelly Welsh and all the crew are supposed to be there but we will have no sport as brother Tim is a teetotaler. He changed very much for the better and you know he wanted it.

Dear brother, I bring this to a close by sending you our best wishes from your loving brother and sister and nieces and nephew.

No more at present from your loving brother and sister,

Michael and Mary Hodnett.

ENDNOTES

1   *The Iberian ran aground off Bird Island on 21 November 1885. It was en route from Boston to Liverpool with a cargo of cattle and a crew of fifty-four, all of whom survived. Bird Island is off the southwestern tip of the Mizen Peninsula*

2   *Con and Brigid were expecting their first child, due to be born in April. "Spike" is the name of the Donovan farm, origin unknown.*

DOCUMENT D15

Brother Con brought Dan up to date on death and life, and reassured him that his new wife was getting along fine with their mother.

15 March 1886 – Cornelius Donovan, Dreenlamane, Ballydehob to Daniel Donovan, Haverhill, Mass.

Derreenlamane
March 15, 1886

Dear Brothers and sister,

I now write these few lines hoping they will find ye all in the enjoyment of good health as the deparcher of this leves us all in at present, thanks be to God for his mercies to us all.

Dear Brother Dan, I received your letter on the last day of February. On that night Tim's child died, the youngest wone.[1] He was sick onely three days. Jane Driscoll, John Sullivan's wife of Greenmount, also died.[2] She was after her confinement. May the Lord have mercy on ther soal.

Dear Brother, there is not much of the spuds planted yet. This month is very wet, hard and coald so no one planted much yet. Dear Brother, they did not many get married this season hear [here] but James Harnety's daughter of Drishane got married [to] Tade Driscoll of Dunman's pear[3] pier] and went there with little money.

Dear Brother we arr all well, thanks be to God for it. Mother is injoyment good health as ever she did yet, thanks be to God for it. Dear Brother, as soon as you get this letter, write and let us now how is Hanna for we feal uneasy until we hear from her.[4] And I hope I will have a good account again then as Bridget is near her confinement. Let me now how Mike [is] or did he get married yet. Let me now how Patrick Driscoll and family [is]. Let me now Ellen or is she in place yet. I felt sorry when I her [hear] she had the soar throath. Her father is trobled until he get a letter from her. He promest a rounce for her as he wanted her help.

Dear Brother, I understand that some person must interfear in telling you about mother and me but as true as God tould you, marriage put never a shange between mother and me and any one could not be kinder to each shodder than bridget and mother is to one nother.

I remean your ever truly,

Cornelius Donovan

ENDNOTES

1   *Tim's infant son, John, died of bronchitis on 28 February 1886. He was nine months old.*

2   *Jane, born 24 September 1848 to John and Mary (Burke) Driscoll of Dreenlamane, married John Sullivan of Greenmount in 1881. Jane Driscoll Sullivan, 32, died 18 February 1886 of exhaustion "after a difficult labor of five days."*

3   *Ellen Harnedy, 18, daughter of James of Drishane, married Timothy Driscoll, son of Patrick of Dunmanway, on 6 March 1886. Patrick was known as "Paddy Og," meaning "Young Paddy," or "Paddy, Junior."*

4   *Hanna Donovan Driscoll, Haverhill, was expecting her ninth child when Con wrote this letter.*

DOCUMENT **D16**

Hanna Cronan expressed her feelings for Dan more openly than previously, and even included a few lines of poetry to win his heart. Dan must have made a lukewarm response, for there were no more letters from Hanna in the box of "Papa's Letters".

2 April 1886 – Hanna Cronan, Andover, Mass, to Daniel Donovan, Haverhill, Mass.

Andover April2:: 1886

My Dear friend Dan,

I now sit down to write you these few lines in hope to find you well. I'm also well but awful mad with you for to say you heeded false stories in the first place. I thought they were above that kind and Dan, I do not think they are for your good. They might want to plaster you on some one of the old maids.

But Dan, I think you are more wide awake than all that. I think you want only an excuse of going back on me. Dan, I know you can get hundereds better looking than me but I might be as good as other will and Dan that's the way with half the world. When they think a poor girl is going to be a kind of lackey, they show there teeth. But I doant thank them a bit. I hope I will not give any one any thing to say so I hope they will mind there own business for the time to come for God knows that fellow I no nothing about nor no other Andover fellow.

Dear Dan, I hope you wont be mad with me for not showing you my picture. I was going to give you one only they were locked in Kate's trunk and the money and I was a kind of scared for she was ill drunk and I was afraid she would spend my money so I will send it to you as soon as I can whether you want it are not. O, Dan, for God's sake, doant name this about Kate. I would not tell this to no other soul living. I hope you are not mad with me. I hope you will soon come back again. I will go to Haverhill in the middle of May for it's the first time you ever asked me to go to Haverhill so

I'm going on that invitation. Please, Dan, if you are gone back on me, I will be an old maid.

Your absence still to me though art dear, I often wish if thou were here,

And still I think if e'er we meet can our love and joy be made complete.

Many eyes may on thee gaze, other hearts may soon forget thee.

But what I have won shall ne'er change, from that it was when first I met thee.

Remember me, Dear Dan. XXX XXX

I hope you will answer this. I will send you my picture with the greatest of pleasure. I hope you will keep it fond and if you gose back on me, I hope you wont frown on the picture. Dear Dan, goodbye. Write soon.

O, I forgot to tell you, Ellie Harnedy got married to Tade Driscoll, Pady Oag's son. Good bye, write. No more at present from your friend, Hanna Cronan.[1] Good by. Burn this please.

ENDNOTES

1   *There were no further letters from Hanna in the Donovan Collection. On 10 January 1889, Hanna married Denis J. Carey in St. Augustine's Church, Andover. Carey was born in Massachusetts, and, like Hanna, worked in a textile mill in Andover. They had a daughter, Mary J., born 22 August 1892. The family cannot be found in the 1900 Federal Census, although there was a seven year old Mary Carey in an orphanage in Lawrence. Such institutions were not only for orphans, but also provided a temporary home to children whose parents could not care for them, as in prolonged illness. In the 1910 Census, there is a Dennis Carey, widower, who was a cook in a boarding house in Andover. He is the right age and of Massachusetts birth to be Hanna's husband.*

Document D17

The Hodnetts send the news that brother Con and his wife Brigid have their first child, a son.

15 April 1886 – Mary and Michael Hodnett, Drishane, Durrus to Daniel Donovan, Haverhill, Mass.

Drishane
April 15, 1886

My dear and loving brother,

I hope you will excuse me for delaying the receipt of your letter. I hope you will not concede to yourself for one moment that it was through negligence I delayed it so long. It was to convey some strang tidings to you. After shorouf [?] regarding it, I have nothing of importance to dictate. I got no chance myself or the grey mare.

Knell Harnedy joined Tade Pady Ogue, or big Pad, that do as brisk with grog and with friends. Jack will tell you all the particulars. It appears that many were not anxious for him where as he took her without a penny in hand but waiting for the gold that is in another man's pocket.

My dear brother, I was very unwell for the last three weeks with a cold and all the family also. It was more like a inflewence than a natural cold but we are all well now, thanks be to God. I am sorry to tell you that brother Tim buried his son John aged 10 months. I suggest you would write him a letter and sympathize with him. He and wife felt bad for him.

My dear brother, on last Sunday there was born for Con a son and John is his name[1]. His wife was very bad. She was anointed for death. In a few hours after her case turned up well.

Your mother is well in her own house living peaceable together and will be taken fonder now than ever. She got half her money yesterday. The remainder will be paid in January next.[2] All your brothers and sisters are well. This is the wettest year that came with the memory of men. The potatoes are not put in yet. They will see summer before finished. Times are very bad at present. Nothing buying or selling in fairs. Though Home rule is contemplated, the farmers of the country will fall to ruin. Butter is between 4 and 6 pence a pound.

My dear brother, I was glad to learn that sister Hannah having an increase in her family, and being well herself and her baby.[3]

My dear brother, we will have a day next Sunday in Spike at the Christening. We will remember you I am sure. The last time w wre in Julia's the following day[4] you will call to mind. When we were graffing in the glen[5] we often speak of you. We don't see any of them since you left. Snday or holiday all industry and puting in the purse.

My brother, I bring this to close by letting you know Mary and the children are well and join in sending you their kindest love. No more at present.

We remain your ever loving brother and sister,

Mary and Michael Hodnett

Write soon.

ENDNOTES

1   *John Donovan, son of Con, was the only one of that branch of the family to come to America. Two of Con's children, Ellen and Dan, went to college and became teachers, a second daughter became a nun, Con III inherited the farm, and youngest son, Mike, became a detective on the Dublin police force.*

2   *It is not clear where this money is coming from. Perhaps it is mother's share of her husband's estate. It is known that when Dan came to America he wore a leather money belt made for him by Tim the Saddler, that was filled with gold coins. Some part of the funds must have been given to brother Michael for he married within a year of Dan's arrival, and soon thereafter purchased a newly built two family house in Bradford. Dan married in 1890 and moved into a recently built seven room house which suggests available funds above and beyond what his work as a laborer would have brought him.*

3   *Agnes Driscoll was born 21 March 1886. Her uncle, Dan Donovan, was her godfather. She was Hanna's ninth child.*

4   *The last family christening that Dan would have attended would have been that of brother John's son, Patrick, born March 1884. Dan helped the family of his sister, Julia Minihane, with their spring planting the day after the christening.*

5   *"Graffing in the glen:" digging the ground with a graf, preparing it for planting seed potatoes.*

Document **D18**
18 April 1886 – Cornelius O'Donovan, Dreenlamane, Ballydehob to Daniel Donovan, Haverhill, Mass.

Derreenlamane
April 18, 1886

Dear Brothers and Sister,

I now take my pen in hand to write you these few lines hoping they will find ye in the enjoyment of good health as this leaves me in at present thanks be to god for his blesson to us all.

Dear Brothers, I mean to tell ye that I become a father of a young son since the leventh of this month. His name is John. Johny and Mother that stod for him.

Dear Brother Dan, the day that the shild was crosten [christened] it was late when we wear home and that night Ellen Brine[1] went away. I went west[2] next morning and she was gone. I would not wish it for anything. Brigid had the gangey made a fortnight before she got sike[3] and it is a very good one and I don't know any one els going and if I do they will get it. When Mike will see it he will ask for another. They are very good tings for the winter.

I sent you the first paper of the new year. Did you get it. Tim's shild was buried in at the south side of father.[4] Tim is now all right since he do took the league of the cross and every one in Ballydehob have it and all around the place and if ye took it two it would be now [no] harm for ye.

Let me know is the worke your at now as good as the last. I think it's a good clean job. Let me [know] what is the pay.

Let me know is Mike in that same job still. We wear very glad to now that Hanna was do[ing] well. Mother was troble until she heard from her and is now glad to have you and Mike together. Brothers and sister are all well. Is not Ellen a good help for her father. They did not three dry days come since the middle of February until the 11 of April so the gardens wear never so late. I have last sat [set] tomorrow and thre or four ackers to be sate yet.

Mother is as wel as ever you see her. She send her blesson to ye all. I have no more to say at present but remain,

Cornelius O'Donovan – Write soon.

Let me have your own address.[5]

ENDNOTES

1   Ellen, daughter of John and Anna (Murphy) O'Brien of Dunbeacon, was the younger sister of Mary who had gone to America with Dan Donovan in 1885.

2   Dunbeacon is west of Dreenlamane.

3   Brigid, Con's wife, had completed a gangey, or knitted sweater, for Dan two weeks before she went into labor with her first child. Guernseys ("gangeys") and jerseys were two styles of heavy sweaters named for the British Islands from which they were traditional, similar to those from the Aran Isles in Ireland.

4   The majority of the Donovan burials, to the present, are in the Dunbeacon Graveyard. Three other children of Tim were buried in Bawnaknockane Burial Ground, north west of Ballydehob on the road to Bantry. Their grandmother, Anne McDonnell is also buried there as is Tim's namesake son, who died in his twenties..

5   Dan had left the Driscoll home and was now sharing a rental with his brother, Mike.

DOCUMENT **D19**

1886 was a very difficult year for farmers in West Cork. Not only was the weather not cooperating but some landlords were pressing their tenants for their rents. Tim told Dan of the sheriff's actions in Dreenlamane. Another version of the story will be told in the next letter.

6 June 1886 – Timothy and Kate Donovan, Ballydehob to Daniel Donovan, Haverhill, Mass.

Ballydehob
June 6 '86

My Dear and fond Brother,

Yours to hand, it gave us great pleasure to see by it ye were all well as this leave me and all the others at preasant, thank god. Dear Brother, I was surprised you did not sea more in your last letter ore let me no more about the friends.

Dear Brother, you want to no how is Johnny getting on. I must tell you sum thing just. As you left him you now that the old man left a good deal of Rent in him wene he died.[1] So I need not tell you where he got it as he shold pay it to get the receipt in his own name sume 4 ore 5 weeks after his death as Peeter Regan and his wife[2] dune there best to have the old mans place but it faild hime. Johnny would be as comfortable as any one belon[g]ing to home if he could put two years more over him. You sea [say] the country cannot be as bad as the report. I can tell you it is eaven worse and a great deal worse than the years of the charity that you remember 5 years ago. Wher as the cow you would get £14 ore 15 for on last yeare, you wold not get more than £5 ore 6 for them this year. Butter for 1/- [shilling] 10d [pence] last year this /4d + /5d + /7d the best. Judge this + you can judge how is the steate of the contry. I am sending you papers.

There was a great day in Derreenlamane this week by the shorrif, bailfs, + all the forse, 25 cares of polocice [police]. They swep what Willy and Wid. Nagle had.[3] Then they went up to Molaagbee to the masters[4] and gave that a clean sweep at a very early oure in the morning. But as it was agin the master the order was, the catle was brought back agin at there own expence as the order shold be agin the father. Sea [say] nothing about it + I will be able to give you more putallers [particulars] in the next letter.

Remember me to all the frinds as well as menchan all is well. Hoping you + all the others is the same. Ever yours,

Kate & T[im] Donovan

[This note was added to the first page of the letter from Tim and Kate.]

Just as I was writing this on Sunday Johnny got his letter + the contents which made him as big agin + will make him all right. May God speare you long. Good by. XXXXXXXXXX

ENDNOTES

1   John Murphy, father of John Donovan's deceased first wife, is listed as lessee of the house and farm land where John Donovan's family lived. Murphy is on Griffith's Valuations and each of the Continuing Valuations forms through 1884. On the form that was filled out in 1886, John Murphy's name is crossed out and (dead) is written beside his name. John Donovan's name is written over Murphy's name, indicating that he is now the lessee and responsible for the rents. What is not known is whether or not Murphy had been living with the large and growing Donovan family, or if he resided with his only son, a policeman.

2   Peter Regan and his wife Catherine (Murphy) lived in Scrahanyleary, a townland to the north east of Dreenlamane. Peter was godfather for John's first child, Ellen, and his wife was godmother for John's second child, Cornelius. Regan was attempting to make a claim on his late father-in-law's farm in the name of his wife.

3   Willy Nagle and his mother, Annie, wiydow of James, were Dreenlamane neighbors.

4   The school master of the Dreenlamane National School was John Mahoney, and Molaagbee was the name of his farm. His father was also named John Mahoney and had his own farm. The seize order had been intended for the father, but because it was delivered t his namesake son, it was invalid, and all the Master's cattle were returned.

Document **D20**

Dan had sent the funds to his brother John that he needed to pay the landlord and avoid seizure of his cattle or his land. John provided more details on the sheriff's raid.

14 June 1886 – John Donovan, Dreenlamane, Ballydehob to Daniel Donovan, Haverhill, Mass.

June the 14, 1886
[Dreenlamane][1]

My Dear brother,

Its with pleasure I set down to write those few lines to you hoping to find you in good health as this leaves us all in at present, thanks be to god for his kind mercies to us all. Dear brother, I mean to inform you that I received your letter which was very welcome to me. You may be sure if it was empty it would be welcome to me.

Dear brother, I went to Durrus[2] to the agents the last time they were out. I asked time till the 9 of June but he would not give me onely till next evening so the third day I had your letter what I did not expect. May God spare you your health and reward you for your kindness. I told the strangers that I got six pounds from you but I showed the letter to me own. Every one prayed for you.

Dear Brother, your money reached me in a very good time. The landlord is coming so hard. I sent it off to him as soon as I got it and it was well for me to have it.[3] All the land are served with letters. No time but 3 days. Any that had high rents they brought writs on them. They were quickest to collect the money. John Mahoney got one but it was in the master's name. It came out so they did not settle till all the force came just at the dawn of day which was a fright to see. They were in bed till James Neagle[4] called them as they were coming to his house. They did not expect them although the order came. They were sure they would go further. They came in the night to old Nagle. He had nothing but they took all the poor Widow had and Will's at the dawn of day to Durrus pound where they were till the court day. Both made a declaration and they were left out. Their name was not in the order but they wont know the day that they will come again. There were about thirty cars of police and bailfs. When they had what they could get west sent to the pound they went east then. The morning was thick with fog and it was so early there was no one out. They took the cows. Will was driving them out. The sheriff put the revolver to his breast and would shoot him if he held any struggle but the master ran and told them to drive away the cows, that there was no one to stop them, so they drove them down to Joe's[5] and brought them back again. He warned that they had no order for his father's cows. They will not bring it in the wrong name the next time. They would give no penny reduction. Any one that could pay it in April got too shillings to the pound but few can pay the prices are so low. The best butter last week was onely 6d. [pence] a pound and from that down to 4 pence and less. Its time to stop of this and say something els.

Dear Dan, this is from your mother. She came up to stay when were [we're] going to write. Mother sends you her blessing. She is very glad how you are turning out. Mother cannot put you out of her mind at all. She is always talking of you. She have her hopes in god that she will never die till she will see you.

Dear Dan, Bridget is no good those too months. She is able to do nothing. Don't you speak about it ever if he dont tell it himself. Don't ever tell that I sent [said] anything about her to you. I can send you the news all ways. If mother was able to catch the pen she would write a long letter to you. Any thing she will say in this don't ever speak about it. My Dear Child, I have no more to say at present to you but sends you my love and blessing and to Mike and Hannah and husband and family, your ever fond Mother.

Dear brother, its all the money I made worth speaking of sence you left home too pounds five shillings of a heifer and five pounds of a colt. I paid that much in the bank and left six due. There were letters coming once a week. I did not care but it was in your name. I took it out and then the letters coming in your name was troubling me. So when Mother was getting a little trifle of her own out she told him to clear out your name and 1 will not forget her allways when I can with the help of god. Don't show this to any one. It is the greatest ease to my mind to have it paid. No one knows she done this for she would not tell it.

Dear brother, I did not ask her to do it. I could not if all went with the cart and more is not. So you asked me to let you know how I stands. I will tell you as well as if you were on the sod. I have six cows and a calf. Two of them ae the heifers I had when you left. I would not have them if I could get any one to buy them. I offered one of them for 2 pounds ten. I could not get it.

They were not well looking, you know, so they remaine with meself and if there was any price for the butter I could do something this year. Its time for me. I worked very hard this winter. I made a road south from the end of the house. I made a great fence on each side. I have a garden in the field of the house.[6] It is promising well yet. I had no garden last season. It was not worth digging the most of it.

Dear brother, I would write to you before now but I did not like to do it. You asked me to let you know did any of the boys leave home since. They did not but Jer[7] was sure he go this year but he got no encouragement from the rest. The master[8] got your letter and paper. He is going to write to you. Let me know how is brother Mike. So he would not ask for me. Let me know how is sister Hannah and husband and family.

Dear Brother, when you are writing to me, anything you want to know you can put it in a note for I should show the letter. We are all well thanks be to god and all joins in sending you our love and blessing. We can never forget your kindness to us. May god never forget you. Don't show this to any one.

Show this to Ellen. I am sending you the paper.[9]

ENDNOTES

1   *None of John Donovan's surviving letters give an address, nor do any of them have surviving envelopes from which a postmark would have provided a location.*

2   *Durrus is a market village north west of Dreenlamane, at the head of Dunmanus Bay which separates the Mizen Peninsula from Kilcrohane/Sheepshead peninsula.*

3   *Dan must have responded to Tim's news about John's need to pay up the back rents on his farm. The amount of money he sent was more than six pounds, and at the rate of about a pound equal to five American dollars, Dan gave John the equivalent to a month's pay. He also may have been giving him a share of the inheritance he brought from Ireland with him.*

4   *James Nagle was born August 1862 to Patrick and Mary (Driscoll) Nagle of Dreenlamane. He was still at the family home, and unmarried, in both the 1901 and 1911 Censuses.*

5   *Joseph Mahoney (Feigh), Dreenlamane. Feigh indicated a subgroup of the Mahoney Clan. Julia Mahoney Donovan, Dan's mother, was a member of the Glacy subfrouop of Mahoneys.*

6   *John Donovan's home and farm is the only one still operating. It remains in the Donovan family.*

7   *Cousin Jeremiah Mahoney, son of Uncle Matthew, did not emigrate until 1890.*

8   *Schoolmaster John Mahoney of the Dreenlamane National School.*

9   *This letter was probably written by John's second daughter, Julia, for the spelling, penmanship, and grammar are a vast improvement over most of John's earlier letters.*

DOCUMENT D21
19 July 1886 – Cornelius O'Donovan, Dreenlamane, Ballydehob to Daniel Donovan, Haverhill, Mass.

July the 19, 1886

Dear Brother

I now drop you these few lines hoping they will find you and all the friends in the best of health as this leaves us all in at present, thanks be to god for his kind mercy to us all.

Dear Brother, we receved your letters which gave us the gretest pleasur to hear that ye wear all in the best of health.

Dear brother, we are all in joyment of the best of health and mother is very well, thank god arid nothing deliths her more than to hear from you often.

Dear Brother, the shild is promising very well as yet and every one compares him to you. We did not a drop of rean these two mounts until these day. So crops wear porely up to this but they are looking well now. Now [no] one dug the spuds yet hear, for they did not come on in time.

Dear Brother, John and family are well. Julia and family are well and she is a near her confinement.

Dear Brother, you naver see the mear [mare] in such stile as she is this day and I don't know which of them I will sell. The mear is so young looking.

Dear Brother, we are trobled about the gangey that   [next third of letter, and right hand side of bottom third are missing – appears to be information about the gangey/sweater that Brigid had knitted for Dan]

And after wearing itmes if it dount be   we   will   make   a nother……. You are taking it off…….up from the bottom in and over your head.

July 24

Dear brother, I wrote this a weak ago and then 1 stopped again to tell you about Julia. She got a young son the 23 of July.[1]

[middle third of this page and left hand side of bottom third are missing.]

I must [go to] the fair with and I am in a hurry. Ive no more to say at [present] but remain youre ever [-loving] brother.

C. O'Donovan

[the following note to John Cronan was included with the above letter in one envelope]

Derreenlamane
July 24, 1886

My Dear friend John Cronan,

I now write you these few lines hoping they will find you and your wife in as good helth as this leves me in at present. Dear friend, as the times is so hard in Ireland this year an a man cannot make sail of anything atall, I wish you would remember me and send me the balance due to me. Your mother lost a cow by Nancy Gogen's gray horse[2] to strike her in the head and she fel dead and they settled at your mother to get two pounds and ten shillings as it been half the value of her. It is anough to tell you how sheap cattle are and a splendid young cow. No more at present from

C. O'Donovan of Derreenlamane
To John Cronan

ENDNOTES

1   *Cornelius Minihane was born to Julia Donovan Minihane and her husband John on the 23 of July 1886. His godparents were his thirteen year old brother Patrick, and his aunt Brigid Donahue Donovan.*

2   *Mary "Nancy" Goggin, daughter of John of Gloun, married Timothy Sullivan, son of Patrick of Gloun in 1885. They were living in Mount Gabriel, south of Dreenlamane, with their nine children when the 1901 Census was taken. The nouns and pronouns in the remainder of the paragraph are difficult to understand, but it seems that it was John Cronan's mother's cow that died, and not John's mother.*

Document D22
15 August 1886 – John Donovan, Dreenlamane, Ballydehob to Daniel Donovan, Haverhill, Mass.

August 15

Dear Brother,

Its with pleasure I sit down to address you with those few lines hoping to find you and all the friends in good health as this leaves us and all the friends in at present.

Dear brother, I mean to let you know I received your letter which gave us great pleasure to hear that you were well and working steady and also that all the friends were well.

Dear Brother, I mean to let you know that the gardens were as fine as ever you see them…this week they are down together it….late when they were….when they were after….earth. The dry weather came and last…..time till they were nearly picking up then they came plenty and kept them growing till they were stalks. I am afraid they will be no good. Sister Julia is well and has a young son, his name is Con. Dear brother, I suppose Ellen will not write any more. Your mother is well and Con and his wife and child are in good health and all your friends are well, thanks be to God. All the children are well and growing strong.[1] Mary[2] is growing well. She……you if I was to…… [If you were to hear] her talk, you would laugh hartly. She……no one els have any…… Dear brother, I suppose it is hard on you to work hard a broad in the heat and cannot take any rest. Its often I think of you when I am working. You must sweat very hard, I suppose. May God spare you the health and keep you from all dangers. Let me know how brother Mike is getting along and sister Hanna and husband and family.

Dear brother, we have a scarce year of   other. Con   £   3 12s [shillings] to take for hay. I gave tripel last year know can I spare any this year ….are not. It is now I am conting it if I can spare an he must have it. I am rearing a heifer for him and so I ought for he did not trouble me since you left for anything he gave me. You need not speak about anything. I have no more to say at present but we all joins in sending you and all the friends our love and blessings and still remain your fond brother and sister, John and Ellen Donovan, Dirreelamane.

[The following was on a separate piece of paper in the same handwriting.]

Dear brother, Mother is well as when you left. She is no trouble to any one. If they don't gain any thing by her, they will loose nothing. It is hard to find fault with her. She is as good for the now as ever she was. You need not be troubled about her. You know she wont be in want. She was not up here since we wrote the last letter to you. Con's wife is as well as ever she was. No Dear Brother, let me know in your next letter how Ellen is or do she take your advice. I don't think she do, or how is she working. Anything you will tell me I will not speak about it. Let me know is herself and Mary together.[3] Dear brother, Mother goes to Mass always when she like.[4] There is no one to hinder her.

ENDNOTES

1   *By this date, John had fathered nine children, eight of whom were at home. A tenth child, Daniel, would be born in September 1886.*
2   *Mary Donovan, John's eighth child, was born in May 1882. Dan Donovan and grandmother Julia were her godparents. Mary/"Molly" was a good student and was to become a teacher at the National School in Dreenlamane, but the head Teacher, John Mahoney, picked someone else. A few years after leaving school, Mary came to Haverhill for a few years, but eventually returned home to Ireland and married.*
3   *Mary O'Brien, from Dunbeacon, had sailed with Ellen and Dan in 1885.*
4   *There was a church (St. Bridgid's) in Ballydehob, but there was also a small chapel in Dunbeacon, serviced by the priest from Ballydehob, that would have been closer to Dreenlamane. This was also the chapel where ulia's daughter Mary Hodnett and her family, and son-in-law Harry Schofield and family worshipped.*

DOCUMENT D23

Dan offered to pay the way to America in 1886 for Kate Hodnett, Mary and Mike's oldest child. Their response underscored just how difficult times were for small farmers. Mike's use of the phrase "mean or pinureus (penurious)" hints at a facility with English that is somewhat unexpected. It is also a reminder that lack of access to education does not indicate lack of intelligence.

7 October 1886 – Mary and Michael Hodnett, Drishane, Durrus to Daniel Donovan, Haverhill, Mass.

Drishane
Oct. 7, 1886

My dear brother,

We received your letter on the 3 ultimo, which gave us great pleasure to hear from you and you being in good health as the receipt leaves us in at present, thanks be to God for his goodness to us all.

My dear brother, I cant but feel greatful to you for your kindness in offering to pay Kate's fare[1] again the spring. You must postpone it for another year as I must tell you that I could not put a pair of shoes on her feet. This is the worst year that ever came in this country. No money can be had for anything. The rest of the young ones are too weak to do anything to support them and also I would like to give her a little insite again the summer and one year would be great strength in her to face a foreign strand and as you are aware I would not like to be mean or pinureus at her departure. I hope to be better prepared in another year's time as you must learn. She is the only help I have. Richie[2] is as good a horse man as you would find in Haverhill of his age.

Dear brother, your brothers and sisters are well and brother John has a young son, Daniel[3] by name. He is two weeks old. Your mother is well. She was here with us those days. She is very troubled that you are so uneasy about her. Believe me that you'd have no occasion. There is no one to control her. She can go and come when she like and is taken fond. She can lie in her own bed in the old place where you were a child. If anything was the matter I would tell you, so don't believe any one that tell you otherwise. She has a shilling in her pocket when ever she likes to spend it. She tells me to tell you so. She will get five shillings to the pound now again of her money and five more again the spring. My dear brother, I am glad that you have study work and is conted [content] and in good health. Kate sends you her love and is very glad to be going to visit you in some future day. I have no more to say at present but we join in sending you our best wishes across the Atlantic from your loving brother and sister,

Mary and Michael Hodnett

ENDNOTES

1   Kate Hodnett, oldest child of Mary and Michael, was born in May 1870. She is probably the one who writes the letters for her parents. Her uncle Dan had offered to pay Kate's fare to America. She, in turn, would help her seven sisters to migrate, typical of the chain migration practice of assistance.

2   Richard Hodnett, only son of Mary and Michael, was born in October 1876. He was the only one of the nine Hodnett children to stay in Drishane, and the only one to stay in Ireland.

3   Daniel Donovan, son of John and Ellen, was baptized 25 September 1886. His godparents were his maternal uncle and aunt, Thomas and Ellen Mahoney of Coomkeen, Durrus. Dan would become a policeman on the Metropolitan force in Dublin.

Document D24

Brother John provided some background on the way in which their father accumulated the funds that kept their mother financially secure following his death.

6 January 1887 – John and Ellen Donovan, Drecnlamane, Ballydehob to Daniel Donovan, Haverhill, Mass.

January the 6, 1887

My Dear Brother,

Its with pleasure I sit down to write you those few lines hoping to find you in good health as this leaves me and family in at present, thanks be to God for his kind 0mercies to us all. Dear brother, you asked me to let you know how the crops were, wether we had as fine a garden as you could look at, but that is all the good it was. They got no time and the kind that come in them were not worth speaking of. This year was not as good as the last but them that have good land have not much reason to complain.

Dear brother, mother is well. She is taken fond and why not, she is as good for the house now as ever she was. As cheap as the stock were those too years he[1] made lots of money. He had so much spared stock and no expenses. Mother is keeping up the house. The mistress will throw nothing out foolish. Don't ever speak of a word of this to any one for fear it would come back.

Dear brother, Ellen sent me too pounds St. Stephen's day. I must feel very thankfull to her. A bad year. If any of the neighbours are going out this year, 1 am going to send you a piece of tobacco. I am very glad to hear that brother Mike is well married.[2] I thought he would ask me to the wedding. I hope you wont do so.

Dear brother, it would give me the greatest pleasure to get your picture. I am going to tell you that I have your name renewed. Ellen is not well since three weeks after he was born. I am sure I went to work too soon.[3] I am better.

Dear brother, how is Mathew's children pulling out. They don't send him anything. He is in great want. I have no more to say at present. We all joins in sending you our blessing and to all the friends and still remain your kind brother and sister,

John and Ellen Donovan

ENDNOTES

1   *Reference is to Con Donovan, senior, father of John and Dan.*

2   *Michael Donovan, 37, married Margaret Leahy 10 November 1886. His best man was named Jeremiah Mahoney, not Mike's cousin, Jerry, who did not come to Haverhill until 1890, but possibly the Jerry who was 0the son of John and Elizabeth Mahoney of Dreenlamane.*

3   *Ellen wrote this letter.*

Document D25

Mike Hodnett continues the litany of woes already expressed by his brothers-in-law, and Dan's niece, Katie, writes her first direct note to her uncle.

10 January 1887 – Mary and Michael Hodnett, Drishane, Durrus to Daniel Donovan, Haverhill, Mass.

Jan. 10th
Drishane: 1887

My dear brother,

We received your letter which gave us great pleasure to learn that you were in good health as the date of this leaves me and family in at present, thanks be to God for his goodness to us all. My dear brother, you need not be so disturbed about your mother. She is well and all your brothers and sisters and families, but Tim's children have the hooping cough. I hope they will get through with the help of God. They are not bad with it. It is favourable as yet "the burn child fears the fire."[1] My dear brother, the times in this country are the worst I ever witnessed. There was a bad crop this year of all kinds not half that was last year. Everything is in a depressed state. No price for anything. Landlords pressing for rent, executions and seizers [seizures] are every day's play. I am of opinion that I will see the Americans before the first of May. I am threatened with evictions. I told them to come on that I could not give them no rent. I owes three years, one of the old and two of the new. The reductions they offered three in the old and two on the new, which if they gave I could not meet them. So if they throw me out I will take a trip across the main wherever herself and the children will take shelter. Still I am not sure of what will be the consequence yet. I would rather they would put me out than take the little heads of cattle. Dear Dan, I must tell you that the gray mare is off of any more pleasure. The parties you know that had a course to Dunmanus, they took her last July out of the hill and drove her in full forse which was honest Bill and more of his companions and left her leg in her shoulder. Since I thought it would wear away, she is worst now than ever. I have no more to say at present. I remain your loving brother and sister, Michael and Mary Hodnett.

My Dear Uncle, I received your present which gave me great pleasure to have them for a New Year gift. Dear Uncle, I am bound to go to the sewing school[2] again the summer to learn the machine as you told me I can work it before. Since I was at school, I was tried at the examination and passed. Dear Uncle, I think it too long unto I will see you. I hope it will not be long. Dear Uncle, you tell me in the next letter what I will carry. So I hope you will send your picture in the next letter to Mamma and I send you my love.

Good bye. Your neice, Kate H.

ENDNOTES

1   *At this date, Tim and Ellen had two children living, Mary Ellen, born December 1883, and James Denis, born October 1886. Both would die in 1888 of the measles. Tim had previously lost two young children to sickness.*

2   *The "sewing school" Kate is attending could be either one that taught the techniques of the new Singer sewing machine, operated by a foot pedal. Or, it could be instructions in how to operate the machinery used in shoe manufacturing to sew shoe parts together. In Haverhill, there were many such jobs available, and they had much to commend them for a shoe stitcher sat down all day to do her work on the machine. When Kate eventually married in Haverhill, she listed her occupation as "shoe stitcher." Unlike all her other female relatives, she did not go into domestic work, but the higher paying factory work.*

Document **D26**

Dan was about to receive a supply of home-made shirts and stockings, hand delivered by a neighbor with family in Haverhill.

4 April 1887 – Julia Donovan, Ballydehob to Daniel Donovan, Haverhill, Mass.

Ballydehob
Apr. 4 '87

My Dear Son,

I mean to inform you that I am sending you 3 shirts, one of flannin and two of Cotton, also I am sending you 4 pair of socks and you will divide with Mick in the socks.

Mrs. C. Donovan[1] is sending you also two pair of socks. I could get no one that wold carry them for me, as small as the parsel is, until Mary Regan[2] told me that she would carry them for me. She is a sister-in-law of Katy Nagle[3] and was a long time next door to me in Ballydehob at John Barry's in Place.[4] So you can go to Keaty Nagle. It is there the parsal will stop. I would send sume more but times are keeping me going today as 20 years ago. Julia left so I have to stick to norsing.[5]

Tim was going to send you some more but she was not able to carry them. I will send what you told Pat Connin[6] when he is going. Remember me to Mick. Tell him that I would like to get a letter from him.

Your ever fond mother, Mrs. C. Donovan

[The following note was written, length-wise, on the fourth page of the letter.]

She will seal on the 6th of April. T. D.]

ENDNOTES

1   *Brigid Donovan*

2   *Mary Regan Harrington was a twenty-two year old widow from Ballydehob.*

3   *Kate Nagle was born in May 1855 to Pat and Mary Nagle of Dreenlamane. She came to Haverhill, Mass., in 1876. She married John Regan, son of Jerry and Mary from the Ballydehob area in October 1889. The Regans were living on Lancaster Street in Haverhill with their six children when the 1900 Federal Census was taken.*

4   *John Barry was a shopkeeper and vintner in Ballydehob. In the 1893 Guy's Directory, Barry was listed as the Rate Collector for the Poor Law Union.*

5   *Julia Donovan was a well-respected midwife. Her name appears over and again as the person reporting births for the civil register in Schull Parish. Her granddaughter, Julia, John's third child, born July 1871, had been helping with the care of Con's new child, and learning midwifery om her grandmother.*

6   *Patrick Cronan, brother of John, sailed for Boston on the S. S. Catalonia and arrived 9 April 1887. He was twenty-one years of age.*

Document D27

Hanna and Pat Driscoll's family residence in Haverhill, The New England House, at the corner of Essex and Locust streets, had been damaged by a fire on 12 February 1887 that destroyed neighboring buildings. A second building owned by Pat Driscoll and adjacent to the New England House was damaged. Both properties were fully insured.

19 April 1887 – Julia and Cornelius Donovan, Dreenlamane to Daniel Donovan, Haverhill, Mass.

Dereenlamane
April the 19, 1887

My Dear Son Daniel,

I now take the great opporsunity of writing you these few lines hoping they will find you and Hanna and husband and family in as good a State as this leaves us all in at present, thanks be to god for his kind goodness to us all.

My Dear Dan, we receved your letter which gave us grate pleasure to now that you wear all well and that ye were notting to the loss by the burning[1] which often gave me a trobelsom mind.

My Dear son, I am now injoyin the best of health, thanks be to God as ever I was, and I now sens my best love to you and Hanna and Husband and family. I have no more to say at present but may the lord guide you. You will get from Mary Reagan two pare of white stockins from Bridget made of our own wool and from mother two pare of blue stockens and three shirts and two pare of brown stockens from Ellen Mahoney.[2] Six pare in all.

From Con Donovan

My Dear Brother, we are all well in health both your brothers and sisters, thanks be to God for it and all the frends and neighbours all round.

Dear Brother, I send a quarter of tobacco by the Widdo Harrington[3] to you and the same to Mike to let you remember old Ireland. Mary

Reagen of Raheenroe died[4] and Nelly Molons is gest going.[5] It is mass time now and I cannt wate any longer. I have no more to say at preasant but I remain your ever truly, Con Donovan

ENDNOTES

1   *The full story of the fire in the Driscoll house was reported in the 12 February 1887 issue of the Daily Evening Bulletin of Haverhill.*

2   *John Donovan's wife.*

3   *Mary Reagan Harrington sailed on the S. S. Bothnia and arrived in Boston on 22 April 1887*

4   *This Mary Reagan was the widow of Denis, and the mother-in-law of Ellen Mahoney, daughter of Uncle Matthew Mahoney, who had been married to Tim Reagan, Mary's son.*

5   *Nelly Molons was Ellen Mullins Minihane, mother of John Minihane of Cussivina with whom she lived. She and her husband John, who had died in 1882, had nine children. Five were still alive in the late 1890s when their grandson, Patrick, recorded their names in an autograph book belonging to Dan Donovan's wife, Mary. The survivors and their birth years were: Frank (1834), Mary (1837), John (1840), Mick (1850), and Dan (1854).*

DOCUMENT D28

Dan had been gone from home for two years, but Mary Anne McCarthy had not given up hope that she and Dan would eventually be together.

22 April 1887 – Mary Anne McCarthy, Roskerig, Kilcrohane to Daniel Donovan, Haverhill, Mass.

Roskerig
April 22nd 1887

My Dear friend Dan,

It is with pleasure I set down to rite you these few lines hoping you are well as this leaves me at present, thanks be to God. My dear Dan, I mean to tell you I received your letter which gave me great pleasure to hear from you as long as I was waiting for to hear from you. My dear friend, I answered every letter you send me and sure I was astonished when I see that you were waiting like me self. It is telling enough. I asked your brother Con one day in Bantry did you get married or did you ever speak about me and he said no but he told me that your sister's house was burned. So I gave over ever again to hear from you but for all god is good.

My dear friend, I was lonesome when I read your letter as I hadent more accounts about you but I hope I wont be long so now.

Dear Dan, I sees Con real often and he asked me several times to go over to his house but I dident go yet. I think I'll go now in the summer. I hope I'll have a nice time but if you were there I should think I would have it Pleasanter.

My dear Dan, I hope you wont delay this and leave me know how are you. I Suppose you will be married before you will receive this but if not I'll be in time for the Wedding. Dear Dan, there dident many get married this year in our Country.

Dear friend, I am thinking to go to America this year but I don't know for certain yet will my mother leave me go this year but please don't delay this and I will tell you all about it in the next letter. My dear Dan, all your folks at home are well.

Dear friend, leave me know how do you like the country your in. My brother Denny is going to America this year and I think I'll go with him but if I'll go I'll not go until late in the season. So I hope if you'll get this you won't delay without answering it. My dear Dan, its often I think of the time when we used to be riting to each other at home but it grieves me that I dident see you in going from your mother's house but for that matter I see you every day. I got your picture framed on Carrighbuy[1] but I dident ever tell who were you or I dident tell to your people. I'll keep it me self until the very day I'll die. Leave me know have you mine always. I was take badly for the old fellow that took it dident know much how, but I hope you'll excuse me.

My dear friend, I'm sending you my heart and love to you. I hope you'll receive them and I hope I'll never die until we will meet again. My dear Dan, leave me know as you ever think you'll come home again. If I was riting to you every day in the week I could not tell you how lonesome I am for you. So I hope you won't delay this now and send me a long letter. So Good by faraway. Remember me. I am send my best love and 6 kisses to you.

For certain yours, truly, Mary Anne McCarthy XXXXXX\\

ENDNOTES

1   *Carrigbue, "yellow rock," was the old name for the village of Durrus.*

Document D29

Mary Anne McCarthy almost had her wish fulfilled, but she was not allowed to accompany her brother to America.

22 June 1887 – Mary Anne McCarthy, Roskerigh, Durrus to Daniel Donovan, Haverhill, Mass.

Roskerigh
June 22nd 1887

My Dear friend Dan,

It is with great pleasure I set down to answer your welcome letter. Dear Dan, I hope you will forgive me for delaying it so long. I got it a week ago. I could not help it.

Dear friend, I mean to tell you Brother Denis went away to America last Thursday and this is Tuesday. So I am not to go at all this year. I asked a passage without me mother knowing it. So they said they would not leave me go this year but believe me I wont ask them in the next year.

My Dear Dan, leave me know will you go to Auburn[1] to our people this year. If you want it, I will send the address of my sisters in the next letter. My Dear Dan, I hope you are well as this leaves me at present.

Dear Dan, I thought I asked you to send a long letter. I thought it a very little you said in the last letter. My dear friend, I hope you wont delay this and leave me know how are you are. Is it very warm in America this year. It is the hottest summer ever came in Ireland.

My dear Dan, leave me know are you married yet or do you think will I be in time to be on your wedding. I hope I will. My dear Dan, I am sending my love and best respects to you and believe me its truth. Dear Dan, I hope I will never die until I'll see you again as it often grieves me I dident see you in you going away. Dear Dan, I hope I will soon hear from you again. When I rites I think I should have it soon again but I know you wont delay it.

Dear Dan, anyone at home don't know you ever wrote to me. My Dear Dan, I am asking you for to send me a pair of ear rings to remember you and any present you'll ask of me I will send it to you and ask it by all means and I'll send it to you. So I hope you wont refuse without sending them. Any kind will do.

My dear Dan, I remember you as well as when we used meet at Carrigbue. I hope I'll soon see you. Dear Dan, leave you come home in the winter and we will be going together then in the next Spring. So I hope you will tell me, will you.

Good By darling far away. Remember me. XXXX Them four kisses by all means to you.

Rite soon to me. Good By.

[Written over the words on the back page] Send a long letter.

[no signature]

ENDNOTES

1   *Mary Anne had sisters living in Auburn, Mass. in the central part of the state.*

DOCUMENT D30
10 July 1887 – Cornelius O'Donovan, Dreenlamane, Ballydehob to Daniel Donovan, Haverhill, Mass.

Derreenlamane
Julia the 10 1887

Dear brother,

I now take my pen in hand to write you these fue lines hoping they will find you all in the best of health as this leaves us all in at prasant, thanks be to god for his merchys [mercies] to us all.

Dear brother, I hope you will escuse me for not writing before now. The reson I was weating for a letter from Mike but we did not get it yet. Dear brother, when we got your pitcher and see it we wear proud to see you so find [fine] as ever you wear.

Dear brother, we or all well in health, thanks be to god and mother is injoying the best of health and she sends her best love to you and Hanna and famely and Mike and wife. My Dear Brother, mother felt very proude over the preasant you send her and seen you so fine looking and you may say she shed some tears and so did us all.

Dear brother, I mean to [tell] you that I dun away with all the breatchy cows[1] long ago for very little and the dog[2] is better than ever and I sold the coalt last September to Tady Reagen's brotherinlaw, Den Reagen[3] for six pounds, and I have a horse foal this year the pitcher of the horse coalt we boath soalt in Bantry if not better.

Dear Brother, this is driest year that ever come. There was not a day of rain sence Febeary until these days and still the gardens are looking well. I could not feed a calf with my own hay this winter, with drieth [drought] and not man could bye it its so dear.

Dear brother, Johny is wandring he is not getting letter from Ellen. I have no more to say at present but I remain your ever truly Brother,

Cornelius O'Donovan

ENDNOTES

1 *"Breatchy" cows were inclined to go over hedges and fences.*

2 *Dan's pet dog, Carlow/Carlo*

3 *Timothy "Tady" Reagan had been married to Dan's cousin, Ellen Mahoney. His second wife was Ellen Reagan.*

DOCUMENT **D31**
24 July 1887 – Julia Minihane, Cussivina, Ballydehob to Daniel Donovan, Haverhill, Mass.

Cussivina
July 24, 1887

My Dear & fond Brother Dan,

Now for the first time I thought it my duty to drop you thouse few lines hoping to find you in the enjoyment [of] good health as this leaves me & Husband & family at preasant. Dear Brother, I reseaved your Pitcure which gave me + all the others great plessure to see it.

Dear Brother, I often thought why you never wrote to me any line since you left. I thought I deserved one as well as any of the others so I sead I would break the ice me self first + steat to you all [th]at I have gon true since you went. In the first place I lost my young horse that you tackled before you went + he never since was. He got spreaned in the back by a fall + he pined away so I was not able to reach any one since but depending on my good Neighbours to do my work.[1]

Dear Brother, I mean to inform you that we bered Nelly Mollen[2] a few months agoe may she rest in pees, Aman. Mother is well and all the others. Remember me Mick + wife, Hanna, Husband + family + [Ellin] + all the frinds as well as mentioned. I have no more to sea, but remain your fond sister, Mrs. Julia Menehane.[3] I will expect a letter in return hoping you will not fail.

ENDNOTES

1   The Minihane farm in Cussivina abutted the fields of Con Donovan's farm in Dreenlamane. It seems curious that Con did not provide his sister and her husband with a horse.

2   Ellen "Nelly" Mollens Minihane, mother-in-law of Julia, lived with her son's family. Her husband, John senior, who died in 1882, had lived there also.

3 *Julia, sixth child of Con and Julia Donovan, born August 1852, married John Minihane in February 1871. Julia was eighteen. Both bride and groom were literate and could sign the marriage register. The couple had twelve children: Frank (1872-1942), Patrick (1873-1951), Mary Theresa (1876-1953), Margaret (1879-1895), Ellen (1881-1882), John, who served in Burma with the British Army where he married and had children (1884 – ?), Cornelius (1887-194?), Michael (1889-1912), Daniel (1890-1965), Julia (1893-c.1925), Nora (1896-post1911), and Margaret Ann (1897-1978).*

Document D32
23 August 1887 – Mary Anne McCarthy, Roskerig, Kilcrohane to Daniel Donovan, Haverhill, Mass.

Roskerig
Aug. 23rd /87

My Dear and loving friend,

It is after a long silence I set down to answer your kind and welcome letter which gave me great pleasure to hear from you. My Dear Dan, I hope you'll excuse me for not writing before now. I would only I was too troubled. My mother is in the infirmary in Cork for the last month with a Cancer that grew on her lip and she is there still. I know you'll feel for me and for her also. Indeed I feel very troubled those times but I hope I'll be better for the future.

My Dear friend, I hope you are well as I would be glad to hear. I hope you'll excuse me for not writing before now. I suppose you think I have forgotten you but I suppose it is by yourself you think of that. If you did forget me I dident you. Dear Dan, don't offend me any more to speak about Police for if I cared for them its long ago, 2 or 3 years. I could have them but to the Devil with all Police in Ireland for my part of them.

Dear Dan, I hope you wont delay without answering this now and leave me know how are you. My dear Dan, I'm sending you the handkerchief. It isent worth sending but I know you don't want them. You can get enough of them where you are but something to remember me. I'm sending my love on it to you for certain. Don't believe otherwise. Its quite true whether you'll accept it or not.

My Dear Dan, I remember you as well as the day we went to holy ground long ago. I hope I'm not deceived with you. Also, my dear Dan, I hope you'll write soon and tell me all about you. Send me a long letter and tell me all the news you know. I will be anxious to hear from you soon. Good By my loving Dan and my only friend. I'm sending my heart and best love to you Remember me far away. Good By. [written across front page: from Mary Anne McCarthy. Write soon. Kisses XXXX XXXX

[Enclosed with the letter is a small piece of lined paper on which Mary Anne has hand-lettered on one side: "Daniel C. Donovan, Haverhill, U. S., Mass." There has been an attempt at decorating the lettering. On the reverse side is:]

When the name that I write is dim on the page
And this little card is yellow with age
Still think of me kindly and never forget
That wherever I am I will remember you yet.

DOCUMENT D33
31 August 1887 – John Donovan, Dreenlamane, Ballydehob to Daniel Donovan, Haverhill, Mass.

August the 31st

My dear brother,

I now take the opportunity of writing the few lines to you hoping to find you and all the friends enjoying good health as this leaves us and all the friend in at present, thanks be to God for his kind mercies to us all.

My Dear brother, I mean to inform you that we received your picture which gave us great pleasure. I would have written to you before this but I posted a letter to you and one to Ellen on New Years Day and never since got any answer from either. I was greatly surprised you did not speak of her in Con's letter. I would write long ago but waiting from day to day thinking she would write some time. When Con was writing I told him to ask you about her. If he did you gave no account of her. She must be dead ore something must happen to her. Don't deny it.

So Dear brother, I hope you will let me know in your next letter. Please don't delay. Write soon. I am glad to hear that brother Mike and wife were well and sister Hannah and family.

Dear brother, if Ellen is alive, do not do not mind telling her to write. If she did not think it worth her while to write to me, let her be, if sickness ore any other thing beside neglect did not prevent her of writing. Mother is well but she is always thinking of you.

Dear brother, Julia left Con. I did not tell her to leave him. I advised her to stay with him.[1] Indeed I knew nothing about her till she was gone down. She would not go if he promised her only 5 shillings a quarter. Its not the same house. They are well and doing well. It's the driest summer that ever came. All the rivers and wells dried up but very few. The ground is burned up, no grass but the gardens are as fine as you ever see them. They were as green as ever yet. Its common here that Mary Brine got married and Ellen B. died.[2] Wheather its true ore not.

No more at present but I remain your fond brother,

John Donovan

ENDNOTES

1   By August 1887, there were nine children at home in John's three room house. Only one, Ellen, had left home. Five of the nine were under the age of ten. His children by his first wife Mary were: Ellen (1868-1938), Cornelius (1869-1934), and Julia (1871-1959). Children by his second wife Ellen Mahoney were: Michael F. (1875-1931), James (1876-1906), John (1878-1916), Timothy (1879-1959), Mary (1882-1959), Patrick (1884-1959), Daniel (1886-63), Kate (1889-1951), and Jeremiah (1892-1937).

2   Mary O'Brien, who made the Atlantic crossing with Dan and his niece Ellen, did not wed until 1893 when she married Leon Comeau, a French-Canadian from Nova Scotia. Her sister Ellen had not died.

Document D34
26 September 1887 – Cornelius O'Donovan, Dreenlamane, Ballydehob to Daniel Donovan, Haverhill, Mass.

Derreenlamane
Septem. 26 1887

Dear brother,

I drop you these few lines hoping they will find you in the in joyment of good health, as this leaves us all in at preasant, thanks be to god for his mercys to us all. Dear brother, I mean to tell you that we are all in the best health thanks be to gog [God].

Dear Brother, Mother is as well as ever you see her in your life and sends her love to you and to Hanah and husband + family and to Mike and wife and was [glad] to now that you wear working study.

Dear Brother, let me now what your doing in the quarry. I sopose you have some hard [work] in it. Dear Brother, keep a good holt of what you or working hard for, and don't anything fool you and have something by your time, for a man without money these times is nothing.

Dear Brother, you asked me had I any help. I have a boy this quarter for 30 s[hillings]. It would not pay to keep them. The lambs that the Cronans[1] boate [bought] frome I sopose they [w]ont ever pay for them. I was trying to get work from them and they say [they] took nothing from me, that [they] gave to Johny to pay for them, and Johny told me he going that he wold pay for them himself and he did.

There is a good fair crop this year, and black ground is best. It is as dry now as it was in June. All that [have] Spring wells are as dry now as ever, but in the hight of the drith [drought] and now as well our two spring wells would keep water the sity Haverhill.

Dear Brother, we all applied to the coart for a fix rent. There is not ten in the parish or in the hole [of] Ireland but have there land in coart how ever we will come off. These hue [who] applied late got great reductions what ever. I have no more to say at preasant but I remain your affectionate] and beloveth Brother,

Cornelius O'Donovan.

XXXX XXXXX XXXX XXXXX

[written on top: write soon, we all joyns in sending you all your blesson.]

ENDNOTES

1   *Probably Jerry Cronan of Derryfunshion, father of Hanna Cronan of Andover.*

DOCUMENT D35
18 October 1887 – Julia and Mary Minihane, Cussivina, Ballydehob to Daniel Donovan, Haverhill, Mass.

Cussivina
October 18th – 1887

Dear brother

I take my pen in hand to write you those few lines hoping to find you in as a good a state of health as this leaves me at present. Thanks be to God for his blessings to us all. Dear brother, I received your letter which gave me great pleasure to hear from you.

Dear brother, I mean to inform you that Johny is well in health. He have the league of the Cross these two years. Dear brother, it was a great loss to me to be without a horse these three years. Me dear brother Dan I mean to informe you that mother is well and she is Always talking about you. She hope In god she Never will die until she see you.

Dear brother, I will never forget your kindness to me. I often thinks of you when I looks west At your old home. All your brothers And Sisters and families are well.

Dear Brother I got your picture framed Beautiful and it is looking splendid. Maggie is delighted About it. She would not leave Mary have any Claim in it.[1]

Maggie is going to school Every day. She is in the third Book. Frank and Pat is not going to school at all. Pat is growing taller than Frank. Johnny sends his best love to you and Hanoria an husband and family and also to Michael and family. Dear Brother remember me to Sister Hanah and family.

Dear Brother, I Mean to inform you that Patrick and Elen Driscoll went out to Texes too years this October. She is house keeping for her Brother. Dan none of them got married yet. Tady, wife and family are well. Sister Julia sends her best love to Brother Mike and wife. Are have they any increase in the family yet. Let me know how is Elen Donovan getting on or have she Constant work.

Dear uncle, Excuse my writing. It was the first letter I ever wrote. I have no more to say at present.

I remain yours truly Julia Donovan. Mary Minehane.
Good By. Write soon. Love to all.

XXXXX XXXXX XXXXX XXXXX

ENDNOTES

1   *Maggie Minihane was Dan's godchild and was staking her own claim in his picture. Maggie would die of phthisis (tuberculosis) when she was sixteen.*

Document D36
18 November [1887] – John and Ellen Donovan, Dreenlamane, Ballydehob to Daniel Donovan, Haverhill, Mass.

November 18th

My Dear brother,

Its with pleasure I set down to write you those few lines hoping to find you in good health as this leaves us and all the friends in at present, thanks be to god for his kind mercies to us all.

Dear brother, I mean to let you know that I received your kind and welcome letter which gave us great pleasure to hear that you and all the freinds were well.

Dear brother, Mother is middling well. She was not up here since April. We delayed this letter for the last three weeks waiting for her. She said she would come when I would be writing to you but she did not come. She is too taken up at home.

Dear brother, its hard times in this country. No price for my stock. If you were well able to sing a song, you would get a cow. No one buying them at all, ever one trying to sell. You would get a too year heifer for too pounds and no one to give that either. There was a fair price for pigs all the year but now they are as bad as anything else. The 8th of November was the worse fair that ever come in Ballydehob.

The land lord is as severe as if the prices were good. I had a notice every week from him. They were giving 3 s[hillings] to the pound reduction. I went to Bantry to meet him on the 14 of October and had a half year's rent. He would not give me one penny reduction. So I came back as I went as I was not able to pay it sooner. I got a notice cost after three days but it did not come yet. I have my land in the court whatever way it will go with me.

Dear brother, I had a letter from Ellen about a week before yours. She said she was well. I did not answer it ore I don't know wheather I will ore not. That was all the task I put on her when she was leaving me, to be advised by you and her aunt, but I see it was no use. My dreams and your letter were alike. I would write to sister

Hannah to turn her away and make her work but I am afeard she would see the letter.

Yours truly,

John and Ellen Donovan.

Document **D37**
7 December 1887 – Cornelius O'Donovan, Dreenlamane, Ballydehob to Daniel Donovan, Haverhill, Mass.

Derreenlamane
December 7, 1887

Dear Brother,

It is with a troublesome and greves mind I drop theses few lines hoping in god it will find you in the injoyment of good health as this leaves me and family, frends an neighbours in at present.

Dear Brother Dan, as I and Mother was in Bantry Tearsday, and we coming home I met Tim Hardnety of Drishane[1] and I asked him had he any nuse and he sed he no good nuse. He sed Wiley is disspare of with a favour [fever] and Dan was robed of thirty pounds of money out of his box.[2] For God Sak[e] and who tould you that[?] Pad Hardnett[3] that come home last night. When I herd it I got stund and cold say nothing. We went in and in and you may say we drank anouf and cried anouf and sence we left Bantry. I could [not] speake one word to my poor old mother for I was shoked up with grefe and mother was gest as bad.

When I thought who [how] you were trying to make your living in frost and snow and in mad heat but never mind. Thanks be to god as you have [y]our health. God will help you in place of it. I new some thing was up for I was dreaming all the time [of] father and Ellen[4] and you. I dreamend I see you in hoult with a man and you could due nothing and I thought I was working with my hands at him and could due nothing. Dear brother if that hopned it is two bad. I hope it did not. I have no more to say at presant but write as soon as you get this letter for mother is so afule trobled about you I wish you all a mery Christmas and a mery new year. I remain your ever truely,

Cornlius O'Donovan Derreenlamane

ENDNOTES

1   *Timothy Harnedy of Drishane was born in 1859.*

2   *Dan had brought a significant portion of money with him from Ireland, his share of his inheritance from his father. He kept the money in a strongbox.*

3   *Possibly a relative of Mike Hodnett.*

4   *"Father," Con Donovan, senior, died October 1882, age 70 of a strangulated hernia. "Ellen" was the first born child of Con and Julia Donovan. She was born in Roskerig in 1839. The first three of the Donovan children were born in the Sheepshead Peninsula where, it is probable, that Con was a cowman hiring out to one farmer or another. Ellen married Henry Schofield of Drishane in 1860, four years before Dan was born. Her only child, Julia, was not born until 1878 and Ellen died the following day of puerperal convulsions (childbirth fever). Her daughter survived. John Donovan's wife, Ellen, had borne a child two months earlier, and she could have been a wet nurse for Julia Schofield.*

DOCUMENT D38

28 June 1888 – Julia Donovan Minihane, Cussivina, Ballydehob to Daniel Donovan, Haverhill, Mass.

Cussavina
June 28th 1888

My Dear brother Dan,

It is with pleasure in mind I take my pen in hand to drop you those few lines hoping to find you in as good a state of health as this leaves me and family in at present, thanks be to god for his blessings to us all.

My Dear brother Dan, excuse me for delaying it so long. I felt very bad when I heard of that great difficulty you came across, but with the help of god you will not feel it after a time. Your mother was very troubled over it. She hope in god she never will die until she see you.

My Dear brother Dan, let me know how is Sister Hanah foot. We are very troubled about it also about her husband's health.[1] I felt very much for sister Hanah, for there is nothing compared like the head of a family. Let me know how is brother Mike and wife. I heard he had a fine boy.[2]

My Dear brother Dan, I hope Kate Hoddnett will be said by you and keep her under your commands.

My Dear brother Dan, I mean to inform you that Ellen Driscoll is writing to me constantly. I am going to send her letter to you and her address. She is always inquiring about you. I hope you will not fail in writing to her. You would be not deceived if you had her.

I have no more to say at present. I remain your affectionate Sister

Julia Donovan

XXXXXXXXX

Good by, write soon, love to all.

ENDNOTES

1   *Hanna Driscoll would bear her tenth child in July 1890. In December 1891, an ailing Pat Driscoll died tragically in a fire in his bedroom. He was 48 years old. According to the extensive newspaper reports of this disaster, Pat had suffered a debilitating stroke some time previously. His may be the health issue to which Julia is referring.*

2   *Cornelius J. Donovan was born to Mike and Margaret Lahey Donovan in February 1888. He was the first of four children in that family. The only daughter, Margaret, died young, and all three of Mike's sons died of tuberculosis before any one of them reached his thirtieth birthday.*

DOCUMENT D39
12 December 1888 – Julia and Cornelius O'Donovan, Dreenlamane, Ballydehob to Daniel Donovan, Haverhill, Mass.

Derreenlamane
December 12, 1888

My Dear Sheldren

Its With Pleasure in mind I Take my pen in hand to Write you all these few lines, Hopening to find you all in The best of health as this Leaves us all in at preasant. Thanks be to god for his kind Mercyes to us all.

Dear Dan, we wear Inpascsantly [impaticntly] weating for a letter for these back six months and did not get any in till this. We new there was no fear of you but Still we wear troble about Hanna and husband to[o] and is still, for you did not tell us how they wear. You only said that Hanna and husband wear well in health but we do not belive that they are, for we hear frome others that they or not and we feels very trobled about them.

Dear Dan, you asked could I make to mass. I could and to you if there was a road. I am not trobled with any of the Ruemattieck panes this long time thanks be to god. I have good fear [fair] health bu[t] I am often trobled about ye since I hear of the faver being around the place but I hope that all the frends will excape from it.

Dear Sheldren I send my love to you all, and Dan when you writes let me now all about Hanna and husband and family and Mike and wife and famely.

From Con, Dear brother Dan I send my blesson to you and hanna and husband and family, Mike, wife and family and let us [know] all about them. Mathew[1] is expecting a letter all the time and did not [have] any yet. I have no more to say at presasant but I remain

Your ever truly brother, Cornelius O'Donovan

ENDNOTES

1   *Uncle Matthew Mahoney*

Document D40
11 January 1889 – Julia and Cornelius Donovan, Dreenlamane, Ballydehob to Daniel Donovan, Haverhill, Mass.

Derreenlamane
January 11, 1889

My Dear Sheldren

I now write you these few lines hoping to find you all in the best of health as this leaves us all in at preasant thanks be to god for his mercies to us all.

My Dear Brother Dan, we receved your letter and was glad to now that you all wear well in health and was glad to now that Mike billed a new house.[1] May it well try with him.

Dear Dan, Mother is still well in health than[k]es be to god for it. She sendes her blesson to you and to Mike and to Hanna and all there families and not forgetting Paddy.[2] Let us now in the next letter how he is getting on.

Dear Brother, Mike Hoddnett and his family is very trobled about Kate since they did n[ot] get any letter from her theyes nine weekes. They say she is ded or sick but I hope she is not.

You asked about children. They or two very good children[3] thanks be to god and Johny is ta[l]king of you and writing letters to you every day and asking you to come home and to bring apples and sweets to himself and you thinks it is last weeke you left him he have so much take [talk] of you.[4]

Julia is heare with me always.[5] All your Brothers and sisters or well. Tell Hanna that we wear glad to get her pitcher and was glad to see her loock so well. I have no more to say at preasant but I remain

Your ever truly Brother,

Con Donovan

ENDNOTES

1 *Brother Michael built a two-family house in Bradford at the corner of Front St. and High St. (later named Germain Ave.). This was near his employment on the B & M Railroad. A few years later, newly married Dan and his wife purchased a recently built home on Locke St. (later named Laurel Ave.) a short distance from Mike. Some years later, nephews Neilus and Mike Donovan and their sister, Ellen Donovan McCarthy would all be living in homes in the same neighborhood.*

2 *Patrick Driscoll*

3 *Con and Brigid had a second child, a daughter Ellen/Nell, baptized 6 March 1888.*

4 *Little Johnny Donovan was born after his Uncle Dan had left for America. He must have heard his uncle talked about often to feel so connected to him.*

5 *John's daughter Julia was helping to care for Con's young children.*

DOCUMENT **D41**
6 June 1889 – Julia and Cornelius O'Donovan, Dreenlamane, Ballydehob to Daniel Donovan, Haverhill, Mass.

Derreenlamane
June 6, 1889

My Dear Shildren,

Its with pleasur I take my pen in hand hoping to find ye all in the best of health as this leaves us all in at preasant thanks be god for his mercies to us all.

Dear Dan, I hope you will escuse us for not writing to you before now. We wear weating for Some one to take the Stockings and could get no one to take them till John O'Mahoncy went away this morning. He took with him three pare of stockings from Mother, one from Julia and two from Mary for you, and a handkerchief for Hanna. Dear Dan, give one pare to Mike and one to Pady.

Dear Dan, I mean to tell you that I sold the old mare May day, she was in foal, for six pounds. She left a good big two year old colt.

You asked about Julia. She [is] now returned to her old lodge since July last. Ellen promised her a ticket but she did not get it or a letter nether.

Tell Kate Hordnett that I got her letter and was glad to now that she is well and going well.

My Dear brother,

Mother and us is all joyings [joining] in sending you your blesson and to Mike and family and to Hanna and family and let me now how is Pady getting on in his health. Sister Julia is near her confindment.[1]

Dear Dan, do not delay the next letter long. I have no more to say at preasent but I remain

Your ever truly,

Con O'Donovan.

ENDNOTES

1   *Julia Donovan Minihane delivered her eighth child, Michael, 9 June 1889. His godparents were Uncle John Donovan and Grandmother Julia Mahoney.*

Document D42
20 August 1889 – Cornelius O'Donovan, Dreenlamane, Ballydehob to Daniel Donovan, Haverhill, Mass.

August 20,1889

Derreenlamane
Dear Brothers and sister,

I now write ye these few lines hoping to find ye all in the best of health as this leaves us all in all present, thanks be to god for his b[l]ession to us all.

Dear Brother Dan, we receved your letter a good while ago but one day barroed [borrowed] anothered, since that I did not write all the while. Dear Dan, we are all well in health thank god for it. The Saddler have a young daughter. Her name is Kate Anne.[1] Mike Hoddnet another young daughter[2] and Johney will have another befor a weake.[3]

Dear Brother, the old Mare was sold back the 9 of June to cavelery for £8. Tade Ones sons of letter[4] bought her the same day coming home for £9.10 and never new her till they came home to letter and they wear mad when they found what they had. She have a nice fole.

Dear Dan, let us now how Hanna husband and family also Mike and wife and family and all the frends and neighbor and not forgetting John Matthew the ankey man.[5] Let me now [how] he is getting on.

Mother have better health than ever she had and was glad to hear from Mary O'Brine that ye wear enjoynt the best of halth and mother send ye all her best love and kind respect. We all joyens in sending ye our blession as we have no more say at prasant but I remain brother Conlius [sic] O'Donovan Dreenlamane.

[written across the top of the fourth page in Dan's handwriting is "Con Donovan."]

ENDNOTES

1   *Kate Anne Donovan was Tim's seventh child. She was baptized 4 August 1889. His children were: Michael (1879- ?), Cornelius (1881-1883), Mary Ellen (1883-1888), John (1885-1886), James Denis (1886-1888), Honora (1888-1972), Kate Anne (1889-1981), Patrick Stephen (1890-1966), Julia (1892-1930), Timothy John (1893-1921), Ellen Sophia (1896-1977), and Mary Eliza/"Lil" (1898-1993).*

2   *Elizabeth Mary, known as "Lil," was born 4 August 1889 the same day that Kate Anne Donovan was christened.*

3   *John and Ellen Donovan's eleventh child, a daughter Kate, was baptized 26 August 1889.*

4   *Timothy Driscoll, son of Owen of the townland of Letter, had sons Jeremiah (35) and John (34), both still unmarried when the 1901 Census of Ireland was taken.*

5   *"John Mahoney, the son of Matthew, the Yankee man." To the Irish, all Americans were Yankees. To American, Yankees were Northerners. To Irish-Americans, Yankees were the Anglo-Saxon Protestants who dominated in their society.*

Document D43
19 September 1889 – Julia, Mary and Maggie Minihane, Cussivina, Ballydehob to Daniel Donovan, Haverhill, Mass.

Cussivina
September 19th 1889

Dear Brother Dan

I take my pen in hand to write you those few lines hoping to find you in as good a state of health as this leaves me and husband and family well at present thanks be to God. My Dear brother Dan, I mean to inform you that Pat[1] Received the paper that you send him. I hope you will excuse me for delaying your letter so long.

My Dear Brother Dan, I mean to inform you that I have Got an increase in the family since the 9th of June last. His name is Michael. John is as well in health as ever you seen. Frank and Pat is as big as their father.

My Brother Dan, let me know have you any knowledge of Ellen Driscoll aug.[2] [She] did not write home this long time. They are very troubled about her. Let me know how is sister Hanoria getting on or is her foot sore always. Also her husband and family. I am surprised that sister Hanoria never rote to me. She have the name as being the best woman in Haverhill. Let me know how is brother Mike and wife and child. I suppose he don't remember me at all. Brother Dan, I mean to inform you that I was very hard up these last five years. Tis God alone now how I managed. I return thanks to God that helped me but we are coming around now. We have a nice young mare now of the age of three years old.

My Dear brother Dan, I hope you will not fail in coming home again Christmas. I remain yours truly, Mary Minehane.[3]

To Dan Donovan XXXXXXXXXXX

Cussivina

My Dear Godfather, I hope you will not refuse me as it is the first time to send me a silk toy. My Dear Godfather, I am in the fifth class now. My Dear Godfather your brothers and sisters are well in health. Your mother do be talking about you every day. She hope in God she never will die until she see you again.

My Dear brother Dan, excuse me. I was not able to send you but one pair of stockings. I was not well at that time. Let me know how is all the inquiring friends and neighbours. Let me know how is Ellin Donovan. Tis a shame for her to forget her sister without paying for her passage. She is a good sensible girl. Uncle John have an increase in the family, a young daughter, and uncle Tim have an increase in the family, also a daughter. Answer this letter as quick as possible. Let me know how is Kate Hoddnett gettig on. Now more to say at present from your affectionate Goddaughter Miss Maggie Minehane. CussivinaX. D. Donovan. XXXXXX

ENDNOTES

1   *Patrick Minihane, Julia's son, would be the first of that family to come to America, specifically, to his Uncle Dan in Bradford, Mass.*

2   *"Aug," or "Og" after a name means "the younger."*

3

DOCUMENT **D44**
8 December 1889 – Timothy Donovan, Ballydehob to Daniel Donovan, Haverhill, Mass.

Ballydehob
December 8, 1889

My Dear Brother Dan,

I just thought to drop you a few lines to let you no that I and wife and family and mother, sisters and brothers were all thanking God for all his goodnesses to us all hoping the arrival of this will find you and all the others the Same.

Dear Brother, how I often thought why you never wrote to me what ever is your reason for it and also it is very seldom you writes to home and you no that would be the only comfort to your mother to get a letter from you often.

Dear Brother, let me no all about Jack Mahony. Jack the Ripper he was called here. He was one of the most purist misers I ever witnessed in one life. Do not tell him I said anything about him at all. Dear Brother, I must inform you that Deny Eagan come home this month from America to get marred to Tady Murphy's daughter of Duneccon.[1] So she refused him so in a few days after, he got married to Ellen Mahony, the master's sister,[2] and he is starting those days agin for America.

Dear Brother, there is one thing I would wish to draw your attention to. You are aware that I got a ring from you and Hanna. I do not were it here as you no it is not the stile of the Contry here, so I was thinking to return it if you tell me it would be taking back by them parteys you got it from and get [a] watch chain [for] the value of it as an exchange.

Dear B., I was delighted about sister [Hanna's] picture.[3] I got it beautifully fremed. But I never could bring me self to no it. Remember me to her and Husband and family, also Mike and wife and child and K. Hodnett. Give my love to them all. Wishing you all a Happy Christmas, I remain your fond Brother,

Tim.

Write soon.

ENDNOTES

1   *Timothy "Tady" Murphy, his wife Mary, and three of his children were in Dunbeacon when the 1901 Census was taken.*

2   *The Master of the Dunbeacon National School was John Mahoney, namesake of the Master of the Dreenlamane School.*

3   *Copies of Hannah's picture, one of which is a large, hand tinted photograph, were in the Donovan Collection.*

Document D45
16 January 1890 – Julia, Mary and Margaret Minihane, Cussivina, Ballydehob to Daniel Donovan, Haverhill, Mass.

Cussivina
January 16th 1890

Dear Brother

It is with pleasure in mind I takes my pen in hand to write you those few lines hoping to find you in a[s] good a State of health as this leaves me and husband and family well at Present. Thanks be to God.

Dear Brother Dan, Excuse me for Delaying your letter so long. Dear Brother we felt very bad when you Said that you would never come home. We were very glad when we heard that Brother Mike built a new house. Let me know how many Children have he.[1] Let me know how is Sister Hannah and family. And also Kate Hodnett. Her people are very troubled about her since she did not write home at Christmas.

Dear Godfather, I am very thankful to you for the ribbon you send your [godchild]. She was delighted about it.

Dear Brother Dan, I hope I will never die until I will see you. Johnny[2] says he will sell the ground and go over. Ellen Driscoll did not write home these twelve months. Let us know if you heard about her since. Your mother was expecting you home and I often heard her saying that she will not forget you. Your [god]daughter Maggie says that she will go over to you when you will be married to mind the young ones. Let me know how is Sister Hannah's leg or is they any thing the matter with it now. Please let me know how is the inquiring friends and neighbours.

Excuse the writing. I was in a hury. I have no more to say at present from your fond neice,

Mary Minehane,[3] Cussivina.

Kisses XXXXXXXXXXXXXXXXXXXXXXXXXXXXXXXXXXXXXXXX
XXXXXXXXXXX

Good bye. Write soon. Love to all.

ENDNOTES

1   Brother Michael Donovan had a son, Cornelius, born February 1888 but his wife was expecting a second child.

2   John Minihane

3   Mary Minihane (1876-1953) emigrated to Haverhill in 1902. There she married Eugene Donovan (c. 1880-1941) from Skibbereen 23 September 1903. The Donovans had five children: Eugene (1910-1973), Helen (1912-1965), John Joseph (1913-2009), Harold (1916-1973), and a baby girl, Florence who died when she was three. J. Joseph was the only one of Mary's children to have children of his own, a daughter Judy, and a son John.

Document D46
15 April 1890 – Cornelius Donovan, Dreenlamane, Ballydehob to Daniel Donovan, Haverhill, Mass.

Dreenlamane
April 15, 1890

My Dear Brother,

I now take my pen in hand to drop you these few lines hoping to find you and all the friends in the best of health as this leaves me and mother and all the family in at preasant, thanks be to god for his mercies to us all.[1]

My Dear Brother, I mean to inform you that Julia is to sail in the 18 inst. in Sipplonia, hoping in god that she will arrive safe.[2]

Dear Brother, I hope you will escuse us for any compleinens for this time for Mother got the cold in her eyes for three month and was bad with them and so did us all get it. Mother is now well in health and sends her love to you and Hanna and husband and family and Mike and wife and shild and all the frends and will ishers. We all feal lonesome for Julia in going and I think herself feals lonesome two and I hope ye will advise her and be kind to her.[3]

I need not tell you about any thing. Julia will tell you about all. Rem[em]ber me to Kate Hodnett and Mary Mahoney[4] and tell her that her mother was unwell those two months with the hen that flue in her wendy.[5] I hope [you] will get a nice place for Julia for she is yet young and soft.

I and wife and mother and all the frends are well and we all sends ye all your blesson. The Master got marred to the Misses[6] and I taught they would be marred. Johney Bill got marred to Lisey O'Brine south Schull.[7] Mike Fain wrote a letter to his sister, Julia, and got no answer this twelve month and this is the address, Mrs. Julia Crowley, No. 116 Gold Street, Boston, Mass., America.[8] I have no more to preasant but I remain your ever truly brother, Con Donovan, Dreenlamane.

ENDNOTES

1   *Someone must have written this letter for Con, perhaps his wife, Brigid, for it does not have Con's usual multiplicity of misspellings that had marked each of Con's previous letters.*

2   *Julia Donovan, John's second daughter, sailed from Queenstown on the S. S. Cephalonia, arriving in Boston on 24 April 1890. She was eighteen years old.*

3   *Julia (1871-1959) worked as a domestic until 1897 when she married Dennis Coughlin (? – 1950). They had four children: John Leo (1898-1951), Daniel "Neil" Cornelius (1900-1986), Dennis Joseph (1902—?), and Mary Veronica (1905-1989). Only Neil had children: William and Margaret/Peggy.*

4   *Mary Mahoney was the youngest of Uncle Matthew's children. She emigrated about 1889, married John McNeal from Prince Edward Island, Canada, in February 1892 and had a son three months later.*

5   *"The hen that flew into the window."*

6   *Master John Mahoney of the Dreenlamane National School married Mistress Jane Donegan of Cussivina, also a National School teacher, on 6 February 1890.*

7   *This John Mahoney (Johnny Bill) was the son of William Mahoney of Raheenroe. He married Lizzie O'Brien, daughter of Daniel of South Schull on 18 February 1890.*

8   *The Crowleys (Daniel and Julia) show up in the 1900 Federal Census, living at 274 4th Street, South Boston, around the corner from the Gold Street address. The Crowleys married in Ireland in 1866 and came to Boston in 1871.*

Document D47
June 1890 – Mary and Michael Hodnett, Drishane, Durrus to Kate Hodnett,[1] Haverhill, Mass.

Drishane
June 1890

My dear child

We received your letter a few days ago and delayed it consequently to give you the full particulars of what took place here regarding our curat priest. His arrest and trial since last Friday will be in record in the history of Ireland for generations to come. In Skull on Friday, in Bantry on Monday, the largest meeting ever was in West Cork. Why not? He was the bravest man of Ireland's sons, father Crowley by name.[2]

I will send you next Saturday paper which will give you the full account. I would like you would send it to your uncle John.[3] 1 would send him one if I had his address.....it as careful as you can. It will remind him of his nation. I would Julia ... hear from ...

My dear child, I am glad you are in good health, study [steady] at work. Your mother and the children are well and all your uncles, aunts and grandmother. This is the wettest summer the oldest man living remember and the worst in crops. The blight has set in already and you could earth them yet in some parts any......more earth them.

My dear child, I have nothing more of any importance to relate hoping soon to hear from [you] again, hoping your uncles, aunt and families are well. No more at present from your fond parents,
Mary and Michael Hodnett.

ENDNOTES

1   *Kate Hodnett (1870-1956), emigrated to Haverhill about 1888. Unlike most of her female cousins, she did not go into domestic work but was employed as a stitcher in the local shoe shops with which Haverhill abounded. She married Garrett Cotter (1868-1910) in 1894. They had six children before Garrett's untimely death from a fall from a horse in 1910. Children were: John (1895-?), Mary Elizabeth/ Lillian (1897-1985), Michael/Milton (1899-1990), Gerald Richard (1902-prel9l0), Helen Irene (1905-1939?), Geraldine Ita (1908-1991). Katie married (2) Joseph Bean (1889-1937) c. 1913. They had a son Joseph who died young of typhoid fever. When Katie's sister, Nora Collins, died in 1925, Katie raised Nora's son, Richard Collins (1919-2006).*

2   *The events above were a part of the Land Reform movement that would end with the Irish once again being allowed to legally own their farms. The story of Father Crowley of Schull Parish can be found in The Mizen Journal, Vol. 9, published in Schull, Co. Cork.*

3   *John Hodnett, Mike's brother, in California.*

DOCUMENT **D48**
14 September 1890 – Cornelius Donovan, Dreenlamane, Ballydehob to Daniel Donovan, Haverhill, Mass.

14 Septem. 1890
Dereenlamane

Dear Dan

We Receved your letter which gave us all great pleasur to hear from you all. Tell Mike that we wear glad when we heard he had a nother young Son[1] and also Hanna.[2] We wear glad to hear that She was well.

Dear Dan, tell Hanna that we felt very much for her troble about Con's excedence[3] but I hope in god it [w]ont enger [injure] him much.

Mother felth very trobled over it. She is well in health thanks be to god for it and is leading a very plasent life. Nothin in the world trobling her but still you now she cannt fele well all the while.

She felt very lonesome intel [until] she got your letter and she sends her blesson to you all. Miss Driscoll would be very thankful to you by sending her brother's address. All the neighbours and frends or well.

Dear Dan, you say it is a very dry Sumer but I say it is the wettest summer that ever I remember and a very bad year of crops. There is Shercherly [scarcely] any Spuds.

Write Soon. I have no more to say [at] present. I remain your ever truele brother[4]

Con Donovan

Please give this bit of a note to Julia that is with this.

ENDNOTES

1   *John "Jack" Michael Donovan born in June 1890. Later births to Michael and his wife Margaret (Lahey) were James Andrew (1892-1917) and Margaret (1893-1897)*

2   *Honora/Hanna Driscoll had her tenth child, Wilfred Leo, on 5 July 1890. He lived until 1973.*

3   *Hanna's first child, Cornelius, was born in Drishane (probably at the home of her married sister, Ellen Donovan Schofield) in September 1864, four months after his uncle Dan was born. Hanna was seventeen. The birth was registered by the midwife, who conveniently was Hanna's mother, Julia. She reported in the Civil Register of Births that the father was "Pat Minihane, a laborer, who has already gone to America.". She listed her daughter as "Hanna Minihane," but no marriage record has been found in any of the local churches. Young Con was very active in local athletics in America, playing on both football and baseball teams. He was also involved in local Democratic politics. In April 1890, Con had gone to Dennison, Texas. While there he was blown from a moving train and fell against a barbed wire fence. He doctored himself and soon came down with blood poisoning. In mid-May, half of his foot was amputated. He recovered and returned home 18 July 1890 carrying with him a gold watch inscribed from his friends in Dennison along with a $100 gift of money. A full report of Con's accident was in the Daily Evening Bulletin, Haverhill, Mass. 21 July 1890, and that is a measure of Con's reputation and popularity in Haverhill. Con died in 1938.*

4   *There is not the slightest hint in this letter that Dan has let anyone in his family in Ireland know that he was planning to marry Mary McCarthy of Ballinlough, Leap, who was a domestic in Haverhill.*

DOCUMENT D49
14 September 1890 – Cornelius O'Donovan, Dreenlamane, Ballydehob to Julia Donovan, Haverhill, Mass.

Dreenlamane
September 14eenth, 1890

My Dear nece,

I receved your letter a few weakes ago but could not write before now as I been in a hurry with the harvest and everything. Dear Julia, we or all well in health thanks be to god for it. The sheldren always talking of you and writing letters every day to you. Dear Julia, when your writing, let me [k]now you or in your health or did your finger get sore since.

Dear Julia, I can reade your writing if it was twice worse then what it is. Mike Field[1] gained the garden.[2] Write soone and write a long letter and I will write a long letter the next time. All your uncles and ants ore well and so is your father. I have no more to say at present but I remain your ever truly Unkle,

C. O'Donovan Give this to Julia Donovan

ENDNOTES

1   *Michael Field, born November 1859 to John and Marty (Driscoll) Field of Dreenlamane, lived on the family farm which abutted the Donovan farm on the north side.*

2

Document D50

Con's note to his niece Julia, Document D49, above, was the last dated letter sent directly to Dan that was in the box of "Papa's Letters," except for a brief note from his niece Ellen Hodnett Conlon, sent in 1907, and two from his sister Julia Minihane, sent in the 1920s, which were added later.

The following undated Document, from Mike Hodnett, appears to have been sent after his daughter Kate went to America, and before any of the other Hodnett daughters joined her. Michael would die in the summer of 1900 by which time three more of his eight daughters had joined Kate in Haverhill.

[n.d.] – Michael Hodnett, Drishane, Durrus to Daniel Donovan, Haverhill, Mass.

Drishane

My dear brother

It has been a very long time since we had as letter from you. It would give us great pleasure to hear from you. Your mother is very impatient at not getting a letter from you. I imagine she thinks that it was Katie that prevented you from not writing. It would be great consolation to her to get a letter from you. No more at present. I remain as ever your loving brother until death.

Michael Hodnett Mary sends you her love, respects across the Atlantic xxxxxxxx

Daniel Donovan

Notes: The Donovan Family in the 1890s

Throughout the last decade of the Nineteenth Century, the various members of the Donovan family completed their families, saw their children emigrate, marry, and start their own families.

Mother Julia Mahoney Donovan: Julia was kept busy throughout the 1890s in her role as midwife and grandmother. Her daughters and the wives of her sons in the Dreenlamane vicinity had a great burst of fertility with fourteen babies born in that ten-year span. When she wasn't moving from home to home to tend to the births and after-care of the mothers and babies, she probably lived with her son Con, or near him in her old family home. Julia died in 1905, aged eighty-eight. Her death was reported by Tim's widow, which suggests Julia was living in Ballydehob at The Saddler's house at that time. Her brother Matthew outlived her, dying in his nineties c.1910.

Ellen Schofield: Ellen's only child, Julia, was born just before her mother died in 1878. She married Denis Burke of Drishane in 1897 and had the first of nine children, Jack, in 1898.

John Donovan: John's twelfth child, Jeremiah, was born in 1892. His two eldest sons, Neilus and Michael, joined their sisters, Ellen and Julia, in Haverhill, MA. Julia married Denis Coughlin in 1898 and had two sons, John and Daniel ("Neil") by 1900.

Mary Hodnett: three daughters, Ellen, Mary Ann ("Mamie"), and Julia, emigrated to join their sister Kate in Haverhill. Kate married Garrett Cotter in 1894, and they had three of their children by 1900. Ellen married James Conlon in 1900. Mary's husband, Michael, died in Drishane, Ireland, of cirrhosis of the liver in July 1900.

Honora/Hanna Driscoll: Hanna's tenth child, Wilfred Leo, was born in 1890. Her daughter, Mary ("Minnie"), married John Carrigg in 1891. Mary Carrigg had given birth to five children by 1900, but only Paul was still alive by that date. Hanna's daughter, Ellen "Nellie," married Charles Ford in 1898 and had at least two children by 1900, one of whom had died. The Driscolls' son Dennis may have married his wife Sarah Bassett before 1900 as they had children born early in the next decade, but the exact dates are unknown. Hanna's husband, Patrick Driscoll, died in a houses fire in December 1891. By 1900, Hannah and her family had moved away from their Essex Street house. They lived near St. James Church in an enclave of other Driscoll families (possibly her in-laws) and her married daughters. Hannah would die in February 1902 of heart disease.

MICHAEL DONOVAN: Mike and his wife, Margaret Leahy, had two sons, Jack and Jim, and a daughter, Margaret, in the 1890s, plus their first son, Cornelius. Baby Margaret died when she was a year old, and Mike's wife, Margaret, died in 1900. Mike's niece, Ellen, daughter of his brother John, moved into his new two-family house in Bradford to help care for his three sons and be his cook and housekeeper.

JULIA MINIHANE: Julia's second daughter, Maggie, died in 1895, aged sixteen. Julia had four children in the 1890s: Daniel, Julia, Nora, and Maggie Ann. Her son Patrick immigrated to Haverhill, MA, in 1896. He married Hannah McSweeney in 1898, and they had their first child, John, in 1900.

TIM DONOVAN: "The Saddler" had fathered seven children by 1890, four of whom had died. He and his second wife, Kate, were far more fortunate in the 1890s with two sons, Patrick Stephen ("Sonny") and Timothy John, and three daughters, Julia, Sophie, and Lil. Tim's namesake nephew, the son of John, had joined his uncle's household as an apprentice saddler. Tim would die in March 1902 of phthisis, a severe form of tuberculosis. His sister Hanna had died only six weeks before him.

CON DONOVAN: Con and his wife Brigid had four children in the 1890s to add to their first two, John and Ellen/Nell. They were Hannah Maria, Cornelius ("Sonny"), Dan, and Michael. The family continued to prosper.

DAN DONOVAN: Dan married Mary McCarthy, originally of Ballinlough, Leap, in November 1890.

[From the *Haverhill Bulletin*, 6 November 1890: Mr. and Mrs. Daniel Donovan held a brilliant reception at their residence, Elm Street, Bradford, last evening, attended by a large number of guests from this city. The presents were numerous and elegant including a substantial remembrance from (his colleagues) on the railroad.]

Included among the ephemera in the Donovan Collection is the receipt from H. C. Tanner, Caterer and Confectioner, for the wedding reception. Guests were served two wedding cakes ($4.50 ea.), 12 Washington pies ($.96), 2 Sheet White Mountain Cakes ($.50), 6 Sheet Sponge Cakes ($.72), 3 Sheet Centennial Cakes ($.36), 10 Loaves Large Cream Bread ($.80), 15 Loaves Small Cream Bread ($.60), 8 Loaves Large Cream Bread ($.64), and 3 Lbs. of candy ($.60), for a grand total of $9.68. To put this in perspective, ten dollars would have been a respectable week's wages for a working man in 1890. And this sum does not include the liquid refreshment provided to the guests.

The newlyweds purchased a recently built, two-story, seven-room house in Bradford on Locke Street (later named Laurel Avenue) close to the Boston & Maine Railroad roundhouse where Dan and his brother Mike was employed. Dan and Mary had three daughters in the 1890s: Julia Agnes (1893), Catherine Marion (1897), and Helen Evelyn (1900). Then tragedy struck the young family. Mary died in September 1900 after a very brief illness of phthisis. The same pulmonary disease would kill Dan's brother Tim two years later.

Mary's young sister, Nora McCarthy, gave up her job as a domestic at a private home in Haverhill and moved to Dan's house in Bradford to care for his young daughters. The following St. Patrick's Day 1901, baby Helen died of a heart problem. Nora stayed on as caregiver for the two older girls and as cook and housekeeper for Dan and, possibly, her brother Tim McCarthy. He had been living in the Donovan home when Mary died.

THE DONOVAN LETTERS

Part II: D51 to D58
1907 to 1929

Document D51
5 April 1907 – Ellen Hodnett Conlon,[1] Somerville, Mass to Uncle Daniel Donovan and family, Bradford, Mass.

9 Beacon
Somerville
4/5/07

My Dear Uncle, Aunt & Cousins,

Just a few lines to let you know we are all well. Hope you are the same. I like here very much it's a very nice place, a beautiful location, but I feel lonesome for Haverhill some times. I imagine when I go out I must see somebody I know. One good thing here their is no body to talk about you.

Now Uncle Dan, I hope to see you all, and that nothing will keep ye from coming to see me Sunday April 14th.[2] There will be no strangers here, only my Sisters[3] & their friends, so be coming with them. Mary or Kate will tell you the time they are coming. Nora, don't forget to come. Marian & Agnes & all of ye. You know how glad I will be to see ye all.

Love from Julia[4] & the children. Kindest regards from Mr. Guthrie. He wants Uncle Dan to be sure & come. Will conclude for the present, hoping to see you all soon. I remain as ever your loving niece,

E. J. Conlon[5]

ENDNOTES

1   *Ellen (1875-1967) was the third child of Michael and Mary (Donovan) Hodnett. She emigrated in 1890. She married James Conlon in April 1900 and they had a daughter, Mary Eileen, in 1901. Then tragedy hit the young family. Jim, a teamster for a local lumber yard, was delivering a load of wood when his horse bolted, the wagon tipped over onto Jim, and he was knocked unconscious. He was taken to the hospital where he was diagnosed as suffering only from bruises. He recovered consciousness and was being prepared to be brought home when he lapsed into unconsciousness again. He was dead within a few hours. An autopsy revealed that his skull had been fractured around the entire circumference. His widow, Ellen, was pregnant with their second child, Geraldine Julia. The family legend is that in her grief she attempted to throw herself into the open grave. Ellen supported herself after Jim's death by turning her home in Bradford into a boarding house, aided by her younger sister, Julia. One of her boarders was a young grocer, James Guthrie.*

2   *Ellen Hodnett Conlon married James Guthrie on 14 April 1907 in Somerville.*

3   *By 1907, five of Ellen's seven sisters had immigrated to Haverhill, Mass. They were Katie Hodnett Cotter, MaryAnn/Mamie, Julia, Nora, and Hannah (later known as Anna).*

4   *Julia, who had been living with Ellen, had been introduced to Michael Finnegan, a colleague of Jim Guthrie. They would be married in September 1907.*

5   *Ellen wrote a beautiful, well-formed hand.*

DOCUMENT D52

"Lil," was the youngest of the Hodnett children, and eighth daughter. Her mother had died in 1908 and Lil had stayed in Ireland to keep house for her brother Richard. In this letter, she gave her sisters in America not only all the details of their brother's marriage, but also included much information about the many Donovan, Burke, and Minihane aunts, uncles and cousins.

27 February 1912 – Elizabeth "Lillie" Hodnett,[1] Dunbeacon to Annie Hodnett, Haverhill, Mass. [Original of this letter is not in the Donovan Collection]

Dunbeacon
Feb. 27, 1912

My Dear Annie,[2]

I received your loving letter this morning, was glad to hear from you and to know ye were well as we are the same. Weall, my Dear, I was very glad ye were so delighted about Richie's marriage.[3] So am I now too. He was married last Tuesday the 20th and you may [be] sure it was a glorious day. I went to Goleen[4] with him as he would not go without me. Also Uncle Con and Mara and Jack Donovan and Neilus Minihan[5] took a car west with us and of course Richie had to have a covered car and Julia Donovan[6] went in with us. It was Jack Donovan stood up with him and a Driscoll girl[7] with Mattie, her first cousin. She asked me too to stand with her but the priest said one would do.

Well, Annie Dear, I could not tell you how lonely I was Tuesday morning and so was himself. Oh, I hate to think how foolish I was but when I thought of all, I had to, and you may be sure I spent a hard week without a soul with me, but thank God, I done all [right].

Well, about Mattie, now I must tell you, she is a Dear girl. No sister could be better to me than her and think so much about me. She has a very quiet disposition and too good for this cursed land. She don't like Ell Jonson. She never came in to see her since she came here but Johnson did and I must say she is a fine girl. She had the head over him that day at the altar and you may be sure she is a fine figure. The Donovans were all delighted with her and thanked God going west to Goleen that it was not Kate Scully. As you now they never liked her manner.

She had a very nice blue costume and a beautiful white hat and veil and looked lovely. I wish you could see her going round the house, and the most thing she is so nice mannered. Richie think everything about her and for herself I need not tell you. Her brother was over to see her Sunday. She has one sister home and a brother and three sisters in America. One of them send her before she came here a Mother of pearl rosary bead to give to Richie. They are delighted about him. We had some of our own cousins that night and they brought a few. Emmiline Barnett and May Driscoll came with them, also. They are very nice girls. I have them promised to go west to them for a few days soon. Rich and Mattie and I are going west Sunday.[8] She would not dare go without me. I think she is a Dear. You need not tee hee, Annie.

I will be the same all the time in the house work away while I am there. She always talks about you. She remembers you well and to see you at Dan McRegans.[9] I hope ye will write to her for indeed, Annie, I am awful fond of her. When I tell her I am going to America in April,[10] she goes crazy. She thinks I will stay home and go back in her place.[11] But don't you say anything about it when you write. She is very innocent, I think. I have told you all about her now. She won't be 25 years until August.

Julia Burke[12] was up to see her a few days ago and brought her a nice teapot and two china cups and saucers and Mary (Donovan) Sweeney gave her a beautiful pink wrap. She is very nice too. She took care of the house, herself and Julia Minahane[13] while we were in Goleen and poor Aunt Julia could not come as Mike is sick[14] with six months and I believe will never recover. He got pneumonia and is awful bad since. Too bad. He is never done with trouble.

Kate Donnell[15] had us invited down. She is very nice and kind to us. Anyway I like her the best. Oh, Annie Dear, you asked me if anyone knew the fortune. Nell Johnson gave it out.[16]

I have no more to say to you now but write soon and if you want to ask me anything, you can put in a bit of a note. So Good bye now from your Darling Lillie. Write soon, Dear Annie. Richie and Mattie sends love to ye. XX

ENDNOTES

1   *'Lillie" Hodnett, the ninth child and eighth daughter of Mary Donovan and Mike Hodnett, was born in 1889.*

2   *Annie Hodnett (1885-1979) emigrated to Haverhill in 1909. She worked as a domestic until she married American-born William Powers (1884-1966) on 25 June 1919. They had three children: Geraldine (1920-2005), William (1923-1998), and John (1927-2007).*

3   *Richard Hodnett (1876-1952) was the only son of Mary and Michael of Drishane. All eight of his sisters emigrated to America and he took over the family farm at the death of his father Michael (1843-1900) and mother Mary (1844-1908). Richard married Martha/Mattie Bennett (1877-1927), daughter of Andrew of Toormore, 20 February 1912 in St. Patrick's church in Goleen. He was 36 and Mattie was 24.*

4   *The Hodnett farm in Drishane was in Goleen Parish which encompassed the western half of the Mizen Peninsula. The village of Goleen, where the parish church was located, was in the southern end of the peninsula.*

5   *"Mara" was Uncle Con Donovan's daughter, Hanna Maria (1891-1972). She would join a religious order and serve in England. Maria left the order in her middle years. "Jack" Donovan was Uncle John's son, the oldest of the males still living at home. He inherited the family farm on the death of his father in 1914, but died of tuberculosis two years later. Neilus (Cornelius) Minihane, Aunt Julia's son, was born in 1886. He took over control of the family farm on his father's death in 1923.*

6   *Tim the Saddler's daughter, Julia. Tim had died in 1902, the second of the Donovan family of nine to die.*

7   *Mary O'Driscoll*

8   *"West." i.e., to Mattie's home at Toormore on the Mizen Peninsula.*

9   *The "Mc" on Regan's name was crossed out in the letter.*

10   *Lillian Hodnett sailed on the S. S. Laconia from Queenstown 14 April 1912, and arrived in Boston on the 25th. Her first cousin, John Donovan, son of Con, was on the same ship. Lil is described on the Ship's Register as 5' 7", fair complexion, fair hair, and blue eyes. She was going to her sister, Mrs. Michael (Julia) Finnegan in Dorchester, Mass. Soon after her arrival, her sister Hanna/ Anna was married to Daniel Murphy. The wedding was the first time all eight of the Hodnett sisters were together, for Katie had left before Lil was born, and Ellen, Mary Ann and Julia had left when Lil was still a young child. The event merited a photo and a story in the local newspaper. Lil's ship had sailed from Queenstown on the same day that the Titanic did on its way to its historic appointment with an iceberg. The two ships would have passed the lighthouse at the tip of the Mizen Peninsula on the same day. Lil and John's ship turned south into the Atlantic (the usual route) and the Titanic headed north in its attempt to set a speed record.*

11   *That is, take over the position Mattie had held.*

12   *Julia Schofield (1878-1955) was the only child of Ellen Donovan. Julia married Denis Burke in 1897. They had nine children. The Schofield/Burke home was a thatched roof cottage on the Drishane/Dunbeacon line, on Dunmanus Bay. Geographically, they were the closest Donovan relatives to the Hodnetts.*

13   *Julia Minihane (1893-1929) was the tenth child of Julia and John Minihane.*

14   *Michael Minihane died 6 April 1912 of consumption. He was twenty-three.*

15   *Aunt Kate McDonnell Donovan, widow of Uncle Tim.*

16   *That is, Mattie's "dowry." Ellen "Nell" Johnson, wife of John, was the next door neighbor of the Hodnetts.*

Document D53

[no date] – Mattie Hodnett, Drishane, Durrus to Annie Hodnett, Haverhill, Mass.

[Original not in Donovan Collection]

Drishane
March 2nd [possibly 1912 before Lillie left for America]

My Dear Sister Annie,

Just a line to you hoping in God ye are well as we are here. I am sending you a sprig of Shamrock. Hope you will get it in time.

Mattie

Document **D54**
16 December 1912 – Ellen/Nell O'Donovan, Ballinspittal, Kinsale to Julia Agnes Donovan, Bradford, Mass.

Ballinspittal Kinsale
Dec. 16th

Dear Cousin Agnes,

I just thought I'd write a note to wish you and Uncle Dan and all a very happy Christmas and a bright and prosperous New Year. I am still at school[1] but when you'll receive this I'll be at my old home.[2] I am closing on Friday for nearly three weeks. The thought of holidays is delightful: but the weather is very nasty. Nothing but rain, rain, rain. However, I think no amount of bad weather could spoil the Xmas joys when we assemble at the old home round the Xmas fire. I know we'll all miss Johnny[3] this year, his first one of absence. But I'm sure he'll enjoy himself very much in your country. I suppose he and your father will chat about "Old Times."

I hope Lillie Hodnett is getting on well. She must be as all her sisters are there to help her and keep her company. Her brother here has a baby boy. I'm not sure if it's a boy, but he has a baby at any rate.[4]

Now dear Agnes as we know so little about each other 'tis hard to write long letters so I'll conclude. Best love to you & your father and all my cousins also to Uncle Mike.

Your fond Cousin,

Nell

ENDNOTES

1   *Ellen/Nell Donovan (1888-1959), daughter of Con and Brigid Donovan, had attended the Teacher Training School in Dublin. One of her instructors was future Premier Eamonn DeValera. She was teaching at the National School in Ballinspittal near Kinsale at the time of this letter. She married a wealthy farmer, Bart O'Donovan. Nell returned to teaching at the Ballinspittal after her four children were born. Her father's property in Dreenlamane would pass down through her son and grandson after her bachelor brothers, Sonny and Mick, died.*

2   *Dreenlamane*

3   *John Donovan (1886-1938), oldest of Con's children, sailed on the S. S. Laconia on 14 April 1912 with his cousin Lillie Hodnett. The Titanic sank the night of their departure! John was 5' 5" with fair complexion, and fair hair and blue eyes. He was going to his cousin Michael Donovan, Uncle John's son in Bradford, Mass. In addition to John, Nell and Hannah Maria, Con's other children were Con (Sonny) (1895-1975), Daniel (1898-1982), and Michael (1900-1972). Sonny inherited the home farm, Dan became a National School teacher, and Mike was a detective on the Dublin police.*

4   *Michael John Hodnett was born to Richie and Mattie on 23 November 1912. His godparents were Mary Driscoll and Jack Donovan, who had stood up for the parents at their wedding. Michael died on 13 January 1913 of bronchial pneumonia.*

Document **D55**

Tim's widow, Kate, continues the updating of the Donovan relatives that was begun by Lil Hodnett, above.

18 June 1919 – Mrs. Tim (Kate) O'Donovan, [Ballydehob, Ireland] to Julia O'Donovan, Oakland, CA [Photocopy of Original in Donovan Collection]

June 18 – 191[9]

My dear Julia[1]

I received your loving letter. I am so glad to hear such good news & this is your wedding day. Julia dear I wish you & Dan[2] all the Joy & happiness that God can give you both & I trust in God you both will be happy. So you have got your own home to live, de[ar?] me & you have Signed your name for the last time Julia O'Donovan. I a[m?] feel lonely dear.

I had Mass here for you at eight o'clock, this Morning & I received for your sake. I do hope you will get the benefit of it. I mailed your letter to Lily.[3] We heard from her today. Sophie[4] will be home in the first week of August. She too has got her. I fear it will break down her health. She is crazy to come home for her holidays. I am glad you are to live so near Anna[5] & Nora.[6] Why Anna is great & to be bridesmaid. I hope to get the picture of the group. Why I look to hear more about Em.[7] I don't hear half enough of him. I will send that present as soon as I can. It is on order. Don't be disappointed dear. I am glad Nora's baby is so good but I guess she will miss you.[8] I wish I was near her or with her. I hope I will some day soon.[9]

M. E. Sweeney was married yesterday.[10] Son[11] & T. J.[12] were at the wedding. Any of the Ladies[13] weren't there. Paddie[14] asked me to his wedding. I am his godmother. I had to laugh at the Idea. Tim is home. He is just the same. No change.

Every body here are well. I am better & intend to take long holidays next month. The Dr. said I should go away for some time. So I am going to Cork the 7th of July. I will remain with Mrs. Donovan.

Son[ny] McCarthy is to be married next week to a Regan girl west some place. Lots of love to Nora & Frank, Anna, Pat & Emmet, & your dear self & Dan.

Your loving, Mother.

ENDNOTES

1   *Julia O'Donovan (1892-1930) was the ninth child born to Tim ("the Saddler") Donovan and seventh born to Tim and his second wife, Kate McDonnell Donovan, Ballydehob. Her godparents were her uncle Con Donovan and Mary Fitzgerald. Julia sailed from Ireland on 12 July 1914 on the S. S. Celtic and went to Oakland, California. Her two older sisters had preceded her, Kate in 1908 and Nora in 1909. Their maternal uncle, Patrick McDonnell from Coolagh, Ballydehob, was an agriculturist who raised carnations in Oakland. Julia, unlike most Irish women on a ship's manifest was not listed as a servant but rather as a "lady." She died of cancer in April 1930, soon after the Census of 1930 was taken.*

2   Daniel Ring (1894?-1970?) married Julia O'Donovan. He emigrated from Ireland to California in 1915 and was a salesman for a bakery. The Rings had two sons, Cornelius Terrence (1920) and James (1922).

3   *Mary Eliza ("Lily" "Marie") O'Donovan (1898-1993) was the youngest of Tim and Kate O'Donovan's children. Her godparents were John McDonnell and Honoria Donovan. She went to California in 1923 with her mother, Kate, her sister Ellen Sofia ("Sophie") and her mother's niece, Bridie Harte. Lil's occupation was listed as teacher. She married Michael Collins (1893-1960) 24 November 1926. Michael worked for a furniture company as a carpet layer. They had three children, Gerald (1927), unnamed baby (1929-1929), and Rosaleen (1933).*

4   *Ellen Sofia ("Sophie") O'Donovan (1896-1977) was the eleventh of Tim O'Donovan's children. Her godparents were John Mahoney and Ellen McDonnell. She was a National School teacher when this letter was written. When she sailed to America in 1923, her occupation was listed as "lacemaker." She married Terrence "Ted" Rogers. They had no children and eventually returned to Ireland to live in a house in Durras, Bantry that Ted had inherited.*

5   *Kate Anne O'Donovan (1889-1981) was the seventh of Tim Donovan's children. Her godparents were uncle Con Donovan and grandmother Anne McDonnell. She was the first in her family to emigrate. She went to her uncle Pat McDonnell in Oakland and was employed as a clerk in a dye works before marrying Patrick O'Donovan about 1914. Pat was a construction worker. They had two sons, Patrick Emmett (1915) and John Timothy (1923).*

6   *Honora "Nora" O'Donovan (1888-1972) was the sixth of Tim Donovan's children and the second to survive infancy. Her godparents were Tim and Ellen McDonnell. She emigrated in 1909 and was living with her uncle Pat McDonnell when the 1910 Census was taken. Her occupation was listed as a dyer in a dye works. She married Frank Schoop of French and Alsatian ancestry about 1913. Frank was a linesman for the streetcars. They had two sons, Frank (1919?) and Gerald (1922?).*

7   *Emmett O'Donovan, child of Kate Anne and Patrick.*

8   *Julia had been living with her sister Nora and family.*

9   *Kate was prescient. She and her other daughters were in California when the 1930 Federal Census was taken.*

10   *Margaret McSweeney married Patrick Donovan, sixth son of John of Dreenlamane.*

11   *Patrick Stephen "Sonny" "P. S." O'Donovan (1890-1966) took over his father's saddlery business after being trained by his cousin Timothy, son of John. He had married Bridget Collins on 6 August 1918 and the first of his ten children, Kathleen, was born on 29 April 1919. She died in 2000. Other children were Tadgh Sean (1920-2009), Diarmuid Kevin (1921-1995), Padraic Cormac (1922-1986), Rosaleen (1924-2005), Maureen Claire (1926-2017), Rita Theresa (1928-__), Brendan (1929-1930), Francis Bernard (1931)-_), and Joseph Aidan (1935-2013).*

12   *Timothy John O'Donovan "T. J." (1893-1921) was the tenth of Tim O'Donovan's children. He died of pneumonia, after suffering from tuberculosis for a number of years. His death prompted his mother and sisters Sophie and Lily to leave Ireland and go to California in 1923.*

13   *It appears that Sonny's wife who had just given birth to their first child, was not present, nor were Kate or her daughters.*

14   *Patrick O'Donovan (1884-1959), was the ninth child of John of Dreenlamane, and the sixth of John and his second wife, Ellen Mahoney. He had his trunks packed to go to America where four of his siblings lived but his older brother John Jr. ("Jack") who had taken over the family farm in 1914 on the death of his father, died in 1916 of consumption. His older brother Timothy had become a saddler after serving as an apprentice to his uncle Tim. Younger brother, Dan, had become a policeman in Dublin and youngest brother Jeremiah was not healthy. So Pat had no option but to stay in Dreenlamane. His wife, Margaret McSweeney, had also planned to emigrate, but married Pat instead. They had six children, John (1920-1960), Michael (1922-1941), Patrick Cornelius (1925-2007), Ellen Philomena (1927-1999), Mary Brigid (1929), and Timothy Joseph (1931-2005).*

Document D56
28 December 1921 – Julia Minihane,[1] Cussovina, Ballydehob to Daniel Donovan, Haverhill, Mass.

28th Dec. 1921

Cussovina

Dear Brother,

I received your letter and it was welcome after such a lot of years and was glad to hear from you. When I got it, it renewed old times. You were so good to bring the pails of water to me. Myself I'm not very strong. I am 70 years next August. 1 am not well these 3 or four years.

I was glad to hear that your daughters were so fine.[2] I would be glad to see their pictures. We did not hear from Paddy[3] these 3 years. I suppose his sons are earning now.

It is good we have peace now after such a long time.[4] I have no more to say until we hear again from you. Wishing you and your family a happy New Year.

From your Sister, Julia Minihane[5] Johny Minihane is keeping strong still.

ENDNOTES

1   It is likely that Julia's youngest child, Margaret Ann (1897-1978), wrote this letter for her mother. Maggie Ann had married Cornelius Helen of Mt. Gabriel in 1915. They lived in nearby Rathruane.

2   Dan's daughters were all grown and employed. Agnes was 28 and an office clerk. Marion was 24 and a bookkeeper. A tall beauty, she had been selected the city's first "Miss Haverhill" in 1917. Marie was eighteen and a business college student as she recovered from a near-fatal attack of peritonitis after a burst appendix. Dan, and his second wife, Nora, also had a son, Daniel Harold, born in 1906. A second son, Cornelius Patrick, had died in infancy.

3   *Patrick Minihane (1873-1951) had immigrated to Haverhill in 1898. He was a tall, handsome man "and he knew it," according to his cousin, Marie Donovan Trainor. Pat married Hannah Sweeney in 1899 and they had four sons: John (1900-post 1951), Cornelius Frank (1904-c.1935), Daniel (1906-1907), and Stephen (1908-post 1951). Pat and his brother Dan Minihane were pall bearers for their Uncle Dan Donovan in 1947.*

4   *The Treaty ending the Anglo-Irish War was signed in 1921. Unfortunately, peace was temporary. Ireland fell into a Civil War between 1922 and 1923. The fighting, especially guerilla war, was particularly intense in County Cork.*

5   *Julia Minihane died 11 April 1929 from a shock (stroke) following an accident. She was 76.*

Document D57
10 June 1923 – Richard Hodnett, Drishane, Durrus to Lillie Hodnett, Haverhill, Mass. [Original letter is not in Donovan Collection]

Drishane
June 10th, 1923

My Dear Lillie,

I received your letter a week ago, and was glad to hear from you. I was afraid that something may be wrong, as I had no letter from you so long. I was very anxious to hear about Nora.[1] I am so glad to hear that she has improved in her health. I am feeling very well myself. Just the same as I was before you left. I feel as young and smart as ever I did. My hair is turning grey now, but there are others much younger far worse.

I am working hard. Times are greatly against everybody. Prices are gone down and taxation is terrible. All the trouble is nearly over now.[2] Half the country boys are in jail. They destroyed the country. People can't stand the taxes. There are a lot of fellows around here going to America this year. Den and Jack Mehegan[3] are going on the 7 of July to Milwauky to Mike M.[4] Pat is very bad.[5] He is very deaf and dumb. He is not in Bantry. He is earning around. They are friends with us now and also the Johnsons.[6] George Harnedy[7] is also going on that day and Maria Johnson[8] and Hannie Burke[9] are also going. Bell and Elie Nugent and Pat.[10]

George Nugent[11] got married a short time ago to a girl in Clonakilty that has a shop.

Well, Lillie, you asked about little Mary.[12] She has got light hair and looks like our family. Francis[13] is in the second class. There is no learning going in the schools, very little English taught now since the treaty. The poor children are persecuted trying to learn Irish.[14]

Johney Minihane was buried.[15] Aunt Julia is feeling well and also Uncle Con is strong. Ellie got married a short time ago to a farmer near the place that she is teaching school. They say that he is very wealthy.[16]

[This letter ends without a signature.]

ENDNOTES

1   *Nora Hodnett (1881-1925) had emigrated to America in May 1901. She married Dennis Collins c. 1914. They had four children: Joseph (1915-1999), Mary (1916-2003), Richard (1917-2006), and John (1920-2007). Both Dennis and Nora contracted tuberculosis. Nora died from it in 1925 and Dennis died a year later. Her sisters, Mary Anne/Mamie and Kate raised the children after Dennis' death.*

2   The Irish Civil War ended in May 1923.

3   *Denis and Jack Mehegan were the sons of Mark and Catherine of Drishane. Denis was born about 1899 and Jack in 1901. Denis, but not Jack, along with George Harnedy, Daniel Leahy, and John Levis, all from the Dunbeacon area, sailed on the S. S. Baltic that arrived in New York 16 April 1923. Denis was going to his cousin Joseph Mehegan in Milwaukee. George Harnedy and his cousin Daniel Leahy were going to Daniel's brother James in the Bronx. John Levis was going to his cousin John Levis in Bayonne, N. J.*

4   *Michael Mehegan was a brother to Denis and Jack. He was born c. 1897.*

5   *Pat Mehegan was born in 1900 to Mark and Catherine. He was not at home when the 1911 Census of Ireland was taken.*

6   *In the Census of 1901, the family of John and Ellen (Daly) Johnson lived next door to the Hodnetts on one side and the Mehegans on the other side.*

7   *George Harnedy was the son of Timothy and Bridget of Drishane. He was born c. 1897.*

8   *Mary/Maria Johnson, daughter of John and Ellen of Drishane, was born c. 1900. She sailed 4 August 1923 on the S. S. Samaria. Her destination was her maternal uncle, Patrick Daly, in Andover, Mass.*

9   *Hannah Burke, Richie's cousin and the granddaughter of Dan Donovan's sister Ellen, was the daughter of Denis and Julia Schofield Burke of Drishane. She was born 28 July 1902. Hannah sailed on the S. S. Samaria arriving 1 September 1923. She was going to her cousin Annie Schofield in Andover. Hannah was 5 foot 5 inches, fresh faced, with brown hair and grey eyes according to the Shipping Record of the Samaria.*

10   *These are the children of Jeremiah (a shopkeeper) and Anne Moynihan Nugent of Derryfunshion. Pat Nugent was born in 1899. Eileen/Elie and Anne/Bell sailed on the President Polk that arrived in New York 15 July 1923. Their destination was their Uncle George Nugent, Bayonne, N. J. Eileen was a typist and Anne a shop assistant.*

11   George Nugent of Derryfunshion was born c. 1896. He was a son of Jeremiah and Anne.

12   Mary Hodnett was born 27 August 1919. Her godparents were neighbors George Nugent and Margaret Mehigan. She never married and lived with her brother Dick. She died in 1985.

13   Francis Joseph Hodnett was born 10 December 1913. His godparents were relatives Julia Burke and Michael Bennett, Mattie's brother. Frank died of tuberculosis in Cork Hospital post 1929. In addition to Mary and Frank, there was also another son, Richard, born 26 June 1916. His godparents were his aunt Elizabeth Bennett and his cousin Timothy Donovan. He never married and died in Bantry Hospital in 1984.

14   This is a very revealing negative aspect of the newly won independence.

15   John Minihane, husband of Julia (Donovan) of Cussovina, died 12 February 1923. He was 82 and died of "senile decay." This death took many years to find in the Vital Records because it was listed under "Cornelius Menihane."

16   Ellen O'Donovan, daughter of Con and Brigid, married Bartholomew O'Donovan of Ballinspittal 5 April 1923. They had four children: Helen (1924-?), Jeremiah/Derry (1925-1998), Cornelius Gerald (1927-2001), and Barry (1929-1999). Ellen continued to teach at the Ballinspittal National School after her marriage. She died in 1959, at 71.

Document **D58**

9 January 1929 – Richard Hodnett, Drishane, Durrus to Annie Hodnett Powers, Haverhill, Mass. [Original is not in Donovan Collection]

Drishane
Jan. 9th, 1929

My Dear Annie,

In answer to your letter which I received a few days ago, no need to say I was glad to hear from you and to know that you and family were well, a blessing we enjoy at present, thank God.

I had a letter from Mary[1] and Julia.[2] Julia send Mary a nice dress and sweater. They were a lovely fit. She is crazy over them. They did not come for a fortnight after her letter, as parcels are held up at Xmas. She is a real good little girl. You would be surprised at the cake that she can bake. The lads also are expert bakers. There is no body does anything for us. We must try and manage the best we can. Every body got enough to do for themselves. It is myself must wash and mend. It's an old saying that a person don't know what they can do until they will have to do it. So, Annie Dear, don't you send any dress to Mary. She got plenty presently. I got some dresses made for her before Xmass. I buy everything in the shops.

It is hard to get along the times are so bad. I will have a hard time to prepare for the Stations[3] again April. I tried to put them back but the priest would not consent to do so as it is my turn to have them. We must do the best we can in the name of God. The priest was good to me in the hour of trouble[4] and he is anxious to have Mass said in the house. The only thing I would need most is a table cloth for the occasion and a couple of towels as I don't know much about buying them. Probably you and some one of the girls may have some old ones. I don't want you to go to the experience of buying them as I feel dear for you. I know what it is to try to get along. If in case any parcel is sent value them low as the tax is 3 shillings to the pound value put on them. There was three shillings on Mary's dress for she valued them to five dollars. They are robbers.

It is with the Nugents[5] I am dealing. I owe a good bill there but the summer is coming and I will be able to clear it off. I got very good little children. They are great for the Fowl. They are hatching for the past year. They have over 60 hens now. Poor Lillie must be feeling lonely now, so far away.[6] She is very good to me. Mary is writing to Geraldine[7] hoping soon to hear from you at your earliest convenience with fond love and happiness to you and Family, I remain as ever, your fond B. Rd.[8]

Love from the Children.

ENDNOTES

1   *Mary Ann ("Mamie") Hodnett (1873-1955) came to Haverhill in 1892. She made at least one trip back to Ireland, returning 25 April 1902 on the S. S. New England along with two cousins: Frank Minihane and James Donovan, and a neighbor, Nellie Burns. Mamie never married. She lived with her sister Katie, worked in the shoe shops, and when her sister Nora died of tuberculosis in 1925, set up housekeeping for three of Nora's orphaned children.*

2   *Julia Hodnett (1878-1967) immigrated to Haverhill in 1897. She worked as a laundress at Bradford Academy, then lived with her widowed sister Ellen and her two daughters. They ran a boarding house at which they each met her future husband. Julia married Michael Finnegan September 1907. They had seven children: Edna Mae (1908-1992), Catherine (1910-2002), Helen (1911-1992), Joseph (1913-1975), Edwin (1915-1998), Francis X. (1917-2000) and Muriel (1924-1953).*

3   *The "Stations" was a tradition of having a Mass said in a parishioner's home for all the neighbors and the family. The practice continues.*

4   *Richie's wife, Mattie, died 8 May 1927 of post-partum hemorrhage after delivering their fifth child, a daughter Elizabeth. The infant was placed with the nuns in Schull where she died about six months later.*

5   *Jeremiah and Ann Nugent of Derryfunshion had a shop, but by this date, it was probably their son, George who operated the store.*

6   *Lil Hodnett was a waitress in the Aldine Hotel, Atlantic City, New Jersey. She would marry Michael Harney in the 1930s.*

7   *Mary Hodnett, born in 1919, was writing to her cousin, Geraldine Powers, daughter of Annie, who was born in 1920.*

8   *"your brother, Richard"*

THE DONOVAN PHOTOS

Michael Donovan with his father, Cornelius, Sr. c.1872, before Michael emigrated to America.

Julia Mahoney Donovan, midwife, nurse, and mother of nine children.

The parish church in Schull, mother church on the Mizen Peninsula. Con Donovan and Julia Mahoney were both baptized here. Their wedding was performed in this church here in 1838

John Donovan.

John's son "Nellus" Donovan and his wife, Minnie Hosford.

John's daughter Julia Donovan Coughlin and her husband, Dennis Coughlin.

John's son Mike Donovan, with cousins Harold and Marie Donovan. Mike was bald due to an industrial accident that removed his scalp, so Marie "assists" with her tresses.

James Donovan, son of John.

Uncle Timothy O'Donovan holding Mary O'Donovan, John, Patrick, Margaret holding Tim Joe O'Donovan (back row). Paddy, Philomena, and Michael O'Donovan (front row).

Margaret and Patrick O'Donovan, Kate O'Donovan Minihane, Molly O'Donovan McSweeney, and Dan O'Donovan with their maternal aunt, Julia Mahoney, at "Darraheen," the home of John Donovan and his descendants

Mary "Molly" O'Donovan McSweeney

Michael and Mary Donovan Hodnett

The original Hodnett family home in Drishane, on the Mizen Peninsula, Co. Cork.

Johannah "Ann" Hodnett, right, with a friend.

Joseph Collins, Mary "Mamie" Hodnett, and John Collins, rear. Mary Collins, front. The Collins siblings were raised by Aunt Mamie after their parents, Nora Hodnett Collins and Dennis Collins, died of tuberculosis in the mid-1920s. Their brother, Richard, was raised by their aunt, Katie Hodnett Cotter Bean.

The eight Hodnett sisters: Mary "Mamie," Katie Hodnett Cotter Bean, Ellen Hodnett Conlon Guthrie, Lil Hodnett, Johannah "Ann" Hodnett Murphy, Julia Hodnett Finnegan, Nora Hodnett Collins at the wedding of Annie Hodnett to William Powers, June 25, 1919.

Julia Hodnett and Michael Finnegan wedding portraits, c. 1908.

Edwin Michael Finnegan, son of Julia Hodnett and Michael Finnegan, with Irish cousins Dick and Mary Hodnett, the surviving children of Richard Hodnett, the only son of Michael and Mary.

Kate Hodnett Cotter Bean with her sone Milton/ Michael Cotter.

Richard and Mary in a donkey cart, likely returning from Church, 1960.

Mary Driscoll Corrigg, first daughter of Hanna.

Honora/Hanna Donovan Driscoll, third daughter of Con and Julia. She immigrated to America in 1865 with her infant son Cornelius.

Connie Driscoll in his office at City Hall, Haverhill. In addition to being an athlete and sports entrepreneur, he was a shoe shop foreman and political activist.

Cornelius "Connie" Driscoll, far left, with a mustache. Connie would go from playing baseball to being part-owner of a Haverhill semi-pro team.

Leo Driscoll was born in 1890, the year before his father's death. After his mother died in 1902, he was raised by his brother Con.

Agnes Driscoll Kershaw, youngest daughter of Hanna, with her husband Richard at their home in Bradford, MA.

Dennis Driscoll with his wife and children. He, his wife, and two eldest daughters would be dead from tuberculosis in the next few years.

Dan Donovan with nieces Julia Driscoll Sheridan and Agnes Driscoll Kershaw.

Michael Francis "Jack" Donovan with wife "Nonnie" Murphy.

James Donovan. He married Margaret Callahan of Lawrence, MA.

Michael Donovan, second son of Con and Julia. He immigrated to America c.1872.

Michael Donovan with sons Jim and Jack, their wives, and a Callahan cousin. All three of Michael's sons would succumb to tuberculosis.

Margaret "Maggie Ann" Minihan and husband Con Hellen. Maggie Ann was the youngest of the Minihan children.

Mary Minihan, eldest daughter of John and Julia Donovan Minihan, Cussivina. Mary went to Haverhill, MA c. 1902. She married Eugene Donovan, Skibereen, in 1903. As a child, she wrote her mother's letters to Dan Donovan.

John Minihan, son of John and Julia. He was a career member of the British Army serving in Burma.

Daniel Minihan, the youngest son of John and Julia, immigrated to the Boston area. Dan was employed by A&P stores for over forty years. He was a pallbearer for his uncle Dan Donovan in 1947.

The twelve Hellens in Ballydehob after their mother's funeral. They came from three continents: Europe, North America, and Australia.

Timothy" Donovan and his wife, Kate McDonnell/O'Donnell. Known as "The Saddler" for his trade, he was the third son of Con and Julia.

Kate O'Donovan, the widow of The Saddler, immigrated to California in the 1920s to live with her daughters.

Michael Collins, Sophie O'Donovan Rogers, Marion Collins, Marie O'Donovan Collins, and Ted Rogers in California.

Kate Anne O'Donovan immigrated to California in 1910. She married Patrick O'Donovan.

Marie O'Donovan Collins in California in the early 1950s. She emigrated from Ireland with her mother, sister Sophie, and adopted sister Bridie Harte in the early 1920s.

The home and shop of Tim the Saddler in Ballydehop in 1996. The house is now a bank.

The only son of Tim the Saddler to survive past the age of 20 was Patrick Stephen ("P.S." or "Sonny") O'Donovan. He and his wife Bridget are shown with eight of their nine children at the wedding of their son Bernard to Helena "Ena" O'Leary in 1958 in Killarney.

Back row: Kathleen, Tadgh, Rosaleen, Claire, Fr. Aidan, Bridget, Sonny, Kevin, and Cormac.

Cornelius O'Donovan was the fourth son of Con and Julia and the designated heir. He was the first in the family to use "O'Donovan." He is shown with his wife, Brigid Donahue. Married in February 1885, Dan Donovan emigrated two months later.

John, firstborn of Con and Brigid and their only child to emigrate. He and his cousin Lil Hodnett left Cobh/Queenstown on the same day as the RMS Titanic.

Michael, born in 1900, was Con and Brigid's youngest child. He became a detective in Dublin. Upon retirement, he returned to Dreenlamane to live with his brother, Sonny Con.

Ellen "Nell" went to college in Dublin, the first of her generation to do so. She became a teacher in Ballinspittal. She married Bart O'Donovan, raised four children, and continued to teach until retirement. Her son Cornelius Gerald succeeded his uncle "Sonny Con" as the owner of the Donovan farm.

Con and Brigid O'Donovan with their son and heir Sonny Con. Con died of bronchial pneumonia in 1929. Brigid would live another ten years.

Con, jr.'s fourth and fifth children, Sister Gertrude (Hannah Maria) and Daniel. Hannah entered a religious order of teaching nuns. She served in England, eventually leaving the order but continuing to live in England. Dan, as did his sister Ellen, attended college in Limerick and became a teacher. His only child, "Brid," was killed in a plane crash while in college. Upon retirement, Dan and his wife opened an inn in Baltimore, south of Skibbereen.

The first time descendants of the three immigrant Donovan children returned to the family home was in 1966. From left, the hired driver, Sonny Con O'Donovan, Marion Donovan Hayes, Maggie Ann Minihan Hellen, and Mike O'Donovan.

The Donovan home, known as "Spike," is surrounded by the family fields. In the 1930s, the stone house was covered in stucco, and a two-story entryway was added.

P. W. TENNANT & SON,   HAVERHILL, MASS.

Daniel Donovan, youngest son of Con and Julia. He immigrated to America in 1885.

Dan's "Greenhorn picture." This tintype was the first picture sent back to family in Ireland to demonstrate how well he was doing in his new country.

Dan had several physical jobs, including construction on the ice house at Haverhill's Round Pond. He is on the far right wielding a sledgehammer.

Dan's future wife, Mary McCarthy of Ballinlough, Leap.

Agnes was named after her paternal grandmother. All Donovan-McCarthy children had a traditional family first name, but each was known by their middle name.

Catherine Marion Donovan, the second child of Dan and Mary, was born in 1897. She was named after her maternal grandmother.

Helen Evelyn, the third daughter of Dan and Mary, was born in January 1900. She died on St. Patrick's Day 1901 of a heart problem.

Agnes, 7, and Marion, 3, in late summer 1900, about the time their mother died of a fast-moving form of tuberculosis. Their uncle, Michael Hodnett, and aunt, Margaret, wife of Michael Donovan, also died in the same outbreak.

Mary holds Julia Agnes Donovan, born in 1893. She was the first daughter of Dan and Mary.

Dan's female friend, Mary Ann McCarthy of Rosskerrig, Kilcrohane on neighboring Sheepshead Peninsula. Mary Ann was an aggressive young lady who pursued Dan up to the year of his marriage.

Dan Donovan, in his later years. His lapel is adorned with union pins, befitting a pioneer member of the local chapter of the Teamsters.

An 1890 postcard of the main road through Ballydehob illustrates Dan Donovan's last view of his hometown in 1890.

Hannah Cronan was Dan's other female correspondent. She had been a neighbor in Ireland and now worked in Andover, MA, a short train ride to Haverhill. Her brother John lived in Haverhill and is mentioned numerous times in the letters.

Part Two:

THE MCCARTHYS OF BALLINLOUGH
AND
THE MCCARTHY COLLECTION

Patrick and Kate McCarthy and the McCarthy Family

When Marie Donovan, the youngest daughter of Dan and Nora (McCarthy) Donovan, was a young child in the Bradford section of Haverhill, she would look forward each week to the visit of her Aunt Ellen McCarthy. Ellen, six feet tall and sturdy in size, was the respected housekeeper and cook for the Spauldings of Summer Street, one of Haverhill's leading shoe manufacturers. Ellen would walk across the bridge over the Merrimack River to Bradford each Thursday, her day off. She would stop at the fish market to purchase a large, fresh salmon. The sisters would prepare the fish for dinner for the Donovans and whatever other boarders or visitors might be expected around the kitchen table. Both of the McCarthy sisters, Ellen and Nora, were splendid cooks and bakers. They had never learned these skills at home in Ireland, where all cooking was done in pots and skillets in the fireplace. When Marie would reminisce about those long-ago family gatherings, she most remembered listening to the conversations after dinner and cleaning up was finished. Ellen and Nora would sit at the wooden kitchen table next to the warm oil stove with their cups of tea and perhaps some "Irish cake" (soda bread with raisins and caraway seeds), smothered in fresh butter.

Young Marie would sit quietly in a chair in the corner, trying not to be noticed so as not to interrupt the flow of conversation. Her mother and her aunt would talk about "home––that unknown Ireland across the ocean. They would talk about their home on a hillside overlooking beautiful Ballin Lake, and their sweet-faced mother, Kate. Their mother always welcomed all of her children's friends and shared in their singing and dancing. And the two sisters would talk about their father, Patrick. Patrick, the "Playboy," whatever that meant.

All Marie knew of her grandfather was derived from the sepia-toned photograph they had of a white-haired, strong-featured man in working clothes, most likely, his only suit of clothes. And this was the man whose memory would start his two daughters laughing. "The Playboy." It's difficult from this distance in time to determine what in heaven's name a semi-literate peasant in post-Famine rural Ireland could possibly do to be labeled a "playboy." Did he gamble, or drink, or behave in some unseemly manner? No one ever explained to Marie. But what was clear was the reality that the McCarthys in Ireland were impoverished. That was why all of the children of Patrick and Kate had emigrated from Ireland to England and America. And for some unexplained reason, Patrick had lost his share of the family farm in Ballinlough. He had to accept charity from the "Guardians of the Poor," in the form of a small cottage with no fields for grazing or growing crops. Whatever income he could anticipate would come from the labor he, and while they were home, his children, could perform for his neighbors, such as his older brother Michael. Or, Pat and Kate could ask their immigrant children to send them money. And they did, over and again, until the British government decided to allot all people over seventy in Ireland a regular sum of five shillings a week, for everyone who could provide proof from the local church (for a price). This manna from Heaven began to arrive in 1909.

The townland of Ballinlough is north of the village of Leap, at the head of Glandore Harbor. It was on the old road, now the N71, from Clonakilty, Rosscarbery, and Skibbereen, to Bantry. Sheahan's Hotel and Post Office, where young Nora worked before emigrating, still stands in the center of the village. When novelist Sheila Connolly decided to set a series of mystery novels in Leap, she was sure to place Sheahan's Hotel in its proper central location. The local parish church is on that old road now known as N70. The parish is known as Kilmacabea. In the townland of Kilmacabea, perched on a hillside north of Leap, are the ruins of an old church and the Kilmacabea Burial Ground.

Ballin Lake, which gives its name to Ballinlough, occupies the greater part of the acreage in the townland. There are few farm sites in the remaining space. The traditional McCarthy site is on the south side of the lake. When Griffiths' Survey was undertaken after the Great Famine, it recorded Jeremiah McCarthy as the lessee. A decade or so later, when the Continuing Valuation, or tax list, was created, not only Jeremiah, but three of his sons: Michael, Timothy, and Patrick, were listed, each with his own house and outbuildings, and a share of the one hundred and thirty- eight acres. There were also two other small houses, leased to Denis and John Hayes, who also had a share of the land. All of the small houses were clustered around a common farmyard. The fields associated with the houses appear to have been worked collectively. Traces of this collective farming appear in letters written to Nora in the 1890s that describe how brother Tim (Tady) had to work on the "mihill" – that is, contribute his labor for some common work, such as haying.

Patrick McCarthy (c.1831-1910) was the son of Jeremiah McCarthy and Honora White. The oldest extant baptismal register for Kilmacabea Parish begins in 1832, so we must depend on Civil burial records to recreate the McCarthy family. The father, Jeremiah, was born about 1789. His oldest son, Michael, was born about 1821. We can assume that Jeremiah married Honora White a year or so earlier.

Jeremiah McCarthy died in 1874 (his wife Honora had died the previous year), leading to a change in the family dynamic. When the next Continuing Valuation was taken in the late 1870s, Michael was the only McCarthy listed at the site. He was living in his father's house. The original farmland had been divided up, and his share was twenty-two acres. Neither Patrick nor Timothy was listed as lessees in Ballinlough. Another decade later, in the late 1880s, Patrick reappeared on the tax list as an inhabitant of a cottage constructed by the Guardians of the Skibbereen Union. His was one of two cottages, each on a site of no more than two square rods, provided by the public agency, on the western side of Ballin Lake. Patrick had sunk in economic status from a farmer to a laborer for other farmers. He would be a laborer until he died in 1910.

There were three other McCarthy siblings in the area in addition to Michael, Patrick, and Timothy: sister Julia Harding who with her husband Harry lived in nearby Kilmacabea, sister Honora (Nora) Keane, who had married Patrick's brother-in-law Daniel Keane of Ballinaclough, Rosscarbery, and brother Denis McCarthy, youngest of the siblings, who was living in Ballinlough when his children were born in the 1860s and 1870s. Denis and older brother Timothy were both dead by 1896 when a reference was made in a letter to Nora that her sister Katie was buried in her grandfather's grave between her uncles Tim and Denis. The remaining brothers and sisters all survived into the first decade of the twentieth century. Michael, the eldest, lived the longest and died in 1911.

All of these family members and their children are referenced frequently throughout the correspondence in the McCarthy Collection, and it is self-evident that this was a close, supportive clan.

Patrick McCarthy married Kate Keane of Balinaclough, Rosscarbery in 1855, in the Kilmacabea Parish Church in the village of Leap, Co. Cork. They had eight children: three males and five females, one of whom died in infancy. The first four children (Jeremiah, Denis, Mary, and Ellen) had left home by the late 1870s-early 1880s, probably about the time period when their father had lost his family farm share. It is likely that the youngest child, Honoria or Nora, had little or no recollection of her older brothers who crossed the Irish Sea to England when she was only a few years old.

Nora McCarthy was baptized in the Kilmacabea Parish church on February 17, 1876. She attended the Knockskagh National School a short distance from her home, where she developed a life-long love of poetry. She worked for a few years in Leap Village at Sheehan's Hotel before immigrating to America in May 1895 when she was nineteen. Nora was accompanied by her older sister, Ellen. Ellen was returning to her post as a domestic servant after convalescing at home for the previous year for some unidentified illness. According to the Shipping Records, their destination was the home of their married sister Mary, wife of Dan Donovan of Dreenlamane, Ballydehob. Dan and Mary Donovan's new seven-room home was in the town of Bradford, on the south side of the Merrimack River across from the shoe manufacturing city of Haverhill, MA.

Like her sister Ellen, Nora worked as a domestic for the Yankee Protestant wealthy class in America. On their days off, the two sisters would go to Mary's house to rest and, in Nora's case, to write letters. She wrote to family and cousins in Ireland and to her "chums," other Irish immigrant domestics like her. Nora was a prodigious letter writer, a practice she maintained all her life. She saved many of the letters she received in her first years in America, which form the base of the McCarthy Family Collection.

There are one hundred and forty-six letters in this edited collection, almost evenly divided between those sent from relatives in Ireland and England (67) and those from friends and fellow immigrants in the United States (79). The total includes some letters sent to Mary McCarthy Donovan before her sister Nora arrived in America. Some envelopes were saved that now have no letters in them. The first letter in the series was from the widow of Jerry McCarthy, the recently deceased oldest brother of the family. It was sent from London in 1884 to Mary at an unknown address, probably in Massachusetts but unknown since the envelope was not saved. The last letters were from cousin Patrick Harding and his family. They were written between 1911 and 1914 and sent to Ellen McCarthy, Nora's sister. The Hardings had assumed responsibility for the burial and final disposition of the belongings of Kate McCarthy, Nora and Ellen's mother, and Paddy Harding's aunt.

For all the hundreds of letters Nora wrote, we have only a few in her own handwriting. If anyone saved others, they have not surfaced. What has survived is one set of four letters that Nora wrote to her sisters during a few weeks of hospitalization at the Boston Eye and Ear Infirmary in 1899. There is also a separate box of letters written to her married daughter, Marion Donovan Hayes, during the 1930s that are very descriptive of the impact of the Depression. The first set of one hundred forty-six letters is included in the McCarthy Collection. The second set falls outside the chronological parameters chosen for this Collection and has not been transcribed and placed in this Collection.

THE McCARTHY LETTERS

Part I: M1 to M128
1884-1900

Document M1

Jeremiah, "Jerry," McCarthy, the eldest of Pat and Kate McCarthy's children, was baptized 3 April 1856. He went to England in the 1870s and married Annie Fitzgerald in 1879 in Uxbridge, Middlesex. In the 1881 English Census, Jerry, Annie and one-year old daughter Catherine (Kate), were living at 38 Warmington St., West Ham, Essex. Jerry was an agricultural laborer. His death from tuberculosis is listed in the December Quarter of 1883.

30 September [1884] – Annie Fitzgerald McCarthy, Plaistow, West Ham, Essex, England to Mary McCarthy [address unknown]

13 Warmington Street,
Barking Road, Plaistow, Essex [England]
September 30 [1884]

My dear Mary,

Just a few lines hoping this will find you quite well as I am sorry to have to tell you it does not leave us at present. My dearest sister, it is with the greatest sorrow I am writing this letter to you to tell you of my darling Jerrie's death but we must put up with the will of God. It is now 8 months since he died and I cannot believe it yet. He was only 10 days ill when he died but I trust in God he is better off. But it is a cruel thing to be parted from the only one you love but I hope, please God, we will meet in heaven yet.

My dear Mary, I wish you would come to England.[1] Yourself and your sister would do well here, and then your Father and Mother would come and we would all be near each other. I suppose your sister told [you] we had a little Patrick [the] last 3d of last September but, worse luck, he will not be able to tell much about his poor dada as he was only two months old when he died. Now, my dear Mary, I hope you will make up your mind to come to England and settle down here. I am sure you would do better here than in America. Write soon and let me know your intentions. Katie sends her love to Aunt Mary also Denny[2] and baby. I must now conclude with fondest love to you from your fond sister but not brother this time.

Annie McCarthy[3]

You musts excuse me for not writing to you before but I am so worried that I could not settle down to do it. Write soon and I will write you a good long letter the next time.

Good by and God bless you.

ENDNOTES

1   *Mary McCarthy and her sister Ellen immigrated to America about 1882/3. Their parents would have been informed of Jerry's death some time previously for his clothes were sent to them.*

2   *Dennis, born in 1882, was Annie and Jerry's second child.*

3   *Annie married Edmund Kiely, a native of Limerick, Ireland, in 1890 in London. In the 1891 Census of England, Annie, children Kate and Dennis, along with Annie's mother and four lodgers from Co. Cork, lived with Kiely, a stoker in a gas works. Annie's baby, Patrick, had died. The Kiely household was on Clifford Road, West Ham, Essex in London's East End. Annie's sister Julia had married and lived on the same street. Ten years later, when the 1901 Census of England was taken, Kate and Dennis were at home and Annie and Edmund had a daughter of their own, Bridget, nine years old. Annie's mother, Bridget, had died in January 1900. Twenty-year old Kate, a dressmaker, went to Ireland in the summer of 1900 to visit her McCarthy grandparents for the first time. (See letters dated 4 June and 6 August 1900.)*

DOCUMENT **M2**

Denis Keane[1], of Ballinaclough, Rosscarbery, was a double first cousin of the McCarthys. His father was the brother of Kate McCarthy and his mother was the sister of Patrick McCarthy. His home was south-east of Leap and south of Rosscarbery on the bay. Denis was a fisherman. He wrote this letter to his brother, Daniel, and his cousin, Bartholomew Crowley, who had immigrated to Bradford, MA. Dan Keane had a reputation as an excellent writer. His younger brother seems to have shared his literary abilities. How this letter ended up in the McCarthy Collection is not known, however, when a fatally ill Dan Keane returned to Ireland about 1894, he left a notebook of the essays he had written for the Haverhill, Mass. newspaper with his McCarthy cousins in Bradford. The letter may have been inside the notebook. Denis' description of a fatal brawl is vivid. A photocopy of the story from the Skibbereen Eagle newspaper is in the McCarthy Collection.

June 1887 – D[enis] Keane to brother [Daniel Keane] and cousin [Bartholomew Crowley], Bradford, Mass.

June 1887

My Dear brother, and beloved friend (Mr. Crowley),

It is profound regret that I narrate to you both the following most melancholy and deplorable tragedy which recently occurred in our midst. It was thus: On Sunday the 8th ultimo as James Kearney of Reenascreena associated with a man whom he much esteemed and venerated and who, among his own neighbours, was held in high respect and renown — James Hayes of Tralong, they proceeded to partake of some refreshment in the public house which is owned by Tom Calnan of Ardagh, and which was formerly held by the Legoe family. They had scarcely chaired or seated themselves when another confederate – John Hayes of Ballinaclough, fell into the respectable society; the three having satisfactorily refreshed themselves, were determined to be on the move towards their respective homes, but very unluckily for each party the doctor (Daunt) of the district appeared, not to exercise any of his medical powers being unnecessary at that moment, though very necessary immediately after, as you will learn further on.

The latter-mentioned gentleman offered a treat which Messrs. Hayes and Kearney kindly accepted, and it is more than probably that several treats ensued. Though James Hayes and the medical gentleman were pretended friends, yet they had not those real regards for each other which would enable to dissolve in an amicable manner, they having on previous occasions very seriously abused each other. A duel now took place between some two rowdies, on the road between the public house referred to and the court-house. The doctor who is of such inferior character, was more than anxious to see the sport and therefore became a spectator; Mr. Kearney, in the meantime, was apprehending that the doctor would get hurt, and was personally going to his assistance when James Hayes endeavoured to prohibit him. Mr. Kearney, resenting this conduct of Mr. Hayes, grew a little hot and spoke in a rather harsh manner to his opponent; those few harmless words were a sufficient provocation to Mr. Hayes' easily irritated temper and the confusion ended

in a fatal struggle. James Kearney was unquestionably a man of enormous strength, and it can be said of James Hayes that he entertained that opinion of himself which a man of remarkable strength and activity should. The rumour which brought this sorrowful tidings to me says that the struggle commenced with fisting, but James Hayes, finding by experience that his then enemy was capable of subduing him, grasped an iron poker and struck James Kearney on the head immediately over the brain and fractured his skull. One rumour says that he struck him only once and another rumour says that he struck him several times, but anyhow there were two wounds inflicted, one of them healed in a few days, and the one which injured the brain was fatal, and caused his beloved parents as well as his numerous friends and neighbours to inter his remains in Ross Abbey on that day three weeks. I wonder if you have not read such a soul-stirring account on the papers.

It was on the 12th day after the occurrence or on the 18th ultimo James Hayes was arrested, till then the medical attendants were not able to satisfy themselves that the man was in danger, and he was conveyed to Cork prison; he was brought for trial on the 1st inst. to the Rosscarbery Petty Session from which he was returned for trial to the Cork Assizes which are to come off about 1st Aug. and will be detained in prison till then, bail being refused. Our knowledge of and acquaintance with Mr. James Hayes have coerced me to say that the benevolent and generous qualities together with the high-spirited and gentlemanly acts, which he possessed, have brought a disagreeable feeling into our hearts in hearing of his detention in prison, and on court-day the community at large expressed to him their feelings of sympathy and tendered him their sincere condolence. We can only say of James Kearney that in him there is lost a familiar face. He was to emigrate to America on the week he got hurt. You will find full particulars of the following narrative in this copy of the Eagle.[2].

ENDNOTES

1   *Denis Keane, a fisherman, was born in 1869 to Daniel and Nora (McCarthy) Keane. He was a frequent correspondent to his cousin Nora McCarthy.*

2   *The Eagle was a Skibbereen newspaper.*

Document M3

James McCarthy was a lateral cousin, probably from a branch in Skibbereen usually identified by their father's name, as in James George, Mary George, Julia George, etc. They were very close to their cousins in Ballinlough and appear often in these letters.

2 August 1887 – James McCarthy, Chelsea, Mass, to Mary McCarthy, [MA]

[Left portion of first page is damaged, and only the last third of the second page exists]

100 Winnisimet St.
Chelsea [Mass.]
August 2nd 1887

Dear Cousin Mary

I received your letter about a week ago and I [was] never so much surprised when [I] read it over as I could not [bring to] mind who it was or probably I never would only for seeing Ballinlough then I knew at once who it was and I felt very glad to have an opportunity of seeing you and Ellie. I suppose I would not know you now [but] I guess I would know Ellie [as] I see her about 18 months ago and I shall feel very happy [to] see her again and you also. I will go next Sunday if [I] live so long and I will tell you all the news. ………….. [missing portion of page] for me to find out Ceder St.[1] I must say good bye for the present. Your Fond Cousin, James McCarthy.

ENDNOTES

1   *There is a Cedar St. in Haverhill and at this time it had many homes that would have used domestic servants. It was located on a trolley line and would have been relatively easy for James to reach Mary. It is also possible that Mary McCarthy was working in Malden, Mass. as there are two envelopes in the Collection, postmarked Malden, and addressed to her future husband, Dan Donovan. There is a Cedar St. in Malden.*

Document M4

Nineteen of the next letters, composed between 8 March 1894 and 27 October 1896 were from Katie McCarthy of Ballinlough. They were sent to her sisters Mary, Ellen and Nora in Haverhill, Mass. and, after his emigration, to her brother Tim in the same place. Katie wrote a neat, legible hand, with adequate grammar and decent spelling. There is a youthful enthusiasm and joy in her early letters, typical of a young woman in her twenties. She takes great pleasure in describing to her siblings the fun and activities of their mutual friends. Her tone darkens in later letters as she copes with her own terminal illness, and the family's financial difficulties.

8 March 1894 – Katie McCarthy, Ballinlough, Leap to sister Mary McCarthy Donovan, Bradford, MA

March 8, 1894
Ballinlough, Leap

Ever fond + loving Sister Mary,

I received your long expected letter a few days ago, and am glad to learn by it that you are all quite well in health, as it is the best of all riches. I am very sorry how you worries so much about matters as worrying too much would not be long ruining your health, so it is my advise to you to take care of your health in the first of your days and not to be troubled about anything, as mother did in the first of her days.[1] She took every trouble to heart too much and so she have the signs of it now. She know what trouble is very well. Now it would kill any person.

Dear Sister Mary, you did not say anything about the baby or Dan Donovan. I hope they are well in health. Mother is troubled as you did not speak of them. I hope ye are all quite well. Let us know is Dan to work or have the same wages still. There are very bad reports of the country in Ireland this year. I have no news to tell you with which to surprise this time. I have a letter written to Ellie[2]a few weeks ago and I have all news told in it. Father and mother also Tim and Honoria also all the friends and neighbors are all quite well. I did not see John Keane since Dan was buried but I heard he came up to Paddy Harding's[3] a few Sundays ago. He did not come over to see me at all, or anyone of them. They are all quite well. Johnny is very fat and strong, you never saw him so well or so fat. Denny expects a letter from you always. Honoria was south[4] at Christmastime. They have no talk of Dan now. It is a great shame for you to worry so much about us. I know of course you are troubled but cheer up, don't be down hearted, take care of yourself and your baby and your husband. I hope Dan Keane is better off than to be in America. I only wish I was with him. I would not be any way troubled if I would die. Sometimes I do be so good I thinks I do be alright until I gets colds every minute and when I gets a cold I'd rather be dead than alive. It is going too long.[5]

Well about the pictures I would have my picture taken long ago only the weather is very cold and I did not walk out since November or I was not able and especially the cold don't answer me at all but if I gets better for the fine weather I will take my picture and send it to you. I have asked for Ellen(s) picture and I expects to get it in the next letter, but if this letter reaches you before Ellen answers my letter I hope you will send the baby's picture with hers.[6] I am afraid Ellen wont answer the letter now as you had the letter sent, but let you tell her answer it, I am very anxious to get letters from ye so let ye write very often.

So now Dear Sister be contented and live cheerful and agreeable. Don't you be so easily troubled but mind yourself and your health. There is enough gone. Mother is very troubled about you for to take troubles to heart so much as you are.

[no signature but in Katie McCarthy's handwriting]

ENDNOTES

1   *Mary was baptized on 8 February 1862, immigrated c. 1883 and married Dan Donovan 5 November 1890. She had her first child, Julia Agnes, on 20 May 1893. Katie seems to be suggesting that Mary is pregnant again.*

2   *Ellen/Ellie was baptized 9 January 1865. She immigrated with her sister Mary, and worked as a domestic in Haverhill, Mass. The letter to her that Katie references was not saved. It probably had the news of the death of cousin Dan Keane. The presence of their cousins, Dan Keane and Bartholomew Crowley in Bradford is probably what drew Mary and Ellen McCarthy there.*

3   *John Keane was Katie's maternal uncle, and the father of "Big Den," John and James Keane of Ballinaclough, and Mary Keane Goodman (1859-1895) of Bradford, MA. Patrick/Paddy Harding (2 March 1853-post 1914) was Katie's paternal first cousin. He lived with his family and parents in Kilmacabea Townland, east of Ballinlough.*

4   *"South" refers to the home of the Keanes in Ballinaclough, south of Leap and Ballinlough.*

5   *Katie, whose birth was registered 20 April 1872, was suffering from Consumption (Tuberculosis).*

6   *The Collection contains a tintype of Katie, a baby picture of Julia Agnes with her mother, and numerous photos of Ellen.*

Document M5
14 October 1894 – Katie McCarthy, Ballinlough, Leap to Mary McCarthy Donovan, Bradford, Mass.

October 14th 1894

My Dear Sister Mary

I just thought to write a few lines to you hoping to find you and the baby and Dan enjoying good health as we are all well. Ellen expects a letter from you every day and I tells her every day to write to you herself. We received the papers yesterday and we enjoyed reading them. It is now Ellen is gaining any thing. She is commencing to get strong now.[1] She got two teeth drawn since she wrote to you before, but she is improving since. Delia and her brother John[2] are sailing out on the 17th Wednesday next. Ellen wants to go with them, but we all and everybody tells her she better stay until spring as she is commencing to get strong, but she does not seem to care for our talk. She likes to be going with Delia, but we tells her if Delia had not gained she would not go so soon but she picked up very quick. Delia had been out visiting for 3 weeks in the County Kerry and when she was returning last Saturday she met with her brother in town and they both entered for the 17th. It is a fast steamer. It is going to New York. Ellen did not know she was going so soon. If she did she would be with her. She says now she will go on the 4th November and Mrs. John McCarthy at Leap[3] tells her to stay until spring and that she will be twice the girl. We all are forcing her to stay but she says sometimes she will and she says more times she will go. So you can see we don't know what to make of her. She says another time she don't know what to do until she will get a letter from you. Father don't like to have any person go on sea so late in the year towards winter. I guess he wont leave Nora go with her this time of the year. Ellen and Delia and John are gone to town today. She don't know that I am writing to you at all. I wont tell her either. I am only telling you what she intends to do, though she don't tell us much of her mind. You would think by her she have no call to us. She seems to be so strange towards us.

John McCarthy's brother's daughter Maggie McCarthy[4] from

Lowell she arrived home about a week ago. She is staying at Leap. She is going to stay until Spring. She tells Ellen to stay also. Everybody is advising her to stay. I cannot tell what she will do yet. Father wont live after Nora and as far as I can judge by him he wont leave her go. I have no news to tell. Ellen had not been in Ballinaclough yet but she was speaking to big Den Keane last Sunday for the first time ever. She met with him in Leap. He told her John Keane is the father of a daughter with a few weeks.[5] James Sullivan, Bohane, Clounties[6] was buried two weeks ago and Patsey Scortia, Keymore north, was buried last Monday.[7] He is a big loss. All the other friends and neighbors are all quite well. Tady is working with Courley Hourihane Bawnfune [8] every day. He is very agreeable and he likes to have Ellen stay until Spring. I have no more to say this time. Hoping you will answer this letter.

I remain your loving sister, Kate McCarthy

I feel myself improving. Good bye. I send best love to all. Don't show this letter to any body. Yourself can judge by it about Ellen. She would not do anything on us.

ENDNOTES

1   *Ellen had returned to Ireland to convalesce from some unnamed illness.*

2   *Neighbors Delia and John Collins sailed from Queenstown/Cork on the S. S. Majestic and arrived in New York City 24 October 1894. Delia, 24, a dressmaker, listed her destination as Haverhill, Mass. John, 23, a laborer, was headed for Boston.*

3   *Johanna McCarthy was the wife of John, a shopkeeper in Leap Village. She is referenced numerous times throughout the letters. She was godmother to Nora McCarthy.*

4   *Maggie McCarthy was the daughter of James and Bridget McCarthy, born September 1872. No known relationship to the Ballinlough McCarthys. She first went to America in 1893. Her new home, Lowell, Mass., was a major textile manufacturing city about twenty miles west of Haverhill. After her 1894 visit, she returned to Lowell on the S. S. Cephalonia, arriving 14 April 1895.*

5   *"Big Den" Keane, was a maternal cousin of the McCarthys. The title "big" distinguished him from "Little Den" Keane, author of Document 2. John Keane was "Little Den's" brother. In a society where it was a tradition to carry on parents' and grandparents' names, distinguishing labels were a necessity to tell one John McCarthy from a half dozen others. Honora Keane was born to John Keane and wife Mary Sullivan of Burgatia, Rosscarbery in October 1894.*

6   *James "Bohanes" Sullivan, farmer, aged 78, died of old age. He lived in Clounties, Kilgaughnabeg district, south of Leap Village. Sullivan was godfather to Mary McCarthy Donovan.*

7   *Patsy "Scortia" Donovan, from Keamore (on the northern side of Leap Village), died of pneumonia 6 October 1894. His death was reported by his daughter, Mary. In the 1901 Census, four other Donovan children were at home with Mary: John, Maggie, Patrick, and Ellie. "Scortia" could be a variation of "Scairte," a clan name of the Donovans.*

8   *Timothy ("Tady") was the sixth of the McCarthy children, born October 1868. He was working for his cousin by marriage, Cornelius (Courley) Hourihane in neighboring Bawnfune. Courely was married to Margaret (Maggie) McCarthy, daughter of Uncle Michael, the patriarch of the family.*

DOCUMENT M6

1 January 1895 – Kate McCarthy, Ballinlough, Leap to Daniel Donovan, Bradford, Mass.

January 1st 1895

Dear brother,

I received your [letter] a week ago and am glad to learn by it that ye are all well, hoping ye enjoyed a merry Xmas as all of us did. We had a good time. I cannot find words to express the joy I felt in receiving [such] a Xmas Present from you. I [don't] know how can I ever return the compliment. You are so good to me, perhaps I would some time, please God. I am. proud to tell you I am improving a little in my health, although its very slow but still I notices the improvement. I drank a health to you Christmas Eve and so did all the family.

Ellen is very well. She laughs a good deal at what you said in the letter about galllivanting season, as it is all true. They are just commencing now to walk out matchmaking. [1]

Ellen is enjoying herself well. She dances every night, but she misses Delia from [her frolics?] *(unreadable – hole in paper)* as they used to get at [talking?] about the Yankies. She is surprised why Delia is not writing to her. She expected a letter from her for Xmas but she did not get it.

Dear brother, I am glad the baby is well and is walking, also Mary. I hope to hear nothing from you but good news and [sure] ly hope the health is good. I have no news to tell this time except we are all well. We all join in sending our best love and wishes from father and mother, brother and sisters, Tim, Norah, Ellen and myself to yourself, Mary and baby, wishing ye all a happy New Year.

I remain your sister, Katie McCarthy

ENDNOTES

1   *The weeks between Christmas and Ash Wednesday marked the traditional season for matchmaking and courting and marriages. There were no marriages allowed during Lent by Church law.*

DOCUMENT M7

Nora McCarthy, youngest of the McCarthy children, went to America in April 1895. She would be the principal recipient of the letters from home that are in the McCarthy Collection. Nora, born in 1876, was the nearest in age to Katie, born in 1872, and the letters to her take on a much lighter note. Nora was part of a group of young people in the Leap area who loved to dance and 'frolic.' And Katie's letters become filled with what she called "newses." It is notable that there is no suggestion of the fabled "Irish Wake," that was reputed to occur when someone was to leave for America. It could be that it was not uncommon for some emigres to return home whether for a visit, to convalesce, or permanently. In this one letter are three examples: sister Ellie, neighbor Delia and Julia from Fro. Also of interest is the passive-aggressive behavior of relatives and neighbors who expected Nora to "make the rounds," and took out their feelings of being slighted on the family.

24 May 1895 – Katie McCarthy, Ballinlough, Leap to Nora McCarthy, Bradford, Mass.

May 24th 1894 [sic] (Leap Fair Day)

My dearest Nora,[1]

As I did not go to the fair today, I just thought to Answer your long wished for letter which I received on Saturday last. Am glad to learn by it you and Ellie arrived safe and in good health. I am very sorry how Ellie was so long seasick as she always dislike it. We did not think ye would have such hard times going across. We were saying all the time that ye would have great comfort laying on the bed, but I can see it is quiet contrary with ye. Well Nora, they got very strict on the emigrants.[2] I am very glad you sent such a newsy letter. Everybody like [it].

Well, Nora, I felt as if you were with me in reading your letter. It was the longest letter I ever read. All the neighbors around come to the house to hear it read. They speaks about you every hour, and tries to carry on some of your old frolics, and especially Mikey.[3] He felt awful lonesome for you, and so did every one of them. As you know it is hard to make them cry but whatever interest they took in you, they were very lonesome for you. Uncle Michael did not come into us since you went. He would not come. He was scolding us for to leave you go.[4] He never believed you would go. Mary in Tullig[5] and Mrs. Crowley and the Lawlors they were all vexed as ye did not go east[6] before ye went. They expected ye every day. They would hardly speak to us now.

Dear Nora yesterday was a holiday.[7] I went to ten o'clock Mass. It was a lovely day. It was five o'clock when I come home. It was a great day in Leap. I never had seen so many shapers from all parishes. I was speaking to Tady Donovan and his wife.[8] They felt awful lonesome for ye. They told me that Julia Hayes at Fro is home[9] this past week. Ellie knows her well. I heard her speak of her often. She is staying at Glandore. I think she aint feeling very well. She is going to stay there all Summer. Well Nora, we regretted you and Ellie very much yesterday. The Slippers[10] and all the fellows around as usual. They went in drinking. They would not leave me home until I should go with them and Tady Don and his wife. They had a merry day singing and drinking until night. I wished you could see them when they come home and especially Tim and Mikey. All the slippers come to our house. I know you would laugh at them. Jack Minihane[11] was going foolish about the room. Just like Ash Wednesday morning. Oh, I wished you could see him. Dan Minihane[12] took me by the hand, and I thought he would never let it go, only talking about you. He was so fond of you. So in respect to you I should have a trait from him. It is seldom with you that you would not be at the fair. Mary Hayes and Julia Mick[13] are gone to the fair today. It is raining now. I would answer your letter sooner, only I was waiting until I would know all about the fair to tell you all the news. Julia Hurley was drawing porter in Mary Anne's[14] so you may be sure Tady did not pay for any half gallon.

Dear Nora, I don't think you said half enough in the letter. You never said anything about Jamesy Donovan.[15] I heard he wrote home and said he was very sorry as he did not go with ye. You did not say whether Mary knew you or not, or you knew her.[16] It was soon they sent you working after going. Hoping you will get along well with it.

I am very sorry to tell you that Johnny Brien[17] is very ill since that night ye were going. He is not expected to recover. Dr. O'Driscoll[18] is attending him. And Thursday the 16th May, Jerry Hayes[19] was coming from the brake with a bundle of furze[20] and he had a scythe in his hand and the bundle on his back. He got a stumble and he fell. His knee came down in the edge of the scythe. His knee is cut through. He was roaring in the brake for an hour before any person assisted him. So all the men of the land was in the bog only Tady Hayes.[21] He ran for the doctor immediately so they should go to Acres' bog[22] for help to bring him home on a door. So they all thought he was dead that he would not live at all, and his parents would (not) leave him into there own house at all,[23] and Mary Collins[24] did not like to leave him in either so mother told her to leave him in because James was not at home at all. So she left him in and he is there still. He cannot stir the leg at all. The doctor attended that evening and is attending him since. He put 9 stitches in his knee, so he is in an awful state the poor fellow. He will never again have the se of his leg. We are very sorry for him. He used to come down every evening and bruise the furze with father.[25] They[26] are scolding one another now again just the same as before, about the doctor's payment.

Dear Nora, we had two letters from Captain[27] since. He says he will soon go to America. He want Patrick Hourihane's address[28] but they would not give it to him. He said he would soon send a present to Tady. We got no letter from London since.[29] Leave me know if ye have her address. If not I will send it to ye. I would send the pictures only I am waiting to get the other ones. Nora, I would like very much to get your green horn picture[30] if you could get it taken. I forgot to say that Courley Connolly's mother[31] was anointed on Sunday last and Peggie Carty also. Courley speaks about you very often and Peggie also. The Bohanes[32] were vexed as ye did not go to see them before ye went. Dan Hickey[33] went off on the first of May. Johnny[34] is not cutting the turf in Acres at all. It is in Acres we have the bog taken this year. We haven't cut it yet. I'd like to tell you everything as I know you would like to hear all about home affairs.

Dear Nora and Ellie, we had no fun since ye went. The fellows do be bowling[35] every Sunday. They removed to Bawnfune road. Tommy Bennett[36] and his crew did not come over since that Sunday in the boreen[37] before ye went, but Bridget, John and Julia[38] come down every Sunday since. Only last Sunday they invited us up last Sunday. So Mary Hayes and Ellie[39] and me we went up. They were talking all the time about you and your career of life. They read your letter. It made them laugh.

Dear Nora, we expects little Denny home this next month coming on. Well, I guess I have all said this time until I'll hear from you again. Write me a long letter and tell me everything. I don't know will Mary answer my last letter. I am expecting she will. Well, Nora, I am after my dinner now, a nice dinner, too, hasty pudding[40] and goat's milk. I'd like you would have a part of it. Hoping Dan, Mary and Julia Agnes, Ellie and yourself are well, I am your ever loving sister all alone far away from each other. I remain your fond Katie. I sends best love to all. Good by to all

(no signature)

Write immediately. Good bye Nora.

ENDNOTES

1   *This is the first letter sent to Nora after she left Ireland. She had sailed with her sister Ellen on the S. S. Pavonia from Queenstown, Cork on 26 April and arrived in Boston 6 May 1895. Both women listed their sister Mary Donovan as their destination. Nora must have written to her family soon after arriving and Katie responded immediately.*

2   *An Act of Congress in 1893 mandated a much more detailed register of each passenger on a ship arriving in an American port. Of particular use to researchers was the new question asking to whom the passenger was going. The answers provide a good source of names and addresses of relatives already in America.*

3   *Michael/Mikey/Mickey McCarthy, baptized 6 September 1873, was the youngest child of Uncle Michael and Mary (Tobin) McCarthy of Ballinlough. He was closest in age of all Michael's children to his cousin Nora.*

4   *Not one of Uncle Michael's children went to America, and only three of his many grandchildren did.*

5   *Mary McCarthy, daughter of Uncle Michael, was baptized 7 February 1860. She married Patrick McCarthy, Tullig, in February 1885. He died suddenly three years later leaving her with two young sons, and pregnant with a third.*

6   *Tullig is in the northeast corner of Kilmacabea parish.*

7   *Leap Fair Days in May were on the 24th and 25th of the month.*

8   *Timothy Donovan, a fisherman from Union Hall, south of Leap Village, married Katie Burns, Union Hall, on 21 October 1888. Katie could be a relative of Ellen Burns Donovan, wife of John, a major leaseholder in Ballinlough.*

9   *The 1901 Census list Patrick Hayes, 67, and wife, Kate, 63, living in Fro. This is a townland near Ballinaclough. The McCarthys of Ballinlough appear to be very familiar with many of the families that lived near their relatives in the Rosscarbery area.*

10   *"Slippers" is a term Katie often uses to describe the young friends of Nora, Tim and herself.*

11   *John "Jack" Minihane. Born in 1869 to Cornelius and Mary Collins Minihane, was from Knockskagh. This townland on the north side of Ballinlough was the location of the local National School. Jack's sister, Kate of Boston (who spelled her name Monohan), was a regular correspondent with Nora. Jack was the only child in his family to stay in Ireland. He is listed in the 1911 Census as married with three children and his widowed mother at home. Jack's father, Cornelius, died of bronchitis 11 October 1886, aged 66.*

12   *There is a Daniel Minihane in Knockskagh in the 1901 Census. He was 46, married, and lived with his parents, wife and four children.*

13   *Mary Hayes was the daughter of Dennis and Ellen Hayes. Julia Mick was the daughter of Uncle Michael. Dennis and Michael shared a common farmyard.*

14   *The 1893 edition of Guy's Postal Directory lists Mary A. O'Donovan as a vintner, or pubkeeper, in Leap. She is not in the 1901 Census. A Julia Hurley of Keamore/Keymore, was born 25 March 1865 to James and Mary (Wholey) Hurley and could be the barmaid who was so generous to brother Tady.*

15   *James Donovan was born 24 December 1869 to Timothy and Mary (Driscoll) Donovan of Bawnfune. He sailed on the S. S. Pavonia with Nora and Ellen. His destination was the home of his cousin, also James Donovan in Lowell, Mass.*

16   *Nora would have been no more than six or seven when Mary left for America, some dozen years previously.*

17   *This could be either John who was 26 in 1895, or John who was 46 that year. Both lived in Knockskagh and both were still alive when the Census was taken in 1901.*

18   *Dr. Michael O'Driscoll, who was 31 in the 1901 Census, was a physician/ surgeon whose home was in the Kilmacabea end of Leap Village, next to the rectory of the parish priest. He is also listed as keeping a yacht in the harbor.*

19   *Jeremiah "Jerry" Hayes was born 28 February 1876 to Patrick and Norry Hayes. Unmarried, he lived with his parents in a house near Uncle Michael.*

20   *A "brake" is a thicket of overgrown brush, such as furze, a type of gorse.*

21   *Timothy "Tady" Hayes, born 26 December 1874 to Dennis and Ellen Hayes of Ballinlough. Tady lived in Knockskagh.*

22   *The bog in Acres Townland was immediately northwest of Ballinlough. The men were digging turf.*

23   *There is an old tradition, or "pishogue," that would not permit a dying or a dead person to be brought into a house for fear it would bring bad luck on the house.*

24   *Mary Collins Hayes was the wife of Jerry's brother, James. Their house was next to that of his parents.*

25   *Chopped furze made a tasty feed for horses in the winter. The plant had to be beaten to soften it up. A later generation would use a hand cranked machine to do the job.*

26   *That is, the Patrick Hayes family.*

27   The "Captain" was Mike Cahalane who, with his sister, Annie, was living in Newport, Wales. He was a close friend of Tady and Mick McCarthy. The only Cahalane family in the area lived in Maulnigarra, two townlands west of Ballinlough. This was the family of Thomas, 60 in 1901, a shoemaker, his wife, Julia, 50, and seven of their children. Another Cahalane, James, 17, was a servant at a neighbor's farm and most likely another one of Thomas' children.

28   Patrick Hourihane immigrated to America on the S. S. Pavonia, 23 August 1891, and lived in Roxbury, Mass. Pat was born 20 March 1869 to Patrick and Kate (Walsh) Hourihane in Knockskagh. When this letter was written, the parents were renting a cottage from John Donovan in Ballinlough.

29   "London" refers to the widow and family of eldest McCarthy brother, Jerry. His widow Annie, was now remarried but kept in regular contact with her in-laws.

30   'Greenhorn" is a slang term for a recent immigrant. A "greenhorn" picture" would be the first to be taken upon arrival in the new home. Usually, the "greenhorn" would not have acquired, as yet, the more modern clothing and hair style of the place. There is both a "greenhorn" picture of Nora, and more than a few of her taken later in the year. The contrast is remarkable.

31   Margaret Driscoll Connolly of Cappanabohy, immediately east of Ballinlough, was the mother of Cornelius (Courley) and Margaret (Peggy) Connolly. She was the daughter of Norry Hegarty Driscoll (whose cottage was next door to the Patrick McCarthys. Mrs. Hegarty's name will appear frequently in the letters.) Mrs. Connolly had married Patrick Connolly of Cappanabohy 26 June 18.

32   The Bohanes were the family of the recently deceased James Sullivan of Clounties.

33   Daniel Hickey, 24, born 10 June 1869 to James and Bridget (Dillon) Hickey of Brulea, sailed on the S. S. Brittanic and arrived in New York City 11 May 1895. Mrs. Kate (Keane) McCarthy's mother was a Dillon, and Brulea is near to her birthplace in Ballinaclough.

34   John Donovan, Ballinlough, had four cottages in the northwestern corner of that townland. The cottage that Pat and Kate McCarthy rented was immediately adjacent to his property. Donovan's farmland abutted that of the next townland, Acres.

35   Road Bowling is a sport peculiar to County Cork. While automobiles have monopolized most of the current roads in Cork today, it is still possible to encounter road bowling on back country lanes.

36   Tommy Bennett, a friend of Tim and Mick McCarthy, was born 30 August 1868 to Thomas and Hesther (French) Bennett of Kilmacabea. He married Ellen Regan, daughter of Daniel of Maulnigarra, 4 June 1898. Bennett was a shopkeeper in Gurteenaduige.

37   *A "boreen" (boithrin) is a small country lane. Kate is probably referring to the land off of the Bawnfune road that went around the western end of Ballin Lake beginning at the homes of Patrick and James Hayes. The path to Katie's cottage on the west side of the lake was off of this lane, northerly up a hillside.*

38   *Bridget, John and Julia were the children of James and Mary (Collins) McCarthy of Gurteenaduige, which is northeast of Ballinlough, thus requiring them to "come down" to visit.*

39   *Ellie Hayes, sister of Mary, was born 21 July 1870.*

40   *Hasty Pudding was a mush made with oatmeal or cornmeal, and often served with brown sugar, maple syrup or other sweetener.*

Document **M8**

Katie's letters to her sisters were as good as a newspaper for providing all the latest local society news.

16 June 1895 – Katie McCarthy, Ballinlough, Leap to Nora McCarthy, Bradford, MA

Sunday evening, Ballinlough Leap
June 16th 1895 (write again soon)

Dear Sister Nora

Yesterday I received a letter from you. Am glad to learn in it ye are all quite well. As for us we are just as you had seen us. I am glad you likes the place so well. You are very lucky and to get a place so near to Mary's[1]. Be contented and cheer up. Don't be lonesome at all. You did not say how many in family in the house or what family are they. As you know, Nora, I'd like to know everything about you. This day three weeks I wrote a letter to you before but I can see by this letter you did not receive it. I told you all about Leap fair. It is now just Mickey is gone out after reading your letter and he laughed enough at it when you inquired about the horse and Fury and Boyo. The horse wont foal at all. Father says now when we do be joking him that it was a false springing she had. Well Nora, next Sunday will be St. John's night. I am intended to go to Ross[2] and Tim. Dannie Mirnane[3] did not cross the water at all. We found out where he was. He is working with Tom Springs at Ross. We expects to see him next Sunday.

Nora, I have no strange news worth relating presently except that old Harry[4] was buried two weeks ago. Aunt Julia is very lonesome for him. Aunt Nora came to see her last Sunday. I had seen big Den today. I think he looks better without the whiskers. Nora, you never said anything about B. Crowley or Mary Keane's family[5] or did you see them at all. Nora, please ask Mary what clothes did she send by Dan Keane that time he come home. I'd like to be sure of it as you can tell her what we got. Don't forget this now, and write and tell me all and everything. I thinks it too seldom you writes.

Well, Nora, I do be dreaming about you and Ellen every night and mother thinks she ought call you every morning to rise for her. She is very weak and downhearted. As you know she would want you always or someone like you because she is not able to stand tramping as you call it.

Johnny and family[6] are living in the big house now and have the grass of Acres let to Miss Collins for 100 pounds for two years. This is what we have heard. Himself and Johanna are friends again. They are walking about the farm this evening. It's a lovely evening. You know, Nora, it's a lonesome evening and to have I get an opportunity of writing the letter without any one coming in. All the fellows stayed above at the cross where the pattern[7] used to be formerly to start a pattern and any girls did not come to them. The Rues[8] were south on the hill and they did not come over at all, or the John's girls[9] did not come either. They would come very willing if we commenced it for them, but the fellows were vexed and so they went away west to Bawnfune road bowling. Jerome John[10] was asking me about the letter and about all the folks over, and the Slippers laughed enough at your letter, and so did Johnny Bawn[11] laugh enough. He sprained his shoulder coming home from Leap fair, and he could not do any work yet. He spends a part of every day with us when he do be going east cutting grass, and he gives some of it to mother.

Well, Nora, the gardens are growing splendid as yet. The stalks[12] in the lower garden are as high as the fence, and the other gardens are promising very good. Also tell Ellie that the part behind the house where she was sticking [13] is the best part of the garden. I guess she remembers that morning she stuck it. Nora, it is talking about you we will be forever again and thinking of you and Ellen also. I am very glad Delia Collins and Katie[14] are such good company for ye, Nora. Make yourself at home with them. Jamesy Donovan sent a second letter 3 weeks ago. He is with his cousin in Lowell and Maggie McCarthy was to see him the first night he went there. She did not write to Mrs. McCarthy, Leap, at all. She says I suppose [you] will do the same as Maggie did. I am surprised why Ellie did not write a few lines to me, and send me her address. You did not send me your own address either. Well, Nora, the baby hair is lovely. Mother kissed it when she got it. I think that [it is] more like the Guinea one than Mary's.[15] Uncle Michael got a letter from Newport yesterday and John Mahony and wife and family taken in one picture. Eight in family, four boys and four girls.[16] They looks nice. Nora, I suppose it is no good for me be asking for your picture still I expects it.

Dear Nora, I knew well Mary would not like the picture. Perhaps I would never again get an opportunity of taking it again.[17] I would not that time either only for the woman being in Leap. Did you know Katie O'Callaghan of Union Hall (Jack at Castlebyre's sister)? She was buried last Thursday in Kilmacabea. She is a big loss, because she got 400 pounds fortune this time three years. She was an only daughter. I will send you the Star.[18] You can read about the funeral. I wonder why Mary did not continue sending the papers. Jerry Hayes is not anything better yet, but Johnny Brien is walking out a little now. He was very ill when I wrote you the last letter.

Dear Nora, your flowers are growing grand. The geraniums are flowered now. Mother takes great care of them for your sake. The southern wood[19] is nearly as high as the window. I did not know they were there at all until about a week ago I saw them there. Nora, tell me is there any other girl in the house where Ellie is or how many in family there, or what family are they. Tell me everything. There was a letter from Johnny John[20] last Sunday. He was eleven days sailing and two days seasick. Nora, I guess the heat is terrible in America now, as it is very warm here. It is the loveliest summer we had this good while.

Tell Ellie that Annie Callaghan is matchmaking with Pake Mahoney[21] (Gemboy). It will be made too. Her trunk was sent to her from America a week ago. They have no notion of going back again. We received no letter from London since or from Denny[22] either. Hoping you will write when you hears from Denny and tell us all about him. I am glad you has such good times with Dan. I suppose the baby can talk very good now. Bat Hourihane can't talk yet. John[23] is going to be confirmed in two weeks time. The bishop is going to come to Leap. William Dick did not go way yet, but Thomas[24] is gone off to England. He beat Thomas Herlihy[25] before he went. Patrick Williamson[26] is gone off to Brazil in a boat from Newport. He will be back again for Christmas.

Nora, Hanna Collins and her sister Maggie are going to America in August.[27] Her father got 90 pounds after Mikey's death.[28] Hanna is going to come to Norry Hegarty[29] 4 weeks before she will go and Maggie Hourihane is coming home for August. Patrick Hourihane sent a letter and money about a week ago. All the friends and neighbors are very well. Tady is not at work at all this past fortnight. He is running in mihills[30] every day. They are in their own bog today, Monday, and I must go with the dinner to them now. They are taking bogstuff. We will have the mihill Thursday. We will regret you that day to carry the dinner to the bog.

James Hayes comes into us often. He asked Tady in his mihill. We are great friends now. I was not able to finish this letter yesterday evening because the Slippers come in when I was writing it. So I stopped writing it then they told me to tell you everything, as you inquired, about the cat. Just last0 Friday night Denny Gallivan[31] brought us a young little kitten. We had not a cat until then.

Well, Nora, I could hardly get paper enough to tell you all I have to say to you. Oh, if only I could speak to you now. All our hens are dying this past week. Did you take care of the chickens for Dan after landing? Has he got many? Nora, I don't know am I putting the right address on the letter or not. Well, I guess I wont say any more this time, hoping to hear from you soon again and tell me lots of news. We all joins in sending our best love and blessing to ye all. All the neighbors wishes ye well. Remember me to Delia Collins. We speaks of her often. I suppose Ellie wont write at all to us. Remember me to her. I have no more to say but write often.

Good bye from father, mother, brother, and sister.

I remains your own fond Katie McCarthy, Ballinlough.

xxxx xxxxx

ENDNOTES

1   *The Donovan home was on Locke St., Bradford, a recently constructed street that connected Main St. to the Boston and Maine railroad depot at the foot of the street. There were a number of large homes on Main Street near Locke St., which would have employed domestic servants like Nora.*

2   *Rosscarbery was a market town east of Leap, and former cathedral seat of the Bishop of Ross.*

3   *Danny Mirnane, a friend of Tim, is mentioned often in the letters.*

4   *Henry "Harry" Harding was married to Katie and Nora's aunt Julia (McCarthy). A farmer in Kilmacabea, he died on 1 June 1895 of old age and debility. His death was reported by his son Patrick.*

5   *Mary Keane Goodman, baptized in the Kilmacabea Parish church 13 March 1859, was the daughter of John and Mary (Hayes) Keane of Ballinadough and a cousin of Katie and Nora, and of Denis and Dan Keane. She immigrated to Bradford, Mass., and married John Goodman in 1884. He was killed in a tragic accident in 1892.*

6   *John Donovan and his wife Ellen Burns had four children at the writing of this letter. A fifth child had died. All were born in Acres before John took over the family farm in Ballinlough. His unmarried sister, Johanna, a dairymaid, lived with them. John had the largest farm in the townland, including the four cottages previously referenced. Three of them had two rooms each, and the third, the "big house," had been the residence of his father Patrick who had gone to live in Acres with his namesake son.*

7   *Patterns or dances were held at the crossroads at Killinga, on the road from Leap to Drinagh, the market town north of it. At one time a platform stood there for dancing.*

8   *The "Rues" could be the daughters of Jeremiah and Julia (Hegarty) Donovan of Bawnfune. Rue/Rua/Rhue is a Donovan clan name. The daughters were Mary (16 April 1875), Johanna (26 February 1877), Julia (6 December 1878), Mary (29 July 1880) and Margaret (10 May 1882).*

9   *The "John's girls" were the daughters of John and Kate Donovan of Bawnfune.*

10   *Jerome (Jermiah) Donovan was the son of John and Kate Donovan, above.*

11   *John Driscoll of Bawnfune was a weaver. The label "Bawn" refers to a light, or blonde-haired person and can be attached to all in the family regardless of color of hair.*

12   *Potato shoots.*

13   *Dibbing sticks are used to set seed potatoes into the ridges(lazy beds) of overturned sods.*

14   *An autograph book that originally belonged to Mary has a page titled "Chums," with the signatures of Delia A. Collins, Katherine F. Collins, Ellen T. McCarthy, Honora McCarthy, and Julia F. Callaghan.*

15   *Baby Julia Agnes had golden blonde hair, like her father Dan, and like a gold English guinea coin. Mary and the other McCarthys had rich reddish-brown hair.*

16   *The Mahoneys of Newport, Wales were the family of Uncle Michael's oldest daughter, Norah, named for her paternal grandmother. In the 1901 Census of Wales, both Mickey McCarthy and his brother, Patrick the Shoemaker, were lodging with the Mahoneys.*

17   *The tintype that Katie sent is in the Collection. She is very thin, evidence of her terminal consumption. All of the McCarthy women were tall, and her height emphasizes her gauntness.*

18   *The Southern Star was a weekly newspaper published in Skibbereen, Co. Cork. Its first edition was in 1889.*

19   *Southern Wood is a shrubby fragrant European wormwood with bitter foliage.*

20   *John Donovan from Bawnfune was the son of John and Catherine. He sailed to Boston on the S. S. Catalonia and arrived on 27 May 1895.*

21   *Patrick "Pake" Mahoney, a farmer from Knockarudane, son of James ("Gem"), married Anne Callaghan of Knockskagh, daughter of John, September 24, 1895. Witnesses were James Mahoney and Kate Callaghan. In the 1901 Census both the mother and 25 year old sister, Hannah, of Annie were listed as lunatics!*

22   *Denis "Denny" McCarthy, baptized 23 April 1859, was the second child, and second son, of Patrick and Kate. He was in Wales when the 1881 Census was taken. He married Julia O'Brien from Co. Cork in 1882 in Wales. Their first two children, Katie and Patrick, were born in Cardiff, Wales. The family immigrated to the coal fields of northeastern Pennsylvania. They eventually made their home in Kingston, PA*

23   *Bartholomew "Batt" Hourihane, son of Courley and Maggie, was born 27 March 1893. John McCarthy. son of Mary and the late Patrick McCarthy of Tullig, was born 12 August 1885. Both boys were grandsons of Uncle Michael.*

24   *William (born 25 February 1865) and Thomas (born 9 March 1874) were the sons of Richard "Dick" Williamson of Knockskagh, a prominent land owner.*

25   *Thomas Herlihy of Knockskagh, son of Denis and Mary (Regan) Herlihy of Cloonkeen, was baptized along with his twin brother, John, on 7 April 1855. He was married to Hannah, daughter of William Williamson of Knockskagh on 2 February 1895.*

26   *Patrick Williamson was the twin brother of Thomas (see note 86).*

27   *Hannah Collins and her sister Margaret were the daughters of Michael Collins of Driminidy, Drinagh. Margaret had emigrated earlier in the 1890s and came home to bring Hannah back with her, as Ellie had done with Nora McCarthy. They lived in Elmira, New York. Hannah wrote over fifty letters to Nora between 1898 and 1900.*

28   *Michael, brother to Hannah and Margaret, born in 1869, died of peritonitis in Elmira in 1894. The ninety pounds received by his father was probably a life insurance payout.*

29   *Honora "Norry" Driscoll was a great-aunt to the Collinses. She rented one of John Donovan's cottages in Ballinlough, in close proximity to the Patrick McCarthys. (See Note 53)*

30   *A "mihill" (meitheall) was a form of cooperative labor at harvest time in rural Irish communities.*

31   *Denis Gallivan was born 4 May 1872, son of Thomas and Mary (Carthy) Gallivan of Mealisheen, Ballinlough's eastern neighbor.*

Document M9

Cousin Julia McCarthy, daughter of Michael and Mary/ Mamey (Tobin) McCarthy, wrote a good, legible penmanship with interesting turns of phrase. When Katie died in 1896, Julia took over the responsibility of handling the correspondence for her illiterate aunt and uncle, Kate and Pat McCarthy.

20 July 1895 – Julia McCarthy, Ballinlough, Leap to Nora McCarthy, Bradford, Mass.

Ballinlough Leap P. O.
July 20th 1895

Dear Cousin Nora,

I received your very welcomed letter on Saturday week which gave me and each of us and likewise your own cottage inmates great pleasure to hear from you from that distant land. And moreover you and your sisters and baby and Mr. D. Donovan enjoying that great blessing which is better than what I can't mention, Good Health, as we enjoys at present. Thank God, but one exception, Nora, poor Kate is feeling bad still. You must think she ought be broken-hearted. (Nora I feel awful lonesome myself along the time to say that Kate don't miss you)

Dear Nora, I hope you will excuse me for not writing before now. Time passes so quick I cannot find one minute's rest except for a wonder but like you often saw something waiting.

Dear Nora, you would be surprised if you could see all of the returned Yanks. Ellie Driscoll came to Grandmother[1] last Wednesday. She is very toney and nothing for her but white clothes. I wish you could see her on the Lakeside. Its then you would laugh that big laugh. I hope you will have so much to say after a time. I am glad to see my old neighbors once more, as Ellie said. Julia Coughlan and Mary Regan, Judy's sister,[2] came home also, and lots more of them but too numerous to mention. You must think this will be an airy spot this summer. Mary Regan is at Maolisheen also. Think on this for a while.

Dear Nora, I can't tell you will Mike write to you this time as he cannot think of any thing little sentence but as much as would fill the Star. You need not be in any trouble about the letters you send as I am on the harbor[3]. Don't dread but they are safe whatever they will contain no matter what. 'Tis the worst we like the best because we knew Slipper too well and her drollery.[4] Dear Cousin Nora, John was confirmed on the 10 of July and goes to ten o'clock Mass now like a man. You could not but laugh at him. John, Jeremiah and Patrick[5] don't know where are you gone to. As for to say you are gone to America, they would only laugh and John would say, "God help us, you are mad."

Dear Nora, I am sorry to tell you that my Poor Father did not go to see the inside of the Cottage since you left, whatever is the reason, and he will never forgive himself as he did not see you before ye left. He waited all the time in Tullig expecting you until it got too late but when he came "what was maddening ye and to leave Nora go" and scolded the Father and Mother. I have no more to say for this time. But we are all well. Maggie and Curley, Bat and Julia, Mary and John, Jerem., Patrick, Father, Mother, Jerry, Dennie, Pat, Mike[6] and more especially myself wishes to be remembered to Mary and Husband and baby Julia Agnes not forgetting Ellie.

To my fond cousin Nora. I can remember old times. I remain your affectionate Cousin, Julia McCarthy

Good by. Write soon.

(written across the top: Burn this when read. Don't show this to any person except Mary or Ellie for fear of a joke. Kiss the baby for me XXXX)

ENDNOTES

1   *Ellen Driscoll was the granddaughter of Norry Hegarty Driscoll. She was born in Staten Island, New York in 1867 to Cornelius and Ellen Driscoll. They are in the 1870 U. S. Federal Census. Ellen had two older sisters, Honora and Margaret. Her uncle Tim Driscoll and family lived in the same three family house in New York. Ellen's family was no longer in New York in the 1880 Census They were in Ballinlough where the mother Ellen died in 1873 of a ruptured uterus. It is during this time that young Ellen would have become friendly with the neighboring McCarthy children. Ellen, a cousin of Hannah Collins, would write some letters to Nora after returning to the States, marrying James Enright, and moving to Washington, D. C.*

2   *The only Coughlan family in the area in the 1901 Census was in Ballyroe, northeast of Ballinlough. Mary Regan was possibly from Killinga, north of Ballinlough. There is a Julia ("Judy") Regan, 22, in the Regan household there in 1901. There is also a Regan family in Mealisheen. A Mary Regan is listed on the manifest of the S. S. Bothnia in September 1894. She stated she was from Leap and going to her brother John in Framingham, a town west of Boston.*

3   *Julia (1869-1949) was working either in Leap Village, possibly at Sheahan's Hotel where Nora had once worked, or in Glandore, south of Leap, at Mrs. Keenan's Hotel. Both villages are on Glandore Harbor. Since letters from America were read aloud to friends and neighbors, Julia is suggesting to Nora that if she has anything to write that she wishes to keep private, she can write directly to Julia who will be able to pick up the letters from the Post Office in Leap.*

4   *"Slipper" is Nora.*

5   *These are the three sons of Uncle Michael's widowed daughter, Mary, of Tullig. John was born 8 December 1885, Jeremiah on 1 February 1887 and Patrick 20 October 1888, three and a half months after the sudden death of his father. Patrick, Jr. was born in Ballinlough at his grandfather's house, but Michael didn't register the birth until the following February.*

6   *Julia's parents, sisters and brothers, and niece and nephews.*

DOCUMENT **M10**

Cousin Michael McCarthy, youngest child of Michael and Mary of Ballinlough, was a high-spirited young man whose letters to Nora are filled with humor and good cheer.

20 July 1895 – Michael McCarthy, Ballinlough, Leap to Nora McCarthy, Bradford, Mass.

July 20, 1895
Ballinlough

Dear Cousin Nora,

I received your welcome letter which gave every one of us great pleasure and as for myself I was more than delighted though sad for your departure but I am very glad. How are you enjoying yourself in that foreign land?

Dear Honoria, I delayed this letter too long from you but time passes away so quickly that I had not any opportunity to write until today because it is raining. And you know that I do be employed at blackguarding and other things as usual on Sundays.

My Dear Cousin Honoria, I felt very lonesome entirely for you on account of the jollification we used to have. I am enjoying very fine times. I do be at the pattern every Sunday and myself and a few more lads went to meet the southern girls last Sunday week and you may say Honoria we gave them fine chasing across the hills. Your father felt very lonesome for you. He said to me one day that he would break his stick and his old shoes on them for sending you away from him. Ellie Driscoll came to Lakeview again. I was at Tullig all the week and did not see her until Sunday so I had a nice talk with her then. She is the same thing all through but she has great tone. I suppose Honoria if you were here now you would have fine laugh.

Poor Jerry Hayes is very bad always. He is almost as bad now as the first days. He cannot scarcely stir the leg yet. I do feel lonesome for him for he was the only fellow that used come in calling me when he was going to mass.

Dear Honoria, I at least thought that the morning ye were going to America should not appear so soon for I felt very lonesome for you and poor Ellie also, for I suppose that I wont have any one of the two of ye next winter that I would go match making for some snowy day.

Dear Honoria, I am drawing now to a close for I haven't enough of paper. I would want the Eagle or Star to tell you all the bladdering as I can not speak to you. We are all enjoying fine health, T. G., except poor Katie. She don't feel well but she will soon be all right too with God's help. John had to get your letter too to read it himself. He is a great man now he is confirmed and Jeremiah and Patrick do be talking mad about their own Honoria. Do not display my letter because Julia says that my letter is a foolish one. Remember me to Ellie. Excuse this bladdering being unaccustomed to letter writing and also misspelled words. We all join in sending best love to all. I suppose you would know a rake. Good Bye Honoria.

Good bye Honoria McCarthy and Good bye to all. Michael McCarthy[1]

XXXXXXXXXXXXXXXXXXX 10 of them for yourself. 8 for Ellie and Agnes.)

With fond love from M. M. rake to H. M. slipper.

Write a fine long funny letter for it is that I would like. I got the letter myself from the post boy, you know him. And Honoria you did not tell me how is your fellow or is he a fine man. Good Bye Honoria. Dear Honoria, I have some of my frolics almost lost too.

ENDNOTES

1   *Cousin Michael (1873-1952) spent most of his adult life in Newport, Wales where he had a trade. Mickey never married. He made regular visits to Ballinlough. Photographs in the Collection show him during a visit home in the late 1920s. He was a tall, well built, handsome man. Mickey was the last of the children of Uncle Michael to die, preceding his dear cousin, Nora, by just a year. Mickey and his sister Julia are the only Ballinlough cousins to correspond with Nora, or the only ones whose letters were saved by Nora. A Skibbereen veterinarian, who grew up in Kilmacabea townland remembers Mickey visiting home in the 1940s. He recalled that Mickey was known as "The mayor of Cardiff" for his style and swagger. (Interview with Dr. Hourihane)*

Document **M11**

After telling Nora that she "have no news to tell you this time," Katie proceeded to describe some sad tales of sudden and unexpected deaths among their friends.

1 August 1895 – Katie McCarthy, Ballinlough, Leap to Nora McCarthy, Bradford, Mass.

August 1st, 1895
Ballinlough Leap

My Dear Sister Nora

Just a few lines in reply to your most appreciated letter, which I received a few days ago. I am glad to hear you are enjoying that great blessing which is the health. Also Mary and Ellen, Dan and Agnes as this date leaves us all quite well, T. God. Well Nora I am glad you have such a nice time over there hoping you will enjoy yourself always. And Delia also. I thought I would have a letter from Ellie and Delia before yours but indeed I got left there as I kept watching the postboy as usual, you know. Well Nora, I was speaking to Julia Hayes[1] yesterday Wednesday. She is staying into Mike Mahony at Leap[2]. She knew me by Mary. She is coming up here on Sunday next. She told me to tell Mary she is going to sail on the 9th of August. That's Friday. She said she promised Mary to write her but she did not have any particular place to stay so she did not mind writing she is going to Haverhill. Mrs. McCarthy[3] is very glad to have an account of Jack as she thought he was dead. She expects a letter from Ellie now. I have no news to tell you this time except that Ellie Driscoll is home and Tady Rick[4] is home and Julia Coughlan also and Patrick Lawlor, the Judge.[5] He is staying at Mrs. Keenans.[6] I heard he sent for all his friends to go to see him. He would not go to the houses at all. He is a great gentleman.

Well, Nora, you wanted to know the relation of Annie Deasy and her husband to each other.[7] Annie and her father-in-law are second cousins, that leaves them second and third. They are near enough to one another. Your comrade Ellie[8] in England is married since June. I know you will be surprised. Well, Dear Nora, we are really sorry for poor Mary Keane[9] or what will her children do. I'd know is there any chance for her. I am very sorry you are out of your place as it was so near Mary's and you having such nice times. I hope you will keep on improving as you are getting stout and fat. Kick up a good time always for yourself wherever you will be. Don't anything trouble you. I am sorry you pays so much taxes for my letters. I wonder what the cause of it. I wont send so much paper any more but I have lots of stories to tell you this time. I need a good deal of paper.

Well, Dear Nora, I'll commence at them and I know you will be sorry for them. Yesterday Johnny Bawn[10] was buried. He was as well as ever he was week ago last Sunday until about 11 o'clock Monday night he got a stitch in his side and he lived until last Monday night. He died about the same time that he was taken sick. The doctor said it was congestion of the lungs. Well, Nora, just imagine in your mind what will his poor wife and five children and his father do. It's a sad case. I am really very sorry for him. I was to see him Monday evening and certainly Nora I could not look at him when I thought of how he used be before and to see him that time. Still, he knew me and called me Katie and asked me how I was getting on.

Again, Dear Nora, one case is bad until the next comes on. Last Sunday, all the Leap people went boating to Baltimore in a fishing boat. So when they were returning some one of them threw turpentine on the fire, so the boat took fire and there was 9 lives lost. They did not have patience and if they did they would be all saved. I'll just mention them to you. Big Den the father of 9 children,[11] and Katie, Jack, Mikey and Dan Callaghan,[12] all the nice Callaghans, Nora. And Willie Burke and Tommie Collins at the Key, and a little girl of the Kellehers from Glandore, and a boy of the Hurley's from Cork Road. Them are the nine. Just think, Nora, what will that mother do that parted them four fine family without a single being to give her a drink of water. And Charles and his wife depending on them also. I'll just tell you who came safe. Charlie Connoly and Charlie Hurley and our post boy and his sister,[13] and John McCarthy and Katie Harnedy and Ellie Hurley, that's big Den's sister-in-law, and Tommie Collins's brother Mikey. And I dont recollect who were the others but there was 27 in the boat and 18 came free, and if them that were drowned had patience they would be safe also. They shouted when they saw the fire, and when the Coast Guard took out a boat to them and while he was bringing them ashore, he told the others to stay where they were until he would come back for them. So Jack Callaghan threw out the smack boat they had with the big boat, and big Den and his own brothers and Katie and William Burke jumped into it and it began to leak and it turned and drowned every one of the lot. So them that stayed in their burning boat were saved.[14]

So Katie Callaghan came ashore on Tuesday and was buried last night about 9 o'clock in Kilmacabea.[15] We went to Myross[16] in Johnny Bawn's funeral and we were back in Leap for 6 o'clock so we waited for the other funeral then it was 8 o'clock when it came into Leap from Baltimore. Father O'Callaghan celebrated Mass in the harbour and Father Fitzgerald celebrated Mass also and while Mass was celebrating Katie Callaghan appeared into the harbour.[17] She never sank because she wore the scapular.[18] She was just as nice as when she was alive. Her shoes were on her and even her hat was on her head. So any of the others were not taken yet and I guess hardly if they will either. Oh, Dear Nora, isn't it terrible and sad. Any body is not able to do anything only thinking and talking about them. Leap is in a gloom, and poor big Den that used call you Susan. I am very sorry for them all.

Dear Nora, I am sorry to be sending such bad news but I know you knew the parties. I hope you will send the picture as soon as you can. I am glad Ellie looks so well. I did not answer your last letter at all because I did not feel like writing. I haven't been very well at all, Nora. I was better when you were home and mother gets her old complaint every day. That is a pain in her heart. She thought she was rid of it until it commenced with her again. Tim and father are just the same. All the friends and neighbors are well. Jerry Hayes will never bend his leg. This is a dull place now, Nora. Perhaps I'd send you the paper for Saturday. You can read about the sad news. Well, I guess I have all said this time. Remember us all to Mary, Ellie, Dan and Delia, and kiss Agnes for me. I wish I had her here now. I remain your fond sister, Katie McCarthy, Ballinlough. Good bye to all, Nora. Please excuse this scribbling. The pen is bad. XXXXXXXXXXX

ENDNOTES

1   *Julia Hayes from Fro (see Note 31) sailed to New York City on the S. S. Campania. She arrived on 23 August 1895 and listed her destination as New London, Conn.*

2   *Mike Mahoney could have been the husband of Mary A. Mahoney, 40. In the 1901 Census, Mary and her five -year old daughter Mary E. were visiting Con Sullivan, shopkeeper, in the village of Leap.*

3   *This Mrs. McCarthy is Kate of Skibbereen, the widow of George who was a relative of the Ballinlough McCarthys. Her son Jack, batized 2 March 1869 in Skibbereen) sailed to Boston on the S. S. Pavonia on 22 March 1895. He intended to join his brother George (born 10 May 1867 in Curragh, Skibbereen), who lived in Lawrence, Mass., a textile manufacturing city immediately west of Haverhill.*

4   *Tady Rick was Timothy Donovan, son of Rickard and Kate (Cushin) Donovan of Gallows Hill/Knockenacrohy, a townland east of Ballinlough. Tady was born 1 December 1880.*

5   *Patrick Lawlor was an Irish-born lawyer in Buffalo, New York. He is listed in the 1900 U. S. Census as living in a hotel. He was divorced. Born in Ireland in February 1847, he emigrated in 1865. The only Lawlors in the area in the Census of 1901 lived in Tullig. In Griffith's Valuations c. 1852 there is a Patrick Lawlor who may be the father of this Patrick.*

6   *Keenan's Hotel, now the Glandore Inn, had the reputation as being the oldest family-run hotel in West Cork.*

7   *Annie Dacey/Deasy, daughter of Peter and Norah (Dillon) Deasy from the Rosscarbery area was one of four siblings to immigrate to Haverhill, Mass. They were cousins of the McCarthys through their mother, Kate Keane McCarthy, whose own mother had been a Dillon. Annie, born in 1872, married James Flavin/ Flahavan, son of James and Kate (Hickey) Flahavan of Ballinaclough on 27 June 1895 in Haverhill.*

8   *Could be Ellen Driscoll, daughter of Patrick of Bawnfune. There is a marriage for an Ellen Driscoll to Thomas O'Connell in the Marriage Register for Cardiff, Wales in this time period. This could also be the same "Ellen Paddy" whose death was reported to Nora in 1899.*

9   *Widowed cousin Mary Keane Goodman of Bradford, Mass., was terminally ill with phithisis, a virulent form of consumption, when Nora wrote this news to Katie. She died on October 1 but Katie would not have known that when she wrote her letter.*

10   *John Driscoll, 46, Bawnfune, a weaver, died of pneumonia on July 29, 1895. He left a wife, Mary McCarthy, born in Co. Tipperary, and five children: Jeremiah, 9, twins Mary Anne and Margaret, 4, John, 1, and Patrick, an infant. His mother, Margaret, died at 75 on 11 February 1889. His father, Jeremiah, also a weaver, lived in Bawnfune, also, and died in 1899. The Driscoll home was on the border line between Bawnfune and Ballinlough.*

11   *Denis Donovan of Keamore was a miller. His widow, Kate (McCarthy) and seven of his nine living children: Charles (born 1885), Denis (born 1886, Kate (1888), James (1890), Jeremiah (1891), Mary (1893) and Eliza (1895) were living there in the 1901 Census was taken. Three children: Denis (1884). Mary (1885), and Jeremiah (1887) had died.*

12   *Katie Callaghan (born 11 October 1874), Jack (born 19 December 1864), Mikey (born ?) and Dan (born 5 November 1877) were four of the children of weaver Dan and Johanna (Hurley) Callaghan. In 1901, Johanna, 58 and a widow, was living with her son Denis, 30, in Keamore.*

13   *John Hurley was the post boy. His sister was Mary.*

14   *The "Southern Star" of Skibbereen published a centenary booklet on the Zephyr tragedy in 1995.*

15   *The old Kilmacabea Parish burial ground is on the site of the ruins of the old parish church. Generations of the McCarthy family are buried there. 4*

16   *Myross burial ground is at the southern tip of the Myross Peninsula, south of Leap. It was a distance from Ballinlough and one wonders if Katie in her weakened condition walked the entire route, or if some kind of transportation was available.*

17   *That is, Baltimore harbor, near where the tragedy occurred. Baltimore is south of Skibbereen on the water.*

18   *A scapular is a religious symbol which consists of a pair of small cloth squares with religious designs or pictures that are joined by shoulder tapes and worn under clothing on breast and back as a sacramental.*

DOCUMENT M12
5 September 1895 – Katie McCarthy, Ballinlough, Leap to Nora McCarthy, Bradford, Mass.

September 5, 1895
Ballinlough Leap (Thursday)

My Dear Sister Nora

Just a few lines in reply to your letter and picture which I received on Monday last which gave us all a great pleasure in reading it and best of all to hear ye are enjoying good health. Well, Nora, I am so glad in having the pleasure of seeing your fond face once more. The picture looks exactly like you but you are not jolly looking at all like I was accustomed to see you.[1] Mother and I cried our eyes out when we had seen you and you could not speak to us. Mother was calling you and telling you to "pull my head" like you used do at any surprise always. Father was reaping with Courley Hourihane that day and we showed him the picture when he come home. We said it was Katie from London and he kept looking at it for a long time and he said she was a nice girl. He said then she was Ellie, so we gave him the spectacles and he seen it better. Well, he says, she is Nora and the tears rolled down his cheeks when you could not speak to him. Just thinking of how you used be to him and you would not make any shape for him that time.

Ellie Driscoll would not know you at all. She said you were like Mary. Ellie looks just the same. She is fat and strong. She is going back on the 15th inst. She is very tony. We can hardly understand her speaking at all. She has told us more stories about America while she is home than our own Yankie[2] while she was with us. I wish you could hear her speak about the Sullivans. She spent a week with them. I mean Nora's people-in-law in the parish of Ballydehob.[3] Cappabeg is the name of the land. She traveled Ballydehob, Skull, Lowertown, Mount Kid while she was up there and she invited them down and hired a car in Skibb, and took them to Catletownsend, Rineen, Union Hall, Glandore, Ross and back to Leap and in to Skib. again. That was something like a drive. She had one pound, ten shilling lost by the day and Norry[4] was mad for to have her be losing the money. Herself and Norry cant agree at all.

Hanna Collins and Maggie[5] are gone off to America and John McCarthy,[6] Leap, will be going with Ellie Driscoll.[7] Maggie Hourihane is home also. Jamesy Hurley our former postboy was burned to death in England and Pad Denis[8] was buried also since I wrote to you last. I like to tell you all the newses. Well, Dear Nora, we are going to have a wedding in our Parish Church on Saturday next, a couple from Cregg by the names of Willie Wolfe and Mary White.[9] 1 guess you know them, and there is an increase in the population of Bawnfune since Monday last. There is a young son born for Con Hourihane. His name is Daniel and Julia [McCarthy] and Jack Hourihane are sponcers.[10] She is very well and strong, and Jamesy Keane's wife is after being delivered of twins. Their names are Dan and Michael.[11] She aint very strong, the poor thing, and Peg. Pohane have a young son. Now, Nora, haven't I lots of newses for you, like you used bring from Leap long ago to me.[12]

Well I think its time for me say something about my dear little Agnes that's so often speaking about me. I hope she is well. I am so glad that somebody speaks about me as my name will soon be forgotten, hoping Agnes will renew it always. I hope I will receive her picture soon. I am glad you have such good times, Nora, always at Dan and Mary. It is too bad you are not working or what will you do for the winter. Mother is very troubled about you Nora as you are idle. It is bad time you went there. Dear Nora, Mother is very troubled about Mary Keane or what came over her at all. She like to get her picture if ye could get it taken. She told Den about her. Little Den said he got no letter from you. Ask her if she would like to come home. The place is not thriving very well for our friends. Well, Nora, we were surprised when we heard that B. C.[13] got married again hoping its all for the better. Well I guess I have all the newses told you. Only for you being writing so often Nora I would not live. I always keep thinking about ye over there and I do be dreaming something about you and Ellie every night regular. Remember me to Ellie. You did not speak of Delia at all.

Well Dear Nora I expect I wont write many letters more to you. I never felt so bad in my life. I have myself given up. Nora you remember that evening long ago that the two of us was talking by the fireside that Dan Sweeney come outside on horseback. You can remember what we were talking about, that troubling me always, and I never visited any doctor since, but I am advised by people to go to the infirmary to Cork, but Nora you know its hard for me to be traveling. Any how I am going to Dr. Somerville this afternoon.[14] Mother and Tim are going with me. I will mail this letter on my way. I have no more to say this time hoping it wont be long until I hear from you again. Excuse this scribble. The pen is bad, and besides I don't feel like writing. We all sends best love to Dan, Mary, Agnes, Ellie, and Yourself.

I remain your fond sister Katie. Good bye Nora, perhaps it is the last. Write soon XXXXXXX

ENDNOTES

1   *Nora had sent home her "greenhorn" photograph, i.e., her first after emigrating. It is in the Collection and shows Nora wearing a simple country dress, with her hair pulled back into a "bun."*

2   *Sister Ellen.*

3   *The Sullivans from Cappahbeg were the in-laws of Ellie Driscoll's sister, Nora, who also lived in Washington, DC. Nora Driscoll'ss husband, John Sullivan, was the son of Denis and Angela (McCarthy) Sullivan. Cappahbeg townland is between Skibbereen and Ballydehob.*

4   *Ellie's grandmother, Norry Hegarty Driscoll.*

5   *The Collins sisters sailed on the S. S. Brittanic. They arrived in New York City on their way to Elmira, NY on 6 September 1895.*

6   *John McCarthy, son of Timothy and Kate (Daly) McCarthy of Leap, was born 11 June 1877. His widowed mother was the "Mrs. McCarthy of Leap" frequently mentioned in these letters. His father, Timothy, could have been Nora's uncle who had died by the time this letter was written.*

7   *Ellie Driscoll and John McCarthy left Ireland on the S. S. Majestic and arrived in New York City on 11 September 1895.*

8   *James Hurley, 24, and his one year old son, Patrick, were burned to death in a house fire in Merthyr, Wales. His father was Patrick Hurley, and his brother John was the post boy in Leap. Patrick Herlihy, son of Denis ("Pad Denis"), of Clounkeen, died 6 August 1895 of pneumonia. He was 68, married, and a farmer. His daughter, Mary, reported his death*

9   *William Wolfe, son of James of Cregg, married Mary White, daughter of William of Cregg, on 5 September 1895.*

10   *Daniel Hourihane was born 3 September 1895 to Cornelius (Courley) and Maggie (McCarthy) Hourihane, Bawnfune.*

11   *Daniel Keane was born at 9 PM and Michael Keane at 9:30 PM on August 8, 1895 to James and Mary (Donovan) Keane of Clontaff. James, a fisherman, was the son of cousin John and Mary (Hayes) Keane.*

12   *Nora had worked as a maid in Sheahan's Hotel in Leap Village before she emigrated.*

13   *Bartholomew Crowley of Bradford, Mass., was the son of Denis and Margaret Keane Crowley and a cousin of the McCarthys and the Keanes. He married for a second time 14 August 1895. He listed his age as 41 and his occupation as a leather dealer. His new wife was Anne McGovern, 40, a domestic born in Saratoga, New York.*

14   *Dr. James L. Somerville of Union Hall, was in the 1875 Guy's Postal Directory listing for Leap as Registrar.*

DOCUMENT M13
3 October 1895 – Katie McCarthy, Ballinlough, Leap to Nora McCarthy, Bradford, Mass.

October 3rd 1895
Ballinlough Leap

My Dear Nora

Just a few lines in reply to your most beloved letter which I received on Monday last unexpected. Am glad to hear ye all are enjoying such good health as this date leaves us all well at present Thank God. I have lots of newses to tell you this time around the neighbourhood. Annie Callaghan got married last Tuesday to Pake Mahony Gemboy. She had a nice wedding. Nine side cars and a covered car and six saddle horses. She was married in a White dress and a wreath and veil and white slippers.

Her sister Katie stood up for her. She was dressed in white also. They were very gay. I know that you will be surprised to hear that Mackey the policeman is going to be married next Tuesday to Miss Mildrid Townsend of Myrosswood. She is reformed a Catholic with him. All her folks are crazy about it. So he have left Maggie Collins behind. Well, Dear Nora, I'd wish Ellie to know that Maggie sent for Jerry Collins.[1] He sailed last Thursday. She paid his fare and three pounds for expenses besides. He went without his parents consent. She was something plucky.

We have another Yankie in our land again, Norry Hegarty's son.[2] He is home after all. He was on the sea coming and Ellie going back. He is just like Norry, small and stout and fat. He is going to stay all Winter. He is home two weeks for Saturday. He brought a gallon of whiskey with him from Skibbereen and a half tierce[3] the following day so you can see what a time we had drinking all the whiskey. Norry is not putting herself out much for him. She says let himself cook for himself. 1 forgot to tell you in my last letter that Molly Walshe come home last June. She did not stay long over there. Her father was buried last week,[4] and Johnny Meenage Corran[5] was buried last Sunday. He was not sick only a few days. They telegraphed to Denny[6] to London so he came and his mother-in-law and child and he was buried before him. It was Monday morning he reached home. So he went off again on Tuesday. We did not see him at all.

Tell Delia that Patk. Crowley[7] have his brother Jack's land now. Jack is out of it. I am glad Delia have such fine times over there. Hanna Hourihane always inquired about her. She told me her cousin Maggie Hourihane is going to pay her fare for spring. She is going to a sewing school until that time. B. C.'s mother is very well for her. I told Maria[8] that he was married again. Well, I thought I would have Agnes picture before now. I am longing to see it. I suppose she is very big now, herself ought to be able to write to me now as I know you have her trained well. I was speaking to Den Keane last Monday in Union Hall. I told him about Mary.[9] It is too bad about her. We are all very sorry for her, but it can't be helped. Well, Dear Nora, I think it is not advisible for you to be giving up nights taking care of her. You ought be careful about your health as there is enough gone. Mother is very troubled for to have you be caring her as it's dangerous. It's too bad about you as you are not working or what will you do at all. Well, Nora, you ought to be ever so thankful to Dan and Mary or how can you ever return them the compliment or how is it that you cant get a place or what will you do. Let me know is it at Ward Hill[10] Dan is working always. It's well for you to have such a good kind brother.

Well, Dear Nora, about myself. I am a little better since I wrote you last. I am attending Dr. Somerville always. The next day I will go down I'll ask him if he would recommend me to go to the infirmary because he can get me in there. But his wife tells me to attend herself regular. He told me I'd get over it by great care and to avoid colds, but I don't believe him. But Nora I sleeps the night as sound as I ever did. The cough never troubles me until morning. Mother is very uneasy about me. You would pity her sometimes, and I pretend to be better than I am. She says she would not care if I'd live the way I am itself. All the rest are well. I guess I have all said this time until I hear from you again. We all joins in sending our best love and regards to Mary and Dan and Agnes, Ellie and yourself, hoping all are well, I remain your ever loving chum, Katie. Good bye to all.

ENDNOTES

1   *Jeremiah "Jerry" Collins, 24, left Queenstown on 27 September 1895 and arrived in Boston 6 October 1895. His passage aboard the S. S. Cephalonia was paid by his cousin Margaret "Maggie" McCarthy, North Marlboro St., Lowell.*

2   *Timothy Driscoll, the son of Norry and the uncle of Ellie was visiting his mother. He, his- wife Ellen, and his three children (Ellen, Mary and Daniel) were living on State Island, New York in the same three family building as Ellie Driscoll and her family when the 1870 Federal Census was taken. He was a coachman in 1870. In 1880, he was in Brooklyn where he was a laborer. The Driscolls had two more daughters, Kate and Maggie, and Mary was now called Nora. When the 1900 Census was taken, Tim was a widower, a fireman, and his two youngest daughters were living with him.*

3   *The dictionary defines a tierce as 42 gallons, so a half tierce was 21 gallons, or a keg of whiskey.*

4   *James Walsh, a 74-ar old farmer from Cloonkeen, died of old age on 17 September 1895. His death was reported by his widow, Mary.*

5   *John McCarthy, 67, a farmer from Corran, died of old age and debility. He had been ill for three months. His widow Catherine reported his death. He was buried 27 September 1895. "Meenig" or "Meenage," is a subgroup of the McCarthys to which the Ballinlough McCarthy families also belonged.*

6   *Denis was the son of John and Catherine (O'Brien) McCarthy of Corran. He was born 6 April 1857. Katie's concern about not seeing Denis suggests that there was a familial relationship between the two McCarthy families. That Denis received the news about his father via telegram is a reminder that these Irish farm families were not as isolated from thei emigrant children as might be assumed.*

7   *Patrick Crowley, 57 in the 1901 Census, lived in Corran South with his wife, Mary, and eight children. There is a John Crowley in Kilmacabea in 1901 who is a 35 year old mason and probably the "Jack" mentioned in the letter.*

8   *This could refer to Maria Crowley, daughter of Patrick and Mary of Corran. She was 25 in 1901, a contemporary of Nora and Katie McCarthy.*

9   *Mary Keane Goodman of Bradford, Mass., was terminally ill with consumption. "Big Den" Keane was her brother. She died October 1 after Nora had already sent her last letter to Katie.*

10   *Dan Donovan was a laborer who in 1895 worked on the construction of a hotel in Ward Hill, located in the southernmost part of Bradford, about a two mile walk from his home, or via the railroad with one depot a short walk from home, and the next depot to the south, close to the Bella Vista hotel, under construction.*

Document **M14**

Katie's detailed description of the "Station" held at Uncle Michael's house is an excellent view of the social relationships within the townland of Ballinlough. It is interesting that only half of the families in the townland are represented. As interesting is the listing of what neighbors from nearby townlands were in attendance. Though a Station's primary purpose was to have a Mass celebrated, there is no mention of the priest who performed the ceremony.

24 November 1895 – Katie McCarthy, Ballinlough, Leap to Nora McCarthy, Haverhill, Mass.

November 24th 1895
Ballinlough Leap

My Dear Sister Nora

I received both your letters and am very glad to hear ye are all enjoying good health as we are all well at present T. God. I hope you will excuse me for not writing sooner as I delayed it a week waiting to have some news to tell you. Well, Nora, yesterday we had a station[1] at Uncle Michael's. We had a good old time the same as usual. You may be sure we missed you from us and mentioned your name often and especially John and Mickey. The children are sure you will be home for Xmas. They had a half tierce and not very many drinking it. I'll just tell you. I think it is talking to you I am. They had Dannie Brien and Katie and Minnie, and Jack Tobin, and Jem Murphy, and Denis Hayes, and all of us, and Johanna and Johnny's wife, and Norry Hegarty and Son, and Corley Connolly, and Courley Hourihane and family, and Mary came from Tullig. That's all was there.[2]

They gave the day and night drinking it. They were singing and dancing all night. So we had a jolly time. And after a long part of the night Gem Murphy asked me where were you that you were not west. He was surprised when I told him you were in America. He never heard a word about it. Julia Murphy is married in America to

John Keohane since the 6th June.[3] Johnny John was playing the fiddle in her house. Katie Minihane[4] wrote home and she said she wrote to you and you did not answer it. She sent for your address last August. Her mother come to the house for it. Mary George received your letter also, but she was waiting to hear from Jack before she would write to you. Her Uncle Mick's wife was buried since she was east a month and she was in Corran for a month also.[5] She has a good time always. Well, Nora, if I could only speak to you now I have lots of stories to tell you. I told you in one letter that Mary White and Willie Wolfe were married. They have a young daughter with five weeks, and Peg Hayes of Carrigeen was buried 4 weeks ago.

Well, Dear Nora, we are all very proud in getting Agnes's picture. She looks nice. She looks very tall in the picture. I was laughing at the way she had her dress taken up and she is so independent looking.[6] Mother took her picture and yours also west[7] yesterday to have Mary see them. You may be sure there was words spoken to you if you could answer them. Any one of them did not know who Agnes looked like. I hope I will see her soon and all of ye. I received the papers on Thursday last and am very glad to find such good intelligence written in them. I can find Agnes signature in them. Isn't well she does not forget me. I am glad to hear you are working. Well, Nora, you were not long when you got employed after the other place. Dear Nora, wasn't it too bad as you were not able to have that place near the girls. When Mick read the letter he was cursing the other girl for to come back there again. I hope Ellie is enjoying good health. Remember me to her. I suppose she will never again write to me. Mrs. McCarthy had written to her before I received your letter. I suppose Ellie wont receive it as she is removed. Well, Nora, it is too bad about Mary Keane.[8] May God have mercy on her soul. Mother and all of us are very sorry for her. She was prayed for last Sunday in the chapel. Den received your letter. I hope her children are well. Her children are a great pity. Bridget Driscoll's sister Annie was buried lately in America also.

Norry Hegarty is very well. Her son is a very nice friendly man. He is advising me to go to America. He would not believe from anything that if I was in America but I would get well by the treatment they gets in Hospitals over there. He says this country is too damp for me, that it is a hard dry climate would answer me.

Sometimes he would not believe anything would be the matter with me. And I says to mother every day that I will go to America for April, and father do be joking me through fun I says it, and certainly, Nora, I says it so earnestly sometimes that I meant it. Tady and Mick has great notions of going somewhere. They do be talking of going away quite often. I am afraid they mean it. I am sure Mick is fully determined to go to America next spring but you need not say anything about it when you writes to him. We have very bad wet weather in this country, every day raining. People cant get the potatoes dug at all. They are very good this year.

Well, Nora, as lonesome as ye are this winter, we are more lonesome. The slippers or anyone don't come to visit us any night now, besides last winter. I do be thinking of ye over there every moment and talking of ye and every night I do be dreaming about you. Well, Nora, the Flavins and Deasey are great creditable people over there. Their both mother-in-laws[9] are fighting here just the same. One of them don't think the other good enough and so on.

Well, I guess its time to draw to a close. I hope Dan and Mary and Agnes are well. Nora, you ought be ever thankful to Dan. It's well for you to have him good and or us too. We all joins in sending our best love to ye all and not forgetting Agnes. Kiss her three times for me. I hope Delia and Katie [Collins] are enjoying good health. Remember me to them. I forgot to tell you about the Mirnanes. Dannie is in Ross still and Nellie and Helena are in Skibbereen and Larry Sullivan is in Moulnigirra. Dannie comes to see us often. Well, Nora, there is not head

or tail to my letter. I'd like to tell you all the news I could. No more at present. Good bye to all. Write soon again and tell me where you're working. I sends best love to all. Your fond Katie. XXXX Mother would like to know is it with her husband Mary Keane is buried.[10] Tell us all particulars.

Good bye, Excuse this letter.

ENDNOTES

1   A "station" was a Mass said in a private home. Families in a townland, or a group of townlands, took turns providing the location and refreshments. The custom dates to a time when it was not always convenient to cover the distance to the parish church. The custom continues to this day, although motor transportation has negated its original purpose. A station was as much a social occasion as it was a religious one, as Katie's letter demonstrates.

2   This accounts for over thirty people in Uncle Michael's house. The 1901 Census, which includes a description of each house, described the house as having three rooms, but with four windows on the front.

3   John Keohane/Cohan and his wife Julia (Murphy) lived in Norwood, Mass., when the 1900 Federal Census was taken. John was born in November 1867 and immigrated in 1894. He was a fireman on a railroad train.. Julia was born October 1867 and immigrated in 1894. Their first child, Dennis, was born August 1895, two months after the marriage date given by Katie. There were two other children, Julia's widowed mother, Mary, and two brothers, Michael and James/ Gem. The last three had immigrated in 1899.

4   Katie Minihane of Knockskagh, known as Monohan in America, wrote nine letters to Nora between 1896 and 1898. Katie was a domestic employed in a number of homes in Greater Boston.

5   The George McCarthys of Skibbereen, including daughter Mary, appear to have been closely related to the John McCarthys of Corran. It is quite possible these two were first cousins of Patrick and Michael of Ballinlough. Mary George, as she was always identified, was a regular visitor to her relatives in Ballinlough. She was baptized in the Kilmacabea church 7 March 1857. Her father was a dairyman who moved about from place to place. Mary and her sister Jane were born in Kilmacabea. The next nine children were born in various locations in Abbeystrewery Parish, Skibbereen.

6   The picture of two-and-a-half-year-old Julia Agnes (always known by her middle name) is in the McCarthy Collection.

7   Mother had walked over to Uncle Mike's house to show his daughter Mary, from Tullig, the pictures.

8   Mary Keane Goodman died of phthisis (virulent consumption) on 1 October 1895 in Bradford. She was widowed in 1892, and at her death, left three young children who were then raised by her brother-in-aw.

9   Norah Dillon Deasy/Dacey of Cregg and Kate Hickey Flahavan/Flavin of Ballinaclough. Norah Dacey came to America early in the twentieth century to live with her children in Haverhill, Mass.

10   Mary Goodman is buried next to her husband in St. James Cemetery, Haverhill. An engraved headstone marks the grave.

Document M15

Christmas 1895 brought both great sadness and unexpected pleasure. The visiting "Yankee,"[9] Tim Driscoll, lifted Katie's spirits with his unexpected celebration and promises of good times in the future. She sounds almost giddy with anticipation of their proposed excursion to Cork. Unfortunately, Katie's consumption was too far advanced, and this would be her last Christmas.

30 December 1895 – Katie McCarthy, Ballinlough, Leap to Nora McCarthy, Haverhill, Mass.

December 30th, 1895
Ballinlough Leap

My Dear Sister Nora

Just a few lines in reply to your welcomed letter which I received on St. Stephen's Day[1] gave us all great pleasure to hear you and Ellen and all the friends are well in health as this date leaves ourselves the same as usual. I must tell you that I did not enjoy Xmas night or Xmas day a bit too good. I was so lonesome as I had no letter received until St. Stephen's day about 12 o'clock the postboy went around. The mails were delayed because of a flood. The train could not run. We had some terrible weather for the past week. Rain falling in torrents and storm continually day and night. Anybody could not go outside doors on Xmas day. We often mentioned the good time we had that day 12 months on the top of the hill.

Well Nora, I must tell you how I spent Xmas night. Norry Hegarty's son come over for me to spend a part of the night with them and I'd prefer to be at home but all excuses would not do. I should go with him, and he had a jar of whiskey for the night, and he would not leave me home until ten o'clock. So Tady should go to meet me. Well he is the nicest and the freest man that ever lived and any day he is going to have a nice dinner he will come for me. He speaks of Haverhill quite often. He was there twice to see Pat Lawler[2] some time ago. Well, Nora all the fellows around went to

Leap on St. Stephen's day. And we never knew anything until we heard the noice coming across the river about five o'clock and what should it be only all the fellows coming and they having a donkey cart and a half tierce of porter. They made it up in Leap and Norry Hegarty's son put 3 or 4 Shillings in it so they got a cart from Patsey Cal. And they drove it up before them. Just like Shrove Tuesday[3]. So they had a jolly time while it stood.

But we had no girls only Julia and me because they came unexpected. But the Yankie promised me and Julia that he would give us a drive anywhere we like. So we are intended to take a trip to Cork on St. Patrick's day. There will be an excursion that day. We will get a return ticket for a half crown. So we are making up for to go. I'll tell you the company. Tim Driscoll, that's Norry Hegarty's son, and Dan Mirnane and Mary George and Julia and Patrick and Mick, also, if he can have the money and Tady and me and William and Denis (Slippers)[4] and we are going to have Ellie Hurley and the melodian, and Julia and me are going to wear hats going up (it's no joking). We have our minds made up for it if we can afford it for that time.

I am glad you has such a good time always hoping you will keep so. I am also glad to hear you are situated again. I suppose it is hard on you to be rising so early. I'd like to know how many in family in the house or is there any other girl in the house.[5] Delia's father got 2 pounds from them. There is lots of money after coming across this Xmas. I hope ye had a jolly Xmas together. We drank a health to ye all on Xmas night and so did Norry Hegarty. I hope you will write to me and tell me all about how you enjoyed the Xmas and what's your opinion of our trip.

Well Dear Nora this place is just the same. Anything would not change it. I have no news to tell this time except that Father Fitzgerald was buried a week ago.[6] I will send you the paper so as you can read about the funeral. And Aunt Julia got her chin bone broken.[7] She fell on the rock going to Leap. The doctor dressed it. I guess she will hardly ever again be any good. Paddy is father of a young son by the name of Henry.[8] All the other friends are all quite well. You know in the next letter how he is. We did not get any letter from London since ye went or from Denny[9] either. Let us know if ye heard from him.

Dear Nora and Ellen we never can return ye thanks enough for your Christmas present as it is very good for poor Ellie after all her expenses. Father is twice the man since he got the letter. He is very thankful to ye for sending the money. Mother is going to Leap now changing it as I don't feel like going myself as I was to Mass yesterday and I am not well since last night. I feel tired. Well I guess 1 have all said for the present, hoping to hear from you soon again. Dannie Mirrnane is with us since Xmas.

Well Dear Nora I have a news for you that Mary Collins[10] is going to have a young one after all, and Ellie Bueg Clounties[11] is gone to the Infirmary with two weeks and she is better too.

I must conclude for the present by wishing ye all a happy New Year. We all joins in sending our best love and respects to you Nora and Ellen, Dan, Mary and Agnes hoping to hear from you soon again. Wishing ye all a happy New Year and good many of them. Good bye to all. I remain your fond Sister, Katie XXXXXXXXX

ENDNOTES

1   *December 26*

2   *Not Patrick Lawlor the judge, but a Pat Lawlor who lived in Haverhill where he was a witness to the first marriage of Batt Crowley 9 September 1875.*

3   *Shrove Tuesday, also known as Mardi Gras. The last day to party before Lent commenced on Ash Wednesday. Also the final day for couples to become engaged before Lenten restrictions went into force.*

4   *William and Denis Williamson of Knockskagh.*

5   *Nora was now working for Mrs. G. E. Batchelder, 36 White St., Haverhill for whom she was a domestic servant.*

6   *Rev. David Fitzgerald, 70, died on 17 December 1895 of congestion of the lungs, after suffering for five years from chronic bronchitis and emphysema. His death was reported by Dr. Michael O'Driscoll who had cared for him. There is a memorial plaque to Fr. Fitzgerald in the Leap Church. "In memorian, Rev. David Fitzgerald who ministered for 32 years as curate, Administrator, and Parish Priest of this parish. He was a pious and exemplary priest, a true follower of his divine Master, and a zealous laborer in the vineyard of the Lord. Died Dec. 17, 1895. A70 years."*

7   *Aunt Julia McCarthy Harding lived with her son, Patrick and his family, in Kilmacabea townland. She more than outlived Katie's expectations for her and died of old age in 1903.*

8   *Henry Harding, son of Patrick and Ellen (Collins) Harding, was born 9 December 1895. He was their first child.*

9   *Christmas monetary gifts from all the emigrant children, including Jerry's family in London, and Denny in Pennsylvania were almost a matter of survival for Katie's parents.*

10   *Mary Collins Hayes was the wife of James Hayes of Ballinlough.*

11   *The only Ellens in Clounties townland in 1901 are the wife, 55, and daughter, 24, of Patrick Sullivan, 65.*

DOCUMENT M16

Kate Monohan/Minihane[1], a friend of Nora McCarthy from childhood, wrote a series of letters to her between 1896 and 1898, nine of which were saved. Kate's correspondence focused on her family, her work as a domestic, and their mutual friends from home. In Ireland, the family was known as Minihane, and in America, they used the Monohan spelling.

3 January 1896 – Kate Monohan, Westland Ave., Boston, Mass, to Nora McCarthy, Haverhill, Mass.

Westland Ave., Boston, Mass.
January 3rd, 1896

My Dearest Nora,

After a long retreat I once more address those few lines to you hoping to find you and your sisters in as good a state of health as the departure of this note leaves us in at present. Thanks be to our divine Lord for his mercies to us all.

My dearest Nora, I hope you will not excuse [me] for my negligence in not answering your welcome letters. Don't think it was through coldness of heart that I did not write sooner. It was not, but I was not feeling well. 1 had a very bad cold for the last three weeks but I am all over it now, thank God. So I hope you will excuse me.

Dear Nora, how did you enjoy yourself during the holidays? I did not enjoy myself at all. I cried my fill Xmas night when I thought of home. How different from home this country is. I suppose you heard Father Fitzgerald died. May his soul rest in peace.

Remember me to Ellie. I wish her the compliments of the season. As for yourself, I cannot express my feelings to you on cold paper or that love which my heart has bore for you. Remember me to Katie and Tim, my old chum, and father and Mother. No more at present from your fond companion, Kate

May your future years be even more happy than those of your past. Write soon to Kate

Good bye. Love to all from Kate.

To Nora, excuse me for not sending you any token of my love as I did not go out yet.

Kisses to Nora XXXXXXX Good night lovely Nora. Wishing you happiness in the country.[2]

ENDNOTES

1   *Kate's family in Knockskagh, Leap were known as Minihanes. Kate and her siblings changed the spelling to Monohan after they came to America.*

2   *Katie Minihane/Monohan, born in 1876 was a classmate of Nora's at Knockskagh National School. The flowery, affectionate language was the style in letter writing between young women at the end of the 19th century.*

Document M17
12 February 1896 – Cousin Denis Keane, Ballinaclough, Rosscarbery to Nora McCarthy, Haverhill, Mass.

Ballinaclough Rosscarbery
12th Feb. 1896

Dear Nora,

We are in receipt of yours of 6th inst, glad to hear that ye were then quite well, as we are still persevering in the enjoyment of good health. Thank God, with the exception of Den's mother. She is ill a considerable time, being the usual way as you may know perhaps.[1] It is a sort of personal illness and scarcely anything could be done for to be recommended for her recovery; as also Mrs. Crowley.[2] I think it is understood that she is rapidly declining; she hardly ever now goes outside doors. I wish you would apply to someone who holds acquaintance with Batty, perhaps Dan Donovan would be kind enough, and to inquire into him what he has to say in reference to a "particular event," that is the remainder of the money which he has, or perhaps Ellie would arrive at some knowledge of his intention.[3]

Dear Nora, about the picture, if there is any difficulty in taking it singly or separately it would be as desirable take a copy of the whole. At all events it would be very handy if it could be furnished. I shall not forget telling you about (Mary Wycherley's) marriage, whom we claimed to be a relative;[4] and which took place on Tuesday last. She is married to a respectable and very wealthy farmer named (Den Donovan) of Barley Hill. Mr. Crowley knows him well. She and Mary held acquaintance, as you may know from her, as also Geoff (her brother) is to be married to a Donovan girl from the Northn. side of Ross Parish. Inform all those whom you think care about them of this.

Danny Murnane has left Ross, and I don't know where he is gone to. Tady inquired of him not long since on a certain occasion and he didn't find trace of him. All are well and especially John and family are happy.

Yours affectionately,

Den

ENDNOTES

1   *Ellen (Hayes) Keane, mother of "Big Den," appears to have been suffering from what was once euphemistically called "female complaints."*

2   *Margaret (Keane) Crowley, mother of Batt Crowley of Bradford, Mass.*

3   *Denis Keane returns to this issue with his cousin Crowley in most of his letters to Nora. It would appear that Den's brother, Dan, had left a sum of money with, or was owed a sum of money by, Crowley. Dan Keane returned to Ireland c. 1893 and died soon after arriving.*

4   *Parentheses are in the original. Mary Wycherley of Ardagh, whose mother was a McCarthy, married Denis Donovan of Barley Hill on 2 March 1896. Ardagh and Barley Hill are townlands north of the village of Rosscarbery.*

DOCUMENT M18

This letter is the first indication that Cousin Den Keane earned his living as a fisherman.

25 February 1896 – Denis Keane, Ballinaclough, Rosscarbery to Nora McCarthy, Haverhill, Mass.

Ballinaclough Rosscarbery
25th Feb. '96

Dear Nora,

We've received your letter and the picture alright and glad to say that we could not express to you the thankfulness of sending it. It is easily identified from any of the others. Mother intends to get it framed along with Mary's as she has got one of them also. I would have given you an answer directly but I wasn't at home for the last week. I was at the fishing myself and Jack Hickey and fishing in the same boat. But it is rather slack as yet. Perhaps it will be soon prosperous. Paddy Harry was here last week and he said that he was told that Tady was going for May. I did not see any of them in quite a while. We are happy to hear that ye are well as we are all well at present especially big Den's father but his mother is always unwell.

John has got another baby, a boy,[1] and is first rate. He is going to have a station on tomorrow. Mother sends a little ribbon to Mary for the baby, as a token of some remembrance. Glad they are well. She knew the picture the first night after opening the letter and it is by the hands and knees she first identified him. I can assure you it is very well taken, and wish to say again we were well pleased with it. There was a letter and two pounds from Mike Flahavan a week ago and said he was first rate. With reference to Crowley, if he intends keeping the money he may but that is not what Dan expected him to do. Dan said he trusted Crowley to send it to Ireland.

Den

ENDNOTES

1   *Daniel Keane, son of John (Den's brother), was born 12 February 1896.*

Document M19

The happiness shown by Katie in her Christmas letter, and the joyous expectation of an excursion to Cork on St. Patrick's Day, were dissipated by March as tuberculosis wracked her body. Her condition was not helped any by her brother Timothy's insistence that he would go to America, though this would leave no one at home to help his parents care for Katie. However, even illness did not deter her from telling Nora of all the parish's pre-Lenten marriages. But, little could hide the difficult financial condition of the McCarthys as Katie details their debts and fears the departure of brother Tady and what little income he could provide.

1 March 1896 – Katie McCarthy, Ballinlough, Leap to Nora McCarthy, Haverhill, Mass.

March 1st, 1896
Ballinlough Leap

My Dear Sister Nora,

Yesterday I received your letter, am very glad to hear such good intelligence from you all, as this date leaves ourselves just the same as usual.

Dear Nora, I was in great hopes of my health when I wrote you last, as I was very strong that time and doing everything and I used clean up my house every Saturday and I did not care anything about it, but I don't feel strong now at all. I feels my heart very weak and my bones also. I was not able to go to Mass for the last three Sundays and the cough increased also, not much in the day but I'll get a good fit in the night and after that I'll fall asleep and be dreaming about you every night regular. I am intended to go to the dispensary[1] tomorrow and get a ticket from the doctor to go to the hospital where I'll get nourishment. We have got plenty tea. We got a parcel of tea from Mike Cahalane from Newport. He is coming home again, but we are drinking the tea without colouring since Xmas. The cow won't calf until June and the goats won't kid until

20th April.

Dear Nora, I have lots of news to tell you, if I only could now. Everyone in the Parish South got married too numerous to mention. Gilhooly[2] got married to the Keohane girl from Derry, and Mickey Brien's daughter Mary is married to big Willie Deasy. And her brother Tady got married to Burchil girl from Brade,[3] and Mike Connolly Corran to Mary Tade,[4] and Mike Driscoll Moultrahane to Ellie Hurley Keelfadeen[5] and Mary Wycherley Ross to Den Donovan Barley hill and G. W. her brother to a girl from Clonakilty. Mary know them. And Jamesy Fitz Ballinaclough to Mary Shannahan Brulea,[6] and little Jer Carthy Cap to a Cullinane girl from the quarry.[7]

I am glad ye heard from Denny. I am proud of his increase.[8] We would be very glad to hear from him. We got no letter from London since the morning ye left or I did not go to Skibb.[9] either since. I'll send the address I have myself: Mrs. Kiley, 45 Clifford Road, Hermit Road, Cannington, London, England.[10] That's the address I've got, and Johnny "George" address is 103 Elm Street, Lawrence, Mass.[11] That's the last address they had from him. I could not get Noney Hayes address[12] or they did not ask for yours since either.

Dear Nora, I don't know what to say about Tim. Father and Mother is consulting about it now just. I'd wish you could hear them now. They are crazy. Tim is not home at all. He is in Clonakilty today and all the lads looking at football playing. He told me yesterday to tell ye send it, and it was a very queer thing for you to speak of taking him out for another year whatever because I'll be surely buried before Xmas again, and if I wanted the priest who will bring him to me or who will bury me. Sure it is not an old stooped crippled father that could hardly move that would do it. And mother again ain't that well.

Dannie Mirnane is working near Skibbereen and he is going to get Tady in at work there and it would be better for ye not to mind him this year. Sure ye should lose 11 pounds by him now and they would rather to help us on a little more this year to get over them few debts and that bank is coming in on the 20 Apr. Now of course your four pounds would do lots of good to us only for the debt. We must give a pound to the rent and a pound to Paddy Carthy for the bog. He has a process warned to us for April, and a pound for Park Con Crown for garden. He was taking it from Johnny[13] a few days before we got the letter. So Johnny would not give it without it in hand, so he had it given over. He could not make up the money. So now, Honoria, where is it gone? Oh, my heart is broken to see it going like that but what would we do only for getting it, and we must bring a half bag of flour for the other one. Don't show this old letter to anyone in the world. I am only just telling you as I know you have all but them forgotten.

Dear Nora, Mother went out this evening picking Shamrock. I don't know is it right or not. I hope you will have it in time. Mother tells you if you can have a pound spared for the 20 April to send it for the bank. There is a fright in the poor thing it should be here for the 20th. We cleared it last year but it was taken again to pay the other bills. All the other friends and neighbors are well. I have no more to say at present. Write soon again. We all joins in sending our love to Mary, Dan, Agnes, Ellie and especially yourself.

I am your fond Katie.

(Excuse me)

Father don't like to have Tim go this year at all. He says too much lost by him.

ENDNOTES

1   The dispensary was in Leap Village. The "ticket from the doctor" would have allowed Katie admission to the hospital in Skibbereen as a charity case.

2   Richard White, the lighthouse keeper in Glandore Harbor, was nicknamed "Gilhooly," and played ball for the Kilmacabea G. A. A. He was the son of William, a farmer from Carrigluskey, and married Mary Keohane, daughter of Jeremiah, a laborer from Barley Hill, in February 17, 1896.

3   Mary and Timothy Brien were the children of Michael of Kilmacabea. She married William Deasy, son of William of Curriheen, on 28 February 1896. Her brother married Ellen Burchell, daughter of Thomas of Brade, 2 January 1896.

4   *Mike Connolly, son of Jerry of Corran, married widow Mary McCarthy Deasy, daughter of Timothy McCarthy of Ballyriree on 18 February 1896. Could Timothy be Nora's deceased Uncle Tim?*

5   *Michael Driscoll, son of Patrick, Maultrahane, married Ellen Hurley, daughter of Randal of Kilfadeen, 15 February 1896.*

6   *James Fitzatrick, Ballinaclough, son of Cornelius, married Mary Shanahan, daughter of Tim, Brulea, on 18 February 1896.*

7   *Jerry Fitzpatrick, Cappanabohy, married Minnie Cullinane, possibly from Maddaranna where there was a slate quarry.*

8   *Brother Dinny McCarthy and his wife, Julia, in Pennsylvania had their third daughter, seventh child, Helen (Nellie) on 9 November 1895.*

9   *Skibbereen was the home of the widow and family of George McCarthy on Upper Bridge St.*

10   *This is the address for the remarried widow of deceased brother Jerry McCarthy.*

11   *John McCarthy, born in Curragh, Skibbereen to George and Kate (Herlihy) McCarthy, was baptized 2 March 1869. Lawrence is the next city west of Haverhill.*

12   *Nora ("Noney") Hayes was born 12 April 1872 to Patrick and Norry Hayes, Ballinlough. She immigrated to Boston in the early 1890s and worked as a domestic, as most of Nora's immigrant friends did.*

13   *John Donovan of Ballinlough.*

DOCUMENT **M20**

Cousin Mick could be relied on to send a cheery note to his lonely cousin, Nora.

6 March 1896 – Michael McCarthy, Ballinlough, Leap to Nora McCarthy, Haverhill, Mass.

March 6th, 1896
Ballinlough

My Dear and Affectionate Cousin,

I must content myself to answer your letter which I received with the greatest pleasure. But I was grieved to the very heart when I saw how ye were employed during the Xmas holidays and especially on Christmas Day. Dear Honoria, you may say it is we that enjoyed ourselves well in fun as usual. We went to Leap St. Stephens Day but we had no dancing in Tom Kingston's loft[1] but we drank some drink and brought a barrel of porter off before us to the Cottage where we had singing and dancing until morning but you may think we thought of you often during them holidays. As for myself, I do feel lonesome every time I do think of the old times when we had all the jollification.

Dear Honoria, many did not get married in the neighbourhood during this Shrove tide only a few such as Michael Driscoll in Moultrahane and Ellen Hurley in Keymore, Michael Connolly in Corran and Mrs. Mary Deasy, Ballyriree. Jerry McCarthy is married to some girl from Madderana. I cannot think of her name but I expect you will hear it. Any amount got married by the seaside but I don't hardly know them but I expect Katie will tell you all of them.

Dear Honoria, any one did not get married in our land so we had no night so we managed to make up a ball but some of the lads disappointed on some occasion or other so we brought 9 or 10 gallons. We had not many girls only Mary George and Minnie Brien and Julia and Katie but we had a night as fine as a wedding. Peggie Connolly and Courley[2] are the same way all through and indeed it would not be any great blackguarding for them if they got married.

Dear Honoria, we had a great day last Sunday at Clonakilty. Patrick[3] and Tim and I and Tim Driscoll and more of the lads were there looking at the Glandore and the Cork City teams playing. The Glandore were beat but all the same we had a fine day. Tim Driscoll is a very fine man and grand company. The Welshes of Clounkeen[4] and John Anglin, Moulnagirra[5] are preparing fast for America. They will be going some day next week.

Dear Honoria, there are great festivals in Ballinlough this week. James Hayeses wife was blessed with a son last Tuesday.[6] I suppose you will have a laugh when you will think of Norrie's[7] talk. For goodness sake, Honoria, excuse me for not writing sooner. You know it is not for want of time but procrastination.

Dear H., I must conclude. My paper is small. We are all in good health and Katie is getting strong too, T. G. John, Jeremiah and Patrick thought you would come home for Christmas. Courley Hourihane and Magg are well, have 3 in family. Mary is well and is east always. I asked Julia would she write. She said one would do, but in any case, she would not spoil her letter with mine.

So Good Bye and Good Luck. I have no room for any more. We all joins in sending our best love to ye all. I cannot forget the day I was going matchmaking for Ellen.

(Good Bye my Dear Honoria. XXXXXXXXXXXX. Give some of them to Agnes) I am, Dear Honoria, your affectionate Cousin MM to HM.

Though many miles divide us,
And you I soon will see,
Remember it is Mickey
That always thinks of thee.

We are planting the potatoes but we wont have any day from you. Dear H. you had a hard day in the big field.

Good Bye and Good Luck. Excuse scribbling. Write soon again.

ENDNOTES

1   *Thomas Kingston was listed as a grocer in the 1893 Guy's Postal Directory for Leap. He is not in the 1901 Census for Leap but was living in Dromillily at the eastern end of Leap Village in the 1911 Census.*

2   *The Connollys were brother and sister from Cappanabohy, and near neighbors of Uncle Michael. They were still unmarried in 1911 when the Census was taken.*

3   *Patrick was Mickey's older brother, and known as "The Shoemaker" for his trade. He lived in Tullig with his widowed sister, Mary, and her three sons.*

4   *There was a John Walsh who owned a house in Clounkeen, but lived with his wife and ten children in Derryleigh in the 1901 Census. Three young people named Walsh were aboard the S. S. Scythia which arrived in Boston on 31 March 1896 but not enough information to verify that they were from Clounkeen.*

5   *John Anlin/Hanglin was born to John and Margaret (Keohane) Hunglin of Maulnigarra in 1873. In 1901, his widowed mother, Margaret, lived with John's brother Jeremiah and family on the family farm. The wife of Patrick Donovan, Bawnfune, was Mary Anglin, John's sister.*

6   *Mary (Collins) Hayes, wife of James of Ballinlough, had a son, Patrick, born 5 March 1896. Godparents were Patrick Hayes and Ellen Sullivan. James and Mary were married 13 February 1892 and this was their first child.*

7   *Honora Hayes, mother of James.*

DOCUMENT **M21**

Katie McCarthy was admitted to the hospital in Skibbereen in early March where she learned there was no hope for a cure for her tuberculosis. Her stay was made doubly unpleasant by her brother's insistence on going to America, despite her terminal condition.

6 April 1896 – Katie McCarthy, Ballinlough, Leap to Nora and Ellen McCarthy, Haverhill, Mass.

April 6[h] 1895 [sic]
Ballinlough

My Dear Sisters Nora and Ellen,

I received your letter on Saturday last. Am glad to hear ye are all well, as this date leaves us just the same. Well, it was almost time for Ellen write a line with twelve months but I never could make off her address. I hope you will send it to me correct. I am glad you all enjoyed Patricks day, as I did not enjoy it very well myself. I am in the hospital for the past five weeks.[1] I just come in the day I posted the last letter to you. So the first evening I come in, the nun[2] told me I was incurable and that I was in consumption and Tady was gone back home that time, so I said if she told me that in time, that I would go back home again. So she told me stay in bed the following morning until the doctor would come, so he sounded me and he said my right lung was gone, but the left alright. So I am in here since and I am not anything better but mother comes to see me quite often. But she was here last Saturday and she brought your letter and I got surprised this morning when mother and father come in to me to write to ye. Tady was vexed Saturday as he had not got his passage in this letter. He expected it so it was he sent them back here again to me to tell ye send it in a hurry.[3] He said he would not work a day here so father and mother have there minds made up to leave him go, but as he is anxious to go, let him. He says he wont taken any clothes with him only the ones he have. He is after buying a frieze trowsers[4] and that what he will take with him. I have no more to say about him only send him the Passage.

Mary Collins have a young son. His name is Patrick. I have no more to say at present. Good by to all. Mother and father are waiting for the letter so excuse the writing. May God bless and love you, Nora Dear. XXX Good bye. I am, Katie

The money is alright.

ENDNOTES

1   The hospital was most likely the Workhouse in Skibbereen as this would be the closest nursing facility to Leap.

2   The Sisters of Mercy, who had a convent in Skibbereen, had provided nursing care at the Workhouse since 1876, alongside the lay staff.

3   Brother Tim/Tady appears quite self-centered with his insistence on going to America when his sister had just been told she was incurably ill, and his parents were financially in need of his help. Katie sounds understandably aggravated and angry. Tady was literate and could have written his own letter, or made the trip to the hospital himself. To be fair, he was approaching thirty, he had no prospects in Ireland either for a farm of his own, or for a marriage. Emigration must have seemed like his last hope.

4   Frieze is a coarse, shaggy woolen cloth with an uncut nap, and very durable.

DOCUMENT M22

Two cheerful letters from Kate Monohan had to brighten Nora's spirits after all the distressing news from home. Her comment that there were more neighbors from home in the Boston area than would be seen at Sunday Mass in Leap very clearly indicates the intense impact of emigration/ immigration on both home and in America.

8 April 1896 – Kate Monohan, Boston, Mass., to Nora McCarthy, Haverhill, Mass.

Boston, Mass.
Wednesday night, April 8th, 1896

My dear Cousin Nora,[1]

I now take an opportunity of answering your welcome letter which gave me great pleasure to hear that you were all enjoying that great blessing which is health of which we can boast of the same at present. Thanks be to God for his kind mercies to us all.

Dear Nora, I mean to inform you that Brother Con is out here since last Thursday night at nine o'clock. He started in to Brother Michael[2] in New Haven. He was thunderstruck when he saw him as he did not expect him out sooner than the middle of April. I did not see him yet but had a letter from him. Brother Patsy[3] is in Boston at present. He wishes to be remembered to you and sisters and to Tim. He come up to Mike Hayeses' wedding[4] and did not go back yet. We had a dandy time there last Saturday night. He got married to Katie Donovan, Tim Donovan's cousin[5] of Bawnfune.

Dear Nora, you asked me if I seen many of the neighbors from home, but my dear child there is more of the neighbors from home around here than ever you see at Leap on a Sunday at church. It would take me a week to mention them all. I did not see Nora Hayes or Nellie Driscoll since I come out until Sunday night. Nellie Driscoll grew very tall but did not change anything in her features. Nora is thinner than when she left home but got very stately. All the Boston folks are well. Sister Maggie sends you and your sisters her best regards. Please remember us to your Sister Nellie. Please pass my best regards to Tim and Katie and Father and Mother and to all the folks. I do not remember those fellows you spoke of at all. I never think of seeing them on board the boat. If I did I should be mashing them.[6] We had all the fellows on the boat crazy. We could mash the whole business both Captain and all.

So I must come to a close by wishing the compliments of the holy season hoping to hear from you soon again. Good bye, love to all. Kisses to darling Nora XXXX

Address 52 G Street, South Boston With best regards from the one who loves you. Good night, Dear, for a while.

ENDNOTES

1   *There is no obvious relationship between the two girls. "Cousin" appears to have been a term of endearment.*

2   *Con Minihane/Monohan was born 15 June 1872. He sailed to New York City on the S. S. Majestic and arrived 2 April 1896. His brother Michael was born 29 September 1863, immigrated in 1889, married in 1898 and worked as a machinist's helper for the railroad in New Haven, Conn.*

3   *Patrick Minihane/Monohan, born 4 August 1867, immigrated to Boston in 1891 and was a laborer there in the 1900 Census.*

4   *Michael Hayes, son of Patrick and Honora of Ballinlough, was born 8 October 1868, immigrated to Boston in 1889, and married Catherine "Kate" Donovan, daughter of Michael and Honora, Bawnfune, 5 April 1896*

5   *Tim Donovan, born 6 October 1873 to Timothy and Mary (Driscoll) Donovan of Bawnfune, was a cousin of Katie Donovan Hayes.*

6   *"Mashing," i.e., flirting with.*

Document M23
30 April 1896 – Kate Monohan, So. Boston, Mass., to Nora McCarthy, Haverhill, Mass.

Thursday, April 30th 1896
Boston, Mass. [52 G St., South Boston]

Ever Dear and loving friend,

I received your long wished for letter a few days ago, was happy to learn from it that you and your Sisters, too, were enjoying that great blessing which is health of which we can boast of the same at present. Thanks be to our divine Lord for his Mercies to us all.

Oh, Dear Nora, you cannot imagine how bad I feel for poor Katie, dear good girl. The morning I got your letter I cried my fill but, Nora dear, don't despair for there is a good God and I trust he will relieve her yet. Let me know in what hospital is she. Sister Maggie felt awful bad at hearing about her. When she read your letter she cried for her Comrade. She did not forget the school days and pleasant times herself and Katie used to have in days gone by. Let us know if Tim is coming out this spring. Sister Maggie thinks he ought to stay home for another year and care for his sister. Let me know if you heard from home since, if so let me know how poor Katie is getting along as I long to hear from her again. When you write again, please pass my regards to Katie and tell her I feel bad for her. Please remember [me] to your father and Mother. I am awful sorry for their trouble. Maria Coakley of Keelinga[1] was buried a few weeks ago. She died of Consumption. Minnie Brien's[2] foot is sore yet, I mean Tim's sister. Mother and Julia, Jerry and John are well and wishes to be remembered to ye all. Mother will feel lonesome for Tim. She thought the world of him. When you write let me know when is he leaving home and the name of the boat. If I got a chance I should like to go to meet him to the Wharf to East Boston.[3] Nora Hayes and Nellie Driscoll and the Donovans of Bawnfune are all well. I have not seen Johnny John[4] since he come over. I gave your address to Nora Hayes. They are working in Newton. All the Boston folk are well. Brother Patsy and Con and Michael, Sister Maggie and Me join in sending our best love and respects to all. Tell me about Julia Driscoll as I hear nothing about her. Write soon again as I would like to hear from Katie. Remember me to Tim. May God speed all travelers. Do he know anybody to be with him?

Kisses to darling Nora XXXX

Write soon. Don't forget, [no signature]

ENDNOTES

1   *Mary (Maria) Coakley was born 8 January 1873 to Timothy and Eliza (Connolly) Coakley. Killinga is northeast of Ballinlough.*

2   *Mary (Minnie) Brien, born 25 July 1870 to John and Julia (Keohane) Brien of Knockskagh.*

3   *Tim 1 arrived in Boston on the same day that Kate sent this letter. However, this is a reminder of the effort that former neighbors in Ireland would make to welcome the new immigrants to America. There is no letter in the Collection telling of Tim's emigration.*

4   *John Donovan, son of John, of Bawnfune.*

DOCUMENT M24

Katie was home from the hospital before her brother Tim left for America. Though she was seriously ill, she filled her first letter to him with cheery news of his friends. She may have been distressed at his leaving, but her natural kindness, so often commented on by others, came through and she did her best to make the most of the situation. She writes only the slightest comment about her own health, but does let Tim know that their cousin Mary McCarthy, Tullig, has had another nervous breakdown.

24 June 1896 – Katie McCarthy, Ballinlough, Leap to Timothy McCarthy, Bradford, Mass.

June 24th 1896
Ballinlough Leap

My Dear Brother Timothy

I received your letter on Saturday last which surprised me very much and every one that read it. They said they never thought you could write such a letter and so did I. Well your letter was written first rate. I hope you will keep practice anymore and keep on writing. Your writing surprised them all.

Well, Dear brother, we are all glad you are landed safe[1] and enjoying yourself so fine. I am glad you met with all the neighbors as it was great encouragement on you after landing. Let me know did you use your currant cake going across or were you dressed up before you met with them. It was too bad how you got the pox. I hope your hand is well by this. Any of the lads did not come to visit us since you left until last Sunday. They laughed enough at what you had said in the letter and how you managed the German fellow.[2] They would like very much to be with you when you were among all the girls. They did not play any ball since the last Sunday you were playing it. It is broken, but they are going to mend it soon again.

They has a pattern at Carrigrour[3] now every Sunday. They had great sport Leap fair day in Tom Kingstown's loft. They broke it down almost. They renewed your name quite often and missed you from them. They were awfully lonesome for you. Patrick Brien and father were home about 6 o'clock that evening.[4] Dannie Mirnane did not come the way since all the fellows enjoyed themselves the night you were going. I hardly know myself what kind of a night had we. I did not see Mary George since. I expected her out here last Sunday but she did not come. I did not go out to anywhere myself. Since you left I feels awfully weak. I never felt so weak. I can't do anything for poor mother. She is very troubled about me. She would not care if I would live with her now.

My dear brother, I hope you will like the country and enjoy yourself. Don't be a bit lonesome. You did not say anything about how Ellie or Nora looked or did Nora change much. It was a good trial for you to know Mary. You ought to be very thankful to her and Dan. They have a nice home for ye all. I am glad Dan was so pleased with the herb.

I sends my best love to him and wishes him many, many a happy year because he is nothing but a good man. Let me know what kind of work will you have, or will you wear your old clothes working. I would like to know all about you. I hope you will be boarding with Mary any way. I have no newses to tell you at present, but the following Tuesday after you going, Mary in Tullig got out of her mind the same as before but she was worse this time.[5] She was from Tuesday until Saturday talking foolish and saying Cousin Tady and Cousin Ellie were gone away and never spoke of Nora and she would not know anybody. So they brought her home to Ballinlough Saturday morning and after coming she did not say anything or would not speak at all. So they brought her the priest Sunday evening and she would not speak any word to him. She did not eat or drink anything for two weeks only trying to go out all the time but she got all right again. You need not say anything about it in the letter for fear they would not like it, and Jerry Donovan of Gurtnidihy[6] his wife is inside in the Asylum since the fourth of June. I had a letter from Nora before yours. She said Ellie would soon write and father is watching the postboy since. He did not cut any more turf since you left. He cant do anything alone. Tim Driscoll wrote to his mother.[7] He said he would be home in 2 months. Well

I guess I have last said. We all joins in sending ye all our best love and blessing to ye all. I remain your fond sister, Kate McCarthy. I hope Agnes is well.

Write soon again. Good bye to all.

We will be lonesome for ever again.

ENDNOTES

1   *Tim/Tady, third son of Patrick and Kate McCarthy, sailed from Queenstown on the S. S. Gallia on 22 May 1896 and arrived in Boston 30 May 1896. There were 512 passengers on the Gallia, with 474 of them in steerage. Tim had $3.00 when he landed and gave his destination as his sister Ellen McCarthy, Locke St., Bradford, the address of Mary and Dan Donovan. Ellen met him at the port and took him to meet his Leap area neighbors who were now in Boston before boarding the train to Bradford. The depot in Bradford was about one hundred yards from the Donovan house.*

2   *There were no Germans on the passenger list of the Gallia, however there were a great number of Scandinavians aboard. Tim, who had never traveled outside of County Cork until this voyage can be excused for not knowing the difference.*

3   *Possibly the Carrigbaun cross roads ("Four Crosses") on the main road from Skibbereen to Drinagh, northwest of Ballinlough.*

4   *Patrick Brien of Knockskagh was a schoolmate of Tim. He probably provided the transportation to Skibbereen for Tim, accompanied by his father Patrick, from where Tim would take the train to Queenstown (Cobh).*

5   *Cousin Mary, who had lost her husband so tragically, leaving her with two very young sons and pregnant with her third, was subject to periodic nervous breakdowns.*

6   *Gurteenaduige. Jeremiah Donovan and Margaret (Connolly) had a daughter Mary born in Gurteenaduige 18 August 1888. This is probably the same Jerry and Margaret who had a large family in Mealisheen. There is no Jerry Donovan in Gurteenaduige in the 1901 Census, but there is a widow Margaret and children in Mealisheen.*

7   *Tim Driscoll had returned to his home in Brooklyn, New York on the S. S. Etruria 11 May 1896. He listed his occupation as a fireman on the Shipping List.*

DOCUMENT M25

Katie's oldest sister, Mary, lived with her husband Dan and daughter in a seven room house. Tim boarded with her and family. Her sisters, Nora and Ellen, spent their days off with them. This letter, with its enclosure to Tim, is one of only a few to Mary that have survived. Most likely, Nora took on the responsibility for writing home and, in turn, shared her letters with her siblings.

3 August 1896 – Katie McCarthy, Ballinlough, Leap to Mary McCarthy Donovan, Bradford, Mass.

August 3rd 1896
Ballinlough Leap

My Dear Sister Mary,

Yesterday I received your letter and we are very much pleased with it. We are glad ye are all well in health as it is the chief comfort of life, as this date leaves father and mother very strong (considering). Mother felt very bad about the time of Tim's departure, but she got better since. She feels well now, as for myself I don't feel well at all, or strong.

Well, Dear Sister, we are glad to hear that Tim is working.[1] I hope he will write himself and tell me all particulars about his work or is it far from his home or how he likes the country. Mother is afraid that he is not contented at all there. She tells him to cheer up and not to be a bit lonesome after this misfortunate old place. 1 have lots of news to tell him now if I could only speak to him. I had no letter from Nora with six weeks. She sent me a pound at that time. I did not answer it at all for she said not to answer it. I hope she will write soon again and tell me everything. It was very nice of Johnny John to call to see ye. I am sure himself and Nora had a great time. I hope Ellie is well in health. I do be dreaming of her quite often. I dreamt one night that she come home. Remember me to her. Do you hear from Denny at all? Ye can have a fine jolly time together. Besides here not a human in or out to us since Tim left.

Well, Dear Sister, I haven't much to say to you this time but I am pleased to get a letter from you. I hope Dan is well. I sends best love to him. I guess Agnes is a great big girl now. Kiss her for me. All the friends and neighbors are well. I will write a few lines to Tim hoping to hear from ye all soon again. We all joins in sending our best love to ye all from father and mother and myself. I remain your fond sister, Katie McCarthy.

Good bye to all.

Ballinlough

XXXX to Agnes.

ENDNOTES

1   The Haverhill City Directories for this time list Tim as living with Dan and Mary in Bradford, but give no information about his employment except to state that he was a laborer.

Document M26
August 1896 – Katie McCarthy, Ballinlough, Leap to Timothy McCarthy, Bradford, Mass.

[n.d. – mailed with previous letter 3 August 1896]

My Dear brother Tim,

I received your money yesterday and was very pleased with it. I did not get it changed yet. Mother was just getting crazy as she was not getting any letter. I am more than thankful to you for your present. I hope you will enjoy yourself the same as always and be cheerful. There was races in Connaugh 1ˢᵗ August. They had great sport. Dannie Murnane called to see us once since you left. It was after Carrigraheen Fair Day. He went to the fair with his master selling a horse and the Regans of Drinagh beat him there. The policemen were looking at them. They knocked Dannie and hurt him very much but the police summoned them to the court and they were only fined 2 shillings 6 pence. He is in the same place still.

Well, Dear Tim, I know you will be sorry to hear of your comrade boys being in jail after Leap Fair night, Jer Minihane and Jamesy Brien Parkbawn and Connie Dan Bohane.[1] They beat Jack Hourihane. Connie Dan followed him up the road and it is with him the others took part, but they say Jerry Minihane did nothing to him. The two Connollys of Knockskagh, Mike and Patsey,[2] went east to Hourihane and told him to summons them and that themselves would swear on them, and so he did and they swore very hard on them in Ross Court so they got two months each of them. The first day of July they were sent in, and Willie Leahy was caught in Cork. He is in also. And Courley Hourihane have Mary Crimeen[3] bound to the peace for twelve months. She paid her rent a month ago and when she went for the receipt he beat her very bad. She was in bed for three days after him and he had the first summons out himself, so he got her bound and Patrick Gem and Tom Kingston[4] are the securities and Courley said inside a Court that Tom was not worth three halfpennys so Tom have him served these days with a writ from Dublin for his character, but I don't know how will it go with them yet. I'd want the Eagle to tell you all. Well, I guess I have all said this time but write often anyway.

Good bye.

I am your own, Catherine

ENDNOTES

1   *Jer was Jeremiah Minihane of Knockskagh. Jamesy was James Brien, son of Patrick and Ellen of the same place, and Connie was Cornelius Dan Sullivan from Clounties.*

2   *Mike, born c. 1867, and Patsy, born 27 March 1876, of Knockskagh were the sons of widow Bridget.*

3   *Mary was the widow of Johnny "Bawn" Driscoll who had died the previous summer. She, her mother, and her five children rented a three room cottage from Courley Hourihane of Bawnfune.*

4   *Patrick "Gem" Murphy was from Knockarudane, east of Glandore. Tom Kingston was a grocer in Leap.*

DOCUMENT M27

Katie's strength was waning. Six months previously she was still able to make the long walk downhill to Leap Village. Now, in August, she cannot even make it to her uncle Michael's a short distance away. Undaunted, she continued to regale her siblings in America with all the news, and a bit of gossip, from home.

19 August 1896 – Katie McCarthy, Ballinlough, Leap to Nora McCarthy, Haverhill, Mass.

August 19th 1896
Ballinlough Leap

Dear Sister Nora

I received your letter on Monday last. We are all very glad to hear ye are all well in health, as we were just getting uneasy about you as you were so long without writing. I hope you will write oftener in future and tell us all the newses. You did not say much about Tim or how he likes the country. Mother is very troubled about him for fear he dont like being there. We are very sorry he have such a hard job for the first time. I hope himself will write soon to me and tell me all particulars about himself.

Dear Sister, I have no news to tell you this time, except that Dannie Connolly was home since I wrote to Tim. He only stayed two weeks. I did not see him at all. From Leap to Glandore he spent the time. He is a great Gent and tell Tim that Tim Daly[1] is home again. He was homesick all the time while he was in America. He speaks very bad of the country. Jerome Pady[2] is loafing also. He wrote home that he had not a cent in his pocket. Its a bad time all the fellows went out. Its greatly with the Deacys[3] how they are increasing.

Dear Nora, I suppose ye have the great heat in the country now, as we think this country very hot this summer. The potato crop is splendid this year. Father and mother are better, mother don't get the pain now at all. She has a lamentation every morning about ye all. She makes me feel bad. I am not a bit better myself, getting weak from day to day. 1 could not go anywhere. Its beyond my best to walk west to Uncle Michael's, so you see how weak I am. Don't ye be a bit troubled about me. I hope Ellie is well. I was dreaming of her last night. Remember me to Tim, Mary, Dan, and Agnes. Hope they are enjoying good health.

Well, Nora, I guess I have not much to say this time until you write again hoping it wont be long. Good bye to all from father and mother and myself. I am your Katie, (write soon). Dear Nora, I forgot to tell you that Mary Bennett[4] at Leap was buried and old Charles the Smith[5] also. I dont think any more died, and another story I have to tell you that big Patrick Dineen[6] is gone away and no account of him and Julia. Peter Driscoll Clounkeen[7] is going to have a kid after him, that for mis-fortune. I have no more news this time. Write soon again. Good bye.

I dont like to have Tim go at all if I could.

ENDNOTES

1   *There are Dalys in Tullig to whom Tim may have been related.*

2   *Jerome Driscoll of Bawnfune, born 17 September 1874, was the son of Patrick and Mary (Donovan) Driscoll. He had been living in Boston, Mass.*

3   *Cousin Patrick Deasey/Dacey married Joanna Horgan 16 October 1890. They had a daughter Agnes in 1893, a son John in 1894 and a daughter Margarita in June 1896. His brother John married Johanna's sister Mary 30 April 1895. Their first child, Marian, was born in April 1896. The Daceys lived in Haverhill, Mass.*

4   *Mary Bennett, 23, daughter of shoemaker John Bennett, died of consumption 11 February 1896.*

5   *Charles the blacksmith. Possibly Charles Callaghan of Keamore where there was a forge. See letter from Katie about the Zephyr tragedy, 1 August 1895, in which she worries what the mother of the four dead Callaghans will do, then adds "and Charles and his wife depending on them also." In the 1901 Census, Margaret Callaghan, a blind widow, is at the home of Mrs. Callaghan who lost the children.*

6   *There are three Dineen families in Shreelane townland in 1901. No others in the area.*

7   *Had Peter been accused of fathering a child? No Peter in Clounkeen in 1901 but there is a widow Mary with five children, ages 14-30.*

Document M28
5 September 1896 – Katie McCarthy, Ballinlough, Leap to Timothy McCarthy, Bradford, Mass.

Sept. 15th 1896
Ballinlough, Leap

My Dear brother,

I received a letter from you and am very much pleased with it. I am very glad to hear you likes the country so well, also that ye are all well in health as we were just getting uneasy about ye on account of the report of all the heat, as it is terrible in N. York. I am very glad you have such fine times. Mick is sorry as he is not with you now, but it is my opinion that any of them will never go to America,[1] but dont any of ye ever send for them, leave themselves go if they wish. Mick is in Tullig now steady & his mother Mary is at home.[2]

Well Dear brother, I have not much news to tell you this time. The jail boys are home. James Brien's father had a half tierce of stout before him the night he came. Jer Minahane looked very bad. Denny Daniel is married to Hannah Regan's sister, Mary Regan.

Dear brother, I was speaking to Johnny McCarthy[3] last night about that man you spoke of in the letter. Johnny did not know any man of that name but he know of a fellow named Mahony that was a great dancer. He told me to ask you where is the man from in Ireland. Try would he know him. He said he did not know any dancer by the name of Harten. Denny Gallivan told me to ask you if you gets the heartburn in America like you used at home. Himself is killed with it. Father is in great hopes since you said that he would work there.[4]

Well Dear brother, the potato crop is splendid this year. I am very glad Nora is improving so well, also Ellen. You did not speak of Agnes at all. I hope she is well, also Dan and Mary. Give my love to them all. I'll just tell you my weight. I got myself weighed on the first of July. My weight was at that time 7 stone and a half, but indeed I aint 6 stone now.[5] I am going back every day. I dont think I'll live to read many letters more from you. Nora got awfully careless in writing since you went. Father and mother is just the same. They sends there love to ye all.

Goodbye to all.

I am your Catherine.

ENDNOTES

1   *Katie was correct. Not one of Uncle Michael's eight surviving children, and only four grandchildren (Jeremiah and Patrick of Tullig, Jerry's daughter Margaret of Ballinlough, and Julia Hourihane of Bawnfume) emigrated to America.*

2   *Mary (Tobin) McCarthy had been caring for her daughter during her breakdown, and Mickey would have been e farm.*

3   *Could be Cousin Johnny "George", home for a visit from Lawrence, Mass.*

4   *This is one of a number of overtures to the McCarthy parents to move to America. With Kate terminally ill, and their other children there, it must have been an attractive offer, especially since Mary and Dan had a seven room house they could have shared.*

5   *A "stone" is a unit of weight in the British Isles equivalent to fourteen pounds. Kate, thus, weighed 105 pounds on the first of July but only 91 pounds on September 15.*

Document M29

Kate Monohan renewed her correspondence with Nora with two letters, a week apart, in October. While most of her writing is about her family, she does make some interesting comments on the hard work of a domestic servant, which was alleviated by the ease with which someone in that line of work could leave one post and seek another.

2 October 1896 – Kate Monohan, Dorchester, Mass, to Nora McCarthy, Haverhill, Mass.

Boston, Mass.
Friday eve, Oct. 2nd

My Dearest friend,

After a long retreat I once more take the pleasure of writing those few lines hoping to find you & your sisters & Brother in as good a state of health as the departure of this note leaves us in at present. Thanks be to our Divine Lord for his mercies to us all.

My Dearest Nora, after all I thought I'd write to you once more to see if you would not answer my letter. It is just now three months since I wrote to you before.[1] I have been patiently waiting for an answer from you but now all hopes failed. So I thought I would drop you a line. I only hope you are not offended at me for anything, if so I humbly beg your pardon. I only hope there is nothing the matter with ye.

My dearest friend, let me know when you are writing how your Brother Tim is getting along. Please give him my best regards also to your sister Nellie & Mary & family & all the folks. Let me know how your sister Katie is getting along also your dear father & Mother. I did not hear from home for quite awhile. I don't know what's the reason they don't write. My sister Maggie is well & wishes to be remembered to you all. Brother Pat has been sick for Some time. He is in the hospital for three weeks but is feeling better now. My self & Pat were going to Haverhill three wks. ago last Sunday but he was taken sick Wednesday of that week. So I do not know when we will get the chance to go again. All the Bostonians are well & send wishes to you & especially to your Brother Tim. They mostly eat my face off that Sunday that Tim come around as I did [not?] bring him in but I excused him as best I could but all in vain. Let me know how he like Yankee land. I guess he looks quite different now. I presume if I met him now I would not know him. I guess he is forgetting the dear old land & the good old times by this time. When you are writing home, pleases give my regards to your father & Mother & to my fond friend Katie in particular. I hope she is feeling better now.

Well, I guess I'll have to stop the Buss & bid adieu to My Dear Companion. I hope you will write. Please write soon & tell me lots of news. Please don't delay as I shall be on the lookout this time sure. G. Bye. XXX

Good By.

XXXXXXX for Nora Dear.

Kate Monohan, 23 Trull St., Dorchester, Mass.

ENDNOTES

1   *This letter is not in the Collection.*

DOCUMENT M30
9 October 1896 – Kate Monohan, Dorchester, Mass, to Nora McCarthy, Haverhill, Mass..

Dorchester, Mass.
Friday eve, Oct. 9th:: 96

Ever dear & loving friend,

After a long retreat I received your long awaited & wished for letter this morning which gave me great pleasure to hear from & more especially to learn from it that you & your brother & sisters were enjoying that great blessing which is health. Thanks be to God for his mercies to us all.

My Dearest Nora, I thought you had quite forgotten me as you did not answer my letters. If you wrote I never received your letter. I know it did not come to G St.[1] because she forwarded all my letters to me but I did not get yours.

Dear Nora, about my brother Pat, he is getting along very slowly as you know Broncittis is a very tedious sickness. I have not seen him since a week ago last Thursday. He is like a skeleton. Sister Maggie was out to see me Monday. She told me he was out of the hospital since Saturday but feels miserable. I am going in town tomorrow to see him. I hope he did not leave the hospital too soon. I will give him Tim's address. 1 know he will be glad to hear from you. You did not tell me whether Tim was working or not. Please let me know in your next letter.

Dear Nora, you asked me why I left my place. I was not feeling well during the whole time I was there. So the doctor advised me to leave there & not to work in town at all. So I am living quite a way out of town. It takes one half an hour to get in on the Steam cars. I have a purty hard place. I don't like it worth a cent. I have a large family to cook for & only four dollars a week. They keep another girl. I do cooking. She is a Down East girl.[2] I don't like her at all. She is a big crank. I may Stay for the winter but have not decided yet. Let me know what sort of a place is Haverhill & what pay do Girls get there. I may go to live out there yet. My sister Maggie is well, so is My brothers Michael & Con. I have not seen Con yet. He is down in Connecticut. 1 may go & see him for Xmas. I wish you & Tim would come in some Sunday as we were disappointed in going there. Patsy is crasy to see Tim. If you come I wish you would let us know in your next letter & we will meet you at the depot.

About my picture, I have not taken any so far but myself and Maggie is going to have them taken soon. I shall send you one but don't you wait for mine. If you have yours taken send me one. Pass my regards to Tim & Nellie & to all folks. It's good enough for the lads what they got. It may give them sense.[3]

The paper would not hold anymore so G. B. Good Bye write soon tell me all newses.

Address to K. Monohan 23 Trull St. Dorchester

ENDNOTES

1   *Address of Kate's previous employer.*

2   *"Down East" refers to Maine.*

3   *This is a reference to Tim's friends from the Leap area who were jailed for fighting.*

Document **M31**

Katie McCarthy wrote her final letter to her family in America on 27 October 1896. There is a great deal of sorrow in it as she tells them that she is dying, in fact on her death bed. Yet, there is also some testiness as she responds to questions from Nora about the use that is made of the money being sent to Ballinlough, and some barely repressed anger that brother Tim has sent little money to help out. But the basic goodness in Katie could not be held back and she made a point to remind Nora to send their mother her Christmas gift in time for the holiday.

27 October 1896 – Katie McCarthy, Ballinlough, Leap to Nora McCarthy, Haverhill, Mass.

Oct. 27th 1896
Ballinlough Leap

My Dear Sister Nora

I hope you will excuse me for not writing sooner but we did not get the money changed for eight days and I did not like to write until we would see everything alright. Excuse me also as I did not answer your last letter. I said Tim's letter would do. I hope ye are all enjoying good health any way. We are very thankful to ye for sending the money as it was badly needed the same as usual, spend beforehand. Tim did not act very good after all. I guess he is able to spend it himself, out of sight, out of mind.

Well Dear Nora, you asked me about home affairs. I should think you should not have them forgotten yet. They are just the same. We pays a part to everybody when we gets the money always, but the bank is without paying yet seven pounds. We are going to pay in 2£ [pounds] next Saturday, and in February it will be in again. We have the cow and the horse still. She does nothing for us only to have a drop of milk. That's the way we are trying to live.

Dear Sister and all of ye, it is hard for me to tell ye that it is in my death bed I am trying to write this letter rather than ask a stranger. I was anointed yesterday so I guess I will never again rise. I am expecting the doctor today. The priest told me to bring him. I am troubled with the diarhoea for the last eight weeks and I am spent away to nothing. I am awfully weak. I have no news to tell you this time but Minnie Brien is married to Dannie Con after all.[1] Mrs. Hayes from Brulea[2] was to see me last Saturday. She stayed the night. If you writes for Christmas write in time to poor mother as I know I wont be before it. I won't write any more this time. I feels tired. All the friends and neighbours are well.

Give my love and blessing to Mary, Dan and Agnes, Ellen, Tim and especially yourself.

Write soon any way. Good bye to all. XXXXXXXXXXX

I remain your loving sister, Katie. Father and mother sends best love.

ENDNOTES

1   *Daniel Collins, son of Cornelius of Driminidy, Drinagh, married Mary (Minnie) Brien, daughter of John and Julia of Knockskagh on 27 September 1898. Dannie was a cousin of Hannah Collins, Nora's friend in Elmira, New York.*

2   *Mary (Fitzpatrick) Hayes, wife of James of Brulea, was 72 when the 1901 Census was taken. She and her husband listed themselves as speaking "Irish Only" on the Census form. Brulea is on the west side of Tralong Bay, across from Ballinaclough. Mrs. Hayes was a relative, or a friend of long standing, who had a traveled a distance to comfort her old neighbor, Mrs. Kate McCarthy and her ill daughter.*

DOCUMENT **M32**

Katie lived one month after writing this letter. She died November 16,1896. The next four letters from Ireland tell and re-tell the story of Katie's dying, her wake and funeral. They are extraordinarily rich in detail with narrations of her final conversations, descriptions of her apparel when she was laid out, details on the participation of neighbors and relatives, and information on how the news was spread to family throughout the area. There is even a touch of the supernatural with the relating of the dreams that Katie's father had before she died. The task of letter writing fell to relatives and friends since Katie's parents were illiterate. Each of the three authors of the four "funeral" letters has her/ his own style and perspective as the story of Katie's dying and death is told, re-told, and told yet again.

21 November 1896 – Patrick and Catherine McCarthy, Ballinlough, Leap to Their Children Mary, Ellen, Tim and Nora, Bradford and Haverhill, Massachusetts

Patrick McCarthy
Ballinlough, Leap
November 21st, 1896

My Dear Children

I am writing you this sad letter which I thought would not come to pass for some years to come but God's will must be to leave us lonely and heart broken.

Dear Nora, poor Katie died on last Monday morning between the hours of 9 and 10 o'clock and left her poor parents in darkness. They were glad she would live with them. She would instruct them in many ways as needed but she being struggling for the past two months she got anxious to die herself. She was anointed three weeks from the day she died and Poor father went for the Priest a second time. That was Saturday before she died. You may picture to yourself that his expense was great.

Dear Sisters and Brothers, Poor Katie died on the 16th November that was Monday between the hours as I have mentioned. She was as steady as ever. She answered all the Litanys as they were read for her by Patrick[1] and told them say prayers for her. She was very anxious to die and wished to die on Friday but lived struggling until Monday. She had large wakes the two nights and days and had a very large Funeral on Wednesday. She willed to be buried nice and to be dressed in white muslin trimmed with blue ribbon, white stockings and Gloves and a wreath and veil and to have whisky in her wake and plenty of other provisions. Yourself know she got every thing as desired and every person liked how she was dressed and said they never saw such a nice corpse and everyone cried for her.

Dear Sisters as ye are I cannot call ye other wise, you must be careful about your poor parents as they are gone through a lot of expence since Tim left home, always attentive to Poor Katie's wants, having tried every place for cures but all failed them. The death came at last and they must be satisfied. I hope she is happy. So now let ye all pray for her as it is the best for her now.

Dear Nora, don't inform Mary of this if you think it will be any hurt to her. She was attended to by her cousins in every way. She was carried away on men's shoulders and had a frightful group of hearty men and women all around her. If you could see them all crying, friends and stranger and the Parish Priest, Father Cunningham,[2] attended the Funeral. He was very nice.

Dear children, I would like to inform you of Katie's conversation before death. Mother said "What will I do, Katie?" "Oh, Mother, Nora will come home to you." "No," says mother. "Well, mother," says she, "Ellie will come," she said. "They wont," said mother. "Well, ye must be alone." She gave up all hopes and was contented to die. May the Lord give her rest. So now don't forget to pray for her and we will do our best for her.

So now dear cousins, I have no more to say for this time. Mother don't like to send you a mourning letter[3] for the first one to take your sences from you so ready. I have no more to say for this time. Excuse my careless letter as I am in a hurry.

From Julia. [4] And from your fond Parents. Good bye.

(We got your papers this morning. It was a lonesome morning with your poor parents.)

ENDNOTES

1   *Patrick McCarthy, known as "The Shoemaker," was the third son of Uncle Michael.*

2   *Rev. Michael Cunningham succeeded Fr. David Fitzgerald as parish priest of Kilmacabea parish, the previous December, 1895. He was 42 years old when Katie died. A "funeral" does not seem to have included a Mass in the church, but rather a prayer service at the home and at the graveside.*

3   *A "mourning letter" would be on black-edged paper in a similar envelope.*

4   *Cousin Julia took over the responsibility of writing letters for her illiterate uncle and aunt until her marriage in 1900.*

Document M33
26 December 1896 – Patrick and Kate McCarthy, Ballinlough, Leap to Their Children in Bradford and Haverhill, Mass.

Patk. McCarthy
Ballinlough, Leap
Decem. 26th 1896 St. Stephen's day

Dear Children,

I am writing you those sad letters but don't like to send you mourning ones as you did not say anything about it so must tell me which would you like. I think them more lonesome and I am.

Dear Nora, tell your sisters and brother they have paid for three Masses for Poor Katie. I hope they will do her good. Mother wanted Katie to be buried with the Glandore[1] [people] and she made her no answer. Now, Tim, mother is surprised you or Mary[2] did not write some line. I hope ye wont be long so to please her. She is awful lonesome.

Dear Cousins, Dennie come to the poor creatures every night since Katie's death and Patk. and Dennie spent all Christmas Night and Xmas Day night with them and Poor Uncle Pad had nothing to say but thinking on the past. I am telling all my story to all of ye as if I was speaking to ye. I hope ye will be pleased with it.

Dear Ellie, it was Mrs. McCarthy of Leap that answered your letter[352] as she asked your address until you would tell her about her sons. Mother tells you write to her as soon as you can.

Dear Nora, I never told you where poor Katie was laid out. She was laid out in her own bed and a small table at her feet for the Candle. She was as nice as we could have her. I have no more to say at Present. Excuse this careless letter from a friend as I have a lot said. Correct errors.

From your parents and Julia. Good Bye.

(Mother and Father tells you to mind your Health. They are afraid of ye fearing death. Good Bye, write soon.)

ENDNOTES

1   *The graveyard at Glandore, south of Leap, was where Mother McCarthy's family, the Keanes of Ballinaclough, was buried.*

2   *Mary McCarthy Donovan was approximately six weeks pregnant with her second baby at this date and probably not up to writing a letter when Nora and Ellen were available to handle such a distressing task.*

Document M34

18 January 1897 – Cousin Denis Keane, Ballinaclough, Rosscarbery to Nora McCarthy, Haverhill, Mass.

Ballinaclough
Jan. 18th, 1897

Dear Nora,

I am in receipt of yours of 14th inst. which gives us the greatest pleasure to hear from you once more, as I had been regretting for the past few months on account of not hearing from you. I would have written to you on Katie's death but I being in doubt as to the certainty of the address which was a sad occurrence and the greatest sympathy is expressed by every one. We were feeling bad enough myself but will do anything you wish.

Dear Nora, your Father and Mother is going to Church regular since Katie's death but some one should accompany Katie all the time back as she didn't like to be one minute alone, was very anxious for company. I hope she is happy with God's Help as she have suffered far in this world.

Dear Nora you can tell your sisters and brothers where poor Katie was buried. She is laid between her two Uncles Tim and Dennie and is down on her Grand Father's grave.[1] I hope you will be glad enough for her company as she often talked of them before death. If she could meet them she would not be lonesome but she got very silent the last two weeks. She had nothing to say but would answer every question as needed and had no conversation as before, had not story or anything, but if all were silent she would turn into the picture she had inside of her head.[2]

Well, Nora, if you had seen her you would almost die for her. She felt so lonesome for leaving her poor parents as they needs her. She was good company for them until she was very spent and then she got anxious to die and willed to be laid out as I have told you before, but liked to live until Xmas to see how would three of them enjoy themselves and to see what would the American presents be for Xmas. But the Lord did not spare her so long. I hope she is better with God's Help.

Dear Nora, poor Johnny Burke of Knockskegh[3] was buried one week before Katie only one week's illness and the Bishop[4] the week after Katie and was not sick at all. He was taken sudden and was carried to Queenstown by his friends. As great as he was that was his end.

So, Dear Nora, Katie's remains was carried by her own friends, I mean her cousins.

They walked through the river,[5] Mike, Park., Jerry and Dennie,[6] and did not mind about the water if it was as high again and all the strangers were surprised as they did not go into the field but they would not and she always talked about how would a coffin go over the river, that they would fall into the river.[7] This was her talk all the time long before death.

Dear Nora, Ellen and Tim and Mary and Dan and Poor Agnes, Poor Katie was tended as well during her illness as if she was Lord Carbery's daughter.[8] And the expense of her wake and Funeral was great. There was four gallons of whiskey spent on her wake and none on her Funeral as 6 gallons would not serve the Funeral, five lbs. Tobacco and 4 dozens of pipes.[9] The coffin was expensive. It cost £1 15s [one pound fifteen shilling] very expensive Hasps[10]. They were to have two priests but one was absent from home.

Dear Tim, your Mother and Father tells you not to be lonesome as poor Katie was attended to as if she had six brothers and six sisters present and she did not give you any blame for leaving her but I am sure sorrow failed her though she did not pretend it. So she is gone from amongst us into a happier home with God's help.

Dear Ellie, poor Katie had nothing to say to anyone or did not speak much about ye but Mother said "Katie, what will I do." "Oh, mother, Nora will come home to you." "she wont," said mother. "Oh, mother, Ellie will come. You won't be alone."

Dear Nora, they received your letter all right and got the money changed. They are very lonesome. The two letters they have got since Katie's death brought tears to the floor from both of them. They are lonesome surely. I am vexed to mother[11] to be trying to cheer her up and we will leave Jeremiah[12] come to her after Christmas as she is sleeping alone in the room. He will accompany her as he has a lot of talk. He will be noisy.

[I'll tell you how we] were informed of it and were at the wake and Funeral. It is Patrick[13] came down to Brulea and then all enquiring friends got an account of it. We all then met together at Cregg[14] from where we started and Patrick waited till every one came. There was any amount of people at the Wake and there was also a very large Funeral in which all were regretting her loss.

Dear Nora, I assure you that she had been buried very well. Perhaps as well as if they were far more superior in wealth. So you may see that everything had been done respectably with regard to her burial. I also heard your mother saying that herself said in the last moments "let ye have whiskey in my Wake" so that is quite enough to you now as regards that matter.[15] Dear Nora, there is no use in being indulged in too much uneasiness at all. I seen Patrick yesterday in Glandore and I asked him how were the old Folks Above and he said they were all very well but as far as sorrow are concerned there is no use in them. I feel satisfied to let you know that on the morning of the Funeral I first became intimate with Mary "George."[16] She was there from the beginning and through all the sorrows. When we fell in conversation we carried on jolly words. We used try to joke each other and I feel proud of her acquaintance. I don't want you to understand that it is how we were any way merry, but we used carry on droll ideas. You can fancy that in your own mind.

Dear Nora, I must also tell you that John's sister-in-law was buried last week for whom all feel very sorry and especially is regretted very much by John. She died from the effects of Cold. She is a great loss. I suppose you did not know her at all.

Glad that ye are all very well and hope ye will not continue in Despair for the future as we feel well at Present. Thank God.

I wish also to make reference to the fishing business for the past season which came awfully wild and stormy, but in the latter end of the time, mackerel were very numerous.[17] Some hauls were as high as 10 thousand, so that the boats had to finish up for want of Demand. The price was as low as 3 shillings a hundred but there was not hake at all. They were a whole failure this year.

Fishermen suffered a lot of hardship in a northerly Gale which prevailed in the month of September last. One boat was lost in

Glandore Harbour. The men came safe. I also had a narrow escape. We went through a great deal of hardship from the effects of remaining hauling too long. All the other boats were cut their nets and were in before the gale. We came to Harbour's mouth. When it blew we lost our sail, that is Kinsale Harbour,[18] were driven 20 miles off and, only for meeting a steamboat which picked us up, would be badly off. We might come. A few more boats were out 3 or 4 days before returning. There was a great alarm in all places.

Yours affectly. Den

ENDNOTES

1   Generations of the McCarthy family have been, and still are, buried at the old Kilmacabea Burial Ground, rather than at the new cemetery in Leap Village. Timothy and Dennis, Katie's uncles, died sometime after 1876 when Dennis' wife gave birth to a daughter. Katie's grandfather, Jeremiah, had died in 1874 and, as was the custom, in a burial ground with very limited space, the more recent deaths would be placed on top of the older coffins. The Kilmacabea burial ground is directly east of Ballinlough.

2   These are very descriptive sentences written by Denis Keane, a fisherman, whose sole education was in a country schoolhouse.

3   John Burke, son of Patrick and Margaret of Knockskagh, aged 25, Katie's school mate, died of pneumonia on 6 November 1896.

4   The Bishop was Most Rev. Dr. Fitzgerald.

5   The Mullaghnagowan River flows easterly out of Ballin Lake and then southerly through Leap Village into Glandore Harbor. It separates the townlands of Mealisheen and Cappanabohy, which abut Ballinlough, from Kilmacabea townland.

6   Michael, Patrick, Jremiah and Dennis, the four sons of Uncle Michael.

7   McCarthy relatives living in the family homestead were gracious enough to show me the traditional path across fields and across the river from Ballinlough, through Mealisheen, and up the hillside to the Kilmacabea parish graveyard in the northern corner of the townland of Kilmacabea.

8   Lord Carbery was the chief landowner of the Barony of Carbery in which Leap is located.

9   Assumedly, the pipes were the traditional small clay pipes ("dudeens"). The custom of providing pipes and tobacco can also be found in Colonial New England burial rites.

10   *The hasps are the metal clasps on the coffin. When Katie's mother was buried fifteen years later in 1911, her coffin cost the same price, according to the bill from P. Minihane, Leap, carpenter, that is in the McCarthy Collection.*

11   *Denis' mother, Norah McCarthy Keane.*

12   *Jeremiah from Tullig. He was almost ten years old when this letter was written.*

13   *Patrick McCarthy, the "shoemaker," son of Uncle Michael.*

14   *Brulea, the home of "Mrs. Hayes," is opposite Ballinaclough on the west side of Tralong Bay. Cregg, the home of the Deasey/Dacey family of cousins, is at the head of the Bay.*

15   *Nora might have expressed concern at the expense incurred for the Wake and Funeral, especially in light of the regular requests for money to cover her parents' debts.*

16   *Mary "George" of Skibbereen was a maternal cousin of Denis Keane.*

17   *According to Guy's Postal Directory, 1875, "The [Glandore] bay is spacious and secure. And during the mackerel season wears a very animated appearance, the fishing roads lying quite near the mouth of it."*

18   *The port village of Kinsale is a good distance, 20 miles or more, east of Glandore Harbor.*

Document **M35**

*Nora "Noney" Hayes, daughter of Patrick and Norry Hayes
of Ballinlough, born 12 April 1872, was a childhood friend
of Katie and Nora. She came to Boston around 1892. She
had three brothers in Boston: John, Michael and Patrick. Like
Nora's other female correspondents in America, Noney was
a domestic.*

[21] **January [1897]**[1]- **Nora Hayes,**[362] **Boston, Mass, to Nora
McCarthy, Haverhill, Mass.**

Boston
January

My Dear Norah,

I received you letter a few days ago from which I learn by it that
you are well. I would have answered it before now but I did not feel
extra well. I have had a severe cold.

Norah, I know [you] must feel quite lonesome for Poor Katie.
Words cannot express to you how sad I felt for Poor Good natured
Katie.

I have just received a letter from Nellie Driscoll,[2] Norah. She is
more than Spoken [for]. She is engaged to be married pretty soon.
She takes in all the Dances and has regular Ball Dresses. I do not
suppose you would know her. She is in fact a very pretty looking
girl and elegant dancer.

Dear Nora, as I intend leaving my place pretty soon, if you
should hear of [a] nice place would you please let me know, Nora,
as I have eight in our family to work for so you can just imagine
what a snap I have. I shall try and go out to see [you] 2 weeks from
Thursday if nothing occurs before then.

Norah, let me know when your heard from [home] and how
they are getting along. Remember me to father and mother also all
the spring chickens. I mean Francis Williamson.[3] Norah, I wonder
if I shall rise any man when I gets out to Haverhill. It will be my
fault if [I] do not. Let me know you got any fellow out there.

I will wind up for the present by saying Good night as I am in awful hurry.

Noney Hayes 7 Waldren Street, Dorchester, Mass.

Write soon. Excuse the lead pencils, also irrboling [scribbling].

Norah, if you got any tintype pictures of yours, I wish you would send me one in the next letter as I am going to send one to you soon.

ENDNOTES

1   *Date from postmark on envelope.*

2   *Ellie Driscoll from Washington, DC, granddaughter of Norry Hegarty, neighbor to the McCarthys on Ballin Lake, Ballinlough.*

3   *Francis Williamson, son of Richard and Ellen of Knockskagh, was living at home with his parents when the 1901 Census was taken. He was 22 in 1901.*

DOCUMENT **M36**

Neighbor Bridget Driscoll of Knockskagh, daughter of Margaret of Knockenacrohy, wrote this letter for the McCarthys. This allowed them to reveal information about problems with financing Katie's funeral that might have hit a bit too close to home if Julia was writing the letter. This also includes the first mention of some otherworldly dreams that Patrick had. Bridget Driscoll uses an interesting technique of alternating the parents' voices with her own words.

6 February 1897 – Patrick and Kate McCarthy, Ballinlough, Leap to Nora, Ellen and Timothy McCarthy, Bradford and Haverhill, Mass.

Ballinlough
Feb. 6th 1897

Dearest Nora, Ellie and Tim

Since my dear Katie died, I'm day after day waiting to send ye all particulars about my darling child who left me and her poor Father sad and lonely with a broken heart. Yes, I need not describe to ye and Mary that poor Kattie was affectionate and kind. We left nothing undone for our darling child. Everything she wished for during her prolonged illness we got for her as we thought from time to time that she would survive and she did herself until she knew her end was fast approaching.

So she made up her mind to leave us for ever, though if it were possible she would

not go. We hope and trust she is happy because she was kind and good and bore her illness to the end with the greatest patience.

Dearest Nora, don't ye worry too much for poor Kattie as it was pleasing to our dear Lord to take her from us all. It is a consolation to us all to know she felt very happy and was perfectly reconciled to die. We left nothing undone for her. You would be consoled to see her die so happy. She had her senses up to the last minute and a short while before she expired she asked "Is that you, Mama?" Oh, we shall never forget her.

Rev'd. F. Cunningham came to see her Sat. eve and administered the last sacraments. She said to me, B. Driscoll, who is writing this letter, that she would like to die while Fr. Cunningham was in the kitchen. I went to see her Sunday eve. The minute she saw me she welcomed me and told me sit by her bedside and asked me how I was getting on. I certainly would not leave her that night but I thought she would not die so soon. Mary Crimeen, Mrs. Driscoll and your Uncle's wife[1] remained with your parents that night. My mother[2] went to see poor Kattie in the morning. She was just after expiring before her so she remained until she was laid out. I certainly could not stand to see poor Kattie departing as I was really very fond of her. Your dear Father and Mother kept up well and I must say from myself that if they had the whole of Ballinlough they could do no more for poor Kattie. She was waked and interred most respectably and looked lovely on the table after 4 long years illness.

Dearest Nora, it would certainly console ye all to see poor Kattie looks so nice on the table dressed in a lovely white robe with the blue bows of ribbon, a Helithrope[3] wreath and white veil, white gloves and stockings. She also had a beautiful casket and was borne on men's shoulders to her last resting place. Really all the neighboring boys and friends were vying with one another to go under her coffin if the distance were three times more as that is what poor Kattie deserved. If you and Taddy were home there could be no more done for her.

Your poor Father and Mother kept up well while she was dead. It is now they miss their darling Kattie as certainly she was very nice. It is now they miss her. It is often she spoke of ye before she died. She used to be trying to console Mother by saying that you would come home to them. Father took her death very much to heart. He dreamt she came to him before they got your letter and told him sing a song for her and a comrade of hers and that they would soon get a good letter from ye. He also dreamt of Jerry two nights before she died and he thought he told him not be troubled for Kattie that she would be happy. May their souls rest in peace.

Good bye, please excuse this scribble.

(Keep this secret as we must live as long as we can.)[4]

The Tuesday before poor Kattie died we had not a shilling to lose by her so poor Father asked some of the friends to take a few pounds for us in bank as we had what we had and what we had not lost by poor Kattie. Some of them were not very willing, so it is Denny Herlihy and Johney Herlihy[5] took four pounds for us. It was very kind of them. We did not tell Michael's a word about it as they did not offer one cent for a help to us[6] but of course they watched while she was dead[7] and did what they could the day of the funeral. We would lose all in this world if we thought we could recover her but such was not God's will. May her soul rest in Peace. Don't ye worry too much for her as it is enough for us to be troubled. We are very thankful to ye for your kindness.

I must tell ye about the cow. We did not like to part her while poor Kattie lived so she got a bad turn after her death. We did our best to fatten her. They being so cheap we scarcely would get nothing for her so we killed her last week when she was not improving much. I know it will console ye to know so much about poor Kattie. Don't forget her in ye'r prayers as she loved ye all. Sincerely I trust she is praying for us all in Heaven where we will all meet and parting will be no more.

Good bye. Hoping to hear from you soon.

Your loving F. and M., P. and K. McC.[8]

(Dada asked Curely to take the money. He said he would not like to refuse him but when he consulted with Peggy he was different.[9] Don't pretend a bit about it. Keep it secret. T. G. your poor father was not refused.)

ENDNOTES

1   *Mary "Crimeen" Driscoll of Bawnfune was the widow of Johnny Bawn Driscoll. Mary "Mamie" Tobin McCarthy was Uncle Michael's wife.*

2   *Bridget's mother, Margaret, appears numerous times in the public records as a witness to births and deaths, indicating she was both a midwife and a "layer-out" of deceased. As such, she played an essential role in the small community.*

3   *Heliotrope, a plant with fragrant tiny flowers.*

4   *This parenthetical statement precedes the final two pages which details those who offered financial help, and those who refused. Nora would have the option to remove these pages before sharing the letter with outsiders.*

5   *The Herlihys were from Knockskagh.*

6   *When considering the oft demonstrated closeness of the McCarthy and Keane relatives, it is remarkable that Patrick McCarthy had to turn to outsiders for a loan.*

7   *The tradition in Ireland, and carried to America by the emigrants, was to sit up through the night with the body of the deceased. The last such "night watch" I personally recall was that of my grandmother, Nora McCarthy Donovan, in October 1953. She was waked from her home, and the male family and friends sat in the kitchen through the ight.*

8   *"Your loving Father and Mother, Patrick and Kate McCarthy."*

9   *Curley Connolly and his sister, Peggy, of Cappanabohy.*

Document M37
15 February 1897 – Mary Ann Donovan,[1] Lowell, Mass, to Nora McCarthy, Haverhill, Mass.

Lowell, Mass.
February 15th, '97

Dear Nora,

I suppose you have by this time forgotten me. I would have written long ago but I lost the address so I felt bad but to my surprise yesterday when I went in to my trunk I found it inside in a little box, which you may be sure I sought for eagerly.

Dear Nora, I would be more than anxious to see ye. Anna McCarthy,[2] I mean Maggie's sister, it is she that works in Carters. Now I mean to let you no I am after leaving their. I am working now by meself with a family by the name of Bagshaws.[3] I can see Anna McCarthy at any time.

She would like to see Teady ["Tady," i.e. Tim McCarthy]. It is not so far to think ye would not come and then we will settle in. She is more than anxious to have ye come up. Tim[4] tells me to have yere brother come. He would like to [be] going down [there].

Dear friend, let me no if it is long since you had a letter from home. I had a letter a few days ago. They or quiet well and wishes to be remembered to ye. Dear Nora, let me no how do you like the weather or how or ye enjoying yourselves. I ave noting strange or new to tell you of save only we enjoy good health hoping ye can say the same.

I must now finish by giving our best love to all hoping to see ye soon. Good bye for the present from your fond friend, Mary A
  Address: Mary A. Donovan
  18 Wilson St.
  Lowell, Mass
  Wright soon and tell me all the newses XXXXXX

ENDNOTES

1   *Mary Ann Donovan, the daughter of Timothy and Mary (Driscoll) Donovan of Bawnfune, was born in December, 1877. There were at least seven children in the family. Five of the seven came to Boston, one died young, and the eldest, Patrick, inherited the family farm in Bawnfune. Mary Ann wrote her letters in a very idiosyncratic manner. She capitalized the initial letter of each line of writing, but not the initial letter of each sentence. Her spelling is often phonetic, and the general tone is of a poorly educated young woman, not at all like the letters Nora received from her similarly-aged friends, and her young relatives who came from the same neighborhood. On the other hand, her handwriting is very well formed and legible. There are five letters in the McCarthy Collection from Mary Ann, dating from 15 February 1897 to 17 January 1898. Her letters have been transcribed with the original spelling but without the unorthodox capitalization.*

2   *Anna/Hanna and Maggie McCarthy were the daughters of James and Bridget McCarthy from the Leap area. They were the nieces of the oft-cited "Mrs. John McCarthy of Leap."*

3   *Mary Ann was a servant for Walter and Margaret Bagshaw, immigrants from England. The household included several children, and Walter's widowed mother at the time of the 1900 Federal Census. Bagshaw was a manufacturer of steel pins.*

4   *Timothy Donovan, older brother of Mary Ann, was born 6 October 1873. The two immigrated to Boston on the S. S. Catalonia, arriving 1 May 1896.*

Document M38
17 March 1897 – Mary Ann Donovan, Lowell, Mass, to Nora McCarthy, Haverhill, Mass.

Lowell, Mass.
March 17 1897

Dear Nora,

I received your kind & most welcome letter in the 29 inst. & was more than delighted to get. Glad to learn by it that ye or enjoying such good health as the writing of this note leaves us at present.

Dear Friend, I hope you will excuse me for delaying an answer to your letter so long but I would have written sooner but I was waiting if I'd get a letter from Nora Hayes but I did not. Let me no if you did. Tim is telling me to tell ye to tell your brother be on the lookout for a place for him. He is going to leave in a few weaks. He has to be up at 3 o'clock every morning.[1] He also tells me to have ye come up some Sunday. Hanna McCarthy wishes to be remembered to ye.

Dear Nora, let me no if you got the shamrock for Patrick's day or had ye to work. We had to. Or did ye enjoy yerselves any. I got plenty to do. I don't be idle. Let me no if ye sees any of the neighbors ye no or how is your fellow or what about Tim's girl.

Dear Nora, I had a letter the 15ᵗʰ of March & the shamrock. They or all well so far, thank god.

Dear Nora, I have notin [nothing] strange or new to tell ye of since I wrote you last. Wright me a long letter & tell me all the newses. I must finish with love to all. So good by from your loving friend, M. A.

To Nora, In fair and stomy weather, I am your friend for ever. M. Address as before – 11 Wilson St., Lowell, Mass.

Give my best regards to Tim, Ellie and in particular yourself. Also your other sister and also James and Tim is sending theirs and Hanna McCarthy. Good bye. XXX

ENDNOTES

1   *Tim Donovan was a farm laborer in Tewksbury, a town adjacent to the city of Lowell.*

DOCUMENT M39

[11 April 1897][1] – Mary Ann Holland[2], Boston, Mass. to Nora McCarthy, Haverhill, Mass.

Boston
Sunday

Dearest Friend Nora,

I received your welcomed letter on last Friday 2 weeks. I was more than proud to hear from you. I wrote to you and Ellie from Taunton[3] the week after we parted [in 1895] and my letter came back to me. I was very much disappointed to think I should loose you and Nelly. But you bet I feel glad again. I am not only 7 months in Boston, my sister is out just a year from this day week.[4] And she did not like Taunton at all. So she wrote to Ireland to some of our cousins and got another Cousin's address. So she wrote here to them and then we both come on to Boston. Our Cousins live in Charlestown. 'Tis there we were going when we met John Collins.[5] We met him in Chelsea going to Charlestown on the car. I knew him the minute I saw him. So I asked him if he was the same fellow and he said yes. The first thing I asked him was about ye and he told me he would get your address from his sister for me. So I never saw him since though I often tried hard to, just for the sake of find ye out. So I am more than glad we are going to be good old friends again.

Dear Nora, I like this country pretty good though I got to work hard enough. I lived in one place while I was in Taunton, a Doctor's house, and when I got to Boston I got another Dr. and I am there still. 'Tis my Cousin Mary's[6] [address] I gave to John Collins & I did not know whether I would like my place or not. But I did. It's to Mary the letter came and she brought it to me, so it was alright. Now, Dear Nora, I am very anxious to see you and Nellie. I would go to see you some time soon if I only knew the way or perhaps ye could come to see me. When you write again you please tell me what to do. Jamesy Donovan[7] must have done pretty well and to have a brother and sister out since.[8] Say, Nora, you keep that brother of yours for me that is if any one else aint got him already. You can hardly read this so I am very troubled with my eyes[9] and I did not write this ever so long. 'Tis Katie writes for me.

Well, I must conclude with fondest love to you and Dear Nelly, from your old friend, Mary Holland. Good bye XX Write soon, Nora.

ENDNOTES

1   *Date determined by postmark on envelope.*

2   *Mary Holland had been a co-passenger on the S. S. Pavonia in 1895 with Nora and Ellen McCarthy. She was born April 1876 to Tim and Ellen (Deasy) Holland from Lislee Parish, Courtmacsherry, Co. Cork. This is an area east of the town of Clonakilty. It is possible that Mary's mother was related to the Dacey/Deasy cousins of the McCarthys. Mary Holland is the only one of Nora's correspondents who did not come from the Leap area. In the 1900 Federal Census, Mary was a servant in the home of Margaret McNamara, the proprietor of a bake shop in Charlestown, Mass. There were five bakers including the proprietor's son, and a saleswoman in the bake shop, along with Mary, and all lived with their employer at 60 Hershey Street, City Square, Charlestown.*

3   *Taunton is in southeastern Massachusetts, near Fall River and New Bedford.*

4   *Katie Holland arrived on the S. S. Gallia in April 1896.*

5   *There was a John Collins on the same ship as Nora and Mary. He was 25, a laborer from Rosscarbery, Cork and was going to his brother in Norwood, Mass.*

6   *Mary's cousin was Mary Connolly of Taunton. It was to her that Mary Holland first went when she arrived in America.*

7   *James "Jamesy" Donovan, born in 1869, was the older brother of Mary Ann Donovan. He was also on the S. S. Pavonia with the McCarthys and Mary Holland.*

8   *Jamesy paid the passage for his sister Mary Ann and his brother Timothy in 1896.*

9   *There is a photograph in the McCarthy Collection of a young woman wearing eye glasses. She is wearing a dress with leg-of-mutton sleeves, a style that appeared in 1895 and disappeared rather soon. The timing, the   style, and the glasses, suggest that this could be a photograph of Mary Holland.*

Document **M40**

20 April 1897 – Mary Ann Donovan, Lowell, Mass, to Nora McCarthy, Haverhill, Mass.

Lowell, Mass.
April 20, '97

Dear friend Nora,

I hope your goodness will pardon me for not answering your kind letter before now but I left my place so I did not feel like writing until I'd no where I'd be to receve your letter.

Dear Nora, I am now working in a family of 4, 2 children & the father & mother. His name is O'Donnell.[1] He lives in Mt Vernon St. They or quiet [quite] particular & hard to be pleased. I am getting good pay, 4 dollars a week. They or a toney kind of people. I am not quiet sure will I stay their yet or not.

Dear Nora, leave me no if Tim is working by this time. As for my brother Tim, he is in the same old tack as usual. And so is James. They all wishes to be remembered to ye. Tim is getting 25 dollars a month now[2] but still he don't care to be their because they don't mend any of his clothes at all. Why don't ye all come up sum Sunday. The Sundays or so fine now. I'd have gone down only for leaving.

When you write let me no when ye or coming up. Anna McCarthy tells ye to come. She is longing to see ye. Ye can come to Carters & we will all meet their as I am not sure of my place yet. The number is 946 Middlesex St. Dear Nora, remember us to all enquiring friends. Leave me no how did you enjoy yourself Easter Sunday, and also Tim. Tell me all the newses. Write soon. You address your letter to Mary A. Donovan, 168 Shaw St.,[3] Lowell, Mass. So, good by. Hoping to see ye soon, from your friend, M. A. Good by. XXX

ENDNOTES

1   *Constantine O'Donnell, 88 Mt. Vernon St., Lowell, was a dry goods merchant.*

2   *This figure compares most favorably with Mary Ann's four dollars a week, which she considered good pay.*

3   *This is the address of Mary Anne's cousin, James Donovan, to whom she and her brothers came when they immigrated. This elder James Donovan, the son of James and Kate Donovan, was born in Ireland in August 1860 and came to America in 1870. He married Jane Mahoney, daughter of Cornelius and Fannie, in 1885 and had three children by the time of the 1900 Federal Census. James was a signalman with the railroad and owned his own home, 0which seems to have been a landing place for a number of relatives from the Leap area.*

Document M41

[3 May 1897] – Mary Holland, Boston, Mass, to Nora McCarthy, Haverhill, Mass.

Boston [across the top of the back side is the address: 78
Lexington St., East Boston]
Sunday

My Dear Nora

I received your Welcomed letter on last Thursday week. Please excuse me for not answering it sooner. I could not help it as I am very busy house-cleaning.

Dear Nora, I am very glad that you and Ellie are well in health. How is your sister that is married? I guess I heard you speak of her on the Ship Coming out. Well, Nora, you know I would not have gall enough to sit for my picture as it would surely break the glass. My Mother is asking for it this long time but she will have to wait until I get good looking.

Dear Nora, if you will, please tell me how I would get out to ye. I might go some Sunday I would have off. Nora, do you remember Tim O'Brien that was coming out with us?[1] I met him in Charlestown a month ago. He is working there and he looks fine. I was more than surprised when I met him. He knew me the minute he saw me, but I could not think at first where I saw him. I was telling him about you and Ellie last Thursday. He said he would like to see ye very much. He is the same jolly fellow all the time.

Well, Nora I am very sorry this day is wet as I was going down to the Cunard Wharf[2] this afternoon. There is a boat coming in and I would like to see them landing. Its most 2 years since we got here ourselves.

Well, Nora, my cousin that's married in Charlestown – that's Mrs. Gleeson[3] – has twin babies since this day week, a boy and girl and she and them are doing fine. She has 4 children now. Nora, the little babies are lovely. I hope this will find you and Ellie and all enjoying good health & I am, thank God.

I must conclude with fondest love to all,
from Mary Holland to Nora McCarthy

ENDNOTES

1   *Tim Brien was a fellow passenger on the S. S. Pavonia. He listed himself as a 22 year old laborer from Castletown Beare, Cork. This village is on the Beara Peninsula, the westernmost corner of County Cork. He had paid his own fare and planned to join his brother, Dan, in Charlestown, Mass.*

2   *The Cunard Wharf was on the East Boston waterfront. Going to the wharf to see the newest arrivals from home seems to have been something of a social occasion.*

3   *Ellen and William Gleeson, Irish immigrants, lived with their three children on Ferrin St., Charlestown in 1900 when the Federal Census was taken. Three other children had died, including the twins born in 1897. William was a freight handler for the railroad. Tim O'Brien, mentioned above, lived around the corner from the Gleesons on Chelsea St., in a boarding house along with his brother Jeremiah. They, too, were freight handlers for the railroad.*

DOCUMENT **M42**
17 May 1897 – Patrick and Kate McCarthy, Ballinlough, Leap to children, Bradford and Haverhill, Mass.

Ballinlough Leap
May 17th 1897

My Dear Children,

I received your very welcome letter on the 10th which gave each of us both and your friends westward great pleasure to hear of your welfare. As for my part — that is Julia — I thought to write twenty times to discover what caused the delay in answering or if in case anything offensive being enclosed in my letter.[1] 1 beg forgiveness as I should not have done so to my Dear Cousins on that distant land, but Thank God, your Poor Father and Mother are easy now as they are easily put to trouble fearing of troubles, even so, if such things should happen, God's Holy will must be at home and foreign.

Dear Nora and Tim, they received your money all safe and are well contented now but before the letter they were troubled day and night, no rest but dreaming of someone or the other of ye, and more especially of Ellie, thinking she appeared to him and could not make enough of her at all, but now he is content in finding ye are enjoying good Health, thank God, as they are at present, but old people must complain as the age is wearisome.

Now, poor Tim, I wish to tell you about this year. Your Father have the cottage field planted with potatoes this time in account of his illness, as I have foretold you in my former letter, but is recovered from that horrible pain. Thank God. So he is commencing to cut the turf, today is the first, and should pay 5 shillings more in addition and should pay up the sum before entering into business as the Bog Master is very strict these days.

Dear Nora, don't spare Mrs. Donovan's happiness or her appearance or her husband's or child's appearance, also Ellie or how she looks. She, that is mother, is for one glimpse of their countenance, and I hope Tim will send home his shadow. I am longing for a peep of the royal family just as well as your affectionate Mother. As for you, Nora, I hope you wont fail in doing so when summer sets in.

Dear Nora, your mother is praying for ye as ye sent the present when most kneeded as poor People has many calls and from which reason you can easily understand and they kneed your aid for some future time as the property is but small[2] and they are getting quite old you must know. And for Uncle Pad, he is very stooped now with sorrow I expect. He think he is quite alone since Poor Katie died, may the Lord have mercy on her Poor soul, Amen.

Dear Tim, you can see your Neighbouring boys. Jerem. John[3] is gone from Bawnfune. He sailed from Queenstown on the 10th May and Patk. Hayes a week before.[4] James Whooley and Nora McCarthy of Maulnigarra is leaving next Thursday morning for Yonkey land.[5]

Mother wish to tell you that Big Den Kean's mother was buried 3 weeks ago[6] after all illness and there is no hopes of Jerry Lawler's recovery.[7] He is confined to bed and is very low. Now as there is any word about Ellie's letter? They will be expecting it day and night as tell her write a few lines soon to ease them for their good. I ask this request and they may be settled in mind.

So now I must come to a conclusion by sending our best wishes to Mrs. Donovan and Husband and Agnes, Ellie and Tim, and especially yourself, Nora, so a fond Good bye from Father and Mother and Julia to their children and Julia's Cousins.

Excuse writing. Write soon in some shape.

ENDNOTES

1   *This refers to a letter sent by Julia to Nora, dated 2 February 1897 for which only an empty envelope survives.*

2   *According to the official Continuing Valuations for 1900, Patrick McCarthy's cottage and small garden were rated at only one pound five shillings for about two rods of property. In contrast, his brother Michael, who inherited the family homestead, was rated at nine pounds ten shillings for over twenty-two acres of land.*

3   *Jeremiah Donovan was the son of the late John Donovan and his widow Catherine Hurley Donovan of Bawnfune. Jeremiah, born 12 December 1871, sailed on the S. S. Cephalonia 9 May 1897. He boarded with his sister Ellen (Mrs. Patrick) Driscoll, So. Boston. His initial immigration seems to have been in 1892.*

4   *Patrick Hayes, born 20 September 1873, was the son of Patrick and Norry Hayes of Ballinlough and brother of Norah/Noney Hanes. He sailed on the S. S. Pavonia and arrived in Boston 2 May 1897. His passage was paid by his sister, Norah Hayes, Williams St., Roxbury. Coincidentally, on the same ship was Dan Donovan's niece, Julia Hodnett, from Drishane on the Mizen Peninsula. (See Donovan Letters). Three other Hodnett sisters had preceded her to Haverhill, Mass.: Katie, Mary Ann/Mamie, and Ellen.*

5   *No James Whooley/Wholey was found on the 1897 shipping lists, but in May 1901 a John Wholey from Leap is listed as going to Providence, R. I., to his brother James Wholey. Others in his family to go to Providence were Maggie, in 1894 and Bridget in 1904. The Whooleys were from Knockskagh. Norah McCarthy, 22, who listed her home address as Skibbereen, sailed on May 20, 1897 to her sister Ellen in Boston. She was the daughter of Jeremiah and Mary McCarthy of Maulnigarra, which is two townlands west of Ballinlough.*

6   *Ellen Hayes Keane, wife of John. No report of her death could be found in the Ross or Kilmacabea (the Leap Area) Registration Districts.*

7   *Probably Jeremiah Lawlor of Tullig. No death notice found.*

DOCUMENT M43
14 June 1897 – Patrick and Kate McCarthy, Ballinlough, Leap to Nora McCarthy and siblings, Bradford and Haverhill, Mass.

Ballinlough
June 14th 1897

Dear Nora, etc.

I received your very welcomed letter on Saturday morning which gave us pleasure to hear from you and to know that ye are enjoying that great blessing, good health, T. G., as we are improved something better than in former days, hoping to be better with your help and God's Help.

Now Nora, these are your Father's words.

Dear Nora, Mother heard nothing about the Funeral until we heard her prayed for at last Mass the following Sunday.[1] They sent her no account of her death so they know nothing about their doings. Mother is very glad ye heard from Dennie[2] as he troubled her very much lately and as for Ellie and Mary she don't blame them for not writing as they may be troubled otherwise, but you can do the whole thing in writing. As for Tim, he grew very careless too soon and ought write a few lines in your letter as the old people would like each of ye would write to them. Ye are in their prayers day and night fearing of any illness as they can't see ye as usual.

Dear Nora, it is at Carrigeeny he cut the turf.[3] Tim knows the place, and have the horse still and the two goats. They are like cows for them. They done away with the dogs as the company left them. They grew careless since the company left them. Their prayer is how are the Americans, the crathers.[4]

Dear Nora, Maria Lawler and Willie of Tullig and Ellie Daley, cousins, and Pat[5] left for America on last Tuesday. They sailed on Wednesday. Maria carried your address to write to you. Well, Nora, she looked like death as is the old custom with people when leaving the old homes.[6]

Dear Nora, we are well in health, T. G., but I am always droll as you see me before you left. As for Denis Hayes they are splendid.[7] Mary is as large as ever as you often talked of her fat cheeks. If you could see herself and Ellie they are as fat as fools.[8] Don't say anything about them in your next letter that I have said, fearing they would chance to see it, but I would tell you anything I could but you are far from me. Tell Tim I always thinks of how he used stretch his long legs on the settle and talk fine and soft.[9]

Nora dear, Father[10] forced me to write these few lines and if it is any insult I am not to blame. He says he need some little portion from each of you for some time to come as his help cannot be much to free some troubles that still remain due. You can keep this private from those you don't wish to know their wants.

So now I must come to a conclusion by sending my best love and for Father and your Mother and my Father and Mother and each of your friends wishes ye well, and for my part, Nora, I can't express what their wishes for ye, as there is a terrible bad report of America and Ireland, God be praised, no demand for butter, slack price on everything lately, but you can understand how things stand from that effect.

To Norah and Company. Good bye. No more at present from Your Father and Mother and Julia Cousin.

Write soon.

Endnotes

1   *Probably a reference to Ellen Hayes Keane of Ballinaclough, wife of John Keane. She had died in late April 1897.*

2   *Denis McCarthy from Pennsylvania, the McCarthys' second son.*

3   *The townland of Carrigeeny is northwest of Ballinlough. As Julia reported in the previous letter, Patrick McCarthy was cutting turf there.*

4   *"The crathers:" the creatures, a common expression in Ireland.*

5   *Maria and William Lawler, of Tullig, left Queenstown aboard the S. S. Aurania on 9 June 1897 and arrived in New York City on 17 June. Maria, 20, a servant, and Willie, 18, a student, were going to Buffalo to their uncle Judge P. W. Lawler. See letter from Katie McCarthy dated 1 August 1895 about Judge Lawler's visit to Leap. Ellen Daley, 23, and Patrick Daley, 19, also from Tullig, sailed with the Lawlers. Their four names follow one another on the shipping list. Ellen was a servant and Pat a laborer. They were also going to Buffalo to their brother Daniel whose address was the same as Judge Lawler.*

6   *There is a suggestion in Julia's comment that the American Wake custom was fading, and considering how often friends who had gone to America came home for visits, the separation was not as permanent as it had once been.*

7   *Denis and Ellen Collins Hayes lived in Ballinlough, near Uncle Michael.*

8   *Mary Hayes, born in 1877, and Ellen Hayes, born in 1881, were daughters of Denis and Ellen Hayes, and childhood chums of Nora McCarthy.*

9   *A settle was a long wooden bench with a high back, often including storage space beneath the seat. Other friends who corresponded with Nora made similar comments about Tim stretching his long legs in front of the fire. He was well over six feet tall, a well built, fine looking man. Unfortunately, the only picture available of him was taken just before he died of tuberculosis in 1909.*

10   *Refers to Nora's father, Patrick McCarthy, not Julia's own father, Michael McCarthy.*

DOCUMENT M44
25 July 1897 – Patrick and Kate McCarthy, Ballinlough, Leap to Nora McCarthy and Company, Bradford and Haverhill, Mass.

Ballinlough Leap PO
July 25th 1897

Dear Nora and Company,

We received your very welcomed letter a week ago, glad to learn from it that ye are enjoying that great blessing good Health, T. God, as we are only middling. Your poor Father and Mother is not strong, you must understand, so she fancy you will come home to see after herself, and poor Uncle says you won't forget him. You will come soon, that his idea all along.

Dear Nora, tell Tim that John was at the Mihill with his Father as a man.[1] The weather is very wet. I expect its very little turf can be saved this year, and the gardens are blighted very early. I fear poor people will be in distress as they will have but little satisfaction after their labour.

Dear Cousins, I am sorry to tell you that we are burying our friends very fast of last days. Poor Tady Donovan[2] have parted with his "little woman" I call her. Uncle Dennie's Mary[3] was buried on the 26th of June and leaves her Husband and little family to mourn her loss. She have been lost in child's birth so you must feel sad and each of you over the matter. We have only to pray for our deceased friends. Poor Katie and Mary, may they rest in peace. Amen.

Dear Nora, your parents haven't much blame to Tim as there is an awful report of America and lots of people coming back this year some of the sorts.

Now, Nora, Mickey did not write to you yet as he is waiting for time and to have some new news for you as he can't make use of his tongue in person, ye should have a long conversation. I have no more to say for him. I haven't seen him this day at all. I must tell you he is a great old browel[4] as you had seen him, no change, but as you have known we are all well so are all our neighbors as you would wish them. Dear Nora, some of them are getting very stylish. I wish you could see them, you would laugh.

Dear Nora and Ellie, your parents are very thankful for your kindness to them and that's how you will encourage them a little now and then, as they have no other consolation in this life but a few lines and a few dollars on and off, then they would be something. They would be satisfied to hear from ye surely and troubled if you delay long without writing.

So now my Dear Cousins I have no more to say at present but your Father and Mother and each of us sends our best wishes and respects to each of you and especially to poor Agnes. To Cousin Nora and Company, Good Bye XXXXXX

ENDNOTES

1   *There were a few young lads named John in Knockskagh who would be about the age to begin harvesting work with their father, including John Williamson (age 7 in 1897), John Wholley (age 8) and John Donovan (age 11). The m;ost likely reference is to John Donovan, the nearest neighbor. The "mihill" was a form of Irish communal, or cooperative, labor.*

2   *Katie Burns Donovan, wife of Timothy.*

3   *Uncle Denis McCarthy and his wife Ellen Mahony had a daughter, Mary, on 29 July 1867 in Ballinlough. Neither her marriage nor her death notice have been found.*

4   *"Browel:" a grouch, a complainer, difficult to live with.*

Document M45
17 August 1897 – Kate Monohan, Dorchester, Mass, to Nora McCarthy, Haverhill, Mass.

Dorchester, Mass
Aug. 17 – 97

My Dearest Nora,

Just a few lines to let you know that I received your welcome letter. Was much pleased to hear from you & more especially to learn from your letter of an increase in the population.[1] Please congratulate Mr. & Mrs. Donovan from me on the birth of their daughter Katie. I hope she will long enjoy her name. I cannot tell you on this cold paper how overjoyed I was in learning from your letter that your dear Sister Mary was all over her troubles, [smudge on paper]. Please excuse this beauty spot, accidents happens a lot. Please pass her my best regards to her & tell her I am proud of her good news. Give my love to Tim & Nellie & Agnes & not forgetting Mr. Donovan & all the Haverhill folks.

Sister Maggie & B[rother] Patsy are well & wishes to be remembered to all also B[rothers] Michael and Connie. I am to inform you that I was down in Connecticut to see Brothers Michael & Connie last Sunday. They are feeling fine. They are sending you all their best regards & especially to Tim as they had been such chums to home. Connie is as fat as a little pig but has grown very little it seems to me. I have not seen Nora Hayes yet. When are you coming to Boston?

307 Norfolk St., Dorchester, Mas

I guess I have all said for this time so I will close by sending you all our best wishes & one wish from Katt and here it is.

If in the storm of life you need an umbrella,

May you have to uphold it a handsome young fellow.

Good Bye, Nora dear.

ENDNOTES

1   *Catherine Marion Donovan was born to Mary McCarthy and Dan Donovan in Bradford on 7 August 1897. She was their second daughter.*

Document M46
6 October 1897 – Patrick and Kate McCarthy, Ballinlough, Leap to Nora McCarthy, Haverhill, Mass.

Ballinlough
October 6th 1897

Dear Nora

We received your letter and money alright and we are very glad how ye are all enjoying good health as we are ourselves at present, thanks be to God. Well, we are very thankful to yourself and Ellie for your good present. We are glad how Mary and family are so well. We are surprised why Tim is not writing to us. When you will see him tell him there is a great failure in the crops this year. The poor people cannot live this year at all without the potatoes. They are scarcely worth digging them at all.

Well, I am sure you will be surprised to hear about the death of James Hayes' wife. She was buried just about the time we got your letter the second of the month. She died in child's birth. She was delivered of a young daughter but the child is living[1] and you may bet she had a large funeral.

Dear Nora, let me know is Tim boarding with Mary still and also let me know what sort of a job has he but we expects to hear from himself soon. Well, I have no more to say at present so I will conclude by sending you all our best love and wishes for the present.

Write soon again and tell us all the newses.

Dear Nora, anyone don't come to us any night but the two old slippers [chums]. 1 suppose you know them of old but Denny[2] spent last winter nights with us while he was at home but he is with Jem Donovan the school teacher now at work.[3]

I remain your affect. Cousin Julia.

From Father and Mother.

ENDNOTES

1   *Mary Collins Hayes, wife of James of Ballinlough, died in childbirth 1 October 1897. She was the daughter of John Collins of Cullane. She and James were married 13 February 1892. They had a son, Patrick, born 4 March 1896, and named for his paternal grandfather. Her baby must have died subsequently, for she is not listed in the 1901 Census of Ireland.*

2   *Denny Gallivan, mentioned numerous times in previous letters.*

3   *James Donovan was the National School teacher for the Knockskagh School.*

DOCUMENT M47
9 October 1897 – Mrs. Katherine McCarthy, Ballinlough, Leap to Norah and Ellen McCarthy, Haverhill, Mass.

October 9, 1889 [sic]
Ballanlough

Dear Norah and Ellen,

I was very thankful to ye for the money ye sent me of late. Though it did not go far for one but it pleased the people so far. But I do not wish to be asking people to be stating my case to you as they think a pound should go further for me than for themselves but the most of that went to pay the rent for me.

Dear Norah, don't blame me for writing this as I don't wish to say much. The whiskey I took from Maggie Collins[1] for the wakes she put 1 [pound] cost on me along with the price of it. I am very glad to hear Mary was well. I was very troubled about her. I am very thankful to hear you called the baby after my Dear Katie, the heavens be her bed. Take good care of her as it was Katie broke my heart. The people here are surprised at Tady if he could help is not doing more than he is. Perhaps I am too hard but I cant do it as I had nothing to make a penny for me. My hens died and you are aware my little cow died. It is easy to put a poor man down.

Dear Norah, if possible to send 3 pounds for the 14 November as it will be calling on me. We should be very thankful to the people who stood to us in sickness and in trouble particularly in death. Dear Norah, let me know how is Agnes and her Father and Mother and the Babie, also Tim, Ellie and yourself.

Dear Norah, don't blame me as you know I have no one to tell my case to only you and you know I did not put any stop to you all when I had it. Your Father and Myself are both getting old and can do nothing for one another. Your Father and the old horse are every day in the bog doing nothing but cussing the bad Weather. He cant get the turf dry. He cant do anything to turn a penny.

Dear Norah, don't show this to anyone but you can do as you like yourself and I don't like sending a poor Mouth. Dear Norah, Mrs. Collins on the Keay[2] wishes to know something about her son, if ye know anything about him let us know in the next letter. I must finish with love to all. Your Affectionate Mother Kath.

McC arthy. [**The following note was included with the above letter**]

Dear Norah,

Just a few lines to let you know I wrote these few lines for your Mother. As you know we always left our business known to one another. I cant ban [?] the rest of the doing [?]. I must tell you I am very comfortable now. I wished you were near me. We would often have a bit of fun. Dear Norah, let me know if ye know anything about George or Jack[3]. I cant say any more at present but pray for me. Your fond friend Mary George[4] Otherwise Mrs John Hurley Bridge St[5] Skibbereen

ENDNOTES

1   *Margaret Collins Hurley, 27, was a shopkeeper in Leap Village. Her husband, Jeremiah, was a baker. Also in the household were Michael and Thomas Collins, nephews.*

2   *Keay: a quay, or wharf. The quay was the harbor area at Leap Village. Would this Mrs. Collins be the mother of Maggie Collins Hurley?*

3   *George McCarthy, brother of Mary George, was born 10 May 1867 to George McCarthy and Catherine Herlihy in Curragh, Skibbereen. George, Sr. was a dairyman. John "Jack" McCarthy was born 2 March 1869. Jack emigrated on the S. S. Pavonia, arriving in Boston on 2 April 1895 where he joined his brother George in Lawrence, Mass. Jack was on the same ship as Ellen and Nora McCarthy, and would have provided them with a male companion not only for the voyage across the ocean, but also for the railroad trip north. Jack's destination, Lawrence, was only two stops from Bradford where Ellen and Nora would depart.*

4   *Mary McCarthy, born 7 March 1857 in Kilmacabea, daughter of George and Kate, was married to John Hurley, a victualler, and son of Charles, also a victualler. The marriage took place at the Skibbereen Cathedral on 21 January 1897. Witnesses were her brother Michael McCarthy and Julia Donovan. Mary George was close to term with her first child when she wrote this letter.*

5   *Mary's mother and five of her brothers were living on Upper Bridge St. ("Bridgetown"), Skibbereen when the 1901 Census of Ireland was taken.*

Document M48
23 October 1897 – Mary Ann Donovan, Somerville, Mass, to Nora McCarthy, Haverhill, Mass.

Summervill, Mass.
October 23rd :97

My Dear friend Nora,

I take the pleasure of writing you those few lines hoping they will find ye in the enjoyment of good health as the writing of this leaves me at present.

Dear friend, I suppose you have by this time forgotten me. I have been often thinking if you were in the same place always so I thought I would wright anyway and to no how my old chum was. I am awful sorry I had not seen any of ye all summer. Leave me no how Tim is getting along. I am living in Boston since July. I had Tim[1] and Jamesy to see me several times. Tim got a week off & he remained in Boston and we had a great time. Boston is a real nice place. We has lots of fun. Leave me no if ye went to see Maggie C. McCarthy, I mean Mrs. Collins.[2] She has a young baby. Its name is Mary. I had Hanna McCarthy down to see me last Thursday. We were speaking about ye. She's longing to see ye.

Well now, my dear old friend, leave me no how you or enjoying yourself, also Tim & Ellie. Give my best regards to them. Did Nora Hayes write to you since? If so leave me no. Will you please give me her address or do you ever hear anything of the Roes.[3]

I think I must close for the present. Write soon. Send me all the newses. Come down some time yourself & Tim and Ellie.

Good by from your old girl M. A. Donovan.

Good bye XXX

Leave me no how is your best fellow.
Address Mary A. Don, 88 Arlington Avenue[4], Charlestown, Mass.

In fair and stormy weather, I am your love for ever. Mary Anne. rite soon XXX

ENDNOTES

1   *Mary Ann's brother, Tim Donovan, worked on a farm in Tewksbury, Mass. when the 1900 Federal Census was taken. Have yet to locate Jamesy Donovan in that Census.*

2   *Margaret "Maggie" McCarthy, daughter of James and Bridget of Leap, married Jeremiah Collins, son of John and Mary, 6 October 1896. They lived in East Boston where Jerry worked on the docks as a longshoreman.*

3   *As mentioned previously, the Rues/Roes were most likely the five daughters of Jeremiah and Julia (Hegarty) Donovan of Bawnfune. They were not living in that townland when the 1901 Census of Ireland was taken.*

4   *In the 1900 Federal Census, Mary Ann Donovan was a servant at the home of John and Mary Mack and their four children, 79 Concord Avenue, Somerville, Mass. John Mack was a fruit dealer, American born, of Irish parents.*

Document M49

11

November 1897 – Patrick and Kate McCarthy, Ballinlough, Leap to Nora McCarthy, Haverhill, Mass.

Patrick McCarthy
Ballinlough Leap
Novem. 11th 1897

Dear Nora,

I received your fond and welcomed letter on last Holiday[1] which gave us pleasure to hear that ye are enjoying good health, T. G. Mother is more than delighted about Mary and her young family. You could not imagine how she thinks of them children and as you said about their colored hair.[2] She likes them more and more but your Father don't make much of any person with his big purpose so they would like to hear all about ye as far as you can tell them as they dreams of queer things.

Dear Nora, our neighbor James Hayes buried his wife and himself and his people are in the greatest clamor as much as ever now. I must tell you all others are well. As for sister Maggie, she is well and have four children,[3] so is Mary and her three boys.[4] And as you enquired about me, I am as you would wish me. As for Mick, I can't get him to write to you as he have not enough of newses for you.

Dear Nora, 'tis not the Post boy reads the letters for Mother. All the same she have no denial gives them to all the neighbors as they likes to see them, so if there is any thing troubling you write a few lines separate. I mean a small note and I promise you she will keep it safe. 'Tis Dennie Gallivan wrote you the last letter.

Dear Nora and Company, ye should have this letter long ere now but your Poor Mother got a sudden attack on last Wednesday Night, so she delayed writing. As for Father he was very troubled about his poor woman, but she is much better now, Thank God. She got the Doctor.[5] He gave her some medicine and ordered some Brandy and chicken broth, so you must understand your letter was good encouragement to them.

Dear Nora, they are very thankful to Tim for his present after such a long time. All the neighbors were anxious to hear from him and all of them asks was it himself wrote the letter. Why didn't he write a few words to leave us know he lives.

Dear Cousins, Mary George have an increase with two weeks, a young man, but can't call him by name.[6] Father and Mother got the money all safe. I find them in good Courage for the winter as this is a very bad year. Its very few have any spuds. They can't see to dig them. Now your poor Father want to get a decided answer or

if any one of ye will come to see after him. Ellen he asks as he fancy Nora think it soon to come, all the same he makes no choice as he wishes ye all well.

So I have no more to say for this time at present. From Your Father and Mother and from Cousin Julia. To their fond children and Grand Children. Write soon and tell us all the newses.

XXXXXXXXXX to the Children from Mother.

ENDNOTES

1   *"Last Holiday:" All Saints Day, November 1, a religious holy day.*

2   *Julia Agnes Donovan had light blonde hair, and new baby, Catherine Marion, was a strawberry blonde.*

3   *Julia's sister Margaret "Maggie" Hourihane. Her children to that date were Bartholomew/Batt, born*

27 March 1893, Julia born 21 June 1894, Daniel born 3 September 1895, and Patrick born 16 March 1897.

4   *The McCarthys of Tullig.*

5   *The local doctor was Michael O'Driscoll of Leap Village.*

6   *Charles Hurley was born to cousin Mary "George" and John Hurley on 28 October 1897 in Skibbereen.*

Document M50

7 January 1898 – Kate Monohan, Roxbury, Mass, to Nora McCarthy, Haverhill, Mass.

Roxbury, Mass. Friday eve.
Jan 7th – 98

Ever Dear and loving friend,

I now embrace this opportunity of writing those few lines to you hoping this will reach you & sisters in the enjoyment of good health as this note leaves me & Sister at present. Thanks be to God for his blessing to us all.

Dear Nora, I arrived home alright Saturday afternoon at 1:30 PM[1] but felt very lonesome for all my Haverhill folks. I enjoyed my trip very much. I did not go back to Dorchester again. I am going to work Sunday eve where my sister Maggie works. It's a purty hard place but still its quite convenient. I wont have any Car fares to pay. How is Mr. Melody?[2] Have you seen him since? Give him my regards, also to Miss Callaghan & Mrs. O'Connell[3] & to all the folks. How is Patsy Moynihan[4] and Tim? Are they working yet. How is Nellie & Mr. & Mrs. Donovan & Agnes & Baby. I am going to write to Mrs. Donovan as soon as I get a chance.[5] All the Boston folks are well & wishes to be remembered to you all. Mr. & Mrs. Donovan & Baby[6] are well & wishes to be remembered to all. Sister Maggie is well. So is Brother Patsy. I have not seen him since I come back as he has to work so I did not see him.

I cannot think of any more this time so I'll close by sending you our best regards & kind wishes from your friend.

K. A. Monohan 70 Weller St. Roxbury, Mass. Good Bye, write soon

May your future years be even more happy than those of our past is the ardent wish of your Sister Kate

ENDNOTES

1   *Katie Monohan had been visiting Nora McCarthy and family in Haverhill.*

2   *Michael Melody, of English birth but Irish descent, had immigrated from England to Haverhill, Mass., in 1884. He was a plasterer. In 1895 he married Margaret Frances Callahan who immigrated at the age of 12 in 1888 from Co. Cork, Ireland to Haverhill.*

3   *Miss Callaghan is either Margaret Callahan Melody, her sister Bess Callahan who lived with the Melodys, or Julia F. Callaghan who is listed with Nora and Ellen McCarthy, and Delia and Katherine Collins as "Chums" in an old autograph book from the late 1890s. Mrs. O'Connell (Kate Callahan) was the sister of Margaret Melody. She was born in 1870, immigrated in 1877. And married Tim O'Connell in 1893. She had three children by 1898.*

4   *Patsy Moynihan: Patrick Minihane ("Moynahan" in 1900 Census) was Dan Donovan's nephew from Cussivina, Ballydehob, Co. Cork. He was born in 1874 to Julia (Donovan) and John Minihane, immigrated from Ireland to Haverhill in 1894, and married Hannah Sweeney in 1899.*

5   *Kate probably stayed with Dan and Mary (McCarthy) Donovan during her visit to Haverhill.*

6   *Possibly Tim Donovan and wife from Bawnfune. Three possibilities in 1900 Census in Boston.*

Document M51
17 January 1898 – Mary Ann Donovan, Somerville, Mass, to Nora McCarthy, Haverhill, *Mass.*

Jan. 17th, 1897 [sic]
Summervill

My most loving friend,

I received your very welcomed letter in the 9 Ulta and was more than delighted to get. Glad to learn by it that ye or all enjoying good health as the writing of this leaves us at present.

Dear Nora, I hope you will excuse me for not writing before now, but I would have answered your letter but I had a very soar hand. I burned it so it kept me from writing to any one. It is getting better now. I feel ashamed to write but I could not help it so I hope you will excuse me. I am only trying to scribble a few lines to you. I felt so glad when I got your letter. I had been in to Boston before the holidays. To my great surprise who should step up to me but Noney Hayes. We had a long conversation. She asked me to meet her in Grove Hall[1] but I never went. She is in the same old place still.

Dear friend, you made inquiries concerning the wellfair of Maggie McCarthy. I had a letter from her sister a few days before I received yours. She told me that they were well and that would soon have another kid.[2] That is all I know of them.

Dear friend, in regard to the Donovans,[3] I don't know the first thing about them. I never heard a word from them. I mean to tell you I never got my pictures taken since but I intend to. Please Nora, send me one in your next letter also Tim and Ellie if they got theirs taken. Don't forget it.

I will send you mine when I get them taken. Jamesy and Tim[4] or coming to Boston next Sunday. I no they would be glad to see yere pictures if I only could see yourself I would be regoised [rejoiced]. I do be thinking from time to time if we would ever see one another, one hear and the other their. Catherine[5] is coming out in spring. I would love to have you see her also your Tim. She was struck in him. Ask him if he thinks of the dancing he used to have with her before he came out hear. I was not in it with them. I hope, Nora, that you will come to Boston this summer. If so you can write and leave me no. I had a letter from Ellie Collins. She is asking me to go to Wakefield some Sunday. Nora, if you might come down, we would go for the fun of it to see the place. I had been their once before. Well, dear Friend, I think I have told you all I could think of. Write me a long letter and tell me all the newses. Don't forget the pictures. I must finish with love to Tim, Ellie, Mary and in particular my old chum. Good by. Tim and James is sending ye their best love.

Address as before:

M. A. Donovan, 88 Arlington Avenue, Charlestown, Mass. Good by from your true friend M. A.

Write soon.

Excuse scribbling. I hope you can read it.

Good by XX

ENDNOTES

1   *Grove Hall is in the Roxbury section of Boston, where some well-known Irish dance halls were located.*

2   *Maggie (McCarthy) and Jeremiah Collins had no child born in 1898 that was listed on the 1900 Federal Census, so either the Maggie miscarried, or the baby died before 1900.*

3   *This could be another reference to the "Mr. & Mrs. Donovan & Baby" mentioned in the previus letter. Tim Donovan was a cousin of Mary Ann and her brothers.*

4   *Mary Ann's brothers.*

5   *Catherine Donovan, born in 1878, was Mary Ann's sister. She sailed from Queenstown on 4 May 1898 aboard the S. S. Cephalonia to Boston. Her destination was to her sister at 88 Arlington Ave., Charlestown, MA. This was the home of Dennis Harrigan and his family. Dennis had been in America since 1854. This was the first address Mary Ann had given Nora, but was not where she was working when she wrote this letter in 1898.*

DOCUMENT M52

20 January 1898 – Kate Monohan, Boston, Mass, to Nora McCarthy, Haverhill, Mass.

Boston, Mass.
Thursday 1:30 PM
Jan. 20th 1897 [sic]

My Dear Friend,

I now take this opportunity of writing you those few lines hoping this note will reach you and all the folks in as good a state of health as the departure of this note leave me and sister and Brother at present. Thanks be to God for his mercies to us all.

My Dear friend, I received your long wished for letter a week ago. Was much pleased to hear you were all well also Mr. and Mrs. Donovan and Agnes and Baby, and not forgetting Paddy Minihan and his loving girl. I presume he is as deep in love as ever.[1] How is Miss Callaghan and Mr. Melody and Mrs. O'Connell? Give my best regards to them all. How is Nellie and Tim and not forgetting Miss Hodnett[2] my best friend. I had a letter from her a few days ago.

Dear Nora, I am to inform [you] that I changed places. I did not go back to my old [place] at all. She was crazy for giving me a vacation. She said I was purty mean to do anything like that. I like my new place purty well but has to work much harder as there is ten in my family but knowing them so well through Maggie. I do not mind the work so much as if it was a strange place. Will send you that photo when I get a chance. Have all said for this time.

Good Bye.

I hope to see you in Boston soon.

Good Bye, write soon.

Address: K. A. Monohan, 42 Rutland Sq., Boston, Mass.

ENDNOTES

1   *Patrick Minihane, Dan Donovan's nephew, married Hannah Sweeney on October 26, 1899 in Haverhill, Mass.*

2   *Katie, Mamie and Ellen Hodnett, Dan's nieces from Drishane, Co. Cork, were all in Haverhill by this date. The next letter from Kate Monohan makes it clear she is referring to Ellen Hodnett, the most recent of the three to arrive in America.*

Document M53
13 February 1898 – Kate Monohan, Boston, Mass, to Nora McCarthy, Haverhill, Mass.

Boston, Mass.
Sunday eve Feb. 13th : 97 [sic]

My Dear Friend,

I once more take this opportunity of answering your very welcome letter which I received some time ago hoping you will excuse me for not answering it sooner but my dear friend it was owing to a sore hand which I had for a week or two past that I have not answered your letter soon. I burned my four fingers & could not handle my pen for some time but they are all better now with the exception of one which is quite sore yet.

My Dear friend Nora, I hope to see you one week from today. I sincerely hope you wont fail in making your appearance also your sister Ellen & Tim & Mr. Donovan as I know there is no use in asking Mrs. Donovan to come.[1] Tell Patsy Minihane to come also as you will be welcome to bring any body you please with you.

Sister Maggie told me she wrote to Mr. & Mrs. Donovan & asked you all to come. Nora, won't you please see Ellen Hodnett & tell her Maggie want her to come to her wedding. I'll not send you my picture now as you can get it when you come up Sunday. Please write as soon as possible & let me know what train ye will come on. If possible, come Saturday night. Write so we can meet you at the depot.[2] P.S. Michael and Connie are coming in Saturday night 0000000000& also some more of our New Haven friends.

Patsy tells ye be sure and come if not he says he shall never again go to Haverhill. You will enjoy yourself to a great extent because you can see all the folks from Home. I'll not say much this time as I can't write very well with my fingers. I do hope they will be better for Sunday.

Good Bye, love to all. Kisses to Agnes & baby. Your friend till death. Please don't fail in coming. Katie

Address:

K. A. M.
42 Rutland Sq.[3] Boston, Mass.

ENDNOTES

1   *Nora and family were invited to the wedding of Kate's sister Maggie to Matthew Donovan, son of Timothy and Mary (Driscoll) Donovan of Bawnfune, on 20 February 1898. Nora's sister, Mary, would not be expected to attend as she had a six month old infant, and a four year old child to care for. Matthew Donovan, born 29 July 1865, was a brother to Mary Ann, Jamesy and Tim Donovan.*

2   *The Boston & Maine train station in Bradford, Mass. was at the foot of the street where Dan and Mary Donovan lived. The train would take them directly to North Station in Boston.*

3   *Rutland Square is in Boston's South End between Tremont Street and Columbus Avenue.*

Document M54
15 April 1898 – Patrick and Kate McCarthy, Ballinlough, Leap to Nora McCarthy, Haverhill, Mass.

Ballinlough
April 15th, '98

My Dear Daughter Norah,

It is time for me to answer your most kind and welcomed letter which I received the 2nd Apr. and did not get it cashed until the 9th. I did not like to write until I would get it changed. I was indeed very thankful to you and more than glad to hear that ye were all enjoying such good health as this leaves us all at present, Thank God.

The weather we are enjoying at present is very fine. We had a little rain about a week ago but it did not continue long. We got very fine weather for planting the potatoes so that most of the people have them planted now.

Norah, there did a lot of young people die in this place this year so that we don't enjoy ourselves at all like we used in days gone by. James Williamson[1] a nice fellow died from the bite of a mad dog. That what the doctor said was the cause of his death. He was only from Friday evening until Monday morning sick when he died. The priest was also with him.

Poor Norah Paddy[2] was buried the Sunday after P.'s day.[3] She was four or five weeks sick. She had great cough so that she did not stand it long. We were all very sorry and lonesome for them so that we don't have dance or anything now. A lot more of old people died this March in this place. They are too numerous to be mentioning them to you. Kate Minihane, Denny Cremeen's wife,[4] was also bitten by a mad dog but the priest, Father Cunningham, ordered her to go to Paris to the head doctors and she did and is alright now. The McCarthys from Skibbereen are all very well so also is your Uncle Michael and family and Gran family are very well too.

I am very sorry for Tim to be so slack in work. All his comrade boys are always asking about him. I did not see Danny Murnane since Tady went until the 2nd of January last he came to see us. It was on a Sunday. It rained very hard the same day so that he renewed my sorrow as fresh as ever. When he came in he did not speak one word for about an hour. I am very glad to know that Mary and her husband and family are well and to hear that the baby is growing so big and fat and also that Tim, Ellen and yourself are well also. I hope the work is better by this time. There is very bad reports of it. This place is getting very lonesome.

You knew Jem Forsham. He is gone to Australia since the day James Williamson was buried. The morning Katie died he was called into the police but he did not pass. He had to come again but he is home since until now. He is gone for good so that there will be soon nobody here. Well, surely Norah, you would laugh if you hear Norry calling James wife Danny Mom.[5] She is scolding them every day. She did not lose the trade yet. I was very sorry that you did not see Nonie Hayes when you went to Boston. Julia Hourihan[6] wrote home and I was very glad to hear that you were so big and fat as she said in her own letter when she saw ye in the wedding and Tim. Nora, Hanna Collins,[7] an old comrade of yours, asked your address and Mary her sister got it yesterday and she left Hanna's to me for you. I'd like to send some nice present to Agnes, and, Norah, tell me for I am ignorant of it myself.

I'll be expecting to hear from ye for Leap Fair[8] again. No wonder for me to be strong, Norah, drinking black tea all the year, but I'll soon have it myself now. Susan and Janey are going to kid soon.[9] Don't be blaming poor Tim for he was nice and kind to his sister and to me. I thought a deal of him. I'd like to have your picture, Norah, and Tim's too. I suppose you have them taken by this for Dennie.

You can keep this letter to yourself if you like. It is I, Ellie Hayes,[10] am writing this to you for Mother. Good Bye from Father + Mother [14 kisses]

ENDNOTES

1   *James Williamson, son of Richard and Ellen Williamson of Knockskagh, died 28 February 1898 of rabies.*

2   *Honoria (Norah) Driscoll, 17, "a weaver's daughter," of Bawnfune, died of phthisis (a severe form of tuberculosis) on 25 March 1898. Her father, Patrick, had predeceased her. Her mother, Mary Donovan Driscoll, reported her death.*

3   *St. Patrick's Day.*

4   *Kate Minihane was the wife of Denis McCarthy of Bawnfune. "Cremeen" is a name for a branch of the McCathy Clan. Mary McCarthy Driscoll, widow of Johnny Bawn Driscoll, was also a "Cremeen."*

5   *Nora "Norry" Hayes of Ballinlough. Her son, James, had married, as his second wife, Kate McCarthy Donovan, on 3 February 1898.*

6   *Julia Hourihane of Ballinlough sailed from Queenstown on the S. S. Cephalonlu on 5 June 1894. Her destination was Portsmouth, N. H. where her sister Maggie lived. Julia was born in Knockskagh 12 September 1875 to Patrick and Kate (Walsh) Hourihane. The Hourihane family was living in Ballinlough in the 1890s.*

7   *Hanna Collins, from Driminidy, Drinagh emigrated from Ireland to New York City aboard the S. S. Brittanic. Her older sister, Maggie, had come from America to accompany her on the ship. They arrived 6 September 1895 and went to Elmira, N. Y. where Maggie and her half-brother, Con, lived.*

8   *Leap Fair was held twice a year, in May and October.*

9   *Susan and Janey were the family goats and, once they had delivered their kids, they would be able to provide fresh milk for Mrs. McCarthy's tea.*

10   *Ellen Hayes was the daughter of Denis and Ellen Hayes of Ballinlough. She was twenty years old when the 1901 Census of Ireland was taken.*

DOCUMENT M55

Hannah Collins wrote more letters to Nora McCarthy than anyone else outside of her family. There are forty-one letters from Hannah to Nora written between May 1898 and October 1900. Another set of letters from Hannah that date from the 1930s and 1940s are in the McCarthy Collection, but are beyond the scope of this narrative. Hannah was the fourth of eight children born to Michael Collins and Mary McCarthy in Driminidy, Drinagh which is a short distance west of Nora's home in Ballinlough, Leap. Her birthday was Christmas 1876. Hannah's great-aunt, Norry Hegarty Driscoll, lived near the McCarthys in Ballinlough and Hannah lived with her for a number of years between the end of her schooling and her departure for America. It was there she became friendly with Nora and her family, and became acquainted with the other young people in the area. It is possible that Hannah, as did Nora, worked in Leap Village, most likely at Sheehan's Hotel. Like Nora, she was a domestic in America and her letters describe both the work demands and the lighter moments of such a life. In addition, Hannah had a boyfriend, Tom Cloake, whom she married in 1901. Thus, her letters are replete with stories of "courting, 1890s style."

12 May 1898 – Hannah Collins, Elmira, N. Y. to Nora McCarthy, Haverhill, Mass.

May 12th, 1898

My Dear Nora,

I received your most kind and welcome letter this morning and was so glad to hear from you as I thought you had forgotten me but I thinks of you all the time.

I wrote home and asked Mary to send me your address but she had not sent it to me. Mary and Patsy[1] has just come out last Tuesday morning. Patsy went home last June. He is a great big man and Mary is a good deal taller than me. She said she was around Ballinlough before she left and she saw your Father and Mother. I suppose they feels quite lonesome. They aint got anybody home with them and I felt awful bad when I heard about poor Katie's death. I hope she is better off. She was always such a nice warm-hearted good girl.

Dear Nora, I am glad you are getting along so nicely. I am sure you are a fine looking girl now. I only wish I could see that Darling sweet face of yours. It would do me lots of good. Give my best love to Tim. How does he like this country? And Ellie and Mary. I remember Ellie seeing her home. Do you go to Mary's house on Sundays and have a nice time?

I am working steady. I am in one place two years and Maggie is working too all the time. Nora, dear, hurry up and have your picture taken as I would be glad to have it. I expect to have mine taken this summer and I will send you one.

Well, my darling Nora, I must finish by saying Good Bye. Write soon again.

Your loving, Hannah

Hannah Collins, 129 East Chemung Place.[2]

ENDNOTES

1   Patrick and Mary Collins, Hannah's siblings, sailed on the S. S. Cymric. It arrived in New York City 9 May 1898. Patsy, who was a United States citizen, had returned to Ireland to accompany his younger sister, Mary, whose fare to America he is listed as paying.

2   In the 1900 Federal Census, this is the address for Nathan Payne, 27, his sister Esther, 23, and his brother Willard, 20. Payne was the Manager of the Payne Machine Company in Elmira.

Document M56
20 May 1898 – Hannah Collins, Elmira, N. Y. to Nora McCarthy, Haverhill, Mass.

Elmira, N. Y.
May 20th, 98

My Darling Nora,

Your very kind and interesting letter reached me a few days ago and I was delighted to hear from you and also to know that you and sisters and Brother were enjoying good health as the date of this letter leave me and the rest of us at present, Thank God.

Nora, dear, I took such pleasure in your letter. It was just fine. It made me think more and more of you and of those happy days when we were together.[1] What a nice time we used to have, but hoping to see you some day or do you ever intend to go home again to see your dear Father and Mother? It is too bad about them to be left all alone in their old days. I am sure you thinks of them many a time. He thought so much of you. Your poor Mother she was so nice. I can never forget her. When you write home send her my best love. It was too bad about all those young people that died around there. It made a great change in the old spot.

I heard James Hayes was married again to a widow woman. He did not think of poor Mary very long.[2] They were all just the same. Did not have much good nature about them. Anything would not break their heart. I wonder if Pake is home yet or do you ever hear from Mary Hayes.[3] Is she out in this country? I suppose Maggie Whooley[4] will send after her. How is your cousin Julia McCarthy or did she get married. Is Jerry and Dennie home yet?[5]

I have never written to poor auntie Norry. I think I am awful mean. I may write and send her a little present soon. My little sister, Nora, is with her now and Mary said she do stay home and not go to school But I told my mother if she did not go to school to take her home and not to have her like I was myself. But I was much older than she was when I went to stay with her. I heard Ellie Driscoll was married.[6] She was home when I come to this country and the night she left they had beer and never told my father and Mother to come.

They did not know she was gone until a week after. Ellie was mean enough to my people after my time with her Grand Mother. Nora, Dear, I am so glad you had such a good time to that wedding but did not feel good the next day when you had to work. I was glad to hear about Julia Hourihan. I remember her well indeed. The little bit of hair made me laugh and the little teeth of hers. But there was nobody at the wedding had a darling face like yours.

Write soon again, Nora. I can't think of any more this time. Will you excuse me, from your loving sister, Hannah. Good Bye.

ENDNOTES

1   Hannah's great aunt, Norry Hegarty, was the immediate neighbor of the McCarthys in Ballinlough. Hannah had lived with her for a period of time before she emigrated.

2   There was only three months between the death of James' first wife and his marriage to his second wife.

3   Patrick ("Packe") Hayes was from Ballinlough. Mary Hayes, the daughter of Denis and Ellen Hayes, was from the same townland. Both had emigrated to Boston.

4   Margaret "Maggie" Whooley was born in the early 1870s to Denis and Julia (McCarthy) Whooley/Wholley of Keamore, Leap. She immigrated to Providence, R. I. in 1894. She was followed by her brothers James (1896) and John (1901) and sister Bridget (1904).

5   Julia, 28, Jerry, 37 and Dennie McCarthy, 35, were three of Uncle Michael's adult children. They were all living at home and unmarried when Hannah wrote this letter.

6   Ellen Driscoll was a cousin of Hannah, and a granddaughter of Norry Hegarty. She had visited Leap in 1895. She married James Enright in Washington, D. C. in April 1899.

Document M57
27 May 1898 – Hannah Collins, Elmira, N. Y. to Nora McCarthy, Haverhill, Mass.

Elmira, N. Y.
May [27], 1898 [date taken from postmark on envelope]

My Own Darling Nora,

Your dear letter I received a few days ago and was delighted to hear from you and also to learn by it that you and sisters and Brother were enjoying good health as the date of this letter leaves me and Maggie and Mary, also Patsy at present, thank God.

Nora, dear, I was surprised when I opened your letter and found that darling face of yours. I think it looks some like you but you are a good deal better looking than that. I know you had it taken when you were a green horn but I guess you look different by this time. I only wish I could see you now. We would have a good talk about the old days we spent together. I thinks of you all the time hoping you do of me just the same.

I am working hard cleaning house every day. I don't like it very well. Mary has gone to work since yesterday. I hope she will like it. She is the same old bold thing yet. She aint got any sense at all. Well, Nora dear, I don't have a very good time. I don't go to any dances. I only been to two since I come out. I don't care to go but every Sunday I go to Mrs. Dempsey's house.[1] You don't know them. Dannie Dempsey that lived near us home, he was a tailor.[2] His mother and sisters are out in this country about ten years. He has got Brothers, too. They are some relation of ours. They do be lots of people to their house on Sundays. We stay there when we aint working. Just like home to us but, Nora dear, you will be surprised to think I got a fellow and he is this country born, too. Aint I smart? He has got light hair and blue eyes. His name is Tom Cloake,[3] so I will have a cloake to keep me warm in the winter nights.[4] Don't you think I'm a great girl? You must tell me about your fellow because I know you got one for they were always crazy about you.

Nora, dear, you wished to know who Ellie Driscoll married. I don't know but I guess its one of the Sullivans.[5] I don't think she sends Aunty Norry much money now. The poor thing is lonesome. You remember how she used to talk about everything to you and said she only live one year more.[6] Give my love to Tadey. I can't call him any other name. Is he just as tall as ever? I suppose he got a girl by this time. Ask him if he will wait for me. I am the same old thing yet. Just as homely as ever. I suppose you never want to go home again. There aint nobody there to make you feel happy. Its often I think of the good time I had to your house and of poor Katie. I cryed when I heard of her death. I hope she is better off.

Well, Nora darling, I must finish by saying Good Bye to you for this time. I remain yours for ever. Hannah XXXXXXXXXXXXXXXXXXXXXXXXXXXX

Write soon again. Excuse bad writing.

ENDNOTES

1   *Ellen Dempsey, 861 Rail Road Ave., Elmira, was born in 1848, emigrated in 1887. She was a widow who had borne twelve children, with nine still alive in 1900. She could not read or write. Three of her children, all born in Ireland, were living with her in 1900 in her rented house.*

2   *Daniel Dempsey, son of Ellen, was living in Driminidy, Drinagh when the 1901 Census of Ireland was taken. There were thirteen inhabitants living in his house.*

3   *Thomas Cloake lived with his widowed mother Bridget and three sisters at 950 Magee Street, Elmira. Bridget was born in 1840 and immigrated to Elmira in 1860. She had borne ten children, eight of whom were still living in 1900. She could read and write and owned a home free of a mortgage. A great-grandson lives in the same house in the present time. Tom, born in New York state in 1870, was an iron worker.*

4   *Hannah will repeat this pun over and again in her letters.*

5   *Elle Driscoll married an Enright, not a Sullivan. Her sister, Nora, who also lived in Washington, D. C. had married a Sullivan.*

6   *Norry Hegarty Driscoll was still alive when the 1901 Census of Ireland was taken. Her age was listed as ninety years.*

DOCUMENT M58
28 May 1898 – Patrick and Kate McCarthy, Ballinlough, Leap to Nora McCarthy, Haverhill, Mass.

Ballinlough
May28th '98

My Dear Daughter Norah,

You must excuse us for delaying an answer to your most kind and welcomed letter and money which I received the 12 May and waited all along the time to have some newses to tell you. I did not get it chequed until the 18th May. I did not miss the time passing on since. The times were very busy too. I am very glad to hear that ye are all very well, yourself, and Ellen and Tim, also Mary and her husband and family. You said nothing about Agnes and Katie in your last letter. I am proud about Tim getting such a good job.

Well, Norah, I was expecting to get the papers all along the time to hear all about the war[1] and how they are getting through it. I was very troubled about ye for fear Dan and Dennie and Tim might be called in. It is in full report about this country that every man will be called. It is long punishment to be waiting for an answer now. It have done great harm over here to us. We would not get any half bag of flour now for less than 23s[hillings] or 24 s[hillings], what we used get before for 12 s[hillings]. It is double the price now and also is the meal, but the meal fell a little in the price of a bag. It is well for the people to have America but for it they would die. Magg Hourihane sent home some money a few days ago. So also did James Wholey and he said they were not a bit afraid of it. The McCarthys of Leap are all well. Mrs. McCarthy herself would like to know who is Johnny's wife.[2] Well, Norah, tell me is Tim's boarding far from Mary's house.[3] Jerome Paddy[4] wrote the other day and said he was going to come home. He is homesick all the time since he left and he'd like to be home.[5] And Katie Paddy is in Cononagh with Mrs. Barry. You knew her. Well, Julia is working, too, and Mick is at home.[6] Maria Crowley is working at Sheehan's Hotel.[7] She inquired often of me about Delia.[8] Do ye see her at all lately? All the neighbors and friends and comrades are all very well, so also is your Uncle and family. Julia was going to delay until Sunday but I thought it too long to wait. She is very busy now, too. She have her nephew over from Newport, her sister's son, William John Mahoney.[9] He is about 19 years of age, a nice smart fellow. He come over for the good of his health. He come over for a few weeks by the Doctor's orders. There did not many from this place go this year but a few, Biddy Leahy and John Cremeen's daughter, Poolroom.[10] We had only a poor Leap Fair this year. There was no fun nor fighting either. The Bishop was at Leap that day examining the children for Confirmation and he confirmed them the day after. There was a lot of children to be confirmed too and very nicely dressed. Jeremiah and Patrick and Hanna Hayes, my sister,[11] were confirmed.

Well, Norah, I must tell you Dannie Rick[12] is married to a Carthy Meenig girl from Caheragh, a fine hearty stylish girl. Well, Norah, I suppose ye have great heat by this time. We had only a very bad May with rain and thunders and hard weather. I was expecting that some one of ye would write, Tim or you, to tell me all about the war. Well, we have no more to say now until the next time. Excuse my writing. I was in a hurry.

So Good bye from Father and Mother.

ENDNOTES

1   *The Spanish-American War was in progress.*

2   *John McCarthy of 27 Springfield Street, South Lawrence, Mass., married Hannah Sheehan on 17 November 1892. His parents were Michael and Mary McCarthy. John was born in 1866 and emigrated in 1885, according to the 1900 Federal Census. "Mrs. McCarthy" was probably Johnny McCarthy's aunt.*

3   *Brother Tim was still boarding with Mary and Dan Donovan.*

4   *Jerome/Jeremiah Driscoll of Bawnfune, son of the late Patrick, and Mary Donovan Driscoll, was born c. 1874. He immigrated to Boston on the S. S. Cephalonia, leaving Queenstown on 8 May 1896. His destination was his sister Maggie Driscoll whose address was South Boston.*

5   *Jerome never did make it back home for he died the following December in Boston.*

6   *Katie, born 24 November 1880, Julia, born 30 August 1884, and Michael/ Mick Driscoll, born 4 May 1886 were Jerome's youngest siblings. Their father had died in 1886 when they were very young children.*

7   *Sheehan's Hotel is still operating in Leap Village. Maria Crowley was either the daughter of blacksmith James Crowley and Mary Donovan of Gurteenaduige, which is immediately north east of Ballinlough. (This Mary/Maria was born 24 March 1884.) Or, she was the daughter of Patrick and Mary Crowley of Corran South, neighbors of John "Meenig" McCarthy. This Maria was born in 1876 and living at home when the 1901 Census was taken.*

8   *Delia Collins, from Ballinlough, was a close friend of Ellen McCarthy and lived in Haverhill, Mass.*

9   *William John Mahoney, son of John and Nora McCarthy Mahoney, was born in Newport, Wales in 1879. Nora was the eldest of Uncle Michael's children by a first wife.*

10   *Bridget "Biddy" Leahy sailed to Boston on the S. S. Pavonia in April 1898.*

11   *Jeremiah and Patrick McCarthy, from Tullig. Uncle Michael's grandsons. Hanna Hayes, daughter of Denis and Ellen Hayes of Ballinlough. She was fourteen when the 1901 Census was taken.*

12   *Daniel Donovan, son of Rickard, married a McCarthy woman from Caheragh. This townland is north-northwest of Skibbereen.*

DOCUMENT 59
9 June 1898 – Hannah Collins, Elmira, N. Y. to Nora McCarthy, Haverhill, Mass.

Elmira, N. Y.
June 9th, 1898

My Own Darling Nora,

Your very kind and welcome letter reached me alright and I was delighted to hear from you and to hear that you and sisters and Brother were well as the date of this letter leaves me and sisters and Brother at present, thanks be to God.

Dear Nora, I am so glad to have you have a comrade girl to go around with you and ye will have a nice time together. I only wish I was with you too. I would enjoy it as I thinks of you every day and of the old days we spent together. How could I forget you, darling?

I am awfully sorry if I offended you about your picture. I think its alright but you are far nicer than that. I know I looks at it every day and makes me think more and more of you. I expect to have mine taken very soon and you will see that homely face of mine once more.

Well, Nora dear, I am working every day and feels tired. I don't have them idle times like I used to in old Ballinlough but I feels good and have my health so I don't mind it. I wish you were here in Elmira. We would have a nice time together. But you would not let me have any fellow. They would all get stuck on you. I suppose you got a dozen in a string by this time or has Tim any girl? Is Ellie working far from you?[1]

I was out Decoration Day[2] and had a good time. We went to a lake.[3] Its five or six miles. They were singing and dancing there and lots of fun. You would enjoy it.

Dear Nora, I felt awful sorry about that Brien fellow.[4] Its too bad about him and especially to die so sudden and unexpected. I suppose his poor Mother and the rest of them will feel terrible about him. Dear Nora, Mary is working in the same place still and likes it pretty well. She is getting along nicely. You would not know her. She is so big and stout. She is a good deal taller than I am. I goes to see her often and she comes to see me.

Dear Nora, what makes you think I am going to step out soon? You mean get married. I don't think I will. I will have to see dear old Ireland first and its many a long year until I get married.[5] I may after you but not before.

Well, my darling Nora, I cant think of any more to say this time with lots of love to you and sisters and Tim,

Your sister Hannah

Good Bye

Write soon again. I am always so glad to hear from you. Excuse bad writing. I wish I could write you a nice letter. This is so funny. Don't kill yourself laughing at it.

Good Bye darling. Think of me often.

ENDNOTES

1 *The house where Nora worked on White Street, Haverhill, was only a few streets away from the place on Summer Street, Haverhill where Ellen was employed.*

2 *Memorial Day, May 31.*

3 *Eldridge Lake, Elmira.*

4 *Timothy Brien, 26, died 18 May 1898 in Boston of pneumonia. He was the son of Patrick and Ellen Welch Brien of Knockskagh. He lived at 105 W. Fourth St., South Boston, Mass. His home in Knockskagh was next to that of Kate Monohan's family. His brother James and family lived there with his widowed mother, Ellen.*

5 *Hannah Collins married Tom Cloake three years later, 9 October 1901. There is no evidence that she ever did make a return trip to Ireland, though her brother Patsy made at least two trips to his old home.*

Document M60
[27 June 1898] – Patrick and Kate McCarthy, Ballinlough, Leap to Nora McCarthy, Haverhill, Mass.

Patrick McCarthy
Ballinlough, Leap
[date from postmark on envelope]
Sunday

My Dear Cousins,

It is Julia is writing this letter for your fond Parents, having received your fond and very welcomed letter on Friday which gave the poor parents and your friends pleasure to hear that ye are well, T. G., as this leaves Father and Mother and your friends at present.

My Dear Cousin Nora, Father and Mother is very thankful to Tim as they had lost all hopes of any money. I hope he will not forget them as richer Parents needs aid if they only could demand it of any one. This is you may be sure a miserable year.

Dear Nora, your Father have the horse and cart and goats still. That's all they have to live out of so poor parents don't looks so well when deprived of their family. They looks wrecked. You can imagine that clothes don't last forever, so I must tell you that's how the old folks look. I would wish you would think of their wants.

Dear Nora, Patrick Brien and company are well, so is Minnie and Husband and Baby.[1] Danny Rick don't live with his Father. I don't know where he lives. We heard about Tim Brien. He was prayed for. Poor Norry Hegarty was glad of Ellie Driscoll being married. Poor Norry don't travel much now. Her sight is failed on her. We have droll times now. James Hayes and his Father and the whole of them are in court every day and was at Bantry sessions those days past Friday and Saturday. Jerry claiming his hire of James and James having the Father and Mother for stealing grass and Hay, so James decreed. The Father and Mother and Jerry got no satisfaction and are to be at Union Hall Court the next day. The place is alive with them.

Dear Nora, we had a visitor for three weeks. William J. Mahoney from England. We had a nice time while we were together but the end of it came and brother Mike went with him to Newport. We are very lonesome for poor Mike as he would remind us of your old tricks. They left three weeks tomorrow morning. Had one letter from him. Jeremiah and Patrick have confirmation and Communions over them now, T. G. I am very glad of it myself and I see you were delighted also. You were fond of them surely.

Dear Nora, Father and Mother is very glad how poor Mary and Husband and Baby are so well in health, and also poor Ellie and Tim. It is good to hear of good Healthy Friends. I am proud of your courage. Don't leave down the name for any friend. Your Father and Pat'k the shoe M.[2] had a great laugh at your idea the McCarthys don't look so bad. Fight for them. I wish poor Katie would live. I hope she is better off. May the Lord give her eternal rest to her soul, amen. Mother is sorry for B. Crowley[3] leaving ye. His mother is still living and is also surprised Dennie[4] don't write to her. Sure, he don't write to you so often. I have no more to say at present. From your affect. Father and Mother and Cousin Julia.

To Nora and Tim, Ellie and Mary and Company. Good Bye
XXXXXX
Write soon. All safe. Good Bye to all.

ENDNOTES

1   *Patrick and his sister, Minnie, Brien were children of John of Knockskagh. Minnie married Dan Collins of Driminidy, Drinagh in 1896. Their first child, Kate, was born in 1896*

2   *Julia's older brother, Patrick, called "the Shoemaker" for his trade.*

3   *Bartholomew Crowley, a cousin on the Keane side, lived in Bradford, Mass. Nora and Dan's daughter, Marie, remembered that her parents and Crowley were estranged when she was a child, but she did not know the cause.*

4   *Nora's brother, Denis, from Pennsylvania.*

DOCUMENT M61
30 June 1898 – Hannah Collins, Elmira, N. Y. to Nora McCarthy, Haverhill, Mass.

Elmira, N. Y.
June 30th, 1898

My Darling Nora,

Your very kind and welcome letter reached me a week ago and I was delighted to hear from you and to hear that you and sisters and Brother were well as the date of this letter leaves me and the rest of us at present, thank God.

Dear Nora, I should have answered your letter before now but I was awful busy cleaning house and we had company. I had to work pretty hard. They has lots of company in summer time which makes it so hard for me. Its awful warm here. I feels the heat very much that I cant hardly work. I am glad you are getting along so well. You had ought not be worrying so much about home. They will be alright when you write to them often but I guess you cant forget the happy days you spent with them. You must try to cheer up and have a little fellow to take up your attention. He would take off all that lonesome from your heart. Don't think I'm awful for saying such funny things to you.

Dear Nora, I was surprised to hear Dannie Rick was married. I remember him well and his jolly ways and Mary told me Den Dempsey[1] was married too. They are all married over there now. Only a few and those that aint are out in this country. Did you ever hear anything about Mike Cahallane or where he is.[2] I cant think to spell the name but I guess you will make it out alright. I heard Mary say Jerry Hayes drinks hard. I was not very much surprised to hear about Nora Hayes and Pad. They are as funny as ever. I suppose you laughed a good deal over that paper. Who did James Hayes marry or do you know? There is great change in old Ballinlough now. It aint like it used to be.

Dear Nora, I had a good time last Wednesday. I was to a wedding. Mrs. Dempsey's daughter was married. I was there and went to the church. She was dressed nice. Did not have any hat just flowers in her hair. They used to live near us home. She was only nineteen years old and a very pretty girl. Mary is working in the same place still and getting along nicely. Maggie is working not far from me. I seen them all often. Patsy is well also. I asked him if he remembered you and he said yes. He is a great big man now. He got fat since he went home. He was a year gone. Well, Nora dear, I am getting tired of writing and cant think of any more to say this time so I hope you will excuse me and such a funny letter as this is.

With lots of love to you and sisters and my dear Tim.[3] Good Bye. I remain as ever,

Your loving sister, Hannah

Think of me often as I do of you.

ENDNOTES

1 *Denis Dempsey, 33, a mason from Knockskagh, was in the 1901 Census of Ireland with wife Hannah, 31, and children John, 3, and Kate, 1. Also in the house, eleven year old Kate Dempsey and 24 year old Kate Donoghue, both listed as "visitors."*

2 *Mick McCarthy mentioned in a letter home that Mike Cahalane was in Newport, Wales with him. Mike is probably connected to the Thomas Cahalane family in nearby Maulnigarra. There were seven children at home and an eighth, a son, who was a servant in a nearby home.*

3 *Hannah, like many of Nora's other female correspondents, was "smitten" with Nora's handsome brother Tim.*

Document M62
29 July 1898 – Hannah Collins, Elmira, N. Y. to Nora McCarthy, Haverhill, Mass.

Elmira, N. Y.
July [29], 1898 [date from postmark on envelope]

My Own Dear Nora,

Your long looked for letter reached me at last which gave me great pleasure to hear from you. I thought there was something the matter with you for I had been dreaming of you twice last week. I was thinking you were sick but I am glad you are well and also your sisters and Brother as I myself is in good health at present and so are the rest of us.

Dear Nora, I am so sorry your comrade girl has gone away. You must feel awiul lonesome now without her. I hope you will have another one soon. I only wish I was with you again. I would feel happy for I am thinking of you all the time. How could I ever forget your darling face. I suppose you are rested up pretty well now after your vacation.

Its so nice for you to have your sister's home to go to when you feel tired or sick. I wish I had a home like that to rest for a while. I have not had a week's vacation in two years. I work all the time and feels tired. I am glad to hear your Mother and Father is well. I feels sorry for poor aunty Norry. She must feel awful bad that she don't come over to your Mother's home for she always liked to go if she was able. I suppose she wont live very long now.

My sister Nora has left her for she did not care to go to school, and Tim was confirmed. You know Nora and Tim are twins.[1] I was surprised to think they are growing so big. We had a letter from home last week. It will be three years next month since I left home.[2] How long are you out? I forget. You must be over four years.

Dear Nora, aint the Hayeses great sport. How they fight all the time. It would be better for James he come to this country long ago than to be like he is. How is Tim getting along or what kind of work does he do? I suppose he is mashing the girls all the time. Well, my darling Nora, I cant think of any more to say this time. I hope you will excuse me with lots of love to you and sisters and Brother.

Good Bye. Think of me often as I do of you. Yours forever, Hannah.

I am almost dead with the heat.

ENDNOTES

1   *Honoria "Nora" and Timothy Collins were born 11 July 1886.*

2   *Hannah Collins, 18, accompanied by her sister Margaret "Maggie", 23, sailed on the S. S. Brittanic from Queenstown. It arrived in New York City 6 September 1895. Their stated destination was Elmira, New York.*

Document **M63**
29 July 1898 – Patrick and Kate McCarthy, Ballinlough, Leap to Nora McCarthy, Haverhill, Mass.

Skibbereen[1]
July 29th 1898

Dear Nora,

We received your letter on the 22nd of July. We were very glad to hear that ye were all quite well as this leaves us at present, thank God. You enquire about Nora Hayes. She wrote home at Christmas and sent one pound to her Norry.[2] The rest is very bleak with each other. The young fellow Jerry processed James for work done and he gained 40 pounds of him at the Cork Assizes.

Dear Nora, we were very glad you enjoyed yourself on your Holiday. Thanks be to God you had a place to rest yourself and to write your letter.[3] I would have written before now but I was waiting for Mikie's address. They were afraid the one they had wouldn't be the right one as he sent off a Character as if he was going to get some situation of some kind or to join the city police of that place, and he did not write since and your father would not like to be delaying the letter so long. We came to Skibbereen today. Julia[4] was busy about hay and churning and the times were busy on them. I did not like to be troubling her in such hurried times. Glad to hear that Ellie and Tim are so well. I know he would like to hear from Mickie. He might get along as well as if he was in America. You might hear from him in a short time. You said that Ballinlough was lonesome now. It is in a way but Norry Hayes keep up the style of the place. She is to be in Union Hall court next week again after being in Cork this week.

Dear Nora, I hope you wont delay this letter. I hope you have heard from Denny by this time and I hope you will be able to get the photos as soon as you can. I would like to get the baby's. The weather is very fine and the people are expecting a good crop of everything this year but it's equal to me. I cannot use any of them because they had like to kill me yesterday. I must conclude now, Dear Nora, with love and best wishes to you all.

I remain your affectionate Father and Mother, Patrick and Kate McCarthy with love.

[the following note, on a separate piece of paper, was mailed with the above letter]

Dear Nora, I hope you wont delay this letter as there is a bill due again the 20th of August. I know that ye have a good deal sent home but Tady know very well that Michael Daly[5] has to get some money each time. He is the only person and of course your father like to keep his credit when he would get one thing and another. He would like to meet his little calls all ways. He want to get some hay for the old horse for the winter. Now is the time to get a thing when the thing is plenty and cheap.

Dear Nora, your father don't like to be without a horse and the old horse is very strong always. She brought us to Skibb today and its Julia George[6] that is writing this letter and her mother would like that you would try and see her family that is in America to advise them to write to her, and if they don't, will you send their address to her if you see them there.[7]

Dear Nora, I hope you won't blame us for being so hard on ye but we can't help it. Don't show this part of the letter to anyone but yourselves. Burn it as soon as you read it. Faithfully yours, in conclusion, I remain Your Affectionate Mother + Father.

Love from Julie George and her Mother, Mary George.

They are all well.

XXXXXXXXXXXXXXXXXXXXXX

ENDNOTES

1   *Nora's parents had gone to the nearby town of Skibbereen to have cousin Julia "George" McCarthy write this letter.*

2   *Nora Hayes, Boston, to her mother Honora "Norry" Hayes in Ballinlough.*

3   *Nora McCarthy took her vacation time at her sister Mary Donovan's house.*

4   *Julia McCarthy of Ballinlough who usually wrote letters for her Uncle Patrick and Aunt Kate McCarthy.*

5   *There was a Michael Daly in Tullig in the 1901 Census. He was a near neighbor of cousin Mary McCarthy.*

6   *Julia McCarthy was born 18 November 1865 in Curragh, Skibbereen to George and Kate (Herlihy) McCarthy. Her father died in 1892 in Bridgetown, Upper Bridge St., Skibbereen where Julia, her mother, and brothers were living when this letter was written. Her sister, Mary "George" Hurley lived nearby.*

7   *In earlier letters that Mary "George" wrote for Patrick and Kate, she mentioned her brothers George and Jack who were living in Lawrence, Mass.*

DOCUMENT M64
25 August 1898 – Hannah Collins, Elmira, N. Y. to Nora McCarthy, Haverhill, Mass.

Elmira, N. Y.
August 25th, 1898

My Darling Nora,

Your most kind and ever welcome letter reached me yesterday which gave me great pleasure to hear from you and to hear that you and sisters and Brother were well as the date of this leaves me and sisters and Brothers at present.

Dear Nora, I did not get your letter until yesterday. I don't know how long it been in the post Office. It was advertised for. I left my place two weeks ago. I got my vacation and I am staying at Mrs. Dempsey's house. I don't think I will go back there anymore for its hard and I was tired out. Did not have a rest in over two years. So I don't feel good yet. I have a cold and Headache those days, but expect to be alright soon. I am glad you are getting along well. I only wish I was with you, darling. I would enjoy it as I thinks of you every day and all our old times in Ballinlough. How could I ever forget?

I thinks those two weeks are so long. I don't do anything but go around every day and have a good time. You say I don't tell you anything about my fellow. He is well. He only lives a little ways from Mrs. Dempsey's house.[1] He comes to see me often. His name is Tom Cloak. Don't you think its funny? He is a Catholic. His Mother came from Tipperary. I think he is alright. He never went with any girl until he met me and say he never will. He is got light hair, pretty near red, the colour of yours, so he must be alright then.

Dear Nora, I am glad Tim is getting along so well. I often thinks of him. Have he got any of his pictures taken yet. I wish you could send me one as I would love to have one.

Mary and Maggie is well. They aint got any fellow yet. Mary is a great old thing. Just the same, as bold as ever. You cant tell her anything. She does be mad at me for having a fellow and she calls him all the old names she can think of and is awful nice to his face.

Well, my darling Nora, I cant think of any more to say this time. I hope you will excuse me and such a funny letter. I am getting poor. I cant afford to buy a writing pen. I got a pencil.

With lots of love to you and sisters and Brother. Your loving chum, Hanna.

Good Bye. Write soon again.

Address: Hannah Collins, 861 Rail Road Avenue, Elmira, N. Y.

ENDNOTES

1   *Tom Cloake's house on Magee Street was one street away from Mrs. Dempsey's house on Rail Road Ave.*

DOCUMENT M65

Hannah Collins had new employers. They were a Jewish family and Hannah was hired in time to experience the Jewish High Holidays. The Irish peasant girl was about to undergo culture shock for these were most likely the first Jewish people she had met. Back home in her Irish countryside even Protestants were few and far between, and generally of a different social status with whom she would have no interaction.

[7] September 1898 – Hannah Collins, Elmira, N. Y. to Nora McCarthy, Haverhill, Mass.

September [7] 1898 [date from postmark on envelope]

My Ever darling Nora,

I received your very nice letter and was glad to hear from you and to learn by it that you and sisters and Brother were well as the date of this letter leaves me and the rest of us at Present.

Dear Nora, I am working again in a week. Its not the same place. They are Jews and are awful funny people but are rich. I had a good rest and did not miss the time going by. I was off three weeks and felt so lonesome to come back to a new place. There are seven in family,[1] five children. I don't know if I will stay there or not.

Dear Nora, I was glad to hear about Nonie Hayes and Pake. I was surprised to think Nonie had forgotten me for I did not forget her or does she look just the same? I suppose she dresses nice. How glad you were to see them, but I suppose it made ye homesick when ye talked about home. Pake Hayes you said will be married soon.[2] I pity his wife. It's a wonder Nonie aint married by this time.

Well, Nora dear, I can't think of anything to say this time. I am just going to bed and am so tired, so excuse me, with lots of love to you and sisters.

Your own, Hanna.

Good Bye. The same address. Write soon. I wish I could see you now dear. Please excuse this pencil. I got your dear old grey locks of hair[3] and you bet I kissed them many a time. I got them safe to remember you.

ENDNOTES

1   *Hannah's new employer was Joseph Sittenfield, a German immigrant, who was a leather dealer. He and his wife had five children, according to the 1900 Federal Census. Their house, at 109 High Street, Elmira, was near St. Joseph's Hospital.*

2   *Patrick "Pake" Hayes did not marry until 16 April 1902. His wife was Catherine Keohane.*

3   *Nora had sent Hannah some locks of her hair. A braid of Nora's hair from the early 1900s is in the McCarthy Collection. The color is a rich auburn, and not the grey about which Hannah had teased her.*

DOCUMENT M66
21 September 1898 – Hannah Collins, Elmira, N. Y. to Nora McCarthy, Haverhill, Mass.

September 21, 1898

My Own Dear Nora,

I got your welcome letter alright and was delighted to hear from you and to know that you and sisters and Brother were well as the date of this leaves me and the rest of us at present. Dear Nora, I am working in the same place still and getting to like it better than I did. They are Jews and are awful rich. They had New Years day last Saturday and had a great time. They had so many presents, just like we have Christmas and they said to me in the morning "I wish you a happy New Year." I thought I would die laughing at them. I got your letter Sunday to Mrs. Dempsey's house. She is a cousin of ours and lived near us home. She is kind to us. We make our home with her and they do be a big crowd there Sundays. It reminds me of our house at home, but not them dear ones you know. Oh, Nora dear, I do be thinking of you all the time and more so when I am alone. How many fine days we spent around the Lake together. How could I ever forget you, darling. I imagine I can see that sweet face of yours. I always thought so much of you. I am glad Tim is well and also your Sisters. Its so nice for you to have your sister's home to go to Sundays and when you are tired or out of work. Why, you are alright. I wish I had some sisters married.[1] Don't you think I'm awful now to say such things. My fellow is just fine. I am going to a show with him tomorrow night. I wish you were here to go too and have another fellow, but I guess you got one alright, and don't tell me you would not have every old thing comes along. Of course I aint particular. Well, Good Bye, from your Hana.

ENDNOTES

1   *Hannah was the first of the Collins girls in Elmira to marry. Her younger sister, Mary, married Charles Dimon in 1908, and Maggie married John McCatee c. 1919. Thus, Hannah, herself, ended up being the married sister with whom the others could spend their vacation time.*

DOCUMENT M67
1 October 1898 – Hannah Collins, Elmira, N. Y. to Nora McCarthy, Haverhill, Mass.

October 1, 1898

My Ever Dear Nora,

Your kind and wished for letter reached me a few days ago and I was delighted to hear from you and above al to learn by it that you and sisters and Brother were well as I hope ye may long remain so and this leaves me and sisters and Brother at present, thank God.

Dear Nora, I am always so glad and pleased to hear from you as your letters are just fine. They makes me think more and more of you. I only wish I could write such nice ones to you. I never used to write to any body but home so I aint much hand from writing a nice letter but hope it will suit you alright. I writes to my Cousin Mary McCarthy from Cornishall. She is in Albany, New York. She is out a year this month. I don't know if you ever saw her home. I guess you did. I am in the same place still with the old Jews and are so funny. They would make you laugh all the time I don't care. It don't make any difference to me who I work for.

Dear Nora, I am surprised Noney Hayes don't write to you. I think she is mean enough. She is careless that way. You has a great time going to see the people getting married. I wish I was with you too. I would like it. What makes you think you won't be to my wedding? You know you would and be the first one there if I was to get married. But you know I aint or may be never would. I am not in a hurry. I would rather live single yet. It's a hard thing to get married, to be bound to a man all the time. Oh, I don't wish to but I got a nice fellow and I guess a one would be kind to me. He is going out of town to work for two months next week. How I will miss him. The man he works for is got a job there so he must go, I guess. He tends masons. Then I will get a love letter once a week.

Mary and Maggie, Patsy are all well, sends you their love. Mary is just the same. Not much different and she acts awful strange to me. She is mad at me all the time. I don't know why because I got a fellow I guess. She is funny. She is taller and stouter than I am a great deal. Well, my darling Nora, I cant think of any more to say this time with lots of love to you and sisters and Brother.

Your old sister, Hana.[1]

> Good Bye.
> The same address. Write soon again.

---

1   *"Hana" is one of the variations of her name that Hannah will use in her letters.*

DOCUMENT M68

9 October 1898 – Cousin Michael McCarthy, Newport, Wales to Cousins Tim and Nora McCarthy, Bradford and Haverhill, Mass.

Newport
October 9th 1898

Dearest Cousins,

It's after a prolonged period I do have the happiness of addressing to ye those few lines hoping their arrival will find ye in a perfect health as I am at present, T. G. And expect that you, Dear Nora, will excuse me for not answering your last letter. I should have answered it but being at Tullig and cared for nothing but fun and enjoyment. Though it being different now still I am enjoying myself well here.

Dear Cousin, I had not the slightest notion to come here but when William John went home and they would not leave me go to America or any place so I just took a notion and went to England so my Mother is killing herself crying but I can't help them now as they know I could not stop in Ballinlough always. So I'm getting on middling well here. I am working with masons as a mason's labourer. And come here in the middle of the strike and got work when thousands were starving with the hunger so I can't complain. I got some nice little girls here too.[1]

Dear Tim, I must tell you that Captain[2] is getting on all right but being idle a few weeks during the strike. He is my old companion. He comes up to me every evening and we do have a fine walk every evening almost. Jemmy come up to see me and we drank some beer. Did not see Annie[3] but once. She is just the same but got somewhat fatter.

Dear Nora, tell Tim that I have all my exercises lost and threw all the foolishness out of my belly at Queenstown.[4]

Dear Nora, we are all well here especially sister Nora. Husband and family[5] are well and wishes to be kindly remembered to ye as they think a great deal of their own friends. Maggie[6] says she would like to go to America to see ye. I must be drawing to a close. Haven't much to say though being in distant lands so we all join in sending best love to all and especially myself for my love for ye will never grow cold, so I must be bidding ye good bye and good bye to all. I am in a hurry. I must see my girl. Good bye from fond cousin M. M. to Cousins.

　　　Write soon again.

ENDNOTES

1　　　*Mick makes frequent references to his enjoyment of girls, but he never did marry.*

2　　　*Mike Cahalane, old neighbor and friend from home, now living in Newport, Wales with Mick.*

3　　　*James and Anne Cahalane, Mike's brother and sister. None of the Cahalanes were in the 1901 Census of Wales.*

4　　　*Mick was seasick on the ferry ride from Queenstown to Newport.*

5　　　*Nora (McCarthy) and John Mahoney had eight children. Their names and birth dates were: William John, 1879; Margaret, 1880; Timothy, 1884; Norah, 1886; Mary Ann, 1888; Michael, 1889; Ellen, 1891; and Patrick, 1896. In the 1901 Census of Wales, Mick and his older brother, Patrick the Shoemaker, were boarding with the Mahoneys.*

6　　　*Maggie Mahoney, who was 18 in 1898.*

Document M69
16 October 1898 – Hannah Collins, Elmira, N. Y. to Nora McCarthy, Haverhill, Mass.

October 16, 1898

My Own Darling Nora,

Your sweet letter reached me alright and I was delighted to hear from you as ever. I am glad to hear that you and sisters and Brother are all well as the date of this leaves me and sisters and Brothers at present, thank God.

Dear Nora, yesterday was Saturday and I intended to have my picture taken only it was such a dark day and it rained a little so I thought I would not mind but I will next Saturday if its fine. You know I will surely break the machine. I am so homely. I can not get out any other day for Saturday is my afternoon. She will not leave me out very much. We have just started house cleaning. I do hate it. I don't have no washing to do or ironing either, so I guess that's the hardest part of the work gone for me. But I have lots of other things to do. I know you feels tired from the big washing you got to do.

I am glad Tim is well. I often thinks of him. How sweet he was. I imagine I can see him dancing. He was such a lively fellow. I bet all the girls are mashed on him. I don't go to any dance. I never danced very much since I come to this country. I am like yourself. I was surprised to think you had forgotten your dance and you was such a good dancer too.

How long is poor Katie dead? I often thinks of her and feels lonesome for her. She was always good natured and kind. I hope she is better off. I am sure Aunty Norry cried a good deal after her for she thought there was nobody like Katie. And your poor Mother left alone without anybody. I suppose you would not care to go back home. Its too lonesome. There aint no young people around. I suppose Mary Hayes[1] is home yet or do you hear from her any more? Mary told me lots about the people around there when she came. I suppose you remember Patrick Brien and Jamesy[2] of Knockskagh. They were working in our land before she left. And Minnie is married to my Cousin Dannie Collins.[3] They got one little girl.

Well, my darling Nora, I must finish for this time so Good Bye, lots of love to you and Tim and the rest. I remain as ever your Loving sister, Hanna

I only wish I could see your sweet face. I would be happy.

Excuse bad writing.

ENDNOTES

1   There is a Mary Hayes, 17, from Leap, on the S. S. Pavonia which sailed in September 1894. She was with Annie Hawley from Skibbereen, and they were going to their aunt, Mrs. Collins, Brookline, Mass. However, this letter above suggests that Hannah's sister saw her in Ballinlough after that date.

2   Patrick and James Brien/O'Brien were the sons of John and Julia Brien. By the time of the 1901 Census, Patrick was married and James, single, was at home with his parents.

3   Minnie (Brien) and Daniel Collins, with their three year old daughter, Kate, and one year old son, Cornelius, along with his parents, Cornelius and Kate, were living in Driminidy, Drinagh in 1901.

Document M70
[30] October 1898 – Hannah Collins, Elmira, N. Y. to Nora McCarthy, Haverhill, Mass.

October [30], 1898 [date from postmark on envelope]

My Darling Nora,

Your kind and wished for letter reached me alright and I was glad to hear you and sisters and Brother were well as the date of this letter leaves me and the rest of us at present, thank God.

Dear Nora, I had my picture taken today.[1] I hope it will be good. Will not be finished for a week yet so I will send you one as soon as possible. Last Saturday was wet so I could not have them taken. Its raining a good deal here and getting cold. I do hate the winter. I am also cleaning house and am awful tired like yourself. I hope you don't have to work so hard. I do be thinking of you every day.

Dear Nora, it was a great surprise to ye to see Johney John.[2] It made you think more of home and the good times that's gone by. I am sure Tim had a great old talk with him and enjoyed seeing him very much. Its too bad he could not stay longer with ye. I remember him well. It's a wonder Bridgie and Julia[3] don't come to this country. I was glad your poor Mother and Father were well but I suppose feels lonesome for ye. We hears from home often.

Dear Nora, you must have some more pictures taken soon, big ones. I would like to have some or did Tim ever have his taken yet? If he did I want one of them. I would love to see his sweet face again. I suppose he is got a nice girl by this time. How is Ellie? Does she work far from you? You has a great old time mashing the fellows

---

1   *A copy of Hannah's photo is in the McCarthy Collection courtesy of the Cloake family, Elmira, N. Y.*
2   *John Donovan, born 4 March 1869 to John and Catherine (Hurley) Donovan of Bawnfune, arrived in Boston 27 May 1895. He had two sisters, Mrs. Ellen Driscoll and Mrs. Patrick Hayes, and a brother Denis living there.*
3   *Bridget Donovan, born 16 February 1874, and Julia Donovan, born 18 June 1875, were single and at home when both the 1901 and 1911 Census of Ireland was taken.*

when you go to church.[4] I wish I was there. Why don't you have a nice fellow? I guess you don't see any one you like yet, but I hope you will soon. My fellow is a little peach. Well, my darling sister, I cant think of any more to say this time.

Hope you will excuse me. Good Bye, write soon again. Lots of love to you and all.

I am as ever yours, Hannah

> Remember me when this you see
> Think me not unkind
> Although your face I cannot see
> You are the dearest in my mind.

You cant read this old writing. Kisses.

---

4   *Nora attended St. James Church, the mother church in Haverhill, Mass. It was located in the neighborhood in which she worked.*

Document M71
9 November 1898 – Patrick and Kate McCarthy, Ballinlough, Leap to Honoria McCarthy, Haverhill, Mass.

Ballinlough
November 9th 98

My Own Dearest Nora and Ellie, Tim, Mary and family,

I received your kind and very welcomed letter in due time and need not tell you how delighted we felt when we found ye were all enjoying good health as the departure of this leaves all here at present, Thank God.

I received the money alright and was very thankful to you for sending it. We are very proud to hear that Dennis is coming to live with ye.[1] It makes our mind easy to think ye are together. I suppose ye won't know Dennie now.[2] Ye are grown out of his knowledge.

About Leap Fair, the times are changed very much. People are getting very quiet. They are all getting sensible now. The fair is not as much as it used to be. I was talking to your Aunt Nora[3] in Rosscarbery. She told me to tell you to write to Batty Crowley to tell him about the affair that was between Dan Cane[4] and himself and tell him send it as he want it now. Little Den[5] is not well himself. I was going to go to see him all the week. That's the reason I delayed your letter thinking I would see him before I would write but the weather was too bad.

Don't ye be blaming him[6] about the horse for he is not losing much by her and we couldn't do without her. It wouldn't do to be asking a horse of the neighbors every time we would want him. He is getting plenty furze[7] from Jer McCarthy Cappinabaugh[8] for nothing. Will Tady have work in the winter in the job he is in? Mickie's mother[9] is anxious what answer did you get from Mickie. Patrick Brien of Knockskagh got married to a girl from Blounbrook. They are expecting to get the place from Crowley. We did not see Dannie Murnane lately. Your Aunt Julia[10] is very hardy always. All the friends and neighbors are well. Your letter was a credit to you the way you loved your father and Mother.

Write soon as we will be anxious to hear for Christmas. Cousins and Friends are all well. It is very nice of Johnny John to come to see ye. We are sending our best love.

Father and Mother

ENDNOTES

1 *Brother Denis in Kingston, Penn. was coming to visit his relatives in Haverhill, but not to live there.*

2 *Nora was only a few years old when Denis left home to go, first, to Wales where he married and had two children, and then to Pennsylvania where he fathered five more children and worked in the coal mines.*

3 *Aunt Nora (McCarthy) Keane was the sister of Patrick McCarthy and was married to Daniel Keane, Ballinaclough, the brother of Kate (Keane) McCarthy.*

4 *Aunt Nora's son, Daniel Keane, who had lived with cousin Batt Crowley, but had returned home to Ireland when he became terminally ill. The financial matter between the Keanes and the Crowley is raised numerous times in the letters.*

5 *Denis Keane was the younger son of Aunt Nora. A number of his letters to Nora McCarthy are in the Collection.*

6 *Refers to Nora's father Patrick.*

7 *Furze is the Irish form of gorse, a spiny shrub with fragrant yellow flowers and black pods. It is a very effective hedge and grows abundantly throughout this part of Ireland. When crushed, it makes an excellent winter feed for horses.*

8 *Jerry McCarthy and his wife Minnie (Cullinane) lived in Cappanabohy, which is immediately east of Ballinlough.*

9 *Mickey's mother, Mary (Tobin) McCarthy, wife of Uncle Michael.*

10 *Aunt Julia (McCarthy) Harding of Kilmacabea.*

DOCUMENT M72
1 December 1898 – Hannah Collins, Elmira, N. Y. to Nora McCarthy, Haverhill, Mass.

Elmira, N. Y.
December 1st, 1898

My Darling Nora,

I received your loving letter last Saturday morning and was delighted to hear from you and also to hear that you and your sisters and Brother Tim were enjoying good health as this leaves us all at present just the same, thank God.

Dear Nora, I was so glad you liked my picture so well. Of course, its awful homely but still you are pleased to see it. You must hurry up and have some more pictures taken as I would love to have a nice one of yours. You make me tired by saying you are so homely because I know better. I don't see anybody is got a sweeter face than yours. 1 don't see why all the boys in Haverhill aint mashed on you. I guess they are too. Hurry up and get a nice fellow or shall I have one made to order for you up here? Now don't laugh at me for saying such funny things. You know me alright. Dear Nora, I had an awful dream about you the other night. I thought I seen you and we had a great old time. It was in this country but after a little while we were back again to dear Ballinlough. Of course, I could not get that sweet place off my mind. I was glad your dear Father and Mother were well but I suppose lonesome without some one of ye with them. I often thinks of your poor Mother. How good natured she was and also your Father. Do you hear from Mary Hayes any more? I suppose there aint any fun around that place any more. I was surprised to hear Patrick Brien was married. There are a great change in that place since we left home. How long are you in this country now? I am three years last September. I guess you were here a year before I was. Well, my Darling Nora, I must finish for this time. Its most ten o'clock. I am going to bed soon. I am tired. I guess I will get married soon. I'm getting tired of this single life. I am only fooling now for he did not ask me yet. Well, I guess he did. Han Write soon.

DOCUMENT M73
16 December 1898 – Hannah Collins, Elmira, N. Y. to Nora McCarthy, Haverhill, Mass.

Elmira, N. Y.
December 16th, 1898

My Dear Nora,

I received your loving letter alright and was glad to hear from you and also to hear that you and sisters and Brother were well as the date of this letter leaves me and sisters and Brothers at present, thank God.

Dear Nora, I am so glad you had your picture taken so I will have one soon to see your loving face. I hope they will be good as I am sure you looks fine, like you always did. You know how I used to tell you when we were home you looked so fine, but I see you did not get the fellow yet. I hope he will come some day soon. I laughed enough at the China man,[1] but I guess he will be a sweet little Irishman. He is the best of all.

Dear Nora, I was to a show this week. It was fine. I enjoys it very much. I goes to a good many of them. Aint Tom lovely to take me there? So you think I will be Mrs. Cloake some day, but I don't know yet. I hope I will have that warm name. Don't you think I'm awful now for talking about my fellow for if you had one you would be just as foolish as I am.

We are having lots of snow here. Its awful cold. I wish the winter was over. I would be glad.

Dear Nora, I hope you will have a merry Christmas and a happy New Year. I wish we were together. We would enjoy it as I often thinks of those happy days we were together in old Ballinlough. I thought you were a year ahead of me in this country but I see you aint. I am glad Tim is well. I want to look out and see if I cant find some thing would make him fat. Does Ellie work far from you? Its so nice for ye to have your sister's home to go to and enjoy yourselves.

Well, my darling sister, its most ten o'clock at night. I am going to bed and am tired. I has to work hard. There are seven in family and myself makes eight, so I don't have much time for myself. So Good Bye, lots of love to you and all. I am as ever, Your Loving Hannah Collins Cloak.

Don't laugh. Wishing you again a merry Christmas/Happy New Year. Write soon.

ENDNOTES

1   *There was, indeed, a "China man" in Nora's life, but not in the way Hannah suggested. He operated a laundry at the foot of Mary and Dan Donovan's street and made regular visits to them to buy one of the ducks they raised. Immigration laws at that time prohibited Chinese females from entering the United States, so the laundry man was destined to bachelorhood.*

Document M74

8 January 1899 – Hannah Collins, Elmira, N. Y. to Nora McCarthy, Haverhill, Mass.

Elmira, New York
January 8th, 1899

My Own Dear Nora,

I received your loving letter yesterday and was glad to hear from you but I am sorry for your sickness as I hope and pray you will be better soon and that you won't have any operation performed. Have you great pain in your ear? Its an awful time. There are lots sick here in Elmira. I hope I won't get sick because I have not got any home to go to and I would feel so bad. I thought the reason you did not write sooner was that you were waiting for our picture as I looked for it every day but did not come. I hope you will be soon well, Darling, to go out and get them as you know how bad I feel for you. Don't you think I am mad at you for I don't blame you. I hope you will write soon again to me as I would like to know if you are better. It was a lonesome Christmas for you when you were sick. I did not enjoy it myself. Never thought it was Christmas at all. Did not have a nice time. I got a lovely silk umbrella from my fellow and a toilet set and also a nice pocketbook. Don't you think that was nice? Mary and Maggie and Patsy are well. Mary felt awful lonesome being the first Christmas away from home. She cryed. We were to our Cousins' Mrs. Dempsey's and had a nice old country cake. I bought Mary a nice dress but she don't thank me very much. I guess I would have to buy her Elmira out and then I could not please her. That's her way. She don't mean it. Well, my darling Sister, I can't think of any more to say this time as it is Sunday and almost four o'clock. I am all through. I am going out soon so I will mail this to you. I go by the Postoffice. So I will close for this time. Hoping you are better now. I will be praying for you all the time so I hope you will be soon alright. If you can, write soon as I will be worrying about you. Good Bye from your own Loving Hanna. XXXXXX please excuse this bad letter

DOCUMENT M75
9 January [1899] – Nora Hayes, Hyde Park, Boston, Mass, to Nora McCarthy, Haverhill, Mass.

My Dear Norah

Please excuse me for not answering your letter before now but I had nothing new to tell you save the death of my sister Katie's Baby,[1] also Jerome Driscoll, Bawnfune.[2] Poor fellow did not realize he was dying. He played cards with Pake until eleven o'clock the night before he died. He was buried from Mike's house.[3]

Nora, I have changed places since I received your last Letter & do not intend to stay only a short time in this confounded hole. I have had no Privileges whatsoever, not even any company. I feel that I am in Prisonment. Nora, how [are] all the folks. Remember me to them also let me know when you heard from home. How is Maggie Noonen.[4] Remember me to her.

I will wind up for the Present as it is getting on to eleven o'clock. Good night.

A quick reply will oblige Nora Hayes 241 West River Street Hyde Park

ENDNOTES

1   *Katie (Donovan) Hayes was Nora Hayes' sister-in-law, wife of Nora's bother Michael. In the 1900 Federal Census, she states that she has had two children but both had died.*

2   *Jeremiah "Jerome Paddy" Driscoll, born 17 September 1874 to Patrick and Mary (Donovan) Driscoll of Bawnfune, died in Boston 20 December 1898 of tuberculosis. He was not married.*

3   *Patrick "Packe" and Michael Hayes, Nora Hayes' brothers, lived in South Boston, Mass.*

4   *Margaret Noonan was born 1 February 1873 to Denis and Ellen Noonan of Dunskullib, which is east north east of Leap, next to Tullig. She immigrated to America in 1896 and was a servant to Helen Howe and her son at 8 Cedar Street, Haverhill, Mass. Nora McCarthy's employment at 36 White Street, Haverhill, was very near to Maggie's place.*

DOCUMENT M76

Nora McCarthy developed mastoiditis, an abscess, in her right ear. She was admitted to the Massachusetts Charitable Eye and Ear Infirmary, 176 Charles Street, Boston on 10 January 1899. Her admissions ticket, which is in the McCarthy Collection, stated that "the Massachusetts Charitable Eye and Ear Infirmary is designed wholly for the POOR and NEEDY, and under no circumstances for those who are not proper subjects for charitable treatment." Nora had to work for her keep, as she describes in her letters to her family in Bradford. The letters from Nora in the hospital to her sisters are the only ones in the Collection that are in her own handwriting, except for a set written to her daughter Marion in the 1930s. They have not been transcribed to date. Nora's handwriting is very well-formed and easy to read

11
January 1899 – Nora McCarthy, Boston, Mass. to Ellen McCarthy, Haverhill, Mass.

Boston, Mass.
Jan. 11 '98 [sic]

My dearest sister

Here I am in at last. I don't know how long 1 am going to be here. I wont say anything about the place but am not very lonely, lots of others with their ears all sore and operations performed every day. The only trouble, we cant sleep much at night with little kids hollering around here all the time. Only one bed vacant for today. A young girl come in today going to have an operation back of her ear where I was so much afraid of mine but I don't think I am out of danger yet.

The doctor examined it twice a day and the nurse souringed it about four times a day but I don't feel much better as yet. I am only afraid I'll have to go under operation but I hope not as its terrible.

Well, I guess one letter must do you both, you and Mary, as I cant get stamps here as I'll have to save my other stamp. I hope Dan got home all right.[1] I did not feel homesick yet but if any chance of an operation I don't know what I will do. So next week I shall write you again and tell you all particulars. I don't see Dr. Hammond. He don't belong up stairs only in the operating room but the others are just as nice. We have to get up every morning at 15:6 o'clock.[2] That's pretty early for patients. It was awfully cold here last night. I wore my heavy dress all the evening. There are two old ladies in my ward and four boys from eight to twelve and one little girl about nine and two children, one a baby about 8 months and myself and the girl come in this fore noon. But the noise of them young ones is terrible.[3] They got all their play things.

Well, I guess I haven't much more to say just the news of the day. The building is quite pleasant. I have to help the nurse to make up the beds and dust around the ward and sweep twice a day and set down all the rest of the time.[4] So I guess I will stand it for a couple of weeks but that's all. There is no occasion of ye coming in to see me as you cant stay but one hour and it is not worth while unless I am going to be in here a long time. I don't think I got any more to say. Dr. Green is our doctor.[5] He just been around visiting us. He likes to plague the old women. I don't know about you writing to me, to the Ear and eye Infirmary, Charles St. Perhaps you need not mind until you hear from me again.

Well, I'll say good bye. Love to all, From your sister, Nora

ENDNOTES

1   *Mary's husband, Dan Donovan, accompanied Nora to the hospital in Boston. Most likely, they rode on the Boston & Maine Rail Road, whose depot was only yards away from Dan's house in Bradford. Once arrived at North Station, Boston, the two would have a short walk to the hospital.*

2   *Six-fifteen in the morning.*

3   *The mixture of ages and genders in Nora's open ward suggests a demeaning attitude to these charity cases.*

4   *Apparently, charity cases had to "earn their keep."*

5   *Nora's admission ticket is stamped with the names "Dr. Green" and "Dr. Crockett." Nora was patient #1390 in Vol. 34.*

Mass. Charitable Eye and Ear Infirmary,
176 CHARLES STREET.

DR. GREEN.   **EAR PATIENT.**

Dr. ....DR. CROCKETT.. Date ....

No. *1390*   Vol. *34*

The Massachusetts Charitable Eye and Ear Infirmary is designed wholly for the **POOR** and **NEEDY**, and under no circumstances for those who are not proper subjects for charitable treatment.

ALWAYS BRING THIS CARD WITH YOU.
☞ COME AT 9 O'CLOCK ☜

Document M77
12 January 1899 – Nora McCarthy, Boston, Mass, to Mary and Dan Donovan and Tim McCarthy, Bradford, Mass.

Jan 12th 99

My Dear sister Mary, Dan, Tim and all included,

I have written to Ellie yesterday and felt blue when writing. I guess I feels better today. I slept good last night and getting more acquainted around.

Well, about my ear, its no better. Dr. Hammond being in to see me this morning. He got another patient in the next bed to mine. She had an operation last night at seven and was very sick. He had to perform the operation. He looked in my ear this morning and said it was much better and I'll soon be going home. (You know he is a smoothe old boy.) I don't mind what he say. I guess he must have spoken to the other doctor as they took extra pains today and this noon a new doctor dug out my ear awfully and put some kind of powder into it.

Well, I am still in hopes not to have operation of the Mastide as its terrible.suppose if it comes on I'll have to go through it. I have met Maggie's cousin (Mikes' wife)[1] here. She is a mother to us all. She had [been] operated twice and is in here since October. But for her I would be lonesome. Another girl about my age, she being living out, too, had an operation today. Just brought up from the operating room. O dear, it is something terrible. Her ear seems so much like mine, that's why I am so discouraged but perhaps I'll get over it all right. She being in here eight days before and the poor girl hated to have an operation so went away and come back again.

I have a chance to get some stamps and will write often as you need not worry. I am worried about mother and father. I been dreaming of them last night. You can answer their letter[2] and send them my picture. I don't believe I'll be back very soon.

The grub is pretty good but is half cold when we gets it. We had boiled dinner this noon and corn starch pudding[3] for dessert. I don't like the meats. My boarding house[4] meat was some better.

Well, I guess I will close this time. No more news for today.

Hope to see ye all soon.

Love to all, from your sister, Nora XXX

ENDNOTES

1   Maggie Monohan, sister of Nora's friend Katie, had married Matthew Donovan. His cousin, Catherine Donovan, had married Mike Hayes (see Footnote 433), Nora's neighbor from Ballinlough. Both couples lived in South Boston.

2   There is no letter from home in the Collection between 9 November 1898 and 20 July 1899, so the letter referred to above was not saved.

3   "Corn starch pudding" is the familiar basic vanilla pudding, or with other flavors such as chocolate or butterscotch.

4   This suggests that Nora did not "live in" at the house in which she was employed although that is the address to which her mail was delivered.

Document M78
13 January 1899 – Nora McCarthy, Boston, Mass, to Mary Donovan, Bradford, Mass.

Boston, Mass.
Jan. 13th 99

My Dear sister Mary,

I have written to you yesterday and told you all particulars concerning matters. I cant believe I want for any thing except some kind of a wrapper as my dress would get all soiled around here. I wipe dishes and sweeps and dusts the ward and makes 1up the beds so I guess I will be all right if you would bring in some more writing paper and envelopes as I don't know how long I'll be here. The doctor is just after fixing my ear. He haven't said much about it. It don't ache but it beats just the same and I cant hear yet. It's running.

Dr. Hammond don't come in every day to see us. He got another patient in our room from Danvers, Mass. I told you about her yesterday.

Well, dear sister, there is not any need of coming in to see me Sunday as I feels all right and you cant see me but one hour from two to three, only one person at one time so you see if two comes in one will have to go out while the other is in my room. That don't suit me. I slept well last night. It is quite comfortable here since but it was so cold that day. I don't need for any food of any kind. We have enough to eat.

I felt kind of discouraged last night as the doctor was fooling with us and asked me to wear my hair down my back. He said if I should have an operation it would be a job to fix it and asked me if I'd like an operation tomorrow. He was fooling but I guess they must have talked between them selves. I told him I did not have the least desire. I would not mind the operation but after, taking the stitches out and dressing the cut. Well, I hope not anyway. Its soar underneath and if it will continue it's a sure sign of operation. But I must make the best of it. I feels so bad to think I should be in here so long, perhaps two or three months. The doctors are so busy they don't come to see us before the afternoon. The nurse is a stuck up thing. I don't like her very well. Her name is Miss Johnson. I guess I wont say any more. I will write Sunday again and if any danger I will write tomorrow.

So good bye and hope ye are still well.

Of course, I should like to see ye but its so much trouble.

Good bye.

Your sister, Nora.

Visiting hrs. from 2-3
Much obliged for the stamps.

Document M79
[31 January 1899] – Nora McCarthy, Boston, Mass, to Mary Donovan, Bradford, Mass.

Tuesday Night

My Dear sister,

I am glad to tell you I got discharged this morning. My ear is doing fine and Dr. said I could go home today and come to his office Thursday as Dr. Hammond is not going to be there for three months more. So I will see him in Haverhill Saturday afternoon. I mean the Infirmary. They got to change doctors and a new class of doctors will be in tomorrow.

I guess he would not leave me go out if I was not well. My ear feels fine. Ellen John[1] come in this afternoon and then I come home with her. I shall stay here till Thursday afternoon and then I'll go home. Dr. Hammond come over at four O'clock yesterday P. M. and dressed my ear. So he come in this morning and looked at it. So he said I might go home. He said he could take off the bandage if he like but thought it better to leave it on. Ellen got a great large fascinator[2] she is going to give to wear so to cover my head all up. I thought I'd better write and let you know I was coming home. Dr. Hammond is just as pleased as I am in being so well.

We had a great old country time eating supper. The men are gone to work again tonight.

Wont say any more. Good bye. I don't exactly know what train Thursday. Don't worry about me. Yours, Nora

Endnotes

1   *Ellen (Donovan) Driscoll, daughter of John and Catherine of Bawnfune, immigrated to Boston where she married Patrick Driscoll in 1885. She was the sister of Johnny John Donovan and others who had also moved to Boston.*

2   *A "fascinator" was a woman's lightweight head scarf, often made of lace or crocheted yarn.*

Document M80
17 February 1899 – Ellen T. Coakley, Boston, Mass, to Nora McCarthy, Bradford, Mass.

Boston, Mass.
Feb. 17 99

Dear Nora

Yours received and pleased me very much to hear from you. I am very glad you was taken good care of. That was what you wanted from the first. I think you done a very wise thing and let Dr. Hammond do what he thought best. He is a very smart man. I hope you will remain well now. Also that you will take good care of yourself.

I would have gone to see you but I got the grippe just after I came home and was very sick myself. Then I went off on a case before I was quite well and got a very bad cold. My patient died so shortened my time. It was a very old lady over 80 years. So you think Mrs. Bachelder is looking well. I am delighted about her doing so well. I did not expect it. I hope by now that Berry has got a position some where. Well, Nora dear, I must close as I have no more to say. Hope to hear from you again.

Very sincerely yours,

Ellen T. Coakley[1]

9 Turner St., Boston Please remember me to your sisters. I hope they are well.

[At the bottom left of the page, in different handwriting, is written: Very sincerely Yours Nora McCarthy]

Endnotes

1   *Ellen Coakley was a nurse who lived in a boarding house for nurses in Boston. She had immigrated from Ireland in 1892.*

DOCUMENT M81

Nora's pleasure at her recovery of good health was offset with the news from Ireland that her cousin Den Keane was terminally ill, from what appears to have been tuberculosis.

25 February 1899 – Denis Keane, Ballinaclough, Rosscarbery to Nora McCarthy, Bradford, Mass.

Ballinaclough Rosscarbery
Feb. 25th 1899

My Dear Cousins,

I am sorry to say that I am hardly able to write a reply to your loving letter. In fact it is an old friend who writes this letter for me. I got a cold last October, and unfortunately, I neglected myself. So I have not been able to work since last November. The Doctor is attending me regularly, but I fear there is no hope of my recovery, but God's will be done.

There was not a stronger man going into Ross, but my strength is gone, you will be very sorry to hear. All the people were very fond of me, and are sorry for my sickness. I know I have their earnest prayers for my recovery, or the grace of a happy death. My poor fond mother and father are bearing with our troubles very well, and are prepared for the worst, should it be God's will to take me from them in my prime of life.[1]

Aunty Peg[2] was buried lately, and Dan her son was in the funeral. She was buried in Ross. Johney and family are very well. He has a son and two daughters.[3] Your mother was here lately, and she spoke of sending for Nora to come home. B. Crowley knows of my sickness and it is unkind of him not to write me a letter. I hope you will write soon, and that you will be all right. It will give me some comfort.

I am glad to hear that all my cousins are well as all my cousins here are well, only myself. But perhaps it my please God to restore my health also.

Write soon to your fond Cousin, Den Keane.

To Cousin Norah

XXXXXXXXXXXXXXX

ENDNOTES

1   *Denis Keane, born 1 April 1869 to Daniel and Nora (McCarthy) Keane of Ballinaclough, was not yet thirty years of age. He was known as "Little Den," to distinguish him from a namesake cousin "Big Den" Keane who was born before him, in 1861.*

2   *Margaret "Peg" (Keane) Crowley, mother of Batt Crowley. Death record not found.*

3   *Denis' brother, John, born 29 March 1863, married Mary Sullivan, daughter of Michael of Burgatia, on 18 February 1893. Witnesses were Denis Keane and Jjulia Collins. Children by 1901 Census were Norah (born 1894), Daniel (born 1896), Margaret (born 1898) and Denis (born 1900.)*

DOCUMENT M82
3 March 1899 – Hannah Collins, Elmira, N. Y. to Nora McCarthy, Bradford, Mass.

March 3, 1899

My Own Dear Nora,

I received your loving letter and your darling picture a few days ago which I was delighted to get. I think your picture is just grand. I am looking at it all the time. You looks so fat[1] and nice. Just as sweet as ever. Well, I am pleased at having it but it would please me a good deal more to see yourself. I suppose you are awful fat now. You seems to have such an awful lot of hair, as my hair did not grow very long. It all came out.

Well, Nora dear, we are all well at present, but I had a cold a few days. Was not very bad. I had a letter from home yesterday. They were all well but my Father was very sick for seven weeks. He had Rheumatism. I guess he is almost well again. He is sick a good deal. He was always so fond of me and I would feel bad if anything would be the matter with him.[2]

Dear Nora, that was too bad about poor Jerome Paddy. I suppose his poor Mother felt awful about him. I wonder what was the matter that they all died so young.[3] His Grandfather died, too, lately. I suppose you remember old Jerry Bawn.[4] He was a funny old man. Well, Nora dear, I guess I laughed a good deal at the friendly words. I well remember Peggie Connolly. I wonder if she got married since we left home.[5] I suppose you will be to Pake Hayes' wedding when it will come on[6] and also Tim. He was a great Pake. I hope he changed since he left home. I guess his intended wife don't know him like we do or she would not marry him. I am glad you are well again hoping you will soon be able to go to work and now, Nora, hurry up and get married so I will go to Haverhill to be your bridesmaid. Oh, aint it awful that I can't see you to say them friendly words. Well, I guess I will close now hoping to hear from you soon again. Please excuse this bad letter.

So Good Bye with lots of love to you from Your own sister, Hanna.

Kiss Tim for me.

ENDNOTES

1   *To "look fat" must have been considered a compliment to these children of famine survivors. The picture that Hannah refers to is in the McCarthy Collection.*

2   *Hannah Collins' father, Michael, died on 11 July 1907 in his home in Driminidy, Drinagh. He was 80 years old and died of "old age."*

3   *Jerome's sister Norah had died in 1898 when she was seventeen.*

4   *Jeremiah Driscoll, 92, of Bawnfune, died 17 January 1899 of old age and debility. He had been a weaver as had his two sons, Johnny Bawn, who died in 1895, and Paddy, who died of an abcess of the liver, age 35, 9 November 1886.*

5   *Margaret "Peggy" Connolly was, she claimed, 39, when the Census of 1901 was taken. She lived with her brother Cornelius "Courley" Connolly, who was 45 in 1901. Ten years later, when the Census of 1911 was taken, Peggie's age was reported as 52 and Courley's as 56.*

6   *Patrick "Pake" Hayes did not marry until 1902.*

Document M83

14 March 1899 – Mrs. Patrick [Ellen] Driscoll, South Boston, Mass, to Nora McCarthy, c/o Mrs. Daniel Donovan, Bradford, Mass.

So. Boston
March 14[tn] 1899

Dear Hanoria,

I hope you will excuse me for not answering your letter before now. I could have written but I am careless, and I have been put about a good deal because we moved lately. It's a little farther up and on the same side of the same street. I was expecting that some one of ye may run into town, so I did not want ye to go astray.

Dear Hanoria, I hope your ear is all better now, and I expect you are working. Let me tell you that the Eye and Ear Infermiry has been moved since you were in Boston. I have been speaking to little Paddy Brien[1] a short while since, and he told me that there is no appearance at all of an increase in Mathew Donovan's family.[2] 1 have no more news at present. Myself, Pat Driscoll and the children are well as are the two lads.[3]

Hoping Mr. and Mrs. Donovan and the children are well, and Timothy, not forgetting poor Nell and of course yourself.

I remain your truly,

Mrs. Patrick Driscoll
116 Broadway[4]
South Boston

ENDNOTES

1   *There is a Patrick Brien in the 1900 Federal Census who lives on West 4th St., South Boston, with his widowed mother Nora, and two sisters, Delia, 26, and Margaret, 24. Patrick worked in a tin factory, Delia was a kitchen worker, and Margaret was a table girl. They all immigrated in 1888.*

2   *Matthew Donovan from Bawnfune, married Maggie Monohan from Knockskagh (sister to Katie), in Boston in 1898. They had no children when the 1900 Census was taken. Ten years later, when the next Census was recorded, Maggie was a widow living in Dorchester with two children. She had borne six children and three were living. There is no indication as to where the third child was living. Maggie was a "laundress" who "worked out."*

3   *The Driscolls had four of their six children living when the 1900 Census was taken. Names and birth years were: Richard, 1887; Joseph, 1889; John, 1890, and Cornelius, 1899. The Driscoll's two lodgers were Ellen's brothers Jerome (Jerome John) and John (Johnny John) from Bawnfune.*

4   *By 1900, the Driscolls had moved to 86 West Fourth St., South Boston in the neighborhood where Tim Brien had lived before his death in 1898. Thirty years later, Catherine Marion Donovan, second daughter of Dan and Mary Donovan of Bradford, married Francis T. Hayes, son of Catherine Donovan Hayes, and nephew of Ellen Donovan Driscoll.*

DOCUMENT M84
15 March 1899 – Hannah Collins, Elmira, N. Y. to Nora McCarthy, Bradford, Mass.

March 15, 1899

My Dear Nora,

I received your ever welcome letter last Thursday which I was delighted to hear from you and to learn by it that you and sisters and Brother were well as we are all first rate at present, thank God.

Dear Nora, I am glad you are having such a nice time with your Sister as I know you enjoys it very much have a fine sleep every morning. That what I would like too. When I was in my vacation last summer I slept every day until eleven and twelve and had a good time. Mary and Maggie and Patsy are well. Mary is the same old thing yet. She is working the College now.[1] It's a grand place if she will stay and they pay good wages. There are lots of Irish girls working with her. It's a female college. She will be alright. I has to work hard myself. I was going to leave this week but I guess I will stay for a while until I will hear of a good place. The old Jews have me crazy. They would make you laugh.

Well, Nora, how very few got married around Ballinlough. It's a wonder your Cousins Jerry and Dennie McCarthy don't get married or Tadey Hayes.[2] He was such a man and thought there was no one like himself. I suppose Mary Hayes has all our fellows in a string now. It's a good thing we aint over there. We would cut her out and especially yourself. You were always so smart for them all.

Well, Nora dear, I hope you will excuse me for not writing sooner as I don't have much time. I suppose you will be to work soon again. Well, I guess I will close now as I can't think of anything to tell you this time. Tom is well and sends you a dozen kisses. I will close now. Good Bye with lots of love to you and sisters and my Darling Tim.

Excuse this awful letter. I am thinking of Tom and can't write. Just think when I will be Mrs. Cloake. Aint that a lovely, warm name. Write soon. I must say something to make you laugh and fill the letter. Good Bye darling, your own

Loving Hannah.

Just as ever was.

XXXXXXXXXXXX

ENDNOTES

1   *Mary Collins was employed by Elmira College, which had been established as a college for women in 1855.*

2   *Jeremiah and Denis McCarthy were still single in 1901 and living at home in Ballinlough. Tadey Hayes, 26, son of Denis and Ellen, and brother of Mary Hayes, Nora's friend, was also at home with his parents. He was still not married when the 1911 Census was taken.*

Document M85
2 April 1899 – Denis Keane, Ballinaclough, Rosscarbery to Nora McCarthy, Bradford, Mass.

Ballinaclough Rosscarbery
April 2nd 1899

My Dear Cousin Norah,

I received your kind & loving letter last week & am very glad you are all right. It was very kind of Ellie to send the money to me for which I return sincere thanks & will & am praying for her & your future happiness. I am not improving anything. I suppose there is no chance of my recovery.

But God's will be done! I am resigned to my lot. The rest of the friends are all well, thank God! I never got my photograph taken, and there is no chance of getting it done now as there is no one round able to take one. I am but a mere skeleton now.

Father & Mother & John & family and Uncle John & Den are very well. I will conclude with love to all & wish all of you health & happiness.

I am your fond cousin, Den Keane.

Miss Norah McCarthy, written by a friend

Document **M86**
22 April 1899 – Hannah Collins, Elmira, N. Y. to Nora McCarthy, Haverhill, Mass.[1]

April 22nd, 1899

My Own Dear Nora,

I received your loving letter a few days ago which gave me great pleasure to learn by it that you and sisters and Brother were still well as the date of this letter leave me and Maggie and Mary at present, thank God.

Dear Nora, we are awful lonesome now as Patsy has gone out of town to work. Its around New York some place. We did not have any letter from him yet but we expect one every day. He got word from a fellow down there to come. He told him he could get three dollars a day but he got two here. That was nice pay, twelve dollars a week. He is a moulder.

Dear Nora, I am in the same place still because I did not hear of any other place. The lady told me she expected to shut up the house two months in the summer so I did not go. It was a grand place. It's a kind of a country place not very far though I think I would like it alright. My place is hard and they are so funny. I gets an afternoon out. Its Saturday, so I will be out this afternoon but will have to come back for supper and I gets Sunday too and don't come back until ten oclock and then I have to wash dishes. I do hate that for I never did until I came here for they have so much company. I only wish you and I was together in one place. We would be alright as I do be thinking of you everyday and all our nice times when we did not have to work so hard.

How is Tim getting along? I suppose he is a fine looking fellow as dark haired people are very handsome in this country as they say.[2] So I am right in it but I'm as homely as ever. We had a letter from home lately. They were well. They did not say anything of

---

1   *Nora was now employed at 117 Arlington Street in the section known as "The Highlands," where Haverhill's shoe manufacturers, bankers, and professionals had their large homes.*

2   *Tim (Tady) McCarthy had dark hair and brown eyes.*

people coming out this spring. Mary is grown awful big and stout. You would not know her. She does be riding a wheel around where she works. She is learning. I suppose she will have one soon. She ought to learn something else first.

Well, Nora dear, I must close now as I have to make the beds and its going to twelve o'clock noon and the lady is out so Good Bye and write soon again.

Hope you will excuse this old letter. Lots of love from your own Hannah.

XXXXXX

Tom is lovely and sends you a dozen kisses. Here they are.

XXXXXXXXXXXX

DOCUMENT M87

24 April 1899 – Gertrude O'Brien,[1] Lawrence, Mass, to Nora McCarthy, Bradford, Mass.

Lawrence, Mass.
April 24, '99

My Dear Friend Nora,

I take my pen in hand to write you a few lines to let you [know] that we are all well up here thanks be to God, hoping the arrival of this letter will find you and sisters, and brother and not forgetting Mr. Donovan, in as good a health.

My Dear Nora, I thought I would write to you as I did not see you the Sunday I was down and I was very sorry I did not. My father was uneasy as he did not get a letter from ye. I hope I will soon see ye again. Father would like to know if ye have heard any thing from Denis.[2]

My dear Friend, please let me know if ye are all working. Father would like to have yours and Nellie's address, so he could write, for he thinks a good deal of ye. We got a letter from my brother John from Boston[3] and he was inquiring for ye all. Father was afraid he did something out of the way because ye did not write to him. Mrs. McCarthy[4] had a letter from Cousin Dan's wife and she sent her picture to her and she told her that Denis McCarthy and his wife was coming this way pretty soon. And father said he hopes they will. Father would like to know when ye would get a letter from him or what time he was coming so he would have an opportunity to meet him somewhere for they told him when he was there that when they would come they would write a letter before them and tell the day they were to leave.[5]

How is Agnes and the baby? I had a good time with them the Sunday I was up. I was so sorry ye were not there. Father and myself was over to my aunt's home yesterday. She keeps a boarding house in South Lawrence, and he was asking them why didn't some one of them get marry and have a man in with them, and they said why, would he get them one, and I told them I knew a fine beauty young man in Haverhill. His name's Timothy McCarthy and they said bring him along and my Father said he would sometime, and please tell Tim about it.

So I must end my few lines as it is drawing late. So, good-bye, write soon. I remain your affectionate Friend.

Gertrude O'Brien 6 Lexington St. Lawrence, Mass.

ENDNOTES

1   *Gertrude O'Brien was the American-born daughter of Daniel and Mary O'Brien of Lawrence, Mass. She was born September 1884 and was one of ten living children in the family. Eight of the ten were at home when the 1900 Census was taken. Her father Dan immigrated in 1870 and her mother Mary in 1872. They were married in 1874. Dan was a day laborer. Gertrude and two older sisters worked in Lawrence's famed woolen mills. An older brother was a clerk in one of the mills. There are two photographs of Mr. O'Brien in the McCarthy Collection. He was remembered for the songs he would perform when visiting the McCarthys and Donovans in Bradford.*

2   *Nora's older brother, Denis McCarthy, from Kingston, Pennsylvania, was married to Julia O'Brien, a sister of Dan O'Brien.*

3   *John O'Brien, born in 1875, was the oldest of the O'Brien children. He was a clerk in a grocery store and lived in a lodging house in East Boston.*

4   *Possibly widow Bridget O'Brien McCarthy, 30, who lived with her six year old son in the house of her mother, Ellen O'Brien, next door to Dan O'Brien and family in Lawrence. Julia McCarthy from Pennsylvania was to visit the following summer.*

5   *Brother Denis McCarthy visited his sisters and brother in Haverhill and Bradford, Mass. for two weeks in late August–early September 1899. There is no mention of his wife, Julia, in the letters from that time that mention his visit.*

Document M87
24 April 1899 – Gertrude O'Brien,[1] Lawrence, Mass, to Nora McCarthy, Bradford, Mass.

Lawrence, Mass.
April 24, '99

My Dear Friend Nora,

I take my pen in hand to write you a few lines to let you [know] that we are all well up here thanks be to God, hoping the arrival of this letter will find you and sisters, and brother and not forgetting Mr. Donovan, in as good a health.

My Dear Nora, I thought I would write to you as I did not see you the Sunday I was down and I was very sorry I did not. My father was uneasy as he did not get a letter from ye. I hope I will soon see ye again. Father would like to know if ye have heard any thing from Denis.[2]

My dear Friend, please let me know if ye are all working. Father would like to have yours and Nellie's address, so he could write, for he thinks a good deal of ye. We got a letter from my brother John from Boston[3] and he was inquiring for ye all. Father was afraid he did something out of the way because ye did not write to him. Mrs. McCarthy[4] had a letter from Cousin Dan's wife and she sent her picture to her and she told her that Denis McCarthy and his wife was coming this way pretty soon. And father said he hopes they will. Father would like to know when ye would get a letter from him or what time he was coming so he would have an opportunity to meet him somewhere for they told him when he was there that when they would come they would write a letter before them and tell the day they were to leave.[5]

How is Agnes and the baby? I had a good time with them the Sunday I was up. I was so sorry ye were not there. Father and myself was over to my aunt's home yesterday. She keeps a boarding house in South Lawrence, and he was asking them why didn't some one of them get marry and have a man in with them, and they said why, would he get them one, and I told them I knew a fine beauty young man in Haverhill. His name's Timothy McCarthy and they said bring him along and my Father said he would sometime, and please tell Tim about it.

So I must end my few lines as it is drawing late. So, good-bye, write soon. I remain your affectionate Friend.

Gertrude O'Brien 6 Lexington St. Lawrence, Mass.

ENDNOTES

1   *Gertrude O'Brien was the American-born daughter of Daniel and Mary O'Brien of Lawrence, Mass. She was born September 1884 and was one of ten living children in the family. Eight of the ten were at home when the 1900 Census was taken. Her father Dan immigrated in 1870 and her mother Mary in 1872. They were married in 1874. Dan was a day laborer. Gertrude and two older sisters worked in Lawrence's famed woolen mills. An older brother was a clerk in one of the mills. There are two photographs of Mr. O'Brien in the McCarthy Collection. He was remembered for the songs he would perform when visiting the McCarthys and Donovans in Bradford.*

2   *Nora's older brother, Denis McCarthy, from Kingston, Pennsylvania, was married to Julia O'Brien, a sister of Dan O'Brien.*

3   *John O'Brien, born in 1875, was the oldest of the O'Brien children. He was a clerk in a grocery store and lived in a lodging house in East Boston.*

4   *Possibly widow Bridget O'Brien McCarthy, 30, who lived with her six year old son in the house of her mother, Ellen O'Brien, next door to Dan O'Brien and family in Lawrence. Julia McCarthy from Pennsylvania was to visit the following summer.*

5   *Brother Denis McCarthy visited his sisters and brother in Haverhill and Bradford, Mass. for two weeks in late August–early September 1899. There is no mention of his wife, Julia, in the letters from that time that mention his visit.*

Document M89
24 May 1899 – Hannah Collins, Elmira, N. Y. to Nora McCarthy, Haverhill, Mass.

Elmira, New York
May 24th, 1899

My Own Dear Nora,

I received your loving letter a week ago today which I was glad to hear that you and sisters and Brother were well as we ourselves are first rate at present, thank God.

Dear Nora, I was glad you left that hard place[1] I hope you will soon find another one that will be nice and easy. I guess you are like myself for I never can get a nice place. I hope the next one I get too will be suitable for me. Its so nice for you have your sister's home to go to when you are out of work or need a rest but I aint got any so I have to work all the time. I hope someday will come when I wont have to work so hard. That is when I will be Mrs. Cloak, that warm name.

Well, Dear Nora, indeed I felt awful sorry about poor Patrick John.[2] Aint it too bad for he was always a lovely boy and so were all of them. 1 am sure they all felt terrible about him. Johnnie must be awful lonesome going home.[3] He will tell your dear Mother how you are getting along and how you changed since you left her. I was surprised to hear Julia Hayes[4] came out to this country, or did she grow any since we left home? She must be about seventeen years old or is she more? And Mary Hayes[5] must be a great masher now. It's a wonder she did not write to you when she left home. She was always stuck on herself but she could not have the fellow she wanted if you like him better.

Well, my darling Sister, I am sure you are having a nice rest now and also a nice sleep in the mornings. I wish we both were together. I would enjoy it very much as I do hate to get up every morning. I am so tired. Well, I guess I will close for this time. Hope to hear from you soon again and to hear you will have a nice place. So Good Bye – lots of love and kisses to you from your ever Loving Hannah.

Give my love to Tim also.

ENDNOTES

1   *Nora had left her post at 117 Arlington Street. This letter was sent to Mary and Dan Donovan's house at 32 Locke St. (later named and renumbered as 77 Laurel Ave.), Bradford, Mass.*

2   *Patrick Donovan of Bawnfune, son of the late John, and Catherine Hurley Donovan, died 21 March 1899. Born 16 May 1864. He was thirty-four when he died of "probably pneumonia" of six days duration. His sister Bridget reported the death. As the eldest son at home, he would have assumed the management of the home farm for his widowed mother. The letter from home informing Nora of his death is not in the Collection.*

3   *Patrick Donovan's brother, known as Johnny John, had been living in Boston. He returned to Ireland after his brother's death to take over the running of the family farm. Other Donovan siblings who remained in Boston included Mrs. Ellen (Patrick) Driscoll, Mrs. Catherine (Patrick) Hayes, and Jerome Donovan. Another brother, Denis, had returned to Bawnfune by the time the 1901 Census was taken. When the 1911 Census was re0corded, the five remaining siblings in Ireland were all single and all living at the family home. All had ages in the thirties, though each age listed was five years younger than what their birth dates indicated.*

4   *Julia Hayes of Ballinlough, daughter of Patrick and Norry, was born 27 February 1881. She sailed to Boston on the S. S. Cephalonia, leaving Queenstown on 26 April 1899. Her destination was her sister Kate who was a domestic in Blue Hill, Milton, Mass. Katie had been born 24 August 1870.*

5   *Mary Hayes of Ballinlough, was born 28 April 1877 to Denis and Ellen (Collins) Hayes. She emigrated in 1894 to her aunt, Mrs. Collins, Pond Ave., Brookline. Aboard ship with her were Annie Hawley of Skibbereen, going to the same aunt, and Kate Collins, 21, from Skibbereen, going to her brother P. Collins, Matthew St., Chelsea, Mass.*

Document M90
10 June 1899 – Hannah Collins, Elmira, N. Y. to Nora McCarthy, Haverhill, Mass.

Elmira, New York
June 10th, 1899

My Own Dear Nora,

I received your ever loving letter alright and was glad to hear that you and sisters and Brother were still well as we are all first rate at present, thank God.

Dear Nora, I am very glad that you had a nice place.[1] I hope you will like it but you will have lots of work to do when those children come to visit. I hope they don't stay too long. Well, Nora, its been awful warm here in Elmira, too. I am just dead with the heat and cant eat anything. I get so thin in summer time but still I like it better than I do the winter. Its terrible how we got to work all the time as you been telling me to get married. I don't care to get married. Its soon enough for me yet. I have to think of my dear Parents and send them a little money often as they have to depend on their children for a while to send them a little money and Maggie and Patsy are older than I am so they have to go first. I had a letter from home this week. They were all well and you will be surprised to hear that Auntie Norry was living with them now. She was anointed the week before they wrote the letter but when they wrote she was getting a little stronger. The poor thing, how lonesome she must be without any of her own children to look after her, but Ellie Driscoll[2] thought all the neighbors around Ballinlough was better to her than my Father was when she was home that time. She was mad at us because I did not stay with Auntie Norry all my life. I know my dear Mother will take all the care she can of her for she was always tender-hearted and kind.

Well, Nora, dear, you must tell me if Johnnie John wrote to you. Indeed he was a nice fellow always and so were all of them but not any too good for you as you are nice enough for any of them. You know I mean all this too. That's so. He is older than you are a good deal,[3] so is my fellow older than I am. Light-haired people are always nice. They have such a beautiful complexion you can never tell their age.

Now write soon before three weeks. Well, I will close for this time with love and kisses to you from your own Loving Hannah.

Mary and Maggie also joins in sending love to you.

ENDNOTES

1   *Nora was now working at the home of Mrs. Abbie Chase, 49 Summer Street, near to her sister Ellen's place of employment.*

2   *American-born Ellie Driscoll was Norry's granddaughter, and Hannah's cousin.*

3   *Johnny John Donovan was born in Bawnfune in 1869, seven years before Nora McCarthy*

Document M91
21 June 1899 – Hannah Collins, Elmira, N. Y. to Nora McCarthy, Haverhill, Mass.

Elmira, New York
June 21st, 1899

My Own Darling Nora,

I received your loving letter last Sunday which gave me great pleasure to hear from you and also to hear that you and sisters and Brother were well as we are all first rate out here at present, thank God.

Dear Nora, I am always so glad to hear from you for your letters are so nice and interesting that I do love to read them. They makes me think of you more and more than ever. 1 am glad you like your new place. I hope you will stay a good while there and its so nice to have Ellie working near you as ye see each other every day.

Well, Darling, I am almost dead with the heat but those last few days has been very cool I wish it would stay so for the rest of the summer. I am sure you feels the heat too. It will make you loose them rosy cheeks of yours, has it not already.

Dear Nora, I seen a green horn[1] the other night. He is from our place home. His name is Jerry Donoghue. He told us about our folks to home as they sent us three silk ties. You know like they used to wear home. They were very pretty.

Dear Nora, I had a lovely time last Sunday. Tom took me out riding. We went out of the city a long ways. He never tells me when he is going to take me out until he comes after me with the horse. And I said to him why he don't, he says he likes to surprise me once in a while. Aint he lovely. He always treats me when we go out together. We are going to have our picture taken together some time this summer. So I will send you one if we do. Mary don't like him very well but I told her I did not get him to suit her. She aint got any fellow yet. She is learning to ride a wheel now. I guess she is worse than she ever was home.

Well, Nora dear, I hope some day will come when we will see

each other again. I would like to go to Haverhill to see you. I wish I could this very minute. We would have a good old talk. I suppose I would not know you now you are such a big young lady but you are still my darling Nora.

Well, Dear, I will close for this time. Hope to hear from you soon again with love and kisses to you and all from your ever Loving sister, Hannah, Good Bye.

Hope you will excuse this letter as I cant think of any more news to tell you this time.

How is Tim? Did he get married yet? I am thinking of you all the time.

XXXXXXXXX kisses.

ENDNOTES

1   *A "greenhorn" was a recent immigrant.*

Document M92
5 July 1899 – Hannah Collins, Elmira, N. Y. to Nora McCarthy, Haverhill, Mass.

Elmira, New York
July 5th, 1899

My Dear Sister Nora,

I hope you will excuse me for not answering your loving letter sooner which I received with great pleasure and was glad to hear that you and sisters and Brother were still well as we are all first rate at present, thank God.

Dear Nora, I would have written sooner but I was busy and did not have much news to tell you so I thought I would wait until after the fourth of July so I could tell you how I spent the day. Well I went to the Park.[1] It's a good ways. We go in the cars. There are a nice lake there too. It's a very nice place and I went to the Reformatory and I seen all the prisoners drill out in the yard.[2] It's a grand building but it don't seem so nice to the poor prisoners and many nice Irish fellows there too. Indeed I felt sorry for them. I did not have to come back for supper. I hope you had a nice time too. I only wish we had our times together. I would enjoy it very much like we always did.

Dear Nora, what is Mickie and Patrick McCarthy doing in England? Dont Patrick work at his trade any more? They were very smart fellows. I was glad to hear that your dear Father and Mother were well. I suppose you will soon have a letter from Johnnie John. He will not forget to write to you. I am sure he thought a good deal of you. He always did and of all the family. I am sure Annie Cahalane[3] is a great girl now but I guess she never had very much love for me. You and her were great chums before I came to Ballinlough but I cut her out then, did I not, Nora.

Did Tim have his pictures taken yet? I wish he would. I would

---

1　　　*Eldridge Park, on the lake of the same name.*

2　　　*Elmira Reformatory, later Elmira Correction Facility.*

3　　　*Cousin Mick McCarthy reported in a letter dated April 1900 that Annie Cahalane was married "about 3 months ago." Annie and her brother Mike were in Newport, Wales, as were cousins Mick and Patrick "The Shoemaker" McCarthy.*

like to see that sweet face of his once more. You must not be asking me for those pictures I told you about because I did not have them taken yet and I dont know if I will this summer. If I do you will get one sure. Well, my darling sister, I cant think of any more to say this time so I will close with fond love and kisses to you from your ever dear Chum, Hannah.

Good Bye and please excuse bad writing. You are my little darling Baby.

Document M93
20 July 1899 – Patrick and Kate McCarthy, Ballinlough, Leap to Nora McCarthy, Haverhill, Mass.[1]

Patrick McCarthy
Ballinlough, Leap
July 20th – 99

Dear Nora,

We received your very welcomed letter on the 8th day of July having delayed it so long owing to busy times spraying gardens and hay making. However, when your poor Father and Mother gets an account from Ye I takes them Careless in writing for them as we would hear ye are all well, Thank God.

Dear Nora, F. and M. received the money all right, are very thankful to you and Ellie for you thinking of them. What notion have Tim I wonder, have he home forgotten like some more? Tell him write. If you can soften him he may return home some time as thousands are after coming home this year, but Uncle Pad[2] says no one will come to himself. I hope he wont have this say always.

Now, Nora, poor Den Keane was buried 1st June. May the Lord have Mercy on his soul and on the souls of our friends. <u>Amen Amen.</u>

Nora, he[3] wont write to his mother or father. We got no letter from Mick or Patk with a month. Were well then and at work. Patk works at his trade.[4] Now, my dear girl, about Father and Mother going to America. Mother would like to go but to get ready, its hard, like to be with ye. As for Father, he says he have no business there as he cannot work. Its hard to live idle in America.

Mother is troubled about Dennie didn't send the picture since. She is fearing he is sick or something. Everything troubles her. Its hard for her be strong and is not either, complains of the old pain with a month or so. You can know it yourself how she is.

Dear Nora, its lucky how you are living near Ellie. It looks like living in one house. About Kate McCarthy address. She is living with Mrs. Brien's[5] where Ellie lodged when she went to meet Tim. This is the account we got. Her mother had a letter yesterday. So I must come to a conclusion by sending our best wishes to Ellie, Tim, Mary, Husband and <u>Babies</u> and especially from Father and Mother to each of you. John John is very nice to every one, talks of ye very often. I have no more to say but write soon again.

From Father and Mother

To Nora

Dear Nora, mother is expecting a good letter from all of ye together for Ross Fair 2nd of August. I hope ye won't fail. Excuse my writing, it is bad.

ENDNOTES

1   *Written across the bottom of this envelope is "Stamped by Agnes Donovan," Mary and Dan Donovan's six year old daughter. The writing is clear and well-formed.*

2   *Cousin Julia McCarthy is writing this letter for her aunt and uncle, Kate and Patrick McCarthy, Nora's parents.*

3   *Probably refers to Julia's brother, Mick, in Wales.*

4   *Patrick was a shoemaker. The label, "The Shoemakers," is still applied to his descendants, though none of them have been followed that trade.*

5   *Kate McCarthy, the daughter of George and Kate McCarthy of Skibbereen, was born 5 June 1864. Mrs. Brien was probably Nora Brien, mother of Patrick, Delia and Margaret of South Boston. That Nora's sister, Ellie, went to Boston to meet Tim, and stayed the night at Mrs. Brien's lodging house, adds another piece of information to the immigration process.*

DOCUMENT M94
[22] July 1899 – Hannah Collins, Elmira, N. Y. to Nora McCarthy, Haverhill, Mass.

Elmira, N. Y.
July 1899 [date from postmark on envelope]

My Own Darling Nora,

I received your loving letter alright and was so delighted to hear from you as sometimes when you delay your letter so long I get worried about you but am glad you and all the rest are still well as I and sisters are first rate at present.

Dear Nora, you don't think of me any oftener than I do of you because there aint a day pass that I dont think of you and feels lonesome for you too. How could I ever forget them happy days gone by we spent together when we were young and foolish. I do be thinking I would not know you now, you are so big and of course you are much prettier than ever but you know I always said you had a handsome face and I still think so. Oh, Nora, your sweet letters makes me think more of you than ever. They are interesting to me that I do love to read them.

Well, Nora dear, I am so tired and almost dead. Its so warm here in Elmira. I am sure you feels the heat too or is it warm in Haverhill? I wish I could lay off and rest a week now. I would need it very much but you see I aint got any home here. Of course, I got some cousins but I don't care for them. Everybody for themselves in this country. I think they aint good natured here like they are home. My Cousin Mary McCarthy has invited me to come down there to Albany to see her and stay and also her Aunt wrote me a few letters to come but she never see me or I her.

Well, Nora, I am sorry your place is so hard. I hope them old people are visiting you will soon go home and give you a little rest. Its nothing but work all the time for us also. I am glad to hear Tim is well, also Ellie and Mary. I would like to see Tim now. So he did not change any since he left home. I am expecting a letter from home soon. Its a wonder Johnnie John did not write to you. I am sure he will yet but he is not settled down. Give him a little while longer. I am sure he did not forget his darling Nora so soon.

Well, my darling, I wish I had some more news to tell you but you don't know any one here to tell you about them. Tom is well and sends you his love. He is going to work all nights next week so I cant see him until Saturday night. How can I live so long without him? He is so dear to me. I am the first girl he ever loved and I guess the last one too. Well, darling, hope you will excuse this bad letter and writing with a bushel of love and kisses to you, I remain forever your old chum, Hanna.

Good Bye, write soon again. Did Jerome John come to see you lately and did Pake Hayes get married yet?

XXXXXXXXXX kisses

Document M95
24 August 1899 – Hannah Collins, Elmira, N. Y. to Nora McCarthy, Haverhill, Mass.

Elmira, N. Y.
August 24th, 1899

My Own Darling Sister,

I hope you will excuse me for not answering your loving letter which I received a week ago but I had been busy all the week cleaning the house for she is going to have company Saturday. They are her cousins from New York but I guess they will not stay long. I hope they don't any way for I will be tired from working.

Well, Darling, I am glad you are still well and your sisters and Brother as I and Maggie and Mary are first rate at present.

Dear Nora, as you said to me, if I had any notion of going home again I would just love to go back to see them again but I suppose I never will. Still I may. I wrote home a few weeks ago but the last letter I had from them Mother and Father said they would have their pictures taken as I asked for them a month ago. I will be delighted if I will get them. I am waiting for another letter from them. I kind of think Auntie Norry is dead because I have been dreaming so much of her lately. The poor thing is very old now.

Dear Nora, so you did not write to Johnnie yet. He may come back again. I am sure he thought a good deal of you as he always like the family so well. So ye all has a nice time playing cards every evening.[1] You were always a great gambler. I only wish I was with you too. I would enjoy it but I cant play.

Well, Nora dear, I hope all of your company are gone by this time so you will get rested. Its company and style with them all. They would make you sick. My fellow is lovely. That is all the pleasure I have when he comes to see me. I would feel lost now if I did not have him. We are going together nearly two years, but, Oh, I hate to get married. I guess not for a long time yet.

Well, did you see any nice fellow you got stuck on? I think its hard to suit you but when you meet the right one it will be alright, but I guess you did not see him yet. I hope you will soon. Well, darling, I cant think of any more to say this time with fond love and kisses to you.

Your Loving Sister, Hanna

XXXX

Please excuse me for not writing sooner and also for such a bad letter.

ENDNOTES

1   *Nora was a life-long devotee of a card game related to Bridge, known as Whist.*

Document M96
31 August 1899 – Patrick and Kate McCarthy, Ballinlough, Leap to Nora McCarthy, Haverhill, Mass.

Ballinlough, Leap
Thursday 31st '99

Dear Cousin Nora,

Your letter arrived here safe on Saturday morning. It is great pleasure to your Father and Mother and your cousins to hear that ye are all well as this leaves your old parents at present. Thank G.

Now, my dear Cousin, Mother received the money alright yesterday Wednesday as it is very good from you to think of them so ready. What about Tim? I never thought him so hard when he was at home.

Dear Nora, I am sorry to tell you that simple storys are no addition to you and I told you what was trouble to each of us and to you also. As for Norry Hegerty's removal, we made nothing of it as few cried, for her was old and displeased with her neighbors as they could not wait on her at all times. She is living with Hanna Collins Father and have money to kick and plenty company now and nothing calling her pocket. Her old house is occupied by a shopkeeper Mickeen Carty of Capponaboha[1] and is doing rolling business.

Johnny John is called sir by lots of people and by myself the first time I talked to him after coming. As for his seasickness, we made no inquiries about it but is looking fine. Julia and Bridgie[2] are wearing style now. You can consider your self and lots of girls too many to mention.

Well, Nora, poor Jer Rick was buried two weeks ago.[3] His is a big loss to his family. Brigid's mother was buried also.[4] The Georges are well. Mary have two children, boys. Their names I can't mention.[5] She is looking fine herself. I had a letter from Mick and Patk last week. Are well. Mick lost your address and asked it of me and will write to you. Then he [is] very slow in writing home too, to you also. Father and Mother are very sorry how Ellie was disappointed if she went to see Katie McCarthy as she is gone to her Brother John.[6] We didn't see your Uncle

Dan since Den was buried or Aunt Nora. Aunt Julia is very well. Can't walk much. Your Father and Mother is middling strong now. I don't hear your mother complain so often. I wonder Dennie don't write to you.[7] Mary Hayes writes often for the time she is gone.

My Dear girl, we had pity for ye all summer. It was very warm here since May, very warm, no rain up to last Saturday. But Johnny John says it is nothing compared to the heat of America. So now, my dear Cousin, I have no more to say for this time.

With best love to all from Father and Mother to Ellie, Tim, Mary and Husband and Children.

Good bye to all from Julia.

ENDNOTES

1   *The 1901 Census of Ireland lists Michael McCarthy, 35, unmarried, egg dealer and grocer, as living in a house owned by John Donovan of Ballinlough. Mickeen was the brother of "Little Jerry" McCarthy of Cappanabohy whose marriage to Minnie Cullinane was reported in a letter from sister Katie to Nora dated 1 March 1896.*

2   *Johnny John Donovan's sisters. In 1901, Bridget was 27 and Julia 26, though they gave much younger ages to the Census taker.*

3   *Jeremiah Donovan, son of Richard, was a carpenter who died at age 60 on 11 August 1899. He lived in Mealisheen, a townland immediately east of Ballinlough. His death was reported by his wife Margaret. In the 1901 Census, there were five children, aged 9 to 20, at home with their widowed mother.*

4   *Margaret Driscoll, a widow aged 80, of Knockenacrohy, died of old age and debility on 12 July 1899. Her death was reported by her daughter, Bridget, of Knockskagh. Bridget had written some of the letters to Nora from her parents when Cousin Julia was not available. Margaret Driscoll had been a midwife, and a neighbor who would assist in the "laying out" of the recently deceased, a service she had performed for Nora's sister, Katie McCarthy.*

5   *Mary "George" and John Hurley of Skibbereen had two sons, Charles and Patrick, by the date of this letter. Two more children, Mary Kate and George, were born before the 1901 Census was taken.*

6   *Kate and John McCarthy were part of the "George" family from Skibbereen. Kate had been lodging with Mrs. Brien in South Boston, but was now with her brother in Lawrence, Mass.*

7   *Either Julia's brother Dennis, or Nora's brother of the same name.*

Document M97
12 September 1899 – Hannah Collins, Elmira, N. Y. to Nora McCarthy, Haverhill, Mass.

September 12th 1899

My Dear Sister Nora

I received your loving letter alright and was glad to hear that ye were all well as the date of this letter leaves me and sisters in perfect good health at present.

Dear Nora, I am sure ye were all glad to see year brother.[1] So he stayed two weeks. That was a good while but I suppose it did not seem more than a day because ye had a nice time with him. Does he live in Pennsylvania? There is where Patsy is in Easton, Pennsylvania.[2] We hears from him often. Last week he went around New York to see Dannie Con sisters[3] and his Cousins and he seen lots of the folks from home that live there too. He had a nice time but he only stayed two days. They wanted him stay a few weeks.

Dear Nora, I am having a great time this month as the Jews are having their New Year again. They would make you laugh. This week we are having a big Holiday.[4] They don't eat anything since the night before until the next night and then when they do eat after fasting so long they have three suppers at once. So you see how crazy they are making so much work for me all the time. I thought I was not going to stay a month with them but here I am over a year already. I have not changed many places since I come out as I am out four years the first of this month.

I am expecting a letter from home in a week as I guess I told you I asked for my Father and Mother's pictures so I hope I will get them but not so soon. I don't expect them in the next letter. I suppose four years made a good change in them. I think they are failed a good deal.

Well, Nora, I suppose your dear Mother will be glad when you tell her about seeing your Brother and especially when he looks so well. I guess I will close for this time with fond love and kisses to you and sisters and Tim.

As ever, Your loving Hannah. Good Bye. Write when you can

as I like to hear from you often. Tom is well and sends you his love also. Mary and Maggie are well. Mary can ride a wheel now but aint got any.

ENDNOTES

1   *Brother Denis "Dinnie" McCarthy, who lived in Kingston, Penn. Nora had probably not seen him since he left home to go first to England and then, with wife and first two children, to Pennsylvania. This appears to have been his first visit to his siblings.*

2   *Easton is in the north-eastern corner of Pennsylvania, near Bethlehem, and the New Jersey border.*

3   *The Collins sisters were the daughters of Cornelius Collins, and sisters to Daniel, of Driminidy, Drinagh. They were Hanna's cousins.*

4   *Yom Kippur and Rosh Hashanah. One must assume that Hann had never met a single person of the Jewish faith before being hired by this family.*

DOCUMENT M98
23 September 1899 – Hannah Collins, Elmira, N. Y. to Nora McCarthy, Haverhill, Mass.

Elmira, N. Y.
September 23rd, 1899

My Dear Sister Nora,

Your loving letter reached me alright and I was glad to see by it that you and sisters and brother were well as we are first rate at present, but I had a very bad cold for almost a week, also a headache and did not feel well but am better now, thank God.

Dear Nora, I also had a letter from home yesterday. They were all well. Also, Auntie Norry was feeling pretty good again. They said she has a letter from Ellie often.[1] I don't know if she sends her any money or not. My Father and Mother had their pictures taken. I did not get them yet as I am anxious to see them. I am sure they will look very funny but still they will be dear to me. T was also glad you had a letter from home and that your dear Father and Mother were well. How many limes I thinks of them too and what a ice good hearted woman your Mother was. Poor Auntie Norry thought so much of her because she was so good to her.

Well, Nora, I only wish I could go to see you this very minute. 1 am always thinking about you. And I love you now as much as ever and you know how dearly I always loved you. I would also like to see Tim now. Did he grow any taller? Has he got any girl yet? My dear Tons is well. I have not seen him since last Saturday. He is working nights........ I am lonesome without him.

Well, Nora, the winter is coming already and I do hate it. I am so cold in winter. I think I love the summer better no matter how warm, but I felt the heat this summer....... Maggie and Mary are well and sends you their best love as they always ask about you. Mary is.............

Well, Darling, I think I will have to close for this time as I can't think of anything more to say. With fond love and kisses to you. Your ever dear Chum, Hanna.

Good bye. Write soon again. XXXXXXX

> My pen is bad, my ink is pale
> But my love for you will never fail, Nora dear.

Remember me to Tim.

ENDNOTES

1   *Ellie Driscoll, of Washington, DC, Norry's granddaughter and Hanna's cousin.*

DOCUMENT M99
8 October 1899 – Hannah Collins, Elmira, N. Y. to Nora McCarthy, Haverhill, Mass.

October 8th, 1899

Darling Nora,

Your dear and fond letter reached- me a few days ago and I was glad to hear that you were still well, also Tim and sisters as I am first rate at present, also Maggie and Mary.

Dear Nora, I am like yourself have not got any news to tell you as you don't know anyone here in Elrnira to tell you about them. Mary is the same old thing yet and did not change any since she left home. She can ride a wheel now. She was to see me the other night and she had one. You would laugh at her.

She aint got any fellow yet. She says they all smiles at me but it don't do them no good. I did not have any other letter from home since. I expects their pictures any time. I hope I will get them soon. Did you hear from home lately or did you write to Johnnie since. I mean yet.

1 had to laugh at Tim. So he did not forget about my feet being so big, but you tell him I wear shoes now every day which makes them smaller. I would love to sec him. Did he have his picture taken yet? So he is very interested in Tom. I guess Tom is alright but you know he did not come from Ireland. I often wish he did but he is awful nice to mc and gives mc a good time. He never went with a girl before me. He will take me to the shows now soon in winter. I just love to go to shows.

Dear Nora, I hears from my Cousin Mary McCarthy often. She want me come down there. I would like to go but I cant. I will have to be cleaning house now soon. I do hate it. This is Sunday and am going out so I will take this letter by the post Office and mail it. I gucss I will close for this time as I don't think of any more to say this time.

With fond love and kisses to you, 1 am as ever your own, Hannah.

Good Bye, Nora dear, and write when you can.

Mary and Maggie sends you their best love as they always ask me when I heard from you.

Please excuse this bad writing as I am in a hurry to meet my Tom.

XXXXXXXXXX kisses.

Document M100
18 October 1899 – Patrick and Kate McCarthy, Ballinlough, Leap to Nora McCarthy, Haverhill, Mass.[1]

Ballinlough
Oct. 18 '99

My very dear child Nora

We received your kind and most welcome letter about a week ago, which was a source of the greatest consolation to us to hear from ye all and especially to hear that ye were all well. I could not describe to you on cold paper how overjoyed we were at hearing that ye all had the pleasure of seeing poor Denic once again. What a pity he was not able to stay longer, I wish he were able to live near ye. We were delighted to hear that he and his wife and family were well. 1 wish we had the great consolation of seeing him once again, but I fear we will be denied of that pleasure on this earth but trust we win all meet in a brighter land where parting will be no more.

What a pity he did not take a trip to see us. It was much the same as seeing him to hear so much about him as I was all the time worrying about him. I was afraid he was dead. Your Father often laughs at me as I often wish I were with ye but he says it is easier to bury me here as he don't need to buy the ground. Did Dennie say he'd write? We were glad to hear that Mary, Husband and family were well, also Ellie and Tim, and though last but not least your own dear self. We were glad to hear that so many of the friends came to sec Dennie. Mrs. McCarthy was delighted to hear that yc met Kate and Jack.[2] It is nice for ye all to be so convenient to one another. Mrs. McCarthy and all the family are well. She wishes to be remembered to ye all. Dennie Herlihy's daughter Kate is expected home this month. Perhaps you might sec her.[3]

Dearest Nora we are very thankful to you for your kind present to us. Father says he'll drink a toast to yc Leap fair day as it is unknown who'll live this time twelve months.[4] He is failing, but he always try to go to Mass. He goes early and will take time. All that you inquired about are well. Cousin Maggie has another young son. His name is Curley.[5] Dan Cullinane of Leap was buried a week ago.[6] Bridget Driscoll's mother died on the 12th of July. She is very lonely now. She intends going to America for Spring. Ye might meet yet. Julia is busy at present. They are digging in the potatoes. Did you hear that poor Ellie Paddy, your once loved companion, was buried?[7] She died in June 3 months after her confinement. Her baby died a week before her.

P. S. Father is anxious to know if Ellie intends to come home again. He intends making a match for her. He did not give up matchmaking[8] yet. I know, Nora, you'll laugh at this.

Good bye. God bless ye all.

ENDNOTES

1   *The writer of this letter is not identified, but it is not one of the usual correspondents for the McCarthy parents. The penmanship is distinctive and is an educated hand with proper use of periods and apostrophes. The first "s" on Miss and Mass on the envelope are the old style long "s" that looks like an "f."*

2   *Mrs. "George" McCarthy of Skibbereen, and her two children who were living in Lawrence, Mass.*

3   *Kate Herlihy had gone to America in 1892 when she was seventeen. What was unusual is that she went via "second cabin" along with her cousin Hannah Leahy. Her father, Denis, paid her way, and Hannah's passage was paid for by the uncle to whom they were both going, Mr. O'Brien, 425 Eastern Ave., Chelsea. Her father died 27 January 1900, aged 66, from bronchitis. This is probably the same Denis Herlihy who helped the McCarthys to cover the expenses of Katie McCarthy's funeral.*

4   *Patrick McCarthy was more prescient than he realized for his daughter Mary Donovan would be dead within a year.*

5   *Cornelius Hourihane was born to cousin Maggie (McCarthy) and Courley Hourihane on 11 September 1899.*

6   *Daniel Cullinane, a 60 year old farmer, died 7 October 1899 of pneumonia. He was ill for eight days. His death was reported by his widow Mary. He had a grocery store in Leap which his widow continued to operate.*

7   *Ellie Driscoll, daughter of Patrick of Bawnfune.*

8   *Ellen McCarthy was thirty-four in 1899, a bit old for matchmaking, and was an independent, well-employed woman. One wonders what her father planned to offer a potential suitor as a dowry since he was always in need of financial help from his children. Ellen would eventually marry a widower, Patrick Quirk.*

Document M101
17 November 1899 – Hannah Collins, Elmira, N. Y, to Nora McCarthy, Haverhill, Mass.

November 17, 1899

My Own Dear Sister,

Your loving letter reached me alright and I was glad to hear that you and sisters and brother were well as we are all just the same here at present.

Dear Nora, I was so busy all the time since I wrote to you last, cleaning house every day, but I am through now and am so glad, as I had to clean all alone. She[1] did not get anybody to help but herself done a little but did not kill herself. Are you through with house cleaning yet?

Dear Nora, I had a letter from home last Monday. They were all well, also Auntie Norry was feeling good. I guess she have a little more care now as my mother says she is very kind to her. I was also glad you heard from home lately and that your dear Father and Mother were well. I guess one time they thought they never would be so lonely. I feels sorry for them to be all alone after all their company. I am sure its very lonesome over there now. There aint many young people around. I shall never forget dear Ballinlough and our old times. I thought more of that place than my own home.

Dear Nora, I was glad to learn that you had such a nice time at that dance. Your brother-in-law is very kind to take you there.[2] I never bother with dance any more as I have never been to any dance since I been in the country, only one, and that was my Cousin's dance they had two years ago. I think they dance too funny in this country.

Dear Nora, Maggie and Mary are well and sends you their best love. Also, Tom is lovely. He is a dear little thing. He likes to hear about Ireland. He also likes to hear people tell stories about it. He has very nice sisters. They are so stylish. Two of them are married to Yankee fellows and are doing well.

Dear Nora, we had a little snow this week. Its getting to look like winter already and how I do hate the winter. Well, I guess I will close for this time with fond love and kisses to you and hope you will excuse me for not writing sooner.

So, Good Bye my darling Sweetheart. I remain forever, Your dear friend,

Hanna Collins Cloak not.

ENDNOTES

1   *Hannah's employer, Mrs. Joseph Sittenfield.*

2   *Dan Donovan had escorted Nora to the dance. At this time, Mary Donovan was about seven months pregnant with the Donovan's third child, Helen Evelyn. Nora and Dan's daughter, Marie, remembers her mother dancing in the kitchen and her father attempting to do the same. Her mother was light on her feet and knew all the complicated steps to Irish dancing. Her father "might as well have had logs where his legs should be!"*

DOCUMENT M102
15 December 1899 – Patrick and Kate McCarthy, Ballinlough, Leap to Nora McCarthy, Haverhill, Mass.

Ballinlough
December 15th '99

My Dearest Daughter Norah

We received your kind and welcomed letter and money alright and were more than glad to hear that you and all of ye are well, enjoying good health as we ourselves are at present, T. G. So also all the friends and neighbours.

Well, Norah, I am glad to know the children are so nice and that ye have such a nice time together. I was proud to know Dennie and his wife and family are all well and that he is looking so fine. And it pleases me to know Ellie, Tim, Mary and Family and husband are also well. About the Ballinaclough folks, I don't know much about them but I had seen Big Den at Leap about a month ago and he was looking first rate. I suppose Katie McCarthy will write home for Christmas. It is nice for ye to be together and have such funny times.

Dear Norah, I'd like to know if cousins Patrick or Mickey had written to you lately. They asked for your address not long ago. They writes home often. They spoke of coming home for Xmas but I cant say whether they will or not. About your Cousin Maggie, she has six children and one she buried.[1] I mean four sons and two daughters living and one son buried. Mary and boys are also well. So also Julia, Jerry and Dennie, father and mother are still well.[2]

Well, Norah, I mean to tell you Mary Hayes sent four pounds for Christmas and James Wholey seven pounds. America is a fright it is so good. The Yankee Johnny John have a pig killed for Christmas and have beaten all the Bawnfune farmers. Pad Hayes' did not get any money yet. It was promised to them. They are expecting it every day.

Norah, how glad I'd be if you came in to me Xmas night. Katie Paddy, Julia, Mickie and their mother[3] are getting on first rate and also Jack's wife and family[4] are just the same. They are living in Bawnfune still. I was expecting to get a letter from Dennie. I suppose he have forgotten about the home altogether. So now I have no more to say at present. I am more than thankful to ye for the Christmas present though I expected one from each of ye more, but all the same I am very thankful to all of ye.

ENDNOTES

1   *Cousin Maggie McCarthy Hourihane's sons were Batt, Daniel, Patrick and Cornelius. Her daughters were Julia and Mary. Mary had a twin brother, Michael, who died when he was ten days old.*

2   *Refers to Uncle Michael and members of his family.*

3   *The widow and family of the late Patrick Driscoll and his wife, Mary, of Bawnfune.*

4   *The widow and family of the late Johnny Bawn Driscoll of Bawnfune.*

Document M103
18 December 1899 – Hannah Collins, Elmira, N. Y. to Nora McCarthy, Haverhill, Mass.

December 18th, 1899

My Darling Sister,

I received your ever fond letter Friday afternoon which gave me great pleasure to hear from you and also to hear that you and sisters were well but am very sorry for Tim being sick so long. I hope he is alright by this time. It seems too bad to have he be sick for he is so jolly and nice. He will have ye laughing all the time. I suppose he is as jolly as ever.

Dear Nora, I have a cold those days, but not very bad. Maggie and Mary are well and sends you their best love as they always ask about you. Patsy is coming for Christmas. We will be glad to see him. I suppose you have written home long ago. I only wrote last week.

Well, Dear Nora, I wish you a merry Christmas and a Happy New Year and a good many of them. I only wish we could be together and have a good time as I well remember our Christmases home and how we used spend them. I would have to be with you all the time. You don't love me any better than I do you as I am always thinking about you. I have a very nice new dress for Christmas. It's a plaid. I did not get any new coat or hat this winter, but I got them last Winter. They are almost as good as ever. So, darling, you had lots of company Thanksgiving. Its so nice to have Ellie work near you. She will help you out.

Dear Nora, I had a letter from my cousin, Mary McCarthy. She was very sick with the Typhoid fever but is almost well again. She is not working yet. She is staying to her Aunt's house as her Aunt is very kind to her. Did you have any letter from your Cousin Mickey in England lately? What is he doing there and is Patrick there also. You don't hear from any of the Boston folks. Did Pake Hayes get married yet.

Well, my darling Sister, I hope you will excuse this bad letter. I must close for the present. So Good Bye. Lots of love and kisses to you and all.

Your ever Loving sister Hanna.

Good Bye and again wishing you a merry Christmas and a happy New Year.

Give my best love to Tim and also your sisters.

DOCUMENT M104

8 January 1900 – Hannah Collins, Elmira, N. Y. to Nora McCarthy, Haverhill, Mass.

January 8th, 1900

My Dear Sister,

Your ever fond letter reached me alright and I was glad to hear that ye were all well as I and sisters are just the same at present. Dear Nora, Christmas has gone and I did not think anything about it. Did not have a very good time. I was to Mrs. Dempsey's Christmas night and went to midnight mass and then came home after. I did not get many presents. I got a ring and a prayer Book from Tom and a pair of gloves from Maggie and an underskirt from Mary and, where work, I got a dress, and aprons, handkerchiefs and I guess that was all I got.

Well, dear Nora, I had a letter from home Sunday. They were all well, also Auntie Norry was pretty well. They sent me Ellie's address as I asked for it. She is married. Her name is Mrs. James Enright.[1] I don't know when she got married. They told me before she was not but they did not know until Auntie Norry came to live with them as she used to say to them sometimes she was and another time she wasn't. You know she used to say so many things. Her and Nora[2] wrote to Auntie Norry for Christmas. They did not say if she got any money or not. When people get married they need all the money themselves, don't you think so. I was glad you heard from home lately and that your dear Father and Mother were well.

So Peggie Connolly's Mother was buried, but she must be very old.[3] I suppose Peggy feels bad now she cant speak any more friendly words. I suppose you will soon have a letter from Mary Hayes. Is she with the Whooleys? I suppose she will marry James. She was a great one for fellows. She thought they were all stuck on her but I guess not. You could cut her out every time.

Patsy was here for Christmas. He only stayed a week. We are lonesome now after him as he said he don't know when he will come here again. He has a good job working every day. He is very sensible and saving lots of money.

Well, dear sister, I will have to close for this time with fond love and kisses to you. I am as ever your true friend, H. C.

Write soon again. I think you are getting very slow.

ENDNOTES

1

2   *Nora Driscoll Sullivan, Hanna's cousin, was born in New York in August 1864. She married John Sullivan of Cappagh Beg, Ballydehob, in Washington DC in 1893. The Sullivans lived on New York Ave., N. W. where John was a saloon keeper. The Sullivan household in 1900 included three children and Catherine Taylor, a 21 year old black domestic.*

3   *Johannah Connolly, 85, a widow of Cappanabohy, died 5 November 1899 of old age and debility. She had been ill for two years. Johanna was the mother of Peggie, Courley, and Michael Connolly, among others, and her death was reported by her daughter Peggie. There is no mention in the December letter to Nora from her parents of this death. It may have been included in a letter sent to Ellie which did not end up in Nora's collection.*

Document M105
[23 January 1900] – Hannah Collins, Elmira, N. Y. to Nora McCarthy, Haverhill, Mass.

My Darling Sister

Its almost time I should answer your loving letter which I received a week ago tomorrow and was glad to hear that you and sisters were well, also Tim, as the date of this letter leaves me and all just the same. [not legible] made for me. Dear Nora, I wrote to Ellie Driscoll in Washington a week ago and I got a letter from her a few days ago. She said she was surprised to hear from me but very glad to think I had not forgotten her yet. She told me she got married last April. She married a man from the county Limerick and is getting along nicely. Have a lovely new home and she says he is so good. She went with him three years. I also told her about you and Tim and that you writes to me so she said to send you and Tim her best love and she also asked me for your address but I have not written to her yet. Will I send her your address. She and Nora wrote to Auntie Norry for Christmas and they sent her two pounds. I think they are very kind to her.

Dear Nora, I am surprised your hair has grown dark but it was not very red any time. I would like to see it. You remember how I always was stuck on red hair especially yours, but Tom has red hair so I don't care. It will be alright. They don't like red hair in this country so mine is just right. Oh, you did not write to Mary Hayes. You are waiting until she writes to you first. Mary was pretty good just the same if she had her own way but as you say her mother was too funny. You are a nice one mashing James Wholey. I never knew that before. Mary did not know anything about that, did she, or she would be jealous of you. I know well you would cut them all out if you try. I only wish we were together again. We would talk about the old days and all the fun we had. I will never forget. You don't love me any better than I do you as I am always thinking of you and wishing to see you. I think I will have to close for this time with fond love and kisses to you. Write when you can, and please excuse this bad letter. I am as ever your true Chum, Hannah

Document **M106**
7 February 1900 – Hannah Collins, Elmira, N. Y. to Nora McCarthy, Haverhill, Mass.

February 7th, 1900

Well My Darling sister

I hope you will excuse me for not answering your ever fond letter which I received a week today which gave me great pleasure to hear from you as your letter is so nice and interesting. I am always so glad when I read it through. Am glad you and sisters are still well, also Tim as the date of this leaves me and Mary and Maggie at present. But Maggie has been very sick in a week. She had the grip.[1] Was very bad. Had the doctor every day but she is getting along alright now.

Dear Nora, I have written to Ellie Driscoll a week ago and sent her your address. Has she written to you yet? So you think she has forgotten about you but I guess not. I also spoke about Katie in the letter as they always liked each other so well. I hope poor Katie is better off for she was always a sweet girl. Many a time I think of her to be taken away from this world in her youth. Also Auntie Norry thought so much of her and of all of ye. She should go west to your house every day if she was able to go at all and of course my self was just as bad to go. I often thinks of the nice tea you and I used to have together when we used to come home after the day. I hope it wont be the last we will have as I expect to see you again some time and I am always wishing for that time to come. Wont I be glad to see your darling sweet face. I suppose you have a nice letter from Mary Hayes by this time. I remember her well. You must tell her about me but I guess she never cared very much for me. I am sure she is a great masher now. She is away from her mother and can do as she please and indeed she was bad enough after the fellows if she had her liberty, but it used to take you to cut her out every time if you like the fellow. I suppose if you were in Elmira you would cut me out too.

Well, my dear, I must finish now so Good Bye as I don't know of any more to say so Good Bye and lots of love and kisses to you.

I am as ever your loving Hannah.
Write when you can.

Please excuse this awful letter.

ENDNOTES

1   *"La Grippe" was an alternative label for influenza.*

Document **M107**
14 February 1900 – Ellen Driscoll Enright, Washington, D. C. to Nora McCarthy, Haverhill, Mass.

Washington, D. C.
Feb. 14th 1900

Dear Nora

I know you will be surprised to hear from me. I had a letter from Hannah Collins two weeks ago and she sent your address, therefore I must say I felt happy to hear from her and thank her for sending your address.

Well, dear Nora, it seems years since I heard direct from home or those there so I will ask you a favour to answer this note and let me know how you are getting along, or [are] you still growing as tall and slim as you used to be. How is Mary and Ellen, also Tim? Give them my best wishes when you see them. I expect all are married and settled down in their own home. If not I hope they will soon be.

As for myself I expect you have heard of me changing my name. I married a Limerick man and a very nice young fellow with that he is two years younger than I am, but that makes no difference.[1] We are fixed very comfortable, thank God. He keeps a saloon or bar room as they call it, so we are getting along nicely so far in it.

Maggie and Nora are well.[2] Sends their love to all of ye. O Nora, how is your poor Father and Mother making out in Ireland or do you hear often from them. I often think of poor Katie. It was too bad she died so young but God's will must be. Do you ever hear from Julia or is she married yet?[3] Are all the boys home yet? Give my love to your Father and Mother when you write to them. Poor Grandmother is still living but have left dear old Ballinlough. I had a letter from her two weeks ago. I know she would be glad to hear from ye. I don't hear a word from home since Grandmother moved to Driminidy and still I think of those old neighbours and onlee wish I could hear from them once in a while.

Well, dear Nora, I have no news to tell you so I will close this note by sending my best wishes to you and Mary and Ellen, not forgetting brother Tim. I often think of that ride he gave me in to Skibbereen the morning I left home.

Good by, write soon, address your letter

Mrs. James Enright

306 4th Street, S. W.

Wa

ENDNOTES

1   *Ellen was born on Staten Island, N. Y. about 1867 to Cornelius and Ellen Driscoll. She is listed as three in the 1870 Census. She took a few years off her age when the 1900 Federal Census was taken and claimed to be born in 1871, giving her the same birth age as her husband, James Enright.*

2   *Margaret "Maggie" Driscoll, the oldest of the three sisters, was born on Staten Island about 1863. Sister Nora was born about a year later.*

3   *Cousin Julia McCarthy, 30, married Patrick Cullinane, 35, of Cahirbeg, Rosscarbery, in November 1899. She had their first child, and only daughter, a year later.*

DOCUMENT M108

[21] February 1900 – Hannah Collins, Elmira, N. Y. to Nora McCarthy, Haverhill, Mass.

February 1900

My Own Dear Nora,

Its with great pleasure I set down to answer your loving letter which I received a few days ago and was delighted to hear from you. Also to hear that ye were all well as the date of this leaves me and sisters just the same. Well, dear Nora, I guess you had a letter from Ellie as she wrote to me last Friday and said she wrote to you at the same time. I suppose you were glad to hear from her. So Mary Hayes has not written to you yet. But I guess she will soon. I was glad you heard from home[1] and that your dear Mother was feeling well but was sorry for your Father being sick. I hope he is alright by this time. So Julia got married. She was always a nice tidy girl but I think she was stuck on herself. Is Mary living home yet? I mean Julia's sister. I suppose her boys are big now.[2]

Dear Nora, so you think I don't say much about Tom. He is the same little darling as sweet as ever and you also think its time I should be Mrs. Cloak. But that will be some day, I hope, but not very soon.[3] I like to have a fellow but I hates to get married and you know I am young enough yet and also I have to send some money to my dear Parents once and a while and if I get married I cant send them any. We aint got a very cold winter here. It has been very nice so far. We will soon have the spring again. I do love the summer no matter how warm it is.

Dear Nora, I was glad you had another little niece to love.[4] I bet they are awful sweet little children. Do any of them look like you? I just love children but I guess I got enough of them where I work. There are five but the youngest is seven years old. They make me tired some times. When I wrote home I sent Auntie Norry your love. I guess she has not forgotten you yet. Ellie wonders how she is living so long. How is Tim? Anyway give him my best love. Has he got any girl yet as he always like them home pretty well. I guess, my darling, I must close with fond love and kisses to you.

I am as ever your
Loving sister Hanna.

Hoping to hear from you soon again and please excuse this bad
writing.

ENDNOTES

1   *The letter from home that Hannah refers to was not in the McCarthy Collection. However, there is an empty envelope in the Collection, postmarked Leap, 7 February 1900.*

2   *Cousin Mary McCarthy's three boys from Tullig were fifteen, fourteen, and twelve in 1900.*

3   *Hannah Collins married Thomas Cloke 9 October 1901. Hannah was a widow by the 1920 Federal Census. Tom had died of pneumonia 12 June 1913, shortly after Hannah had given birth to their son, Edward (23 April 1913).*

4   *Helen Evelyn Donovan, third daughter of Mary and Dan Donovan, was born 31 January 1900.*

DOCUMENT M109
7 March 1900 – Hannah Collins, Elmira, N. Y. to Nora McCarthy, Haverhill, Mass.

March 7th 1900

My Own Dear Nora

Your dear and fond letter reached me alright and I was delighted to hear from you same as ever. Also glad you and all were well as I and sisters are just the same at present.

Dear Nora, I was very glad you had a nice time at the entertainment but I guess you were awful tired the next day as I am if I stay up one night. You would think I had not slept for a week. Well, dear Sister, so you wrote to Ellie. I am sure she will be delighted to hear from you as she thought so much of the whole family. I suppose Tim was also glad to hear about Ellie. I have written to her about a week. I am worried I had not a letter from home lately. I should have got one a week ago. I don't know what is the matter with them for they never delayed so long.

Well, dear Nora, we had lots of snow here the first of March. I had a nice sleigh ride Sunday and enjoyed it as this was the first good slaying [sleighing] we had this winter. Have ye lots of snow in Haverhill and did you have a sleigh ride? I think Mary Hayes is mean don't write to you after all the good old times ye had together but I suppose she has too many fellows now. She aint got any time to write. She thought all the fellows home were stuck on her but I guess not. While you were around you could cut her out of all of them. I suppose if you were in Elmira you would cut me out, too, but I wish you were with me even if you would.

Well, darling, I must close for this time as I cant think of any more to say but I must tell you that I love you more than ever and always did and will forever. Maggie and Mary are well and sends you their love as they often ask about you. Mary is the same old foolish girl. I don't think she has changed much since she left home. Good Bye. Write soon again. I am always so glad to hear from you. I remain forever your sister, Hannah.

Document **M110**
13 March 1900 – Patrick and Kate McCarthy, Ballinlough, Leap to Nora McCarthy, Haverhill, Mass.

Ballinlough
March 13th 1900

My Dearest Daughter Nora

In reply to your most kind and very welcomed letters which we received, the money letter the [?] of March and in a week after the other one. They gave us great pleasure to know ye were all getting on so well and also enjoying good health as we ourselves are at present and all the friends and neighbors. And more so to know ye increased in the population. I am very proud Mary and her baby are so well, T. G. About Julia's husband, he is not any relative of Mike Cullinane.[1] They are not one Cullinane at all. Short time ago, Ellen Cullinane, Mike's sister, inquired of me about Mary, how she was doing. She said she thought a deal of her. It is too bad about Tim not being working, but he cant be blamed. The winter is bad. I misses him, too, but I hope he will get work soon. We are glad Ellie Driscoll is doing so well. I am glad you told me about Dennie for I was very troubled about him.[2] 1 dreamt of him a few nights before I got your letter. The poor fellow got enough of it all the time but am glad he is all right now and at work again.

Dear Nora, you must excuse me this time for not sending you the Shamrock for P's day. The weather was very cold and I was not able to get it. We had snow for a week and the days were very cold. Though the weather is hard enough now, too, every one sticking the potatoes. But Nora be fond of the little girls. I'd like little girls. Ye have not half enough of girls for they are good. I guess she will have hair like guinea one.[3] 1 mean to tell you, Nora, the Keohane girl I spoke of before to you is married to Jack Donoghue, a Blacksmith working in Charles' forge.[4] I am sure all the children are cracked about for you were the show for coaxing them. I hope you wont fail at all. Father have a cold day today drawing out dung with Black Puss, you know him well. He went for him yesterday. I am more than thankful to you for the money for I was in the want of it, though Magg Sheahan[5] never refuses me for whatever I ask of her. So now I must conclude for the present until some other time hoping to hear soon again. Wishing ye all success especially to you, Nora, from Father and Mother to our fond child, Norah.

XXXXXX M XXXXXX F, Good Bye.

[this note, from Mrs. McCarthy, Leap, is in a different handwriting from the main letter]

Dear Norah,

Just a few lines to let you know that I had a letter from Kate about two weeks ago. She said she was in good health and had a nice place in a hospital.[6] I am more than thankful to you to be enquiring about her as I would like to have she write to you so that you could mention her in your letters. No more at present, hoping ye are all well. Remember me to Ellie and Mary.

Your fond Friend, Mrs. McCarthy, Leap

[the following note, in Mrs. McCarthy of Leap's handwriting, was on a small square sheet of paper included with the above letter]

Dear Nora

This is Kate Mc address is with her Brother John.
Good Bye
Write Soon

Mr. John McCarthy[7]
No. 21 Springfield St.
South Lawrence, Mass U. S. America

ENDNOTES

1   *The only Cullinanes in the Leap area according to the 1901 Census were Mary (Burke), 47, the widow of Dan, who was a "farmer and grocer" in Leap, and seven children, ages five to twenty. There was also a servant in the house.*

2   *Few of the letters from Denny and family were saved. What is there were some written by Denny's eldest child, Kate, in the early 1900s. Other letters may have been sent back to Denny's family in later years, as the two families remained very close.*

3   *"Guinea" as in gold, like the English gold piece known as a guinea. Young Agnes was described as having "guinea" hair. Sister Marion's color was strawberry blond. In the few photos that have survived baby Evelyn, who died a year later, her hair appears to be dark like her mother, Mary.*

4   *John Donohue, 30, blacksmith, and his wife Julia (Keohane) lived in the townland of Keamore on Leap Harbor. They had a three month old son, John, at the time the 1901 Census was taken.*

5   *Margaret Sheehan was a shopkeeper and post office assistant in Leap Village. Her brother, John, ran Sheehan's Hotel and many of the shops and homes in Leap Village. He was also the "Baron" of the Leap Fair.*

6   *The hospitals in Lawrence, Mass. at this time, included the Lawrence General and the Clover Hill.*

7   *According to the 1900 Federal Census, taken on the 7th day of June, John F. McCarthy lived with his wife, Hannah, and three children (John F., Jr., 6; Michael J. 4' and Mary 1) at 21 Springfield St., Lawrence. John McCarthy and Hannah Sheehan were married 17 November 1892. John was the son of Michael and Mary McCarthy. Also in the household were Hannah's 24 year old sister, Mary, and a boarder, but not John's sister Kate, who probably had lodging at the hospital where she worked.*

Document **M111**
14 March 1900 – Ellen Driscoll Enright, Washington, D. C. to Nora McCarthy, Haverhill, Mass.

306 4th St. S. W.
Washington D. C.
Mar. 14th 1900

My very dear Nora

Your most welcome letter I received on the first inst. Can not express how glad I was to hear from you and all the rest of the family, also to hear that ye were all keeping well and having a good old time enjoying yourselves. There is nothing better than to keep lively while we can as we are sure to be dead long enough. O don't I feel sorry to hear of all those nice young people being dead and gone, but God's will must be. Poor Patrick John. I feel so sorry to hear of his death. I have not heard from home since grandmother moved so it is quite a while now. I heard that Bridget Driscoll's Mother was buried also and that Bridget was to be married this Easter but I doubt it very much, I think. Though old she is, she had better try and come out here then to be half starved over there.

Well, dear Nora, so Julia got married. I laughed until I cried when you called him an old buck.[1] Well, just look at Hurigahn,[2] Peggie's husband, a fine looking girl as she was to be married to such a man.[3] I often think they were foolish that did not come to this country.[4] Did Mary get married again or is she in Ballinlough? Don't you know Mary Tobin was oughfull mean to those girls.[5] She was afraid any body would steal them. But I always thought they were able to take care of them selves.

O, Nora, poor James Hayes is getting his share of trouble all along. I feel sorry for the poor fellow. I often think of the way they used to talk of me and him. No doubt I liked him but not as much as they thought I did because I could be married to him before ever I came to this country if I wanted to. I have never regretted it, thank God, as I am happy to be away from all of them only my self and my old man to contend with. Nora, dear, get married and don't be an old maid as I thought I was. Come on your wedding trip to Washington and I ashure you I can give a nice comfortable reception. Washington is a lovely place but few from home are there. There are a great many from around Skibbereen that I know but none from our own place. I often think how nice it would be to go to Boston as there are so many that I know there. Katie and Maggie Harding were in to see me the other night.[6] They are looking well. Katie is married and has two children.[7] They are just like they were home getting mixed in with things that don't belong to them at all. For that reason the friends don't care much for them. Maggie is working the Printing Office getting big money, but Kate is spending it for her as her husband has gone to Central America.

O, dear Nora, how glad I was to hear that Denis was to see ye. I remember him very well. He used be hugging the girls just like Tim, a great big rogue. I am glad to hear that Mary is well and have such a comfortable home. No doubt she deserved it as she all ways was a good girl. What in the world is the matter with Ellie to think she don't stir herself up. She must not be so chousey as no doubt the woods are full of men but the right one seldom comes along. Give Ellie and Mary my love. Tell them how glad I am to hear from them, also Tim. No doubt I should remember Tim as he done many a favour for me. As for poor Katie, I hope she is in heaven. I often think of her, how nice and good she was to me, but I hope we will meet in heaven. The poor thing, she felt so weak when I was home.[8] She used to cry when she could not walk like used to. No doubt your poor mother is heartbroken after her and in fact all of ye. Give my love to your mother when you write and don't forget Patrick Francis as you used to call him.

Well, dear Nora, I must Apologize for not writing to you before now but I will promise to be more punctual the next time, so I will close with love hoping to hear from you soon again. I remain your loving friend and old neighbor. Write soon.

Ellie T. Enright
306 4th St. South West
Washington, D. C.

ENDNOTES

1   *Patrick Cullinane was five years older than Cousin Julia when they married.*

2   *Hourihane*

3   *Courley Hourihane was nine years older than his wife, Margaret McCarthy.*

4   *Not one of Uncle Michael's children came to America, and only two of his many grandchildren did so.*

5   *Mary Tobin McCarthy was Uncle Michael's wife.*

6   *These Harding sisters were not the daughters of Nora's Aunt Julia McCarthy and Uncle Henry Harding of Kilmacabea.*

7   *Kate Harding married Edward Byam, a machinist, in 1894. They had two sons at the time of the 1900 Federal Census. Sister Maggie, unmarried, lived with them.*

8   *Ellie visited Ballinlough in 1895.*

Document M112
5 April 1900 – Hannah Collins, Elmira, N. Y. to Nora McCarthy, Haverhill, Mass.

April 5th 1900

My Own Dear Sister

Your loving letter reached me alright and I was glad to hear from you same as ever. Also glad to know you and sisters and brother were still well as the date of this leaves us all at present.

Dear Nora, I would have written sooner but I was waiting to tell you about I leaving my place. I expect to leave next Tuesday. I was tired out from the old Jews. They had such funny ways but still they were very nice to me. She wanted me to stay in some evenings for her because she was out all the time. I told her I was not a nurse girl to be taking care of kids. They are old enough to mind themselves.

Well, I have another place. It's the second house to where Maggie works. I think I will like it there. He is a minister. There are six in family.[1] I will be near Maggie and will be with her all the time. Well, I was glad you heard from home lately and that your dear Father and Mother ere getting along so well. You must remember me to them and also send them my best love.

So Jerry did not get married yet[24] He must look pretty old now. I suppose our dear Ballinlough aint the same any more. Its so lonely. All the young people are gone. Do you ever intend to go back again? Oh, my darling Nora, I wish I would see your loving face this minute. I would feel happy as I do be thinking of you every day and night and praying for that day to come when I will see you or do you think we shall meet again. Mary does be talking of you often. Sometimes she comes to see me the day I get your letters and she reads them. She says she don't care to read any other letter I get only yours, but I don't let her see all of them. She has a fellow now, but not steady. You would laugh enough if you seen her. I think she is worse now than when she was home. She talks so funny.

When you write, address my letter to 462 Franklin Street in care of Maggie Collins as I don't know the number of my house so I will be sure to get it there.

Good Bye and think of me often.

ENDNOTES

1   *Hannah's new employers were Rev. Daniel Campbell and his wife, Effie, 466 Franklin St., Elmira. Their four children, 11-19 in age, were born in Kansas.*

2   *Jeremiah McCarhy, oldest son of Uncle Michael, did not marry until 1904 when he was forty-three.*

Document M113
[12] April [1900] – Michael McCarthy, Ballinlough, Leap to Nora McCarthy, Haverhill, Mass.

Ballinlough
April [12,1900]

My Dear Cousin Nora

It is with pleasure I do write those lines just to let ye know that I come back to the old spot for a few weeks vacation to see how they were enjoying times in old Ireland but found they were the same 3s 4d[1] with a few alterations, as I expect you have heard all about them, that our Julia got her name changed to Mrs. Cullinane, living at Cahirbeg. It is a nice little place but I had seen it before I went to England. And also a lot of the neighbors have departed to eternity and more gone to America, England and every place. So Ballinlough and around the Neighbourhood seems very lonesome now, as there is no fun like was in the old times so I could not stop long. I will be going back again in 13th April. That will be a fortnight loafing around Ballinlough.

Now, Dear Nora, about answering of the past letters. I hope you will excuse me as I happened to lose the address, got it from home twice to write to you as I think we must have a conversation in different countries as paper is not so dear. But at the time when I got your address from home I met with an accident. I got the Erisyplas[2] in the head but got over it all right, T. G. So for goodness sake, excuse me as I will keep you going reading my letters in America. Do not write when you will receive this as I will write as soon as I will land in Newport again and tell you all the newses.

We are enjoying fine times in England. Patrick got a sound job as I expect you know what it is. He is a foreman in a shop. Got 6 men and 2 apprentices under him so he done a good work to go to Newport. M. Cahalane is just the same but doing more work than formerly, but poor Annie got married about 3 months ago. So I asked her how she like her marriage life. So she said she like it well. But as for myself I am enjoying the finest times at all with plenty of work and fun which Irish men wants in strange countries.

Now, Dear Nora, I must tell you about the parents at home. Your father failed very much with 2 yrs but the poor fellow said he would go to Newport with me, making fun. But your mother is just the same as I fancy she is as strong as ever. But my father and mother are failed all together. So now I must be drawing to a close by each of us sending our best wishes to ye all and wishes also to be remembered to ye all as ye fancy we have by this time forgotten ye. Ye are as fresh as ever talking in our thoughts and always talking about ye in Newport.

So no more at present from your fond Cousin M. M. to Cousin N. McC.

ENDNOTES

1   *Three shillings four pence: an old expression meaning nothing has changed.*

2   *Erysipelas: a streptococcal infection of the skin.*

Document M114
26 April 1900 – Hannah Collins, Elmira, N. Y. to Nora McCarthy, Haverhill, Mass.

April 26th 1900

My Own Dear Nora

Your wished for letter reached me alright and I was glad to hear from you. Also glad you and sisters and all are well as the date of this letter leaves me and all just the same at present. Dear Nora, I am in my new place and like it very much. It's a very big house and of course lots of work but still I like it a good deal better than the other one I had. They are awful nice people and the lady is going away this week to be gone over a month. Aint that nice for me. I'll have a fine time when she is away. I guess I wont kill myself. Well, dear sister, I am glad you have a nice new suit. I hope you will wear it with pleasure and that you cut the Ice at last. I laughs at your dear letter. I also have a new suit too. It's a grey, very pretty.

Dear Nora, I have not heard from Ellie Driscoll in three weeks or more. Did she write to you since? We had a letter from Patsy last week. He was very sick with the grippe but is almost well again. My brother, Dennie, is coming out the first of May but not here to Elmira. I suppose Patsy wont bring him here to see us very soon as it costs a good deal from Pennsylvania to Elmira. I think Dennie is awful small yet.[1] I also think he should stay for two years more but he was crazy to come here. Maggie and Mary are well and sends you their love. Mary speaks of you often and says what a handsome girl you were. Nobody like you. Well, dear Nora, I only wish I was going to see you now. I would feel happy or do you think we shall ever meet again after all the nice days we spent together. I guess I told you about my Cousin Mary McCarthy that is in Albany. She was sick with Typhoid Fever last November and she is not able to work yet.[2] Just think, such a long time to be idle. She said she did not tell her parents about her being so bad but I think she will have to go home again if she don't feel better soon.

Well, my sweet heart, I cant think of any more this time. Hope you will excuse me for such a bad letter and write soon again.

I am as ever your own, Hanah

ENDNOTES

1   *Denis Collins was seventeen when he immigrated to America.*

2   *When the Census was taken in Albany, N. Y. in June, Mary A. McCarty [sic] was an inmate (patient) in Dy. Peter's Hosopital, Albany. She was born October 1878 and her occupation was a domestic. Her year of immigration was not listed.*

Document **M115**
2 May 1900 – Patrick and Kate McCarthy, Ballinlough, Leap to Nora McCarthy, Haverhill, Mass.

May 2nd 1900

Dear Nora

I received your kind and welcomed letter a few days ago and we were glad to hear ye were all well as the departure of this leaves us at present, thanks be to God. You will be surprised to hear that your cousin Mickie was home from England lately. He was home for a fortnight. He is gone away since Easter Monday. He is a very big hearty man. He said it would be better for Tadey to be in England than America. It is very good now since the war started.[1] I am glad Tadey is working and that Dennis and family are all well as I was very troubled about them. I did not like to be delaying this letter very long as the times are very dull here at present. The only help I had was the fowl. They are all dying. They were as a cow for me and we had no making of money.[2] You never said how Mary was getting on and her baby. I was talking to Kate McCarthy's mother. She had a letter last Saturday from her. She have a very nice place. Excuse this short note as I am in a hurry now. I have not time to be coming to Leap tomorrow. We are promising money to Mrs. McCarthy this long time so I hope ye will send some money now as Leap Fair is coming and don't show this to any one only your self. I hope ye will all join us and send something good. Good bye. Write soon.

From Your loving Father and Mother to our fond family.
XXXXXXXXX

Endnotes

1   *Refers to the Boer War in South Africa, 1900-1902.*

2   *Nora's mother earned extra income by selling eggs, as she would have by selling milk and butter had she a cow.*

Document **M116**

5 May 1900 – Ellen Driscoll Enright, Washington, D. C. to Nora McCarthy, Haverhill, Mass.

306 4th St. South West
Washington D. C.
May 5th 1900

My very dear Nora

In reply to your most welcome letter I received on the 25 inst. and can not express to you how pleased I was to hear that each and all of you were so well and happy. A blessing all of us enjoy at present, thank God.

O, Nora dear, I am so sorry to think that I cant send any pictures to you as really I have not an old one of mine. It is true I had some taken since I changed my name but they all are gone. Where to I can't tell and as for my having any more of them taken I expect I shall wait. You can guess the reason yourself. Catch on?[1]

But, Nora dear, if you will remember me and send me your own I will be ever so pleased even though it be a tin type. Tell Ellie if she have any of her that I would love dearly to get one. Also Mary and Tim. Give my love to all of them. I remember Mary and Ellie as if I saw them yesterday. I am glad to hear that Mary is so well fixed as she was always a very good girl. Nora has another good man. She is as happy as she can be. Have a lovely home and a girl to do her work, but what do you suppose? I got a colored maid. She is as black as the ace of spades but a good worker. Washington is a great place for them. The only thing about them, they smell so bad and steal all the eye can see, but mine is a Cathelick. I know you wont laugh at her.

Dear Nora, I was so glad to hear that you had a letter from home and that they are all well over there. Give my love to your father and mother when you write. I would be glad to hear from Uncle Johney's wife.[2] Poor thing has her hands full I expect.

O, Nora dear, wouldn't I love to go to Boston and see some of the old neighbours from around home. Remember me to them if you should go there this summer. I was glad to hear that Brother

Denis was well and had such a fine family. I don't remember very much about him as he was in England some time[3] before he came out here.

I will close this note as it is half past eleven and time I should be in Blanket St. so will say good night with the hope of hearing from you soon again.

I remain your loving friend and old neighbor.

Ellie to dear Nora.

ENDNOTES

1   Ellen was pregnant with her first child, a son, Joseph.

2   Probably Mary McCarthy Driscoll, of Bawnfune, widow of "Johnny Bawn" Driscoll who had died suddenly in 1895, leaving Mary with five young children to raise.

3   Denis McCarthy was in Newport, Wales in 1881 when the Census of England was taken. Since Ellen can not remember him, he probably left Ballinlough some years before 1881.

DOCUMENT **M117**
11 May 1900 – Hannah Collins, Elmira, N. Y. to Nora McCarthy, Haverhill, Mass.

My Own Dear Nora,

I received your fond letter almost a week ago and was glad to hear from you same as ever. Also glad yourself and sisters & brother Tim were still well as the date of this leaves me and all at present.

Well, dear Nora, I am always so pleased when I read your dear letter. I enjoy it so much for you tell me all the newes that I do like to hear about. I am also very glad to hear you are having such nice times and enjoying yourself so well. You are just right to go to all those places. I see you have not forgotten your dance yet. I bet you & Tim can beat them all dancing. I am sure Tim is as lively as ever as he was always jolly.

Well, Nora, I was glad you heard from your Cousin Mickie in England and so Annie Cahalane is married. I was surprised but I guess she is not very young. She must be older than we are and the Captain[1] is not married yet. I think its most time he should be but I guess he never cared for any girl but you & your sisters. He certainly thought he would be joined in that family as I remember Auntie Norry told me one time about him telling her that he used to hear from your sister Ellie and that your Mother knew about it and thought it would be alright.

Maggie & Mary are well & sends you their love. They never had their picture taken yet but when they will you will be sure to get one. They told me you will have to send them yours first. It don't do for them to have I have one of yours. They want one too. We had a letter from Patsy a few days ago. He is well. He said he expected Dennie out the last of this week.[2]

Well, I must finish for this time hoping you will excuse me for not writing sooner also for such a bad letter.

I am so ever your loving sister, Hannah.

Have you heard from Ellie lately as I did not hear from her since I wrote to you before.

Good Bye my own little Sweet-heart, forever.

ENDNOTES

1 *Mike Cahalane, who was also in Newport, Wales with Cousin Mickey.*

2 *Denis Collins, 17, sailed from Queenstown (Cobh) on May 20 and arrived in New York City on May 26. He listed his destination as his brother, Patrick Collins, in Easton, Penn.*

Document M118
1 June 1900 – Hannah Collins, Elmira, N. Y. to Nora McCarthy, Haverhill, Mass.

June 1st, 1900

My Own little darling

I hope you will excuse me for not answering your loving letter sooner which I received over a week ago and was pleased to hear from you same as ever. Also, glad you and Sisters and all were still enjoying the best of health as we are at present.

Dear Nora, I had a good time Decoration Day,[1] I was out all the afternoon. Did not come back for supper. Tom took me all over and I also went to the Lake. Its almost five or six miles on the cars. I also had a very nice time last Sunday. He took me out buggy riding. We went out in the country. It was a lovely place. The hills looked so nice and green. It reminded me of sweet Ballinlough hill over the Lake where you and I spent many a happy Sunday. I am lonesome for those happy days many a time.

Well, Nora, I had a letter from Ellie last week. She was well but she said she had been sick for some time but is alright again. I did not get her letter here. It stayed in the Post Office three weeks, I guess, as she addressed it to the other place where I was before. She also said she hears from you often and that you were the same Nora as ever, full of fun. Well, you has a great time mashing the coach man. I suppose ye has lots of fun together. I should say he would be mad at you not speaking to him on the street. You keep the right side of him and go out riding with him sometimes, but I guess he aint pretty enough for you. Well, has Tim got any girl yet? I guess they are all stuck on him he is so jolly and nice but you must tell him that he is the only boy I ever loved, but he never cared for me. Did you ever hear from Mary Hayes since? I think she is terrible to go back on you like that after all year good old times together, but I guess she is too busy with the fellows now. She aint got time.

Well, dear Sister, I must close for this time. Hoping to hear from you soon again.

I remain as ever your loving sister Hanah, and hope you will excuse me for not writing sooner.

ENDNOTES

1 *Memorial Day (May 31)*

Document **M119**

4 June 1900 – Patrick and Kate McCarthy, Ballinlough, Leap to Nora McCarthy, Haverhill, Mass.

Ballinlough
June 4th 1900

My Dear Nora

We received your most welcome letter and was more than glad to hear from ye. Indeed, we ware not blaming ye because ye have a lot done for us, but we are old and feeble now[1] and we cant help spending a little money when there was debts on us. We would like to meet a little that would be due once. If you wont pay you wont get. So, Dear Nora, I wont waste what ye sends me. I am fonder than what you think of your money. I know you are working hard for it. So whatever we will do we wont blame you in future for it. Its time for you to spare something for yourself whatever we will do. Only Jerry's daughter said she would come to see us[2] and we would like to entertain her as well as we could. That's all. I would like she stays. She don't feel well and she would like to come to Ireland.[3]

Your father would like to have Ellie come home but your father don't understand anything. Mickey was a great man when to home. He went back again after a few days. I am enclose Cousin Katie's letter from England. I hope you will excuse us this time only I would like to be reasonable before her. A little from each wouldn't be much. Tell Mary to think of me.

Dear Nora, remember us to all the friends and tell Tady to have sense and not to spend his money. He know how I stood and he going away. Excuse me this time. Do ye hear anything about the Georges from Skibbereen?[4]

Enclosion.

I remain your Affectionate Father and Mother
Kate and Patrick McCarthy

ENDNOTES

1   *Patrick was about seventy in 1900, and Kate had just had her sixty-sixth birthday.*

2   *Katherine McCarthy was the daughter of Pat and Kate's late son, Jeremiah. She was born in 1880 in Poplar. Essex. England (East London).*

3   *Apparently there had been regular communication between Ballinlough and Jerry's widow in London, but this is probably the first visit to Ireland of anyone from Jerry's family since he left home in the 1870s.*

4   *The envelope for this letter was postmarked Skibbereen, and had been written for Pat and Kate by cousin Julia "George," hence the inquiry about her siblings in Lawrence, Mass.*

DOCUMENT M120
[Spring 1900] – Kate McCarthy, London, England to Patrick and Kate McCarthy, Ballinlough, Leap

45 Clifford Rd. Hermit Rd. Barking Road East

My Dear Grandmother

I am sure you will be very much surprised to hear from me but I have been going to write to you ever since I can remember but never succeeded until now. So I hope you will excuse me for never writing before. I was 20 years of age last month so you may know I am big. My brother Denis[1] is very tall. He is 17 and is growing very much like my Dadda used to be, but we are both tall. My grandmother[2] died last January, and I have not been very well so my mother told me I could come to Ireland in the summer. So if I come I should like to come to see you. I hope my grandfather and all my Aunts and Uncles are all quite well as this leaves us at present, Thank God. My mother sends her love and wishes to be remembered to all at home. Please write an answer to my letter and say if you would like a photo of us and if you would we will have some done. We had some taken once before to send to you but they came out very bad so we did not send them but we will this time if you would like them.[3]

I must now say good bye and may God bless you. Hoping you will excuse me for not writing before, I remain your
Sincere and fond Grandchild Kate McCarthy
Please answer my letter.

[The parents used the fourth page of London Kate's letter to append the following note. The first 14 words are in a different handwriting from the remainder of the page. Letter was sent from Skibbereen]

Ye will be surprised to see this letter. I am sending this letter to have you see it. I lost all my hens and it's a great loss to me. I would be able to do something only for that. I would not be to hard on ye every minute. Your good mother was glad to know that you were well. Its Julie George is writing for me this time. Remember us to Ellie Driscoll. I am glad she is well married.

Faithfully yours, Mother and Father.

ENDNOTES

1   *Denis McCarthy, son of Jerry and Annie (Fitzgerald) McCarthy, was born in Middlesex, England in 1882.*

2   *Bridget Fitzgerald, Annie's mother. who was born in County Cork, Ireland.*

3   *There is a set of pictures in the McCarthy Collection: one each of Jerry and Annie, and another of the three children (a young Kate, baby Denis, and infant Patrick who died about his first birthday in 1883.) The children are shown with an older woman, probably their grandmother Fitzgerald, as that picture and the one of Annie are numbered sequentially by the photographer. However, Katie from London is writing about the possibility of new photos being taken.*

Document **M121**
21 June 1900 – Hannah Collins, Elmira, N. Y. to Nora McCarthy, Haverhill, Mass.

June 21st 1900

My Own little darling

I guess you think I am getting tired of writing to you as I have not answered your ever fond letter before now but time goes so quick and I has a good deal to do but still I am always thinking of you no matter what I am doing. Well, Nora, I was glad to hear that you and sisters and Tim and all were still well as we are at present, thank God.

Well, dear Nora, I got so lonesome when I read your dear letter that I had to cry thinking of you and all our good old times. I would love to go to see you but I guess its too far. I am sure we would have a good old talk. Well, I see you are still enjoying yourself going to dances and weddings.[1] You are just right to go and have a good time while you are young. I guess you must have a fellow, too, but you don't tell me about him as I know they are all stuck on you, but you don't care. I know you.

Well, Nora, my brother Dennie has come. He is in Easton, Pennsylvania. I don't know when he is coming here to see us. I suppose he wont for a while as it costs a good deal from there to Elmira but we would like to see him. I wrote home yesterday and sent money. I suppose they feels lonesome after Dennie. They only got Nora and Tim home now.[2] Did you hear from home lately, and how are your dear Father and Mother getting along as I shall never forget them. They were so nice.

Well, Nora, my Cousin Mary McCarthy is getting along pretty good now. She told me she would be able to work soon again but just think of her being sick since last November. Its terrible. She told me her people wants her come home but she says she don't like to go home for she likes this country so well. But she must go if she don't feel well soon.

Well, my own Nora, I must finish now by sending you my best love and hope you will write soon again as I like to hear from you often. I am, as ever, your old chum,

Hannah.

ENDNOTES

1   One wedding that Nora McCarthy might have attended in Spring of 1900 was that of Dan Donovan's niece, Ellen Hodnett, who married James J. Conlon on April 25, 1900 in Haverhill, Mass.

2   Tim Collins left Ireland for Elmira in 1908, the year after his father died. Nora Collins came in 1921, probably after her mother's death, although neither mother nor daughter is in Driminidy, Drinagh in 1911 when the Census of Ireland was taken.

DOCUMENT M122
3 July 1900 – Ellen Driscoll Enright, Washington, D. C. to Nora McCarthy, Haverhill, Mass.

306 4th Street S.W.
Washington, D. C.
July 3rd 1900

My very dear Nora,

In reply to your loving letter I received several days ago was more than pleased to hear from you also in hearing that each and all the friends were well.

I was glad to hear that your poor Mother was keeping up so well, also to learn that your niece was going to visit dear old Ballinlough. No doubt it must be very dreary over there by this as all the old sports have left there. I often set down and picture things that have gone by over there and wonder if there is any fun at all to be had there now, but I guess not. All the old fogies remained back and all that had life in left there. Tell the truth or not, you are glad to be away from there having a good old time among yourselves in this clean country.

I often picture Johanna Pady[1] and the eirs [airs] she used to put on in days gone by. Nora, dear, you ought to see her when I was home hailing [hauling] turf on her back with a big old bag and then putting a b[ig]C[2] in her chins with it. That is the truth. Read this to Tim. He will say it is true. And big Mick eating the raw potatoes. Just picture the Connellys, Peggie and Aunty and Courley, and Stocken, the old horse that they used to pride in so much.

O, Nora dear, I have to stop as they certainly were a Circiuse [circus] over there. And aunty and Peggie would hide the tea underneath their petticoats for fear any one would get a cup.

Well, dear Nora, I must change the subject. I had a nice letter from Hannah Collins yesterday. She is very well and mentioned you in the letter. Said that you write such nice long letters to her and tells all the news from home. Well, dear Nora, I laughed hearty when I read your letter when you mentioned your head of hair. I can picture each one of you just as if I saw ye yesterday, except Dennie and Jerry, the Lord have mercy on him. Well, it was kind for you to have lovely hair. It was in year family. If any of mine came out, I would be bald headed.

Well, dear Nora, my husband said he would like to meet you. He thinks exactly what you are, full of fun and life. He said if ever you would come close enough to him he will give you a good hugging but your best fellow would not leave him do anything like that.

I have to finish this note as it is supper time and will close with lots of love. Remember me to all the friends. Write soon again. I remain as ever,

Your old neighbor, Ellie.

ENDNOTES

1   *Johanna Donovan of Ballinlough, daughter of Patrick, never married and lived with her brother John and family in the vicinity of the McCarthy home. She gave her age as 45 when the 1901 Census of Ireland was taken, but ten years later she had added more than ten to her age and declared she was 61.*

2   *Possibly a "big chew of Tobacco?"*

Document M123
5 July 1900 – Katie T. McCarthy,[1] Kingston, Penn. to Aunt Nora McCarthy, Haverhill, Mass.

July 5th 1900
Kingston, Pa

Dear Aunt Nora

I hope you will excuse us for not answering your letter before now as it is putting it off all the time as I believe I am getting careless about writing anymore but I hope I will do better for the future.

Well Dear Aunt, I have not got much of anything to say after all. I have had good time of three weeks in Scranton[2] as I did not start to work yet and no signs of any settlement[3] but I don't care if we don't start for the summer as it is so terrible warm up here that we are very near melted but we must not complain as long as we get along good and have no sickness at present, thank God.

Dear Aunt, Ma[4] said she has not decided yet wether she will go down their or not yet, but she hopes she will be able to go with the help of God. Dear Nora, you told us you had a good time in Pat Dacey's[5] and Pa heard it, he said he wished he was there. He would have a good time, too. When we read your letters to Pa he always says he wish he was down their.[6] It must be a lovely place because he is always saying he would like to live there but he says it might be a long time but I hope it will not be although I like this place very much but I would like to see you all. Pa says you are very jolly. I guess you are tired reading this letter as there are nothing of anything in it but I hope the next one will be better.

Dear Nora, I would love to see one of you come up hear for the summer but I guess you won't come this summer but I hope Ma will be able to go down there before long. Our Maggie[7] received her first Holy Cummion [Communion] a week Sunday. She is a big girl and is home two. We are having a good time now with us all home but I am getting paid right along every week from the union.

Well, Dear Nora, I have not got any more to say this time but I am ashamed of this letter. I hope you will excuse it. I hope you are all in good health and all enjoyed the forth[8] well on.

We all send our best regards to yourself, Tim, Ellie and the Dovonan [Donovans] and hope you are in good health and also hope Mary and the baby are getting along good. Pa and Patrick are still working.[9] I guess I will put my letter to a close wishing you all good bye and hope you hear from your mother and father and that they are well too. So Good by

From your loving neice. Katie T. McCarthy

ENDNOTES

1 *Katie McCarthy was born in Wales in May 1884, the first born of Denis and Julia McCarthy's children. Her father, and each of his brothers, stayed with tradition and named their first daughter after their mother Kate. Kate was seventeen when she wrote to her Aunt Nora, who was only a few years older than she. The tone of comfortable familiarity suggests this was one of many letters back and forth between the Massachusetts and Pennsylvania McCarthys, but very few of them have survived.*

2 *Katie's maternal aunt, Ellen O'Brien, had married Robert Donovan in 1900.*

3 *Kate worked in a lace mill. Evidently, she and her fellow workers were on strike.*

4 *"Ma," (Julia O'Brien McCarthy) was born in Ireland in 1862. She married Denis in Wales. She would visit in Bradford in August 1900.*

5 *Patrick Dacey, a maternal cousin of the McCarthys, lived in Haverhill, as did other of his siblings. The occasion of Nora's "good times" may have been the christening of John Dacey's son, Peter, born 30 April 1900.*

6 *Katie's reference to Bradford, Mass., north of her home in Penn as being "down there,"., is reminiscent of New Englanders referring to Maine as "Down East."*

7 *Margaret "Maggie" McCarthy, the third McCarthy child, was born in Pennsylvania in 1887.*

8 *Fourth of July*

9 *According to the 1900 Census, Denis was a coal miner, and Patrick, born in Wales in 1885, was a "door boy" in the mine.*

Document M124
19 July 1900 – Hannah Collins, Elmira, N. Y. to Nora McCarthy, Haverhill, Mass.

July 19th 1900

My Own little darling:

I hope you will excuse me for not answering your ever fond letter which I received over a week ago and was glad to hear from you same as ever. Also glad yourself and sisters and Brother were still well as the date of this letter leaves us all at present.

Dear Nora, I had a letter from Ellie last week. She is well, also her sisters she said. Its terrible warm here. I am just dead with the heat. I suppose you are the same. I do hate to work those days but I have to. My lady has come home and is working me too hard as I didn't do a thing while she was gone but have a good rest. I went to bed every after noon and when I didn't I went out. She was gone eleven weeks.

Well, my darling, so you want me come to see you. I will promise I will some time but I don't know when it will be as I am always praying for that time to come.[1] when I will see your loving face again. Wont we have a great old time talking about our foolish days when we were young. I guess I would not know you now. You must be a great lady, but I am just as homely as ever. How is my dear Tim as I love him just the same. Also Ellie and all the rest of your people. I was glad you heard from home that your dear Parents were well. I often thinks of them. They were so good.

Nora's brother-in-law went home a few weeks ago and is going to Driminidy. She sent a dress to my sister Nora. She did not send any clothes to her Grand Mother. She don't need any as I suppose she don't go out any wheres now. She sent her a little money. Its just as well. And Nora sent a dress to my Mother. Don't you think they were very kind to remember them.

Well, dear Nora, I remain as ever your sister,

Hanah.

Good Bye

466 Franklin St. and please excuse this bad letter. XXXXXXXXX
Well, my darling, I must close this time so Good Bye with lots of
love to you my dear one. And write soon.

ENDNOTES

1   *Hannah did visit Nora in Bradford in the 1930s. If there were other visits,
that information has not been found.*

Document **M125**

6 August 1900 – Patrick and Kate McCarthy, Ballinlough, Leap to Nora McCarthy, Bradford, Mass.[1]

August 6th 1900
Ballinlough

Dear daughter Norah

In reply to your most kind and welcomed letter which we received a few weeks ago and we are more than glad to know ye are all well, enjoying good health as we are ourselves at present, T.G. Well, I hope Dennie's wife is with ye by this time.

Well, Norah, I am glad to tell you Katie came home the 6th July though we expected her the 5th. We went to meet her to Skibbereen on the 5th and we took Con Bohane of Leap[2] his car to meet her and she was not to meet us that day but she came the day after, herself and a boy from Limerick,[3] a friend of hers. They remained only a few days. She felt very lonesome when she came. They had a returned ticket and a Tourist's ticket to travel around every where they like. She went to see her mother's friends.[4]

Well, Norah, I would have answered this letter sooner but she promised me to come back again the latter end of July and she did not come at all. She was a nice girl. She was nearly as tall as Katie.[5] She put on my cloak and she took it up very well.[6] She had great fun at it. She had great fun also at my likeness when she see how I was dressed and the cap on me.[7] She took it with her to take a larger one out of it. She said she would return it again after she go back home. She would stay longer here but she thought the place lonesome. She did not like the comerade boy go at all. She like to keep his company as they were going to travel round, for he was going to Limerick to see his own friends when he see her safe here with us. So she went with him. He was a friend of hers.

Jerry[8] said she had eye brows like Tim. She was a black-haired girl. She said her brother would come over next summer to see us. He is working in a gas office. She looked very well. I had not much time to prepare the house. She came unexpected. I whitewashed and papered the room, myself and Mary Cremeen.[9] I did not think she would come until August. The day they were going back I was going to go to town with them and she said to me over in the road, Grandmother, don't go at all. You don't look strong. So her Grandfather went with her then. We were very glad to see her. She liked to walk around the lake. She wore black clothes after her Grandmother [Fitzgerald] who was buried lately.[10]

ENDNOTES

1   *Both the front and back of the envelope for this letter has numerous attempts to imitate the handwriting of the sender. The copyist was probably young Agnes Donovan who was seven that summer. The letter was sent to Nora at her sister Mary's house.*

2   *Cornelius Sullivan, who had a shop in Leap Village.*

3   *The step-father of Katie from London, Edmund Kiely, was from Limerick. Perhaps this young man was a relative of his.*

4   *Katie's mother, Annie Fitzgerald, had been born in England. Her "friends" could have been her new husband's relatives.*

5   *Nora's sister who had died in 1896.*

6   *Probably the traditional collared "Munster Cloak" with a large attached hood.*

7   *The sepia print of Mrs. McCarthy in the Collection shows her wearing a plaid shawl and a white cap with long streamers on it.*

8   *Jeremiah McCarthy, oldest son of Uncle Michael.*

9   *Neighbor Mary McCarthy Driscoll of Bawnfune, widow of Johnny Bawn Driscoll.*

10   *The letter appears to be missing a final page.*

Document M126
29 August 1900 – Hannah Collins, Elmira, N. Y. to Nora McCarthy, Bradford, Mass.

August 1900

My Darling Nora

I received your ever welcome letter alright and was glad to hear from you same as ever also glad you are still well. I am very sorry for your sister Mary's sickness.[1] I hope in God she is better now and will get over it alright as it would be a terrible thing if any thing should happen to her and her little children. What would they do? And of course the rest of ye all would be awful upset about her.

Well, dear Nora, I hope you will excuse me for not writing sooner but I was off two weeks in my vacation and had a good time but I thought of you just the same so your letter stayed a week in the house where I worked before I got it. I am back again a week. I was very home sick to get back to work again. I had too good a time and its hard enough where I works but I will have to be satisfied as I don't like to change places too often.

My darling, I am thinking of you day and night. So you were dreaming of me. I have been dreaming of you many a time, always wishing for that time to come when we will embrace together as usual. Oh, how happy I would be to see your loving face just now.[2]

Dear Nora, I have not heard from Ellie in over five weeks. She is slow about writing but I had a letter from home a few weeks ago. They were pretty well, only

my Father was very bad with the Rhemmiatism [rheumatism]. He couldn't walk without a stick. Auntie Norry was pretty well. They also said the Sullivan fellow called to see them and was a very nice young man. I told you before about him. Nora's brother-in-law. They also said his mother was to see the, How is Tim and Ellie? Give them my love. Did ye hear from home lately, and how are your dear ones over there?

Well, I must close for this time, so Good Bye. Lots of love and kisses to you and all.

I am as ever,

Your loving sister, Hannah.

Please write soon and let me know how your sister is.

ENDNOTES

1   *Mary, who had delivered her third child at the end of January, had contracted phthisis, a particularly virulent form of tuberculosis, commonly known as "galloping consumption" because of how quickly it brought on death to its victims.*

2   *Such overly sentimental, romanticized expressions between women was quite usual in this time period.*

DOCUMENT **M127**

18 September 1900 – Patrick and Kate McCarthy, Ballinlough, Leap to Nora McCarthy c/o Dan Donovan, Bradford, Mass.

Ballinlough
September 18 1900

My Dear daughter Nora,

As I intend to answer your most kind and very welcomed letter which we received about a week ago, it gave us great [pleasure] to know how ye were getting on. About Mary, I feel bad and troubled for fear anything would be to matter with her. You did not say what was her ailment.[1] But I hope she will be alright at the time this letter reaches you. It was too bad to be sick all the time in this hot weather. I am glad Tim and Ellie are well. I suppose Dan and the children were upset on account of Mary being sick.

Well, Dear Nora, about your niece Katie [from England], I never thought I would ever see her. When she came I done all I could for her and for the fellow that was with her. They did not trouble me long. Some say they were married and I don't know which. I was going to ask her but I did not mind she wore a gold ring.[2] When she was leaving she said she'd write and she did not ever since. She was very nice to us, she gave us a half sovereign each[3] the morning she was leaving as a present.

I forgot telling it to you in my last letter. Nora, if you care about writing to them, write to her mother. I think it is the safest. Mrs. Kiely. I am also glad to know Dennie and his wife and family are well. I am sorry the Collins girls have left that place.[4] I am sure ye feel lonesome.

Well, I'd like to see a few lines from Tim and Ellie in your next letter. I feel very troubled about Mary and also your father. It's a long time to be in trouble until an answer is back for this. I don't know what I am doing but I hope she is well by this time. And if a road was leading to that place I'd walk all the ways to go to see her and all of ye but its too bad there is not.[5] Well, Nora, you sent me no address. It must be you were very much upset but however I'll address it to Mary and Dan.[6] Tell me how is Agnes, Katie, and the baby. Tell me do Agnes mind the baby.

I'd like to see them all. The friends and Neighbours over here are all well. Excuse me for not answering your letter before now. I was too troubled. I did not know what I was doing. I'd be glad Mary would write one line in your letter also to see her hand writing. Well, I must conclude for the present. Have no more to say until some other time. Hoping it wont be long. Write soon. Good bye and good luck. Wishing ye all Health, Wealth, and Prosperity from Father and Mother. Good Bye. Write soon. XXXXXX from Mother to her loving daughter Nora.

ENDNOTES

1   *Unknown to her parents, Mary McCarthy Donovan had died at her home on 9 September 1900 at 10:45 A. M. Cause of death was phthisis, a particularly virulent form of tuberculosis, commonly called "galloping consumption" for the rapidity with which it brought on death. The McCarthy Collection contains the newspaper accounts of both her death and her funeral, as well as the undertaker's invoice of $112. It would take about a week for a letter to go, via steamship, from Massachusetts to Ireland, so the parents would have received the sad news within a few days of sending the above letter.*

2   *Katie was not married. According to the 1901 Census of England, she was single and living with her mother and step-father. Her occupation was a dressmaker.*

3   *A sovereign was a British gold Pound piece worth twenty shillings. A half shillings would be valued at ten shillings.*

4   *Delia and Kate Collins, Ellie's friend who were from Ballinlough and now worked in Haverhill.*

5   *A similar expression was in a letter twelve years earlier from Dan Donovan's mother to him.*

6   *Nora had left her place of employment to care for Mary and her children at the Donovan home in Bradford. She lived in this house until her death over a half century later.*

Document **M128**
October 1900 – Hannah Collins, Elmira, N. Y. to Nora McCarthy, Bradford, Mass.

October 1900

My Darling Nora

I received your fond and welcome letter alright and was glad to hear from you same as ever as I did not expect to hear from you so soon as I delayed your last letter so long but I thought of you just the same as you are always in my mind. I am so sorry for you as I'm sure you are worring yourself too much. Now, Nora dear, don't be worring so much you will get sick. I know you cant help it but still its no good. I hope in God your poor sister is better off.[1] Also poor Katie. I often thinks of her, how nice she was. Poor Auntie Norry thought so much of her too, and of your Mother and the rest of ye. Oh, how they will feel to home after your Sister. Did you write to them yet? I suppose you don't know how to tell them such a sad news. I am sorry for the dear little children. I hope they are feeling well now. They are a great care for you, Nora, especially the baby being so young. Is she cross at night?

So you expect to leave after Christmas. I would love to go to see you but I guess I can't but hope to see you some time. Don't worry about me if you aint got any place for me to go. That will be alright.

Dear Nora, I had a letter from my Cousin Mary McCarthy a few days ago. She aint feeling well yet. Just think, she has been sick so long, a year this month. She said she will have to go home soon and she don't like to go for she likes this country. Her people are worried about her and wants her to go home. I would like to see her before she went. Perhaps I'd never see her again. Maggie and Mary are well and sends you their best love as they always ask when I heard from you. Poor Tim, I feel sorry for him. Give him my love and I thank him very much for wanting me come down to see ye. He was always good natured.

Well, dear Nora, I think I will have to close for the time with lots of love and kisses to you my dear one., so Good Bye. I am as ever your own Hannah XXXXXXXX

Give Tim one for me, X, as he always like to rub his mustache to the girls. Write soon.

ENDNOTES

1   *Mary was thirty eight years old when she died, though her death certificate and the newspaper obituary listed her as thirty four. Hannah's condolence is the only reference to Mary's death in the McCarthy Collection of letters. This was also the last letter from Hannah Collins to be saved, until the late 1930s following a visit from Hannah to Nora. One assumes they continued their correspondence in the intervening years.*

NOTES: THE MCCARTHY FAMILY 1900 TO 1906

No letters exist in the McCarthy Collection between the above and 1906, neither from family in Ireland nor friends in America. And from 1906 until 1914, only McCarthy family letters were saved from the parents, from niece Katie in Pennsylvania, and from cousin Jeremiah McCarthy. The only surviving reference to the death of Mary McCarthy Donovan is in Hannah Collins's letter above.

A similar censorship had taken place with the box of letters sent to Mary's husband, Dan Donovan that constitutes The Donovan Collection. Those letters span the time period from a month after Dan's departure to America in May 1885 until November 1890. The correspondents were his mother, three brothers, two sisters, and two female friends. There is not one word in any of the saved letters commenting on Dan's forthcoming marriage to Mary McCarthy on November 6, 1890. No other letters sent to Dan, except one from his sister, Julia, from the 1920s, were saved. Yet, it is abundantly clear that communication between the relatives in Ireland and Dan continued as evidenced by the steady stream of his nieces and nephews that immigrated to Haverhill, Massachusetts throughout the 1890s and early 1900s, many with assistance from "Uncle Dan."

What is the reason for this blanket of silence? It is a sad but romantic tale. Nora McCarthy had been with her sister Mary when she died. She stayed on in the home to care for Mary's three little daughters, who were seven, three, and nine months old when their mother died so unexpectedly. Nora may have intended to return to her previous employment by December, as Hannah Collins noted above. But something happened to change her plans. Perhaps it was the poor health of baby Helen Evelyn. Perhaps there was no alternative. Someone had to care for the children while Dan worked as a laborer for the Boston & Maine Railroad. Tragedy struck the family for the second time in less than a year on St. Patrick's Day, 1901. Baby Helen died of a heart ailment. She was one year, one month, and seventeen days old. Costello and Shanahan, Funeral Directors and Embalmers, provided the tiny white casket that went next to her mother into the newly purchased burial lot in St. James Cemetery, Haverhill. The bills for both funerals and the burial lot are in the McCarthy Collection.

Nora continued to care for the surviving children and to be the housekeeper for Dan. Fourteen months after Baby Helen's death, Nora became pregnant. A daughter, Honora Mary, was born on February 6, 1903. The baptismal register of the parish church, St. James, in Haverhill, lists the parents (in Latin) as Daniel Donovan and his "wife," Honora McCarthy. However, there is no marriage recorded in the parish register. A search in the city records of Haverhill uncovered the marriage of Dan and Nora in May 1903, three months after the baby's birth. The marriage was performed by John Lowell, minister of the West Congregational Church in Haverhill's West Parish, a good distance from the home in Bradford. According to the Baptismal Register, Dan and Nora were married at the time of the birth of baby Honora Mary (always known as Marie). Perhaps the couple had what is known in the Catholic Church as a "secret marriage," which would be a sacramental marriage, but one not recognized by secular law. To legitimize the marriage, they would need to go through a public ceremony. Why it was performed by a Protestant minister and not a justice of the peace is unexplained.

Marie never knew that the marriage had been performed three months after her birth. She did remember that she was never told that her beloved father had a previous wife, who was her mother's sister. Nor was she ever told that her two older sisters had a different mother. Mary was not talked about in front of her or her younger brother, Daniel Harold, born in 1906. There were occasions when her father had imbibed a bit too much, and he would begin to weep and call out Mary's name. Nora, mindful of the young children present, would hush him up. Mary and Dan's wedding portraits hung in the front parlor. Because the resemblance was strong between the McCarthy sisters, Marie assumed that it was her mother's portrait. Other incidents occurred during Marie's childhood when relatives or neighbors let slip mention of Mary. When a puzzled Marie would question her mother, she would be told, in classic Irish fashion, "Hush, don't ask questions."

Marie was an adult before she learned much of the story, but never the whole story. That was slowly recovered as work began on editing these letters. Fortunately, Marie lived well into her nineties. She was able to identify Mary in pictures that survived along with the letters in the McCarthy and Donovan Collections. What she was sure of was that her mother, Nora, adored Marie's father, Dan. The Donovan family was always the most faithful of Catholics, and Catholic priests were close friends and regular visitors at their home. Yet, Dan and Nora were married by a Protestant minister. The answer to that, and to the attempt to "hide" Mary's existence, may lie in the Church's teaching that a widower could not (or should not) marry his deceased wife's sister. Marie Donovan believed that eliminating Mary's name from the public talk was intended to unify the first and second families. It worked as far as she and her brother Harold knew. Considering how many relatives and friends knew of the two marriages, especially Mary's elder daughter Agnes, who was seven when her mother died, it is a wonder that she did not learn the reality of the situation until she was an adult. Nora's grandchildren were never were told about Mary and would not have known if not for a historian granddaughter's interest in family archives and her discovery of the treasure trove of old letters.

THE McCARTHY LETTERS

Part II: M129 to M148
1906-1918

DOCUMENT M129
3 March 1906 – Patrick and Kate McCarthy, Ballinlough, Leap to Nora McCarthy Donovan, Bradford, Mass.

Ballinlough, Leap
March 3rd 1906

Dear Nora,

We were waiting day to day thinking that we would hear from you. How could you forget your poor father and mother like you are.[1] We n ever thought you would give us up like you did. Your poor father feel it terrible as he was fonder of you than any of them when you were at home. Nora, I hope you're well and strong. I'm sure only for there's something wrong with you, you wouldn't be so long without writing. How are the little children and your husband getting along? If ye are happy, we are satisfied.

Nora, I must trouble you and Dan to try and send me something to help us on. The winter was very hard and your poor father isn't a bit strong and it is troubling him very much to have you forget him like you did. We didn't plant any potatoes for the past two years as Guano is very dear.[2] Only for Ellie we would be badly off. The poor thing is dead from us. Tim have forgotten us altogether.[3] Have you any account of him? I don't hear from Denny either.

God help us, all of you are forgetting us in our old age. Nobody to look after us. After all we reared now not to have one who think of us only Ellie, and she can't stand always sending to us. Nora, I hope you will write. I couldn't wait any longer as I'm anxious to hear about the children. Are they going to School? I suppose Mary[4] is a big girl now. Tell me all about them when you write. I'm sending a little Shamrock for Patrick's day. God help us, we haven't heart nor courage to do anything.

Mary Hayes is home. I was blaming her for not going to see you before she came. She put her father and mother on their legs. She is full of money. She is going back again next month.[5] She said she would go to see you when she'd go back. Is Agnes going to school always?[6] Nora, write to your poor mother and father always and don't forget us. I don't think we will be troubling you long more.

It would make us happy to hear from you again. Don't stop up writing any more. Write on and off to us and let us know how you are getting on. Hoping to hear soon.

From Your fond father and Mother,
Mrs. Patrick McCarthy

ENDNOTES

1   *There is no way to determine if Nora had written any letters to her parents since 1900. However, based on her pattern of writing in the past, it can be assumed there had to be some correspondence. And, if not Nora, then there would have been letters from sister Ellen and brother Tim to home, and her parents indicate that Ellen had been sending them money.*

2   *Guano is a fertilizer made from bird droppings.*

3   *Tim, who had been living with Dan and Mary at the time of Mary's death, married Ellen Donovan 3 November 1904. Ellen was Dan's niece, and had immigrated with him in 1885. She had been keeping house for her Uncle Michael Donovan and his young sons following the death of Michael's wife in 1900. Tim and Ellen had a daughter, Catherine Marion, 11 March 1905 and a second daughter, Julia Helen, in 1906.*

4   *Nora's daughter was christened Honora Mary, but was always known as Marie, using an Irish pronounciation (Ma-ree). When she was delivered to her first grade classroom by her older sister, Agnes, she heard Agnes tell the teacher that the child's name was the much fancier "Lenora Marie." And so she remained, legally, until her death at the age of 96. All the children in the Donovan family, and in brother Tim's family, were given family names for their first names but were known by their middle names.*

5   *Mary Hayes, daughter of Dennis and Ellen of Ballinlough, returned to Boston on the S. S. Ivernia April 1906. Her contact was her cousin, Simon Collins, East Boston, and her employer was Augustine Ivers, Newton Highlands, Mass.*

6   *Agnes would complete ninth grade in 1908 in the local public school, and go on to Saint James High School, Haverhill, Class of 1911. As part of the attempt in later years to alter the age record, someone "edited" an autograph book belonging to Agnes (and originally to her mother, Mary). On a page in which Agnes noted her name and graduation date from the ninth grade at George Cogswell School, she listed her age as 15. The 5, written in pencil, was later overwritten in ink with a 2, removing three years from Agnes' age.*

DOCUMENT M130
6 August 1906 – Katie (Dennis) McCarthy, Kingston, Penn. To Nora McCarthy Donovan, Bradford, Mass.

August 6, 1906
Kingston, Penn.

My Dear Aunt Nora,

I hope you will excuse me for not writing to you before now as I have been very careless about it. Ma[1] has been at me all the time but I did not know how to start. Sometimes I get the streak and imagain [sic!] I don't know how to write a letter.

Well, Dear Nora, it is very warm here for the last few days but we should not complain for it has been lovely weather so far. I am not working for the last week and do not expect to work this week but I am going to stay right at home because it costs to go away and we cannot afford very well to go away. I had been thinking for the past year if every thing went all right I would be taking a trip down there but its all off now, but I am satisfied if every thing will go all right for awhile.

Pa is working every day since the suspension we had up here. Well, we are all doing well now and are trying to get straightened out the best way we can with the help of God.

Dear Aunt, we do have some very nice times at our home and I often wish you could be here to enjoy it. There's a friend of Pa's living a little way from the house and he is very well to do also a very bright man. His name is Con Cronin.[2] He gave us a violin for a present and he comes up to see us every Sunday since Pa was hurt. He plays the violin nicely and we have the violin and the piano playing together and its lovely to hear it and often some of the boys come and they can sing so we have a very pleasant time in a nice way.[3]

My Aunt Ellen (O'Brien Donovan), her husband and the children[4] were down for Fourth of July and spent a few days with us and we certainly had a delightful time while they were here. We keep her little girl down for a week. She is growing very big and is lovely little girl. In fact her children are all nice.

Dear Aunt, tell Agnes we hope it won't be very long and with God's help that she will be coming on to spend a few weeks with us.[5] Oh, how we would enjoy that visit. I am sure we would be delighted to have her with us. I suppose the baby[6] is big by this time and you will be finding more and more to do all the time for there are a family you can find something to do all the time. Last week we were kept busy all the time. Ma and I worked hard every day while Margaret sewed and we were going all the time. They tell me I am a perfect old maid for I am a crank around the house, but I try to make every think look as pleasant as I can. We have not elaborate things but I like to have things look respectable.

Well, Dear Aunt, I am filling this letter up with nonsense and you will say there is no sence [sic!] in it. I just imagine I am talking to you personal now and just think of it I have never seen you yet. Well we will imagine we did see one another. We are all done up after yesterday. It was so warm. Ma went to a place called Harvey Lake for the day. We stayed around the house enjoying ourselves or trying to with Mr. Cronin and Pa, then last eve I went for a trolley ride, but it was very warm all day that we were all played out.

Dear Aunt, we received a letter from Ellie quite a while ago and I am just going to answer it now. She will surely think I have forgotten her. Have you heard from Ireland since. I guess they will never forgive us. Ma was saying she would try now and send them something for we don't like to write unless we send something for it is such a long time now. I guess you hear about Tim, or does he live near yet.

Well, Dear Aunt, I will be coming to a close or I will keep up my old nonsense longer. I hope Dan is keeping well and of course yourself. I also hope he has a good work. I mean steady work. The poor men they have to keep up all the time and work all the time. But I guess we all have to do our share, women as well in a different way. Now write soon and don't do as I done, delay this letter, for I will be anxious to hear from you so with fond love to all friends and to Dan, yourself and children,

Good Bye, Your Loving Neice [sic!], Katie McCarthy.

I wish you XXXXXXX

Excuse all mistakes. There are many of them.

ENDNOTES

1 *Katie's mother, Julia O'Brien McCarthy, was the daughter of John O'Brien and Margaret Houlihan. She died in 1920.*

2 *According to the Federal Census of 1900, Cornelius Cronin was born in England of Irish parents and came to America in 1870 with his wife of two years, Catherine. They had a son and an adopted daughter in 1900. Con was an Agent and his son a motorman on the street cars.*

3 *Both Katie's older brother, John, and her future husband, John McGroaty, belonged to singing groups. Sister Margaret played the piano.*

4 *Ellen O'Brien, Julia McCarthy's sister, and her husband, Robert Donovan, were born in Wales. They immigrated the same year, 1889, and married in 1900. By 1906, when Katie wrote this letter, the Donovans had three children: Elizabeth, 5; Robert Jr., 4; and Patrick, 2. The Donovans lived in Scranton, Penn. Where Robert was a coal miner, as was Denis McCarthy.*

5 *It would not be until 1917 that Agnes, with her sister Marion, will make their visit to their relatives in Pennsylvania. It was the same year that Marion had been selected the first "Miss Haverhill" in a local beauty pageant.*

6 *Daniel Harold, Nora's second child, and Dan's first son, was born in January 1906.*

DOCUMENT M131
9 December 1906 – Katie McCarthy, Kingston, Penn. To Nora McCarthy Donovan, Bradford, Mass.

Dearest Aunt Nora

Well, I will not be a bit surprised if you do be cross at me this time for it certainly is quite a while now since you wrote and to think I did not answer, but as I often said before, it is that we do not think abut you and indeed very often speak of y ou all. I started t write you a letter a few weeks ago and had so very little to say I really was ashamed to send it. And I destroyed it and I guess this one will not be very much better.

Dear Aunt Nora, we received yours and Agnes postal cards and we prized them very much because you are to thoughtful and they are very nice. I was not going to write you yet for another little while but I was afraid you might be wondering if there were anything wrong but <u>Thank God</u> that we had a good summer and up to the present time. We are just getting on our feet fairly well and I pray that every thing will continue for a while and this is what I wish you all also. I hope you have had good luck since we last [heard] from you and pray you will all be well and enjoy your Xmas which is near. We have not wrote to Ireland yet for we did not like to send an empty letter and could not very well send them anything so now we are going to send them a little for Xmas. I suppose they will think by this time we have forgotten them entirely.

Well, Dear Nora, which I often think you might think I am very bold for addressing you as Dear Nora, but I feel as though I am talking right with you. We are having lots of cold weather just at present and the working up here are doing good now and we are all tr ying to do the best we can for ourselves, but me I guess I will stay to the old Mill until some poor John comes and takes me. But they all tell me I am going to be an old maid[1] for I am too cranky and that they pity the man that will ever take me. But I tell them the man that misses me does not know what he is missing. But we are joking all the time. I could not explain all the fun we have sometime. Our Marg. [Margaret] is full of fun. Ma just hates to

......................[remainder of letter is missing.]

ENDNOTES

1   *Ironically, Katie was the only one of the three McCarthy sisters to marry.*

DOCUMENT M132

8 January 1907 – Patrick and Kate McCarthy, Ballinlough, Leap to Nora McCarthy Donovan, Bradford, Mass.

Ballinlough
January 1907

Dear Nora,

We received your very welcome letter and present for Xmas. We were delighted to hear from you [after] so long a time. We never thought you would forget us so much. I hope now as you wrote at all you always think of us.

Dear Nora, your poor father have an awful hard time. Your mother got hurt by a horse six months ago and is laid up since. She got her hip out of joint and is that way since. She is out of bed now for the past month and is going around the house with a stick. There isn't a bigger pity in the world than the both of them old and weak, as they are without one to look after them.

Ellie is very kind to them. The poor things, they want somebody to help them. Your father can't do any work now. He is kept going inside trying to do your Mother's work. They are very thankful to you for the help you sent them. Denny send 1 pound too. Your father and mother are very glad you are so happy.

They are satisfied too as you are looking after Mary's little children so well. The eldest girl must be very big now. They are very glad too to hear you have a little Baby boy.

Your Uncle Michael is stronger than your father.[1] Jerry is married and have two sons.[2] Patrick the Shoemaker is working at his trade in Tullig.[3] Julia have three sons and a daughter.[4]

Dear Nora, I hope you wont ever again be so long without writing as you know it is a pleasure to hear from you. Dear Nora, if you see Tim tell him I told him come home and look after me now in my old age. He would do as well here now as he could get an acre of good ground. I have to give it up as I cant work now. Tell my Grandson I'm very thankful to him to think of me for Xmas. I'm afraid you will never see me or your Mother again as we cant last long more now. We are failing entirely. Hoping yourself and all the

Children are well and write soon again to your loving father and Mother. We are very glad your Husband is so good and kind to you.

ENDNOTES

1   *Uncle Michael McCarthy, born about 1821, was approximately nine years older than his brother Patrick.*

2   *Michael's oldest son, Jeremiah, married Mary Neill, born 31 March 1878 to James and Mary of Kilnacally, on 14 February 1904. Jerry was 43 years old. Son Patrick was born 8 March 1905 and son Michael was born 29 May 1906. Jerry and Mary would have seven more children.*

3   *Patrick, third son of Uncle Michael, would not marry for another ten years, when he was also in his forties.*

4   *Julia McCarthy married Patrick Cullinane of Cahirbeg 27 January 1900. Their sons were John (born 2 February 1902; died 2 April 1905). Denis (27 October 1903 – 4 July 1981), Patrick (26 March 1905-8 March 1984), and Michael1 December 1906 – 21 June 1977). Ma ry Ann, the only daughter, was born in January 1901. She became a religious sister and died in 1974.*

DOCUMENT M133

6 March 1907 – Patrick McCarthy, Ballinlough, Leap to Nora McCarthy Donovan, Bradford, Mass.

Ballinlough
March 6, 1907

My Dear Daughter

We received your very welcomed letter a few days ago. We were very glad to see by it that you are all well. Your mother is not at all well. I don't think she will ever be any good. She cannot go around the house without the use of a stick. It would be a comfort to us if Ellie would come home but I suppose there is no use in us asking her to come. I asked her in my last letter to come.

I suppose we wont ever move from where we are now until we go to the grave. Your father is failing in a fright. I don't think he will live long more. I don't think he will see any other St. Patrick's Day.[1] Your Aunt and Uncle were buried.[2] There wasn't two months between them both. Paddy Harding's Mother is buried also.[3] Pad Hayes was buried a few weeks ago.[4] Jerry is married to a girl of the Neills from Kilmacabea, James Bohane's brother-in-law's daughter.[5] He have two sons. Courley Hourihane and Courley Connolly are very good. Mickey is at home always. Denny is married in Drinagh.[6] James Hayes and family are well.[7] The Leap people are very well.[8] They got an account last Sunday that another of their Sons was buried in California. It is Katie McCarthy that writes for me always.[9]

I'm glad your children are growing so big. Your eldest girl will soon be a great help to you. I'm sending a little Shamrock.[10] I hope you will get it for Patrick's Day. I don't ever hear from Tim.[11] I'm sorry for him. I hope you will always write to us now as we would like to hear from you always. I didn't get any letter from Denny since Xmas. It's a comfort to know your husband is so good to you.

Love from father and Mother to yourself and children.

Your loving Father, Patrick McCarthy

ENDNOTES

1   *Patrick would live to see another three St. Patrick's Days.*

2   *Probably refers to Nora (McCarthy) and Dan Keane of Ballinaclough. Deaths not found in civil register.*

3   *Julia (McCarthy) Harding died 3 March 1903, aged 90. Her death was reported by her son Patrick Harding, Kilbeg.*

4   *Patrick Hayes, formerly of Ballinlough, died of old age and debility 11 February 1907. He was a 75 year old farmer, whose wife, Norey, was still alive. He had been living in Knockanenacrohy, the townland east of Ballinlough. His death was reported by Margaret French. There is a Margaret French, 25, living with her mother and two sisters in nearby Cappanabohy in the 1901 Census.*

5   *James "Bohane" Sullivan had been godfather to Mary McCarthy Donovan in 1862. His death was reported in a letter from Katie McCarthy to Mary in 1894. His first marriage was to Julia Neile which made him a brother-in-law to James Neil.*

6   *Dennis McCarthy, second son of Uncle Michael, a farmer, married Maryanne O'Regan, daughter of James, a farmer of Drinagh West, on 24 February 1903. He was forty-one years old. As with his brothers, Jerry and Patrick, he waited until well into middle age before attempting matrimony.*

7   *James Hayes, son of Pad, had lived in Ballinlough. In the 1911 Census of Ireland, James, his wife, and his daughter Kate lived in a house in Keamore on Leap Harbor owned by Charles Donovan. James was listed as a caretaker.*

8   *Either Mr. and Mrs. John McCarthy of Leap, or widow Kate McCarthy, 48, a publican, with six children at home when the 1901 Census was taken.*

9   *Possibly Katie McCarthy the daughter of widow Kate. She was 18 in 1901 and 24 in 1907.*

10   *The shamrock sent in 1907 is still in the envelope in which it was mailed.*

11   *Tim McCarthy, his wife Ellen Donovan (Dan's eldest niece), and their two daughters were living on Kimball Street, Bradford in 1907. Ellen's sister, Julia Coughlin, and many of her cousins (Dan Donovan's nieces and nephews) lived in the same neighborhood near the Merrimack River. Tim was a laborer. It was about this time that he contracted the tuberculosis from which he would die in 1909.*

Document M134

4 August 1907 – Katie (Dennis) McCarthy, Kingston, Penn., to Aunt Nora McCarthy Donovan, Bradford, Mass.

August 4 – 07
Kingston, Pa

My Dear Aunt Nora,

I don't know how I am going to write to you because I feel terrible blue. I am thinking about you all day and talking about you all.

Dear Nora, I cannot tell or express my feelings when I reached this dear old town. It was then I began to realize the beautiful place I had just left.[1] Well, Nora, my journey was just grand after all. I felt very lonesome all the way to Boston and Ellie[2] and I did very little talking as I felt very bad and did not feel like talking at all. But when I reached Boston all the excitement I seen while there I rather forgot where I was. Well, we had our suppers in the station. Ellie paid for them and it was fine. Then we only purchased our tickets when it was time for the train to leave. Then it was seven thirty when I got to the boat, got my state room and then came out to look around all by myself until about nine o'clock when I met a very nice young man from here. He had been to Boston for home [sic!] week. I can't tell you how I felt when I seen somebody I knew. He stayed with me until ten thirty then I retired for the night and done just what Dan told me, laid facing the boat and I rested fine. Tell Agnes I sleep better than I did in a few nights but I thought of you all every time I would waken and wonder if you were worrying about me as I was getting along fine. I said to myself somebody's prayers are heard from me, for Nora I did certainly enjoy my trip on the boat. I could never begin to try and tell you how grand it was with all the beautiful lights, the beautiful carpets and the band playing all the time.[3]

Well, I arised the next morning about six o'clock, got dressed, eat my breakfast and got ready to leave the boat. It landed in N. Y. about seven that morning and the young man I meet on the boat escorted me to the ferry. So I had no trouble for the ferry took me right to the train. The train left about quarter past eight and I arrived home about three very tired and much more tired when I got to bed that night after all the talking.

Dear Nora, my mother and father have both said I will never get such treatment again and Nora as I said before I am just beginning to realize it. It is just like a dream to me today when I think of being down there to see you all and for nearly..........[Two pages missing]...... good time we had I had them laughing. He [4] said he go out there to live and not live here in this dirty place.[5] I know when I speak about you all he feels bad for he just sits and thinks.[6]

Well, Dear Nora, I am wondering what you are doing now. I hope you are happier in one way than I. Tell Dan that my fellow is near me now.[7] I mean the same town but I am lonesome. But I am lonesome all the time I guess. Now he will know I was not lonesome for him all the time. Tell him sometimes, but not all the time, as I am lonesome today and what for? Why, for my dear friends that I left far away, and it only seems like a dream that all that I was with you all just a short time ago and now so far away. Well, that's the way. Now the next I have got to say is I do not know how I am going to return you thanks for the treatment you gave me, but I will do something sometime.

Well, Dear Nora, I will have to be coming to a close and hope you will be able to understand this letter as I am in a hurry to write to Ellie now. Nora, I am going to work tomorrow morning. I ho pe I will get along all right. Now hoping this letter finds you all well. I want you to write me as soon as you can for I will be anxious. I wish youxxxxxx Good by for this time with love to yourself, Dan, Marian, Agnes, Marie, Harold.

Your niece, Katherine
XXXXXX

ENDNOTES

1   *Katie had just made her first visit to her relatives in Bradford.*

2   *Nora's sister Ellen McCarthy who had accompanied Katie on the train to Boston and then to the waterfront to board her boat to New York City.*

3   *Katie probably took the steamer from Boston, that sailed around Cape Cod, into Long Island Sound, to New York City.*

4   *Katie's father, Dinny McCarthy.*

5   *Kingston was in the anthracite coal mining region of northeastern Pennsylvania.*

6   *Originally, Dennis "Dinny" McCarthy had planned to come with his family from Wales to his relatives in Massachusetts. However, as the family story reports, he met someone on the boat while crossing the Atlantic, who persuaded him to head for the coal mines of Pennsylvania instead. This must have been difficult for his wife, Julia, for she, too, had relatives in Massachusetts, Lawrence, to be specific*

7   *Katie's future husband, John McGroaty.*

DOCUMENT M135

25 August 1907 – Katie (Dennis) McCarthy, Kingston, Penn., to Nora McCarthy Donovan, Bradford, Mass.

My Dear Aunt Nora

I received your last letter and as usual I certainly enjoyed it, but I suppose you will think I am forgetting you again when I have not answered your letter before now, but don't think for a minute I have forgotten you, for I think more and more of you every day and wonder what you are doing at certain times of the day.

When I think of you I often wonder if you are all hustling like you were when I was there but I guess I had you all keep busy while I was there. And poor Dan, I guess he is keep busy all the time with the bossy.[1] I have not had a good drink of milk since I came home. I get lots of milk to drink but [not] like got from you.

Well, Dear Nora, I felt very sorry to hear that Harold was sick. I suppose that's why he was so cross, but I hope he is all right now. Poor little Marie, I wonder about her too, and Marian and Agnes. I can see Agnes at the station yet, when I think of the day I left and I certainly think of Dan and cannot forget how much he made of me. I tell the people up here, I will never again be treated like I was when I was down there. Only last night, after I came home, we were all talking a out you and Agnes. My mother thinks she is just lovely.

Well, Nora, I am working every day since I came home and I am beginning to like [it] much better as I get more accustomed to it. The first Saturday night I worked after coming home I felt terrible. I was deathly sick all that day and night so I got some medicine and felt much better the next day and ever since. Then my friend Nellie Foley came to our house on Sunday and we all went to the lake with our fellows. I have been having some very nice times since I came home. Some of the girls I worked with in the Mill had a nice time for me one eve and we had a lovely time. And this week m John and I were to the opera and also to a wedding. I have been on the go ever since I came home. Marg[aret] tells me I am Miss Prim since I came back and am working

ENDNOTES

1   *Dan Donovan, though his home was in a built up part of town, kept a cow for many years. He had a small barn in his limited back yard, and he pastured the beast in a field at the head of his street. His youngest daughter, Marie, remembered selling cans of the cow's milk to the neighbors as a means of earning extra income for the family.*

DOCUMENT M136
30 October 1907 – Patrick McCarthy, Ballinlough, Leap to Nora McCarthy Donovan, Bradford, Mass.

Ballinlough
Oct. 30th 1907

Dear Nora

We received your very welcome letter a few weeks ago and was sorry to see by it you lost the cow but troubles will come to everybody. I know it was a great loss to you. Your Mother is just the same, no improvement, going around the house with a stick. We are done altogether this year.

The crops are failed in everybody this year. Flour and meal are 2 shillings a stone.[1] The people will die altogether this year.

I didn't do anything in the bog this year and your mother was laid up. We wrote to Ellie to ask her come home but she couldn't come as there is nothing here for her. I didn't hear from Denny or Tim at all but we hear Tim had two Daughters.[2] I hope yourself and family are in good health.

Only for Ellie's help your mother and myself would be in the workhouse. She is the only one that is thinking about us. Your Mother is gone entirely since we got Ellie's letter saying she wouldn't come home. All the friends around are well. Jerry got three sons now.[3] They are getting on very well.

I would have answered your letter long ago but was wanting to hear from Ellie to know what she would do. I haven't any more to say this time. Hoping ye are all well. Give our love to the children. Hoping to hear from you soon again.

Your Broken hearted father.

Endnotes

1   *A "stone" is equal to fourteen pounds weight.*

2   *Tim's second daughter, Julia Helen, was born August 1906.*

3   *Jerry McCarthy's third son, also named Jeremiah, was born 9 October 1907. He had died before the 1911 Census was taken.*

DOCUMENT M137

2 January 1909 – Patrick and Kate McCarthy, Ballinlough, Leap to Nora McCarthy Donovan, Bradford, Mass.

Ballinlough
Jan 2nd 1908 [1909]

Dear Nora

Your very welcome letter to hand a week ago and was more than happy to hear from you and very thankful for your present. We had a letter from Denny also and 1 pound. Ellie didn't forget us either. We are very thankful to all of ye not to forget us for Xmas. Your poor father was very sick five weeks before Xmas. We all thought he was gone. The doctor was attending him. He wouldn't get anything to use only brandy and corn flour. He was very bad but he is sitting up by the fire now. I don't think he will ever do any more good. I should put him in the Hospital only for the help Ellie sent me. I had to spend it all on him getting nourishment but, Thank God, he is a little better now.

I know you will be glad to hear that we will get 5 shillings a week each of us from the government.[1] All the old people around that is over 70 years will get 5 shillings. We had to pay 5 shillings for the certificates of our age to the priest. I'm 75 years for April and your father 78 years.[2] We are old and worn and no one to look after us. We didn't hear anything about Tim from either of ye. I suppose he is dead.[3] Jeremiah McCarthy is going to write to you and Ellie.[4] He is thinking of going to America.

We are very glad ye are well. I suppose Agnes is a very big girl now.[5] You will soon have help in her.[6] You can't stand all the work you have to do yourself without some help. I hope you wont be so long without writing any more as we do be troubled when we don't hear from ye. Hoping ye are all well and write soon again.

Your fond father and mother.
Love to the children.

ENDNOTES

1   *The British Parliament passed the Old Age Pensions Act of 1908. Pat and Kate McCarthy would receive five shillings apiece each week. This would amount to two pounds per month, or about what some of their children sent them for a once a year gift. In their straightened circumstances, this Act provided a tremendous aid and a great relief.*

2   *Katherine Keane [McCarthy] was baptized in the Kilmacabea parish church on 29 April 1834. Patrick was born about 1831, but the Kilmacabea Parish register that survives begins June 1832.*

3   *Kate's premonition was premature, but Tim would be dead before the year was out. He died on New Year's Eve, 1909.*

4   *Cousin Jeremiah McCarthy, of Tullig, was the second son of Mary, and grandson of Uncle Michael.*

5   *Agnes was indeed a very big girl. She and her sister Marion would each be five feet nine in height and both were large bosomed women like their mother. Younger sister Marie would top them both at five feet eleven inches, however she was built along the slimmer lines of her mother Nora.*

6   *Agnes graduated from St. James High School, Haverhill, in 1911 with a certificate in business studies. She went to work as an office clerk for S. Starensier Shoe Company. She never married and became the chief wage earner for her parents for the remainder of their lives. Agnes worked for the same employer for 56 years until she retired at the age of 74 in 1967. For her retirement gift, her employers gave her and her sister, Marie, an all expenses paid six week trip to Ireland. The two sisters spent their time visiting their relatives in Leap and Ballydehob. This was the first visit of any of Dan and Nora's family to their Irish homes.*

DOCUMENT M138
[Winter 1909] – Cousin Jeremiah McCarthy, Tullig, Leap to Nora McCarthy Donovan, Bradford, Mass.

Tullig
Leap Co. Cork

Dear Cousin Nora

I am sure you will be surprised to read a letter from me and I am writing it with the greatest pleasure in telling you that all of us are enjoying the best of health, T. G.

Dear Nora, I feel very proud in telling you that it is a great year in old people, every one that is gone 70 years are entitled to a pension of 5 shillings per week. They all were paid New Years Day.

Dear Nora, I think the old Folks would like to hear a letter from you oftener. I was great company a last year to them. I was working in Ballinlough. I always walked towards them every night. I am sure you would laugh enough if you had to see us a few nights before Xmas, myself and Johnny Brien[1] and Uncle Pad.

Dear Nora, I was very unlucky last year. I tried for the Police and got a 1st class pass in education and then was called in on the 4th July and the last moment was sent home on account of a few bad teeth. I come home and drew them and I tried for the Dublin Metropolitans and the very same happened. I come home very lonesome. I am earning since with Jerry[2] there being enough at home. There is my two brothers and uncle.[3] It come very hard in me to stop in Ireland since so I am just prepared to go to America for the commencement of the spring, that is if I could get into any job of work. I would like to know. So I felt very lonesome when I saw all my comrades going. I am almost sworn not to be before them. I hope you will have welcome before me.[4] I am writing to Ellie also.

No more to say at present but I will write a longer letter the next time. Write without delay.

Address: Jeremiah McCarthy Tullig Leap Co. Cork and write soon.

ENDNOTES

1   *John Brien of Knockskagh.*

2   *His uncle of the same name, in Ballinlough.*

3   *At home were older brother John, who would inherit the farm, and was twenty-three, and younger brother Patrick who would follow Jerry to America. He was twenty. Their uncle was Patrick the Shoemaker who had yet to marry.*

4   *Jeremiah would board with Nora and Dan for a while when he arrived in America. He was there when the 1910 Census was taken.*

DOCUMENT M139
5 March 1909 – Patrick and Kate McCarthy, Ballinlough, Leap to Nora McCarthy Donovan, Bradford, Mass.

Ballinlough
March 5, 1909

Dear Nora

Your very welcome letter to hand a few weeks ago and was very glad to see by it you and family are well. I got a letter from Ellie last week and 1 pound to pay the rent. She don't ever forget us coming on Patrick's Day. I was delaying your letter to see if I would hear from Denny but he don't think atall of us. I answered his letter when I wrote to you but didn't hear yet.

We are getting on middling now. The help we get every week is very good to us. I would send you the shamrock but your father or myself couldn't pick it with the frost and snow. I couldn't go myself but your father would try and get some little bit for you but for the weather and he is afraid of the cold and he isn't very strong or I suppose never will be. I'm very glad that Tim isn't buried We were sure he was by the dreams we had of him. We are very old now. It is no wonder. You would be sorry for us to be alone and not to have any one to look after us or speak to us in our old age.

I suppose Agnes is a very big girl now. I didn't see Jeremiah since he wrote to you. He said he would write to Ellie too but she didn't say anything about it in her letter. I hope you wont be troubled about us as with God's help we will get on alright but mind your health and the children. Hoping you will write to us often as we do be anxious to hear from ye. With love from father and mother

Document M140
26 April 1909 – Cousin Jeremiah McCarthy, Tullig, Leap to Nora McCarthy Donovan, Bradford, Mass.

Tullig
April 26th 1909

Dear Cousin Nora

I think it about time for me to write to you now. I am sailing from Queenstown on the 5th of May[1] Ellie is going to meet me. She gave me my tickets also.

You need not trouble. I'll find you out.

I am your Fond Cousin,

Jeremiah

Mrs. Norah Donovan

ENDNOTES

1   *Jeremiah sailed on the S. S. Saxonia and arrived in Boston on 13 May 1909.*

Document M141
October 1909 – Katie (Dennis) McCarthy McGroarty, Kingston, Penn. To Nora McCarthy Donovan, Bradford, Mass.

Kingston, Pa.
October 1909

My Dear Aunt Nora

I received your most welcome letter and present this morning with very much surprise. Cannot thank you enough. I never thought of you doing any thing like that for you have enough to do. My mother was cross at you to do such a thing. She said you had too many places to put to do where there are so many to look after and only one man working. But I hope and pray you have the best of luck and health.

Well, my dear Aunt, I hope you will pardon me for not writing to you before now but this is the first chance I have had for a month and now I am writing to all my friends. I just wrote to Ellie in ans[wer] to her letter. She sent me ten dollars.[1] It was too much for her to do. I had a letter written to send you when I received your but neglected in mailing as we were so busy at the time.

Well, dear aunt, here I am settled down in my own house at last, a married woman. Don't feel any change only I am very lonesome for my dear home for I had a lovely home and our family is just lovely. Thank God. It makes me feel good when I go home and see them all. They miss me very much. It will take a long time for me to get over it. Our Marg is a fine girl, very sensible and great worker and very cool head. I pray they will all continue being good.

Well, dear Aunt Nora, I wish you could have been here, you and Dan, the morning I was married.[2] Not that I want to boast but I know you would feel proud of your niece. We were married with a High Mass, pipe organ playing. Our priest spoke highly about us. Never done such a thing before at a wedding. He spoke how we prepared for to enter into marriage and what edifying lives we lead and the people should take us as an example. Everybody in the church thought it was just lovely and said we should feel happy. Now you must know what a good fellow I have and I hope he will continue. His people are very pious.

Well, my mother had a lovely wedding Breakfast for us and had a few of our nearest friends. Jno. [John] had a good many of his relatives which were all very nice people. Our Marg was my Bridesmaid and the best man was a dear friend who holds a position as manager in clothing store in the city. He gave us a beautiful couch. I received some beautiful presents, four pieces of cut glass, set of silver ware, pictures, rocker, linen, four bed spreads, and from Jno.'s mother a $45.00 brass bed, from his brother $40.00 side board. Every thing went off lovely, then I went away at three o'clock that afternoon to New York and stayed two weeks. Never enjoyed myself better. I almost forgot. I received a beautiful watch and chain from Jno. that morning as my wedding gift. The day was beautiful and had beautiful weather until we returned home. I will never be able to pay my people back. They done so much for me and now they have me down every Sunday since I came back. We spent the day there yesterday and my mother said write to Ellie and Nora right away. So I said I intended writing today.

I am not living far away although it is not the same town. It is a very busy place but not near so nice as where I lived. They say every body has something to bother about. Well, this is my bother, if I were only living near home. I am or have nothing else to bother me so far. Jno. McGroarty is one of the kindest fellows and so considerate. He works with his brother right on the same street which we live. We are living on the Main St. He comes to dinner[3] everyday so only for that I would not know what to do with my self. Every body expected to see me all excited that day but to their surprise was very cool and felt very happy. The girls which I worked with at the store gave me a center piece which took every body's eye, also china dishes and pair of best linen towels. One of the managers gave me a table cloth worth dollar and a half a yard with dozen napkins to match and the girls I worked with two years ago at the mill came and surprised me a few nights before with a granite shower.

Well, dear aunt, I could write and write. If you were only here so I could talk to you and tell you all. Of course, this is only some of the parts. Now it is all over and it seems just like a dream but when I received your letter this morning I thought I would let you know I received it alright while I had a few spare moments. We have been very busy cleaning and sewing. So now hoping you will still continue praying I will close this time thanking both you and your loving husband.

Good morning, from your loving niece.

Kathryn
Love to all XXXXXXX

[on reverse of last page: "This is what I had written to send you."]

Additional Notes:

Patrick McCarthy died on 7 May 1910. He was 79 years of age and his occupation was listed as a farmer on the Civil Register. His widow, Kate, reported his death. At some date during that year, daughter Ellen/Ellie traveled to Ballinlough to be with her mother. She was in Haverhill when the 1910 Census was taken on 21 April 1910 and she was in Ballinlough on 12 September 1910 when she purchased some items from shopkeeper Margaret Hegarty in Leap Village. The receipt for one pair of socks, 2 ½ yards of sheeting, 4 yards of flannel and some thread is archived in the McCarthy Collection.

Ellie was still at her mother's home when the 1911 Census of Ireland was taken in the spring of that year. The Census form states that Kate had been married for 56 years and that she had borne eight children, of whom only three (Ellen, Nora, and Dennis) were still living. Kate's age was 77 but Ellie adjusted her own age. She had been born in 1865 but she told the Census taker that she was 35 years old, thus removing eleven years from her age.

Ellen McCarthy boarded the S. S. *Franconia* in Queenstown on the 17th of May and was back in Boston by May 24, 1911. She treated herself to a second-class cabin. The shipping lists required by the United States Immigration Office had become more detailed than those of the 1890s when Ellen last crossed the Atlantic. From the manifesto for the S. S. *Franconia*, we learn that Ellen was five feet eleven – very tall for a woman at that time – and that she had a dark complexion, dark hair, and brown eyes. She was in good health and was neither a polygamist nor an anarchist!

There is a family story that Ellen "slipped out" of the cottage in Ballinlough without saying good-bye to her mother, thus breaking the heart of the old lady and bringing on her death two months later. The family story continued that Ellen was returning to the States to "marry Hegarty." Marie Donovan Trainor, Nora's daughter who told this story, had no idea who "Hegarty" was, and when Ellen did eventually marry it was to Patrick Quirk, a widower from County Limerick, and a man much shorter than her regal height.

Kate McCarthy died of "senile decay" on 24 July 1911. She was 78 years old. Her death was reported by her nephew, Patrick Harding of Kilmacabea. Patrick was the son of Julia McCarthy Harding, Kate's sister-in-law. Paddy Harding handled all of the funeral preparations and forwarded the accounts to Ellen. The letters and accounts that follow this Note were sent to Ellen McCarthy where they were kept in her strong box that in time passed on to her heir and executrix, her niece, Agnes Donovan.

ENDNOTES

1   *Ten dollars was a week's wage for many laboring people in 1909'*

2   *Kate was 26 and her husband, John McGroarty, was five years older. John worked in a furniture store.*

3   *The mid-day meal. The evening meal was "supper."*

DOCUMENT M142
28 July 1911 – Patrick Harding, Kilmacabea, Leap to Cousin Ellen McCarthy, Haverhill, Mass.

Ballinlough
July 28th, 1911

It is with the greatest feeling I take my pen in hand hoping you are well. Dear Ellie, your Dear Mother died on Monday and was buried on Wednesday to Kilmacabea. She died very happy, was very well prepared. We could do no more. Mary[1] cared for her well. She was very lonesome for her, may God have mercy on her soul. Dear Ellie, she sent for me to tell me what I would do for her. I have done all she said.[2] We did not expect her to die so soon.

Dear Ellie, Mary called all the friends in: Jerry McCarthy, Mary Nail, Mary Tobin, Mary Bawn[3] and they were all around her and she dying. She had her perfect sense until the last moment.

Dear Ellie, she was speaking of ye the days before she died. Father Lawton that anointed her, he was delighted how clean and tidy the old Woman was. Mary, he said, you are very good. Mother said no one could do better for me than she have done. She never will forget her. The Priest went on his holidays before she died. We had Father O'Hea[4] at her funeral and paid him 1 pound for coming. We wired and sent news to all the friends and so they came. She had a large respectable funeral and Mrs. Dealy and all the Friends were delighted to see her so well, so clean and nice. Pad Minihane of Leap made a fine coffin. Paid him 1 pound 5 shillings, a little balance due.[5] I went to Bennett.[6] I went to Mam[7] for some Whiskey for the Wake. I got nothing. I got one gallon whiskey for the wake in the sisters.[8] Jerry was with me. I gave no funeral whiskey but to Friends. I thought it too much expence on you. The sisters were very kind.

Dear Ellie, your Mother gave me two pound fourteen shillings, witness. I could do no more. Tell me what will I do with the house.[9] Mary will write in a few days. I have no more to say at present.

From your affectionate Cousin, Patrick Harding

I am staying with Mary in the Cottage until I will hear from you.

ENDNOTES

1   *Mary Harding, daughter of Patrick and Ellen Collins Harding, was born 31 December 1896. The implication is that fifteen year old Mary had been living with Kate and caring for her.*

2   *It is interesting that it was to Paddy that Kate turned, and not to any of Uncle Michael's family who lived nearby. Perhaps Ellen had made prior arrangements with Paddy and his daughter while she was in Ballinlough.*

3   *Jerry McCarthy and his wife Mary Neill; Mary Tobin McCarthy, wife of Uncle Michael; and Mary Driscoll of Bawnfune, widow of Johnny Bawn Driscoll.*

4   *Rev. J. J. O'Hea was the Leap Parish Priest, and Fr. Lawton was the Parish curate.*

5   *"For coffin supplied to Mrs. McCarthy, Ballinlough, o ne pound 15 shillings. Cash paid. With thans." Original receipt from P. Minihane, Leap.*

6   *Samuel J. Bennett was a shopkeeper in the Keamore portion of Leap Village.*

7   *Mamey Tobin McCarthy*

8   *Receipt in McCarthy Collection from Julia A. McCarthy, General Grocer, Wine and Spirit Store, Leap, for one pound, four shillings eleven pence received from P. Harding on July 21st, 1911.*

9   *According to the records f the Continuing Valuation (tax) Office, the McCarthy cottage was leased from the Guardians of Skibbereen Union. After Kate's death in 1911, the owner was listed as the Skibbereen R. D. (Rural District) Council and was occupied by various people until it was purchased from the Council in 1951 by its last lessee. It was declared vacant in 1952, and then purchased by one of Uncle Michael McCarthy's grandsons. When the Valuation did its survey in 1978, the property was owned by John McCarthy, a great-grandson of Uncle Michael. The cottage has since been leveled, and the land incorporated in the McCarthy holdings in Ballinlough.*

Document M144
25 November 1911 – Patrick Harding, Kilmacabea, Leap to Ellen McCarthy, Haverhill, Mass.

Kilmacabea
November 25th, 1911

Dear Ellie,

I received your Welcome letter and was very glad to hear from you as the departure of those few lines leaves us all in at present, thank God.

Dear Ellie, I am sending those few bills so you need not be uneasy about them. I

paid them all as far as I went through. I paid one pound 5 shillings the first day, in a few weeks after I paid the balance and the same to Julia A. McCarthy. You need not speak of anything I took anymore. I paid for all. You may be sure they will not call again.

Dear Ellie I would write before now. I had a very sore foot. It is all right now, thank God. There is no news at present. You will not be surprised to hear Michael Mcarthy of Ballinlough was buried a few weeks ago.[1] Your business was carried out as good and as respectable as his was.

Dear Elie, we left no thing undone for your kind and Loving Mother. All the neighbors say the same. May god have mercy on her soul. I paid for Mass for her All Souls Day.

Dear Ellie, I cannot express in words how bad she was, Mammy. She did not know the thirst of [the] poor woman. What she gave her one day the rinsing of the barrel, the old woman[2] threw it out. The old woman and Mary kept an account about 32 weeks. They thought there was some money coming to them in place of that it was coming to Mammy. Pay no bill to Mammy for it is not due. She could not be Paid.[3] Benett told me he got your money. He will write himself.

From your Cousin,

Pat Harding

Kilmacabea, Leap

ENDNOTES

1   *Uncle Michael McCarthy's death was registered on 27 November 1911 a few days after Paddy Harding reported it to Ellen McCarthy. Michael was the last McCarthy of his generation. Cause of death was old age, and his age was given as 90. He was the son of Jeremiah and Honora McCarthy and eight of his ten children were living when he died*

2   *Paddy is either referring to Kate McCarthy or to his wife Ellen, who along with their daughter Mary, had cared for Kate.*

3   *This is not a flattering picture of Mammy Tobin McCarthy*

Document M144
25 November 1911 – Patrick Harding, Kilmacabea, Leap to Ellen McCarthy, Haverhill, Mass.

Kilmacabea
November 25th, 1911

Dear Ellie,

I received your Welcome letter and was very glad to hear from you as the departure of those few lines leaves us all in at present, thank God.

Dear Ellie, I am sending those few bills so you need not be uneasy about them. I

paid them all as far as I went through. I paid one pound 5 shillings the first day, in a few weeks after I paid the balance and the same to Julia A. McCarthy. You need not speak of anything I took anymore. I paid for all. You may be sure they will not call again.

Dear Ellie I would write before now. I had a very sore foot. It is all right now, thank God. There is no news at present. You will not be surprised to hear Michael Mcarthy of Ballinlough was buried a few weeks ago.[1] Your business was carried out as good and as respectable as his was.

Dear Elie, we left no thing undone for your kind and Loving Mother. All the neighbors say the same. May god have mercy on her soul. I paid for Mass for her All Souls Day.

Dear Ellie, I cannot express in words how bad she was, Mammy. She did not know the thirst of [the] poor woman. What she gave her one day the rinsing of the barrel, the old woman[2] threw it out. The old woman and Mary kept an account about 32 weeks. They thought there was some money coming to them in place of that it was coming to Mammy. Pay no bill to Mammy for it is not due. She could not be Paid.[3] Benett told me he got your money. He will write himself.

From your Cousin,

Pat Harding

Kilmacabea, Leap

ENDNOTES

1   *Uncle Michael McCarthy's death was registered on 27 November 1911 a few days after Paddy Harding reported it to Ellen McCarthy. Michael was the last McCarthy of his generation. Cause of death was old age, and his age was given as 90. He was the son of Jeremiah and Honora McCarthy and eight of his ten children were living when he died*

2   *Paddy is either referring to Kate McCarthy or to his wife Ellen, who along with their daughter Mary, had cared for Kate.*

3   *This is not a flattering picture of Mammy Tobin McCarthy*

DOCUMENT M145
13/8/13 – Mary and Katie Harding, Kilblary, Dunmanway to Ellen McCarthy, Haverhill, Mass.

Dunmanway
Aug. 13th, 1913

My Dear Ellie,

I suppose you wil be surprised to hear from me after such a long time not writing to you. Hoping you are all well and happy as we are. Thank God for it. Dear Ellie, We lefte Kilmacabea about a year and a hafe ago and came to live to Dunmanway and are feeling very happy since all of us are working well but the wages are very low. Dady often thinks of when he ust [used] go to Ballinlough to see your poor mother, God have mercy on her Soul.

Dear Ellie, Katie[1] and me were thinking that you would send the prise of a dress to us, as you know that it is know joke to keeps us in clothes and every thing elce and low wages. Dear Ellie, Henry[2] would like very much to go to America and so would I. I suppose you are lonely for Mother and all the rest of your companions like we were when we came here first. I have no more to say at Present hoping this letter will reach you all in the best of health. So Good by from Mary Harding, and sisters and brother. My address:

Mary Harding, Kilblarry Grove
Dunmanway, Co. Cork, Ireland

Best love from Mary and Katie, Julia,[3] Henry, dady, Mother
XXXXXXXXX

ENDNOTES

1   *Kate Harding was born 8 March 1899 and was fourteen at the writing of this letter. Mary was sixteen.*

2   *Henry Harding was born 9 December 1895 and was seventeen in 1913.*

3   *Julia Harding, named for her grandmother Julia McCarthy Harding, was born 10 March 1901.*

DOCUMENT M146
9 December 1914 – Mary Harding, Kilblary, Dunmanway to Ellen McCarthy, Haverhill, Mass.

Kilblary
Dunmanway
Dec. 9th, 1914

Dear Ellie,

I am sure you will be surprised to hear from me after such a long time. I hope you are all well and strong.

Dear Ellie, I taught [thought] you would answer mu last letter. I was expecting to hear from you. We are all well and strong. Thanks be to God. We don't ever think of Leap now but always thinks of your poor mother, god have mercy on her soul. Dada always [talks\ of you and he said to write you might answer this time.

Excuse my short letter for I have no more time. Wishing you all a merry Christmas and a happy New Year. We all join in sending our best wishing to you all. We are all afraid of the Ware[1] at present.

Please answer very soon.

Good by from Mary Harding, Kattie and Julia, Henry & Mama, Kilblary, Dunmanway

ENDNOTES

1   *World War I began on 1 August 1914. Young Henry would have been of an age to fight.*

ADDENDUM I:

Document **M147**

Three autograph books, from the turn of the Twentieth Century, are in the McCarthy Collection. The oldest of the three had belonged to Mary McCarthy and dates to the early years of her marriage to Dan Donovan. Mary's name has been erased from a few pages, but the writing is still visible. The book has great value, not only for its connection to Mary, but for the names and comments of the various friends and relatives who all seemed to find their way to the Donovans' house at 32 Locke St., Bradford (later renamed and renumbered as 77 Laurel Ave.). This autograph book passed into the hands of Mary's older daughter, Agnes, and occasionally something new would be penned. One such occasion occurred on September 3rd, 1915. After quoting Longfellow for two pages, Nora McCarthy Donovan then wrote this verse:

September 3, 1915 – Nora McCarthy Donovan, Bradford, Mass.

"Last night we had a lovely time with Rev. Fr. John O'Brien
The best of all was Thomas Bough[1]
And Lord Thomas Noonan led the crowd[2]
Mary & Kiddo & Marion too,[3]
With Jeremiah[4] they had something to do
Johney and Agnes[5] done their best to entertain all the guests
As for poor Danie O.[6] we had a long wait
As Bridget surely went to a wake.
We played and sang until a late houre
And then we parted perhaps for evermore.

The Hostess

Mrs. Donovan September 3rd, 1915"

ENDNOTES

1   *Tom Bough was a Haverhill policeman and the brother of schoolteacher Mary Bough, a close friend of Agnes Donovan. They lived in Bradford.*

2   *Tom Noonan was an undertaker, and carried himself with all the style and dignity of one in such a profession.*

3   *Mary Noonan, a St. James High School classmate of Marion Donovan; Kiddo was Mary and Tom's younger sister, Margaret Noonan; Marion was the second of the Donovan children.*

4   *Cousin Jeremiah McCarthy who had immigrated in 1909.*

5   *John Donovan, son of Con, had immigrated in 1912, and Agnes Donovan.*

6   *Dan O'Brien of Lawrence.*

ADDENDUM II

DOCUMENT **M148**

Another delightful creation of Nora Donovan that was saved in the McCarthy Collection was written on a page from a Trial Balance Bookkeeping workbook. She had each of those seated around the kitchen table with her predict what he or she would be doing in twenty years.

February 22, 1918 – Nora McCarthy Donovan, Bradford, Mass.

"This is the 22nd of Feb. 1918 (George Washington's Birthday) at 32 Laurel Ave., Bradford, Mass.

Julia A. Donovan has received her Policy today, 20 year endowment. Hoping we will live to enjoy and well in health to celebrate her $1000 One Thousand dollars in 1938.

Today the whole world is at War and lots of suffering in the world.

Father is reading the paper at the stove. Marion is studying Short Hand. Agnes is knitting a sweater for Harry Hirshberg[1] and is in great glee.

Marie is studying her School lessons.

Harold is bothering every one talking about the War. He is twelve years old. Mother is knitting a sweater for Harold and also writing this to remind us of Twenty Years from tonight.

This has been a very cold day, 7 below zero. This morning Nonie Donovan[2] was down from Lawrence with her baby Eileen, two years old. She is very cunning.

(Signed)
Honora Donovan

1938

Catherine Marion Donovan

Age 20 years, work for Eli at the Rosengard furn. Co., Haverhill, Mass.
U. S. A. My name in 1938 Marion ??

Julia Agnes Donovan
Age 24 yrs. Work for Simon Starensier at 21 Railroad Sq., Haverhill, Mass., U. S. A.
My name in 1938 Agnes R.

Lenora Marie Donovan
Age 15 yrs., 9th grade of school
Take care of Simon Starensier baby (Estelle)
1938 expect to be teaching school

D. Harold Donovan
I am going to be a Cowboy in 1938.

ENDNOTES

1   *Harry Hirshberg was related to, and worked for Agnes' employer, Simon Starensier. The company's office was in Railroad Square, Haverhill.*

2   *Nora "Nonie" Donovan was the wife of Dan's nephew, Michael John "Jack" Donovan, son of Michael. Jack born in 1890 would die of tuberculosis before his thirtieth birthday.*

THE MCCARTHY
PHOTOS

Katherine "Kate" Keane, of Ballinaclough, Rosscarbery (south of Leap).
She was born in 1834, the daughter
of Denis Keane. She married Patrick
McCarthy in 1855. Kate died in 1911.

Patrick McCarthy of Ballinlough,
Leap. Pat, born c.1831 was a younger
son of Jeremiah McCarthy and Honora White. He was a farm laborer who
worked for others. Pat died in 1909.

Entering the village of Leap from the east. This road is now the National Route N71
along the southern coast of Cork. Ballinlough, home of the McCarthys, is to the
northwest of Leap.

Annie Fitzgerald, English-born of Irish parents, lived outside of London. She married jerry McCarthy, had a daughter, Kate, and two sons, Denis and Patrick. Her youngest child died soon after his father. Annie eventually remarried.

The three children of Jerry and Annie with their grandmother, Bridget Fitzgerald. Shown are Katie, Denis, and baby Patric, with their grandmother behind them. After Bridget died in 1900, Kate visited Ireland to meet her father's parents. A letter to America noted she was still dressed in mourning for her late grandmother.

Glandore Harbor, on the west side of Glandore peninsula, south of Leap Harbor. It was a center for fishing, including Denis Keane, a cousin and correspondent of Nora McCarthy.

Wedding picture of Denis McCarthy and Julia O'Brien, wales, 1881. while there, they had their first two children, another Kate and a son Patrick. Soon after, they left for America. Denis had planned to go to Haverhill, where he had relatives. Instead, a fellow passenger on the ship persuaded him to go to the coalfields of Pennsylvania.

Denis McCarthy, the second son of Kate and Pat, was born in ballinlough in 1859. like his older brother, Jerry, he left home for England. he went to Wales where he met and married an Irish woman, Julia O'Brien.

Julia O'Brien McCarthy and her daughters: Helen ("Nelly"), Katie, and Margaret. This formal photo was probably taken around the time of Katie's wedding to John McGroarty, c.1909. Katie was the only one of the three daughters to marry.

"Mr. O'Brien of Lawrence" was eventually discovered to be Daniel O'Brien, Julia O'Brien McCarthy's brother. He was remembered as someone who loved to sing and often came by train from Lawrence to visit the Donovans and engage in a night of songs. His daughter, Gertrude, was a correspondent of Nora McCarthy.

Nelly McCarthy and her father, Denis. Nelly was an elementary school teacher in Kingston, PA, until her retirement. Margaret kept house in Kingston for Nelly and Denis following the death of Julia McCarthy in 1923. Once his children had their own careers, Denis left the coal mines and became a school custodian. He died in 1935.

Agnes and Marion Donovan made their first visit to their relatives in Pennsylvania in 1917. Front: John, baby Joseph, and Nellie McCarthy. Center: Marion Donovan and Margaret McCarthy. Rear: Grace, Patrick, Aunt Julia, Agnes Donovan, Tim McCarthy, John McGroarty and his wife Kate, and Uncle Dinny McCarthy.

McCarthy family and in-laws. Rear: Patrick, his wife Grace, John McGroarty and Katie, Timothy, and Margaret. Center: Julia and Denis. Front: John, Helen with Pat's son Joseph, and youngest brother, Dennis.

Mary McCarthy, eldest daughter of Pat and Kate, born in 1863. She immigrated to America with her sister Ellen c.1882.

Mary adapted to the styles of America quickly, an example of which is this very stylish winter hat and coat.

On November 1889 in Bradford, Mary married Dan Donovan, formerly of Dreenlamane. Within a year, they had purchased a newly built house on the newly built Locke Street. The street was later renamed Laurel Avenue.

Ellen, the second daughter of Pat and Kate McCarthy, came to America c.1882 with her older sister Mary. Ellen was a striking woman at six feet tall with thick dark hair and brown eyes, as did her brothers Jerry and Tim.

Ellen in the late 1880s. She was a domestic servant, working in the large houses in Haverhill, ma

Ellen McCarthy, seated right, with best friend, Nellie Connolly, seated left. Behind them is her brother Tim who immigrated in 1896. Standing on the right is Delia Collins, who was also from Ballinlough, Leap with the McCarthys.

Ellen McCarthy and Nellie Connolly in their "head housekeeper" outfits in Haverhill, pre-World War I. Ellen worked for A. Spaulding, a dominant industrialist in the city. The house, an architectural gem on Summer Street, is now a funeral home.

Ellen Donovan, daughter of John of Dreenlamane, had come to America in 1885 with her Uncle Dan. That is how she met Tim McCarthy. They married in 1902.

Timothy McCarthy, known as Tady, or Tadgh, was the last of the McCarthys to leave home. He had been an agricultural laborer in Ireland, like his father. He helped support his parents long after his older brothers had left home. He came to Bradford, MA in 1896, where he boarded with his sister Mary and her family.

Helen, born in 1906, was seriously ill in 1908. Her parents had this photo taken to remember her. Helen survived, but her father died in 1910 when his two little girls were six and four.

Tim and Ellen had two daughters, Catherine Marion, born in 1904, and Julia Helen, born in 1906. The girls, known by their middle names, are lower right in this neighborhood birthday party photo.

Katie McCarthy, born in 1872, was the principal letter writer to her sisters Mary, Ellen, and Nora in America. She wrote for her parents, but also her own letters with splendid descriptions of life in Ballinlough.

Katie was diagnosed with tuberculosis in her early twenties. Her long, painful fight against the deadly disease provides interesting insights into medical practices in Ireland at this time. In addition to Katie, three other siblings, Jerry, Mary, and Tim, died from the same disease. This photograph was taken in the summer of 1896, a few months before she died at 24.

Leap Harbor on the southern shore of Ireland on the Irish Sea.

"Nora" McCarthy, fifth daughter of Pat and Kate. This is her "greenhorn picture," taken soon after her arrival. Her sister Ellen had returned home in 1894 to recover from some unnamed illness. When she returned to America in April 1895, she brought Nora back with her.

This photo of Nora was taken a year or so later. The change in her appearance between the two images is notable.

Nora McCarthy, right, with her childhood friend, Mary Hayes of Ballinlough. Mary had immigrated to Boston about 1894.

Daniel Harold Donovan, first son of Dan. Like all his siblings, Agnes, Marion, and Marie, he was always known by his middle name. A second son, Cornelius Patrick, was born in 1910 but only lived a short while.

Nora McCarthy married Dan Donovan in 1903. Their first child, Dan's fourth daughter, was born the same year. She was christened Honora Mary for her mother and her aunt Mary. But she was always known as "Lenora Marie." Three years later, a son, Daniel Harold, was born.

Agnes Donovan, aged about ten, after receiving her first holy communion. Copies of such celebratory photographs would be sent to grandparents and relatives in Ireland and Pennsylvania.

Dan Donovan, with Harold, Nora, and foster child James Carey. James had been on an "orphan train" sent from Boston by the archdiocese. The local priest, aware that Nora had just lost a baby, persuaded the Donovans to take the boy to keep Harold company. After a year or so, he returned to the orphanage in Boston.

Marion and Marie Donovan, about 1913, when Marion would have been confirmed in the church, and Marie would have received her first communion. Soon after, the rules in the Catholic Church were changed, allowing confirmation when a child was twelve and first communion when a child was seven.

Agnes Donovan's graduation from Saint James high school in Haverhill. She went directly from school to an office job at the S. Starensier Shoe Company in Haverhill's Railroad Square. She worked for the company until her retirement in 1967. Her employer rewarded Agnes for her years of service by giving her an all-expenses-paid trip for two to Co. Cork, Ireland.

C. Marion Donovan selected the first "Miss Haverhill" in 1917. She and her sister Agnes celebrated by making their first trip to their relatives in Pennsylvania. Their Uncle Denis had made previous trips to Bradford, but this was the first time meeting his family.

L. Marie Donovan in the 1920s. Marie had almost died when she was sixteen from a burst appendix followed by peritonitis. She was unable to finish high school due to extended hospitalizations and surgeries in these days before penicillin. Eventually, she would earn a diploma from a local business college and began a life-long career as a bookkeeper.

The three McCarthy siblings: Nora, Denis, and Ellen, during a post-World War I visit by "Uncle Dinny" from Pennsylvania.

The Donovan family at their home on Laurel Avenue in Bradford, 1916. Front: Dan, Harold, and Nora. Rear: Agnes, Marie, and Marion.

The three in-laws: Dan Donovan, Denis McCarthy, and Patrick Quirk ("PQ"), who had married Ellen McCarthy.

Nora McCarthy Donovan, "Norry" Hayes and grandchild, and Nellie Connelly. Rear: Ellen McCarthy and Dan Donovan. Dan was above-average in height, but Ellen, at six feet, towers over him. Norry Hayes was a Ballinlugh neighbor of the McCarthys. Ellen and Nellie are in their "head housekeeper" uniforms, as befitting their status.

Jeremiah "Jerry" McCarthy, Tullig, Leap, was the son of Mary of Tullig, Leap, and grandson of Uncle Mike. He would come to Bradford and live with his cousin Nora Donovan until he married. Jeremiah was a great talker, singer, and Irish step-dancer.

Patrick McCarthy with his older brother Jeremiah. Their brother John remained on the family farm in Tullig with his widowed mother, who lost her husband while pregnant with Patrick.

Annie Dacey Stanton, from Ballinaclough, Rosscarbery, was a maternal cousin of the McCarthys. Annie, her two brothers, and eventually, their mother all came to Haverhill. A Sunday walk across the river to "visit the Dacey" was a regular feature of life for the Donovans.

Michael, "Mike," "Mickey," was the youngest son of Uncle Mike McCarthy. A close cousin to Tim and Nora, his letters to Nora are witty and fun-filled. Mike was the only son in his family allowed to leave home. He only got as far as Newport, Wales, where his older sister, Nora Mahoney, and her family lived. When he would return to Ireland to visit, he was such a dapper dresser that he was nicknamed "the Mayor of Newport, Wales."

Julia McCarthy Cullinane of Cahirbeg, Rosscarbery was the youngest daughter of Uncle Mike. She handled the correspondence for Nora's parents after Katie McCarthy died. She and her brothers didn't marry until the beginning of the twentieth century, decades after their three older sisters had done so. She is shown with her daughter.

In August 1928, Pat McCarthy, formerly of Tullig, Leap, returned home from Bradford, MA. Pat drove from the port of Cobh/Queenstown in this splendid roadster, adding to the delight of his visit for his uncles Jerry, Patrick the shoemaker, Mike, his aunt Julia McCarthy Cullinane, her husband Denis, and his Cullinane cousins. Jerry is in the driver's seat, Denis, Mike, and Patrick are in the rear. The young men are the Cullinane sons.

The Cullinane men in their work clothes. Seated: Patrick the shoemaker. Standing: Mike, Denis, John Curran, and Cullinane sons.

Also visiting their relatives was a cousin from Newport, Wales, Nora Flaherty Curran and her husband, John. Nora's mother, Nora McCarthy Flaherty, was the eldest daughter of Uncle Michael. Kneeling: Denis Cullinane, Patrick, and two Cullinane sons. Standing: Cullinane son, Margaret McCarthy (the future Mrs. Jerry Murphy of Bradford, MA), Mike, Nora Curran, Julia Cullinane, and John Curran.

The twenty-first-century McCarthys. John McCarthy inherited the traditional family farm from his father, Jerry. He and his wife, Eileen, raised their family in the old farmhouse. The property passed to his son, John, and his wife, Noelle, upon John's death. Shown are John's widow Eileen, Jerry, Ann, Mary, Margaret, and John McCarthy. To complete the circle of Donovan-McCarthy connections that began this book, Ann McCarthy married Pat Hickey. Pat's brother John is married to Joanne Donovan. Joanne's parents, Tim Joe and Joan, inherited the original farm of John Donovan, eldest son of Con and Julia Donovan.

Kate Monohan, from Knockskagh, immediately north of Ballinlough. The family was known as Minihan in Ireland. Kate, who came to Boston in 1896, changed her name to Monohan, as did all her siblings.

Mary Holland, from Clonakilty, east of Leap, had met Nora and Ellen McCarthy onboard the ship while the three were sailing to America. There are a number of letters from Mary, and from Kate Monohan, in Nora's collection.

Hannah Collin's future husband, Tom Cloke, of Elmira, was American-born. They would marry in the early 20th century.

Hannah Collins, from Driminidy, Drinagh, had met Nora when visiting her great-aunt norry Hegarty, a next-door neighbor to the McCarthys. She had immigrated to Elmira, NY, in 1895. More than seventy of the letters in the McCarthy collection were from Hannah to Nora.

Mary was Hanna's younger sister. Mary joined her sister in Elmira c.1897 and worked as a domestic at Elmira Academy, the future Elmira College. One of her first accomplishments at "Americanization" was to learn to ride a bicycle.

Afterword

Margaret (Peggy) Lynch-Brennan

I went to my mailbox one day, and in it, I found a package from Dr. Patricia Trainor O'Malley. It contained letters that Hannah Collins, an Irish immigrant domestic working in Elmira, New York, wrote to her friend from home in Ireland, and fellow Irish immigrant domestic, Nora McCarthy. Nora was Dr. O'Malley's grandmother. Who was Dr. O'Malley? How did she know I was looking for anything and everything, especially letters, regarding Irish women who worked as domestic servants in America in the nineteenth and early twentieth centuries? It turned out that it pays to advertise! At the time I received the letters, I was a doctoral student in American history at the University at Albany, State University of New York, and I was in desperate search of primary source material for my planned doctoral dissertation on Irish immigrant women who worked in domestic service in America. A friend of my husband's suggested that I make up a "student" business card indicating the material I sought. I took the friend's advice, had "student" business cards made up, and disseminated them anywhere and everywhere. My husband posted my card on the Internet, and Dr. O'Malley saw it there. She then mailed the letters to me, a complete unknown! I could not believe my good fortune.

My path to a doctorate in American history was not the usual one. I began my career as a classroom teacher and remained in education until I retired from the professional staff of the New York State Education Department (NYSED). While working as a teacher,

I earned a Master's Degree in American History. Subsequently, my father, Daniel Joseph Lynch, Jr., encouraged me to go on to study for a doctoral degree. By the time I decided to do so, it was 1993, my father was dead, I was 43 years old, and I was employed full-time at NYSED.

In the first semester of my doctoral studies, I read that most Irish immigrant women in the nineteenth and twentieth centuries worked as domestic servants in private homes when they first arrived in America. Although all my ancestors were Irish, I never knew this. It explained why, however, at a family reunion in the late 1960s, I heard my great aunts whisper disapprovingly about a cousin who was working as a chambermaid in a hotel for the summer. Surely the memory lingered with that older generation of when such work was ostensibly the only work Irish girls did before marriage. My great aunts must have found it quite unseemly that in the 1960s when the younger female relatives were going to college, they would choose an occupation that was once synonymous with being an Irish female. I was hooked: I decided to write my dissertation on Irish immigrant women who worked in domestic service in America.

As I began my research, I found that not one book was written on the topic, and I soon learned why: archives contain next to nothing written by Irish immigrant women, especially those who worked as domestics. I found secondary sources, but few of the primary sources I needed to write a dissertation. Eventually, I learned that both the late Dr. Arnold Schrier of the University of Cincinnati and Dr. Kerby Miller of the University of Missouri-Columbia owned collections of Irish emigrant letters. Each generously let me read their collections for use in writing my dissertation. I am indebted to both of them. In particular, Dr. Miller's help was a godsend, and he became a friend over time. Dr. Schrier also alerted me to another useful primary resource: the interviews conducted with Irish immigrants housed at Ellis Island.

My delight in having access to the primary resource material of Drs. Schrier and Miller was offset by the fact that helpful as it was, it was still insufficient to form the basis of a dissertation. And then, I received Dr. O'Malley's package of letters written by Hannah Collins to Nora McCarthy. And, as it transpired, the Collins' letters were only a part of the much larger collection of letters that comprises this book. Dr. O'Malley kindly permitted me to use both the Collins' letters and the letters from the more extensive collection (including the Katie McCarthy letters and the letters written to Nora McCarthy by her friends and fellow Irish immigrant domestics) in writing my dissertation. Over time, Dr. O'Malley and I kept in touch; she became my very dear friend, and I assisted her in translating, interpreting, and formatting the letters in this collection. Eventually, I transformed my dissertation into a book entitled *The Irish Bridget: Irish Immigrant Women in Domestic Service in America, 1840-1930,* published by Syracuse University Press in 2009.

Since my book was published, Hannah Collins and Nora McCarthy, in my estimation the stars of this collection, have acquired posthumous fame. They are known, not only to readers of my book but to those who have attended the many, many presentations I have given and continue to give in, which I not only quote Hannah and Nora but show their photographs as well. Multiple times those who read my book became interested in the O'Malley collection (the term I used when referencing the letters in my book), contacted Dr. O'Malley or me asking to view the letters. Dr. O'Malley generously shared the letters with them, including, among others, staff of the Lower East Side Tenement Museum in New York City and Delia Cruz Kelly from the University of California, Irvine.

Theatre is another venue through which Hannah Collins and the McCarthy women have gained fame. I was lucky enough to attend an event at the West End Museum in Boston in 2019, including a dramatic reading of Katie McCarthy's letters. Another program featuring a dramatization of the correspondence between Hannah Collins and Nora McCarthy took place on St. Brigid's Day, February 1, 2021. More such presentations are planned for the future.

The lives of Hannah Collins, Nora McCarthy, and their fellow Irish domestics are testimony to the efforts of Irish immigrant women, particularly those who worked as domestic servants, to acculturate their families. When I interviewed her after receiving the letters, Dr. O'Malley said that as a result of their experience in domestic service, her female relatives determined to have "a piano in the front room. . . . to have a good dining room set and good china and good silverware. . . . You had to set that fine table. . . . And it had to be done just right." They insisted that their children speak English with "the right accent. . . . We'd be drilled in how to pronounce things. . . . Get the culture." But perhaps most importantly, they determined to elevate their families through education. For the domestics in Dr. O'Malley's family, "That was the big deal, to get them [their children] into high school" (1997). In the end, their drive to raise their families into the American middle class was largely successful because the Irish became "the most affluent gentile ethnic group in America" (Greeley 1988, 231).

WORKS CITED

Greeley, Andrew M. 1988. "The Success and Assimilation of Irish Protestants and Irish Catholics in the United States." *Sociology and Social Research* 72: 229-37.

O'Malley, Patricia. 1997. Interview by author. Tape recording. October 16.

Margaret Lynch-Brennan, Ph.D., New York State Education Department, Retired, and Independent Scholar. Dr. Lynch-Brennan is the author of The Irish Bridget: Irish Immigrant Women in Domestic Service in America, 1840-1930 (2009).

Dan and Nora Donovan

Made in the USA
Coppell, TX
28 September 2021

63105459R00312